Conceiving Freedom

Conceiving
FREEDOM

*Women of Color, Gender, and the Abolition of Slavery
in Havana and Rio de Janeiro*

CAMILLIA COWLING

The University of North Carolina Press CHAPEL HILL

Set in Miller by Integrated Book Technology. Manufactured in the United States of America. The paper in this book meets the guidelines for permanence and durability of the Committee on Production Guidelines for Book Longevity of the Council on Library Resources. The University of North Carolina Press has been a member of the Green Press Initiative since 2003.

Library of Congress Cataloging-in-Publication Data
Cowling, Camillia.
Conceiving freedom : women of color, gender, and the abolition of slavery
in Havana and Rio de Janeiro / Camillia Cowling.
pages cm
Includes bibliographical references and index.
ISBN 978-1-4696-1087-0 (cloth : alk. paper)
ISBN 978-1-4696-1088-7 (pbk. : alk. paper)
ISBN 978-1-4696-1089-4 (ebook)
1. Women slaves—Cuba—Havana—History—19th century.   2. Women slaves—Brazil—
Rio de Janeiro—History—19th century.   3. Women slaves—Legal status, laws, etc.—
Cuba—Havana—History—19th century.   4. Women slaves—Legal status, laws, etc.—
Brazil—Rio de Janeiro—History—19th century.   5. Antislavery movements—Cuba—
Havana—History—19th century.   6. Antislavery movements—Brazil—Rio de Janeiro—
History—19th century.   7. Havana (Cuba)—Race relations—History—19th century.
8. Rio de Janeiro (Brazil)—Race relations—History—19th century.   I. Title.
HT1076.c69 2013
306.3'62082—dc23   2013025582

Portions of this work have appeared previously, in somewhat different form, as "'As a Slave Woman and as a Mother': Women and the Abolition of Slavery in Havana and Rio de Janeiro," *Social History* 36, no. 3 (2011): 294–311, reprinted by permission of Taylor & Francis Ltd, http://www.tandf.co.uk/journals; "Debating Womanhood, Defining Freedom: The Abolition of Slavery in 1880s Rio de Janeiro," *Gender and History* 22, no. 2 (August 2010): 284–301, © 2010 Blackwell Publishing Ltd., reprinted by permission of John Wiley and Sons; and (coauthored with Celso Castilho), "Funding Freedom, Popularizing Politics: Abolitionism and Local Emancipation Funds in 1880s Brazil," *Luso-Brazilian Review* 47, no. 1 (Spring 2010): 89–120, © 2010 by the Board of Regents of the University of Wisconsin, reprinted courtesy of the University of Wisconsin Press.

To my parents,
Mark and Amani Cowling,
with love and gratitude

Contents

Acknowledgments, ix

Note on Currency, xiii

Introduction, 1

PART ONE. GENDER, LAW, AND URBAN SLAVERY

1 / Sites of Enslavement, Spaces of Freedom, 23
*Slavery and Abolition in the Atlantic Cities of Havana
and Rio de Janeiro*

2 / The Law Is Final, Excellent Sir, 47
Slave Law, Gender, and Gradual Emancipation

PART TWO. SEEKING FREEDOM

3 / As a Slave Woman and as a Mother, 71
*Law, Jurisprudence, and Rhetoric in Stories from
Women's Claims-Making*

4 / Exaggerated and Sentimental?, 97
Engendering Abolitionism in the Atlantic World

5 / I Wish to Be in This City, 123
Mapping Women's Quest for Urban Freedom

PART THREE. CONCEIVING FREEDOM

6 / Enlightened Mothers of Families
or Competent Domestic Servants?, 151
Elites Imagine the Meanings of Freedom

7 / She Was Now a Free Woman, 174
Ex-Slave Women and the Meanings of Urban Freedom

8 / My Mother Was Free-Womb, She Wasn't a Slave, 198
Conceiving Freedom

Conclusion, 214

Epilogue, 220
Conceiving Citizenship

Notes, 223
Bibliography, 273
Index, 311

Maps and Illustrations

MAPS

Havana, 1881, 24

Rio de Janeiro, 1864, 24

ILLUSTRATIONS

Statue depicting Mariana Grajales, Havana, 4

"Female fruit seller," Cuba, 1871, 33

"The Quitandeira," Brazil, 1857, 33

Cartoon depicting the conditions of Rio de Janeiro's
streets in 1885, 38

Satirical depiction of emancipation ceremony, 82

Official portrait of first emancipation ceremony, 82

Political cartoon depicting the sale and potential separation
of slave families in Brazil in 1885, 102

Image depicting benefit concert of Nadina Bulicioff in
Rio de Janeiro, August 1886, 113

Image depicting the slaves Joana and Eduarda,
owned by D. Francisca de Castro, 119

Image of "Slavery," painted as an enslaved woman being
transported through the countryside, 136

Cartoon depicting black market women's role in a strike at
Rio de Janeiro's marketplace, October 1885, 172

Cartoon depicting the forcible shaving of the heads of suspected
fugitive slaves, Rio de Janeiro, November 1885, 175

Acknowledgments

Any book is a journey; this book, in particular, has involved a great many. I have been fortunate to have a great deal of help along the way. Writing the acknowledgements is a happy reminder that, while research can be a long and sometimes lonely road, we travel it in wonderful company.

My travels took me to many rich archives and libraries. I would like to thank the staff of all of them. Especial thanks to Julio López and his colleagues at the Archivo Nacional de Cuba, who work so hard to keep this wonderful archive open despite daily practical difficulties; Sátiro Nunes at Brazil's Arquivo Nacional, Rio de Janeiro; and Manuel Martínez of the Biblioteca Lázaro, Recinto Río Piedras, University of Puerto Rico.

Before I could even pack my bags, institutional and financial support had to be found. The following institutions have provided crucial academic affiliations: Caribbean Studies Centre, London Metropolitan University, UK; Cuba Research Forum, University of Nottingham, UK; Instituto de Estudios del Caribe, Recinto Río Piedras, University of Puerto Rico; Pontífica Universidade Católica, Rio de Janeiro; and Faculty of History and Philosophy, University of Havana. I have been very fortunate to receive research funding from the Institute for the Study of Slavery, University of Nottingham, UK, and two successive research grants from the Leverhulme Trust, UK. I am grateful for additional funding support from the School of History, Classics and Archaeology, University of Edinburgh, UK, and the Department of History, University of Warwick, UK.

In the UK, a number of scholars have supported this project since its inception. Tony Kapcia and Dick Geary each took me under their wing as a Ph.D. student and have given unfailing support ever since. Tony has read several incarnations of this book, with unflagging patience and good humor. Nancy Naro encouraged me from the start, and kindly read and commented on this manuscript. Jean Stubbs stopped me from giving up early on, and, with characteristic grace and energy, has helped me out and inspired me ever since. Perhaps one day I will work out how she does it. Matthias Assunção, Manuel Barcia, Jane-Marie Collins, Catherine Davies, and Gad Heuman have given great advice and help in different ways. Diana Paton kindly read the manuscript and gave very insightful comments.

In Rio de Janeiro, I had the good fortune to meet a wide circle of inspiring scholars. Martha Abreu, Hebe Mattos, and Mariza Soares generously allowed a baffled young Brit who was still grappling with her Portuguese vocabulary to attend their postgraduate history classes at UFF, and commented on my work. Perhaps the most important lesson I learned at those Monday sessions in Niterói was how little I knew. Keila Grinberg shared her research with me from the moment I arrived in Rio. Sidney Chalhoub (in Campinas) and Olívia Gomes da Cunha opened doors, allowing me to discuss my ideas at their seminars. Sidney Chalhoub kindly read this manuscript and made very helpful suggestions. From São Paulo, Maria Helena Machado gave support and inspiration. In Rio, Bruno Cerqueira, Ivana Stolze Lima and Chico, Carlos Luiz Soares and Marília, and Eduardo Silva gave help and encouragement. I learned a lot from exchanges with a dynamic cohort of younger scholars, including Rodrigo Amaral, Robert Daibert Jr., Juliana Barreto Farias, Silvana Jeha, Moacir Maia, Iacy Maia Matta, Ynaê Lopes dos Santos, and Giovana Xavier. I would never have enjoyed the highs, or made it through the lows, of life in the *cidade maravilhosa* without the unfailing friendship of Denise Adell, Fabiana and Gustavo Brochado, and Paulo Fontes.

In Havana, I received help and advice at different moments from María del Carmen Barcia, Gloria García, Oilda Hevia, Jorge Ibarra Cuesta, and Ana Vera. Bárbara Danzie León has given me her support and friendship since the very first day I arrived at the ANC. María de los Ángeles Meriño Fuentes and Aisnara Perera Díaz have shared their time, groundbreaking work, and incorrigible humor. The Salas family and Chon welcomed me into their home. Carlitos and Luisito gave their friendship and endless kindnesses. Jon and Eldy Curry-Machado, Felicidad Machado, Helen Marsden, Anna Russell, and Miguel Salas gave help and friendship between London and Havana. Elsewhere in Cuba, I have been welcomed into homes, archives, and museums by Urbano Martínez and Leo in Matanzas, Olga Portuondo in Santiago de Cuba, and Hernán Venegas in Trinidad.

The settings of this book are Rio and Havana, but while researching it I have accumulated debts in many other places. In Puerto Rico, many thanks to María del Carmen Baerga, Astrid Cubano, Jorge Duany, Humberto García, and Gwyn Weathers, a *boricua* at heart. Doña Ruth Torres and her family gave me a warm welcome. In Spain, I benefited from the friendship of Leida Fernández Prieto, while Claudia Varella gave me great feedback on my work. Jessica Millward, Jeffrey Needell, and David Sartorius kindly read my work or helped me formulate my ideas. Dan Rood gave helpful comments on chapters of this book, but I learned even more from our long chats outside the archives in Havana and Madrid. Celso Castilho's roguish humor, beady historian's eye, and warm heart have provided constant support and inspiration.

To Jorge Giovannetti, I and this book owe a tremendous debt of gratitude. On so many Atlantic journeys, and in so many fascinating places, he gave endless help and boundless enthusiasm. Jorge and his work continue to be a source of great inspiration to me.

Friends in the UK have given advice in long-distance phone calls, flown to visit, and put me up in their homes for long periods. From far away, they reminded me that the UK is still a place I can call "home." They have been hearing patiently about this book for so long that they have probably given up expecting to actually see it in print. To Miranda Atkins, Nancy Campbell, Jo and Dan Friedland, Pru Hobson-West and Gavin White, Cat Kernot and Chris Bowman, Helen Mabelis and Alan Saunders, and Mark Walton and Carinne Piekema, my heartfelt thanks.

As well as taking me to distant shores, the journey brought me to new places in Britain. I was welcomed into the University of Nottingham's Department of Spanish, Portuguese and Latin American Studies. I got quality chats and fabulous cooking from Sarah Davidson and Helen Oakley, and inspiration and sore muscles from Juliet Line and Capoeira Angola Nottingham. In Edinburgh, I've had the support of great colleagues—particularly Ewen Cameron, Martin Chick, Louise Jackson, Charlotte Hammond Matthews, Iona Macintyre, and Paul Quigley—and of new friends; thanks to Liz Cripps and Judith Mabelis. As this book goes to press, I am looking forward to joining a wonderful new set of colleagues at the Department of History, University of Warwick.

The manuscript has been much improved thanks to the careful reading and very helpful comments of the two reviewers for the University of North Carolina Press, Keila Grinberg and Christopher Schmidt-Nowara. Many thanks to them, and to Elaine Maisner and the wonderful team at UNC Press, for making this a much better book.

This book is dedicated to my parents, Amani and Mark Cowling, who helped me take my first steps on the journey. They have given me so much more than I could ever say. Their resilience and generosity in the face of their own troubles inspire me to tackle my own much smaller ones. Mark Cowling kindly read and gave helpful comments on the manuscript. Sophie and Ralph Cowling have supported me always, adding a touch of mischievous humor whenever things were getting too serious.

The last phases of the journey have been very happy ones, because they have been shared with Manny Olaiya. Manny's sturdy support has lightened my load, and his infectious laughter has gladdened my heart. With him at my side, even as I was deeply immersed in the past, I learned again to feel courage in the present and hope for the future.

Note on Currency

In the period discussed in this book, Brazilian currency was the *mil-réis* (1,000 *réis*), written 1$000. A *conto* was 1,000 *mil-réis*.

Currency in Cuba was the *peso*. Inflation was very high in the 1870s and 1880s, with values especially fluctuating for money in notes (*billetes*). Amounts in *billetes* were typically worth less than those in gold. All amounts quoted in this book are in gold, unless otherwise stated.

Conceiving Freedom

Introduction

The Supplicant demands that action on this matter be taken,
not only for the authority of this Court to be respected, but also for the
child Maria to be handed to her.
—Joaquim Monteiro, on behalf of Josepha Gonçalves de Moraes,
Rio de Janeiro, 26 July 1886

One sweltering August day in the Caribbean summer of 1883, in Havana, Cuba, a freedwoman named Ramona Oliva made a petition to the offices of the island's governor general. She requested custody of her four children, María Fabiana, Agustina, Luis, and María de las Nieves, who were being held by Ramona's former owner, Manuel Oliva, on his farm in Matanzas, in the sugar-growing heartland of western Cuba. Ramona had purchased her own freedom the previous year, but she could not rest until her children could enjoy the rights she thought should apply to them under the new laws for the gradual abolition of slavery that had been enacted by Spain for colonial Cuba.[1]

Almost exactly one year later, in August 1884, in Rio de Janeiro, Brazil, freedwoman Josepha Gonçalves de Moraes embarked upon a court case to wrest custody of her ten-year-old daughter, Maria, away from Josepha's former owners, José Gonçalves de Pinho and his wife Maria Amélia da Silva Pinho. Josepha filed her statement in the same month of the year as Ramona, yet, unlike her Caribbean counterpart, she was perhaps shivering rather than sweating as she walked the city's streets to visit the lawyer who drafted her petition. August was the middle of Rio de Janeiro's winter, when its shores were often lashed by storms whipped up over the grey,

1

brooding Atlantic, bringing drizzle and chilly winds that swept across the city.[2]

The contrast in the seasons alone reminds us of the sheer physical distance—over 4,000 miles—that separated these two women. Both lived in what today we call "Latin America," a region whose similarities appear evident when viewed from the outside, yet which often unravel when viewed from the vantage-point of any one of its many nations or of their many distinct regions, languages, and cultures. Even today, a direct flight from Rio to Havana—the same distance as from London to Calcutta, or from New York to Istanbul—would take a long, tiring nine hours. Josepha's and Ramona's petitions were made in two different languages, within legal and bureaucratic systems that had developed along contrasting historical trajectories, in two countries whose differences could hardly be more apparent.[3] Yet each woman's actions and aims, and the circumstances from which they arose, were also strikingly similar.

In fact, in each city, women claimants like Josepha and Ramona made up over half—and probably a significant majority—of the enslaved and freed people who approached the law during the gradual process of emancipation that occurred in both Brazil and Cuba over the 1870s and 1880s.[4] In each case, historians have revealed much about how enslaved people's relationship with the law helped both to accelerate the course of emancipation and to define what freedom would come to mean.[5] Women appear in significant numbers across the pages of their works, yet we know less about how and why they came to make specific contributions to these processes.[6] Their stories—or rather, the parts of their stories about which we can claim to know something—are woven throughout this book. Ramona and Josepha are only two examples among many women who appear in these pages, whose individually small but cumulatively significant actions helped shape the course of emancipation and construct freedom's meanings in these last two American slaveholding territories.

Focusing on an arena of social and legal change where women were so prominent is interesting because much of what we know about enslaved people's attempts to attain freedom or change the conditions of their enslavement—marronage, crime, armed conflict—tells us primarily about the actions of enslaved men.[7] Tales of long, dry courtroom battles may appear less compelling than, in Jane Landers's words, "a daring and dangerous escape from closely supervised plantations, followed by a harrowing chase" that "is most often depicted as a male endeavor, as in the case of war."[8] Such are the images that often spring to mind as representing enslaved "resistance," even as historians have increasingly moved away from dichotomizing "resistance" and "accommodation." Yet quiet, ongoing attempts to free oneself or one's child through legal means, made in increasing numbers as slavery's institutional and political edifice began to crumble, collectively presented a challenge that was, in its way, at least as significant as other, more dramatic actions. Nor should legal routes out of enslavement be thought of as "merely" individual strategies.[9] Close reading and contextualizing reveals how they were the product of collective networks of support and communication, while legal developments as a whole were intimately connected to the broader sweep of political changes that occurred with gradual abolition. In the large, fluid cities of Rio de Janeiro and Havana, newspapers informed influential city residents of the progress of slaves' court cases; individual petitions influenced politics and jurisprudence; and slaves' relatives sought connections with entities as diverse as abolition societies, British consuls, the Brazilian royal family, and Spanish colonial officials.

Engaging with women's specific actions in this regard helps us notice how, in two different societies, slavery was a gendered concept—both in theory and in the practice of daily life. This in turn opens a series of crucial questions for understanding the broader dynamics of these and other postslavery contexts. In what specific ways did women experience enslavement and why? Did they seek particular routes toward freedom, and what impact did their actions have on the overall transition process in each case? How might shifting, contested notions about masculinity and femininity have affected the quest of the enslaved for legal freedom, or helped shape the very definition of what freedom came to mean? How did gendered norms intersect with changing ideas about race and citizenship to influence or reflect social and legal change?

Taking seriously slave agency within broader abolition processes has helped two generations of scholars to shed light on slaves' and freedpeople's roles in seeking citizenship and national belonging. In the same way, paying close attention to women's activities can both reveal their contributions to broader national developments and shed light on the changing politics of gender that underpinned those developments. Free Cuban woman of color Mariana Grajales, the much-lauded mother of independence fighter Antonio Maceo, is commemorated in Cuba today as a symbol of women's contributions to abolition, independence, and nation-building.[10] Yet as Mariana sacrificed her sons to die in the wars for independent Cuba, so countless other women engaged in protracted legal struggles to ensure their children might live lives in freedom. In Brazil, Princess Isabel's image as the "Redeemer," who freed the nation's slaves

Statue depicting Mariana Grajales, Havana. Photo taken by author, 2008.

when she signed the law of final abolition in 1888, was carefully molded by abolitionists and by the imperial family over the 1870s and 1880s. The "Redeemer" image was lauded by sycophantic historians long afterwards and then radically undercut by revisionist historians and activists in the 1980s.[11] Yet Isabel was only one of many women who helped engender Brazilian abolition.[12] As well as the elite "ladies" who graced the charity events of abolitionist high society, such women also included former slaves like Josepha. Engaging with their stories means telling the broader story of Atlantic abolition in a new way.

WOMEN, URBAN SLAVERY, AND URBAN FREEDOM

Josepha's case unfolded in Rio de Janeiro, the imperial capital of a proudly independent nation; Ramona's was filed in Havana, the beleaguered seat of Spain's power over its most treasured remaining colony. Neither woman was a native of the city in which she found herself, yet the context was significant for each. Both cities were intimately connected to plantation-based economies whose main wealth was created in the countryside; yet each also had a long tradition of urban slavery. These were "African" or "black" cities whose daily functioning depended on armies of enslaved and free laborers of color, and where an observer walking down a single street might hear multiple African and European languages being spoken.[13] And unlike the plantations that surrounded them, these cities—like other large cities of the slaveholding Americas—were home to large numbers of enslaved and free(d) women of color, whose work underpinned the rhythms of urban life.[14]

If Rio de Janeiro and Havana both relied on slavery, they each also had venerable traditions of freedom. These traditions had developed along different historical trajectories. For the first three hundred years of its history, Brazil occupied a unique place among the slave societies of the New World in terms of its relatively high levels of manumission. To Luiz Felipe Alencastro, this was a deliberate strategy of "social engineering" on the part of the Portuguese, linked to the creation of a large sector of free people of color.[15] Cuba also had relatively high levels of manumission historically, but had developed into a full-fledged, plantation-based slave society only from the late eighteenth century onward.

In each context, long before the gradual emancipation processes that are the focus of this book, women of color were at the center of the practices of miscegenation and manumission. It was through their bodies that the violence of physical and cultural intermixture occurred.[16] Yet, as studies of manumission for the Americas—and particularly a flood of quantitative studies on Brazil—have shown, women and their children were also more likely than men to gain manumission.[17] In this sense, Brazil and Cuba both stand out in the nineteenth century as intensive slave societies that, nonetheless, also had relatively high rates of manumission. Yet in both cases, those who had the best chance of attaining manumission had a quite similar profile to other areas of the slaveholding Americas: women gained legal freedom in greater numbers than did men, and urban slaves were more likely to become manumitted than their rural counterparts.

Yet the thousands of manumission documents left to us by these "juridical" or "legal" cultures tell us more about manumission as an *outcome* than as a *process*.[18] The dynamics that produced that outcome are often hidden from us, the owners simply arriving at a notary's office to record the person's manumission. In fact, historians are increasingly tracing the part played by enslaved people themselves in pushing for manumission, whether in tortuous negotiations with their owners that were not recorded on the final manumission letter, or whether through savings and self-purchase, often hidden behind slaveholders' formal declarations about "benevolently" conceding manumission.[19] Behind each statistic, then, lies a story. But how can we go about telling these stories?

In a minority of cases, enslaved people or those who claimed ownership of them disputed their legal status. In both Spanish America and Brazil, at least in theory, slaves had more systematic access to legal recourse than was provided in other parts of the Americas, although, in practice, there were severe limitations to how much the enslaved could make use of them.[20] Although access to such mechanisms was limited everywhere, it was more possible in large cities—especially the capital cities—than it was in small towns or the countryside, where owners' power held more undisputed sway. The paper trail that these legal struggles left behind has, for several decades, been being used by scholars of both Brazil and Cuba to reveal how and why enslaved people might seek their own freedom.[21] Such documents are relatively few in number, representing only the tip of a much larger iceberg of unrecorded daily negotiations between enslaved people, their free relatives, and owners. Yet in allowing us to trace the stories of women like Josepha and Ramona, they help us peek behind the manumission statistics to think about the attainment of legal freedom as a journey, not simply an outcome. They also allow us to appreciate how this journey was shaped at least in part by women's own actions and aspirations. Following this longer trajectory, the 1870s and 1880s ushered in a series of legal, social, and political changes in each context that brought women to the forefront of the quest for legal freedom in important new ways.

GRADUAL EMANCIPATION AND THE
WOMB IN BRAZIL AND CUBA

The settings in which gradual emancipation would occur in Brazil and Cuba were very different, but they were also closely linked. The exponential growth in each case of slave-produced plantation crops for export during the nineteenth century—mainly coffee in Brazil and sugar in Cuba—responded to broader Atlantic developments. As the rest of the Americas saw slavery gradually eliminated, Brazil and Cuba along with the United States South experienced a "second slavery" which, rather than representing an anomaly or anachronism, was partly stimulated by its very eradication elsewhere.[22] At the same time, the "second slavery" societies were also profoundly, if differently, influenced by the currents of Atlantic abolitionist thought and organizing. For Christopher Schmidt-Nowara, "This simultaneous apotheosis and unique vulnerability of Latin American slavery is the defining feature of its last century of existence."[23] This longer-term influence of Atlantic abolitionism began to be felt especially strongly in both Brazil and Cuba once slavery was abolished in the United States following the Civil War, even as the specific circumstances in which each country found itself made for two very different routes toward gradual emancipation.

Cuba, Spain's treasured "Pearl of the Antilles," was the largest of the Caribbean islands, rich in sugar and in the slaves who labored to produce it. Cuba had not previously been among the major importers of enslaved Africans, but from the end of the eighteenth century, intensive sugar cultivation for world markets led to an exponential rise in slave imports, transforming Cuban society. Almost 770,000 slaves arrived on Cuban shores from Africa between 1775 and 1866.[24] By 1868, Cuba produced 40 percent of the world's cane sugar.[25] The island's enslaved population reached 199,000 by 1817 and jumped to 436,000 by 1841.[26] By this point, slaves and free(d) people of color comprised 58 percent of Cuba's one million population, outnumbering whites. This exacerbated fears of Cuba becoming "another Haiti" and led to calls to end the trade.[27] In response to British pressure, Spain signed treaties banning the slave trade in 1817 and 1835. However, the Cubans continued to import slaves until at least 1867. Between 1851 and 1866, nearly 164,000 Africans entered Cuba as slaves.[28] In 1873, with gradual emancipation already underway, one Havana-based British consul complained of the "unconquerable hankering these people still have for the Slave Trade."[29]

Throughout the 1860s, the Spanish ruminated on how to address the slavery question, especially as the United States Civil War (1861–65) brought the institution to an end there. Matters were brought to a head, however, by the outbreak of rebellion in the east of the island in October 1868. It took Spanish troops over a decade to put down the anticolonial rebellion, which finally ended with an uneasy peace only five years before Ramona made her petition. Revolution both on the island and in metropolitan Spain transformed the politics of the Spanish empire, whether in Spain, Cuba, or Cuba's sister colony of Puerto Rico.[30] It had been the Cuban rebels who first declared slavery abolished in the course of the war, ensuring that, more than ever, the issue of slavery would be inseparable from the broader question of the relationship between metropolis and colonies. In the east, Afro-Cubans joined the rebel armies in large numbers, fighting both for freedom from slavery and freedom from Spain.[31]

Meanwhile, a staggering nineteenth-century coffee boom meant that Brazil became as important to the growing number of coffee drinkers in Europe and North America as Cuba was to their increasingly sweet tooth. By the 1870s, coffee accounted for about 70 percent of the wealth generated by exports.[32] With it, the boom brought African slave imports on a scale that was unprecedented, even in this much larger and more deeply rooted slave society. Unlike in Cuba, slavery had played a central role in Brazilian economic, social, and political life for hundreds of years. A close connection to, and counterpoint with, Angola had shaped the very construction of Brazil as a Portuguese colony.[33] During more than three hundred years of the Atlantic slave trade, around 45 percent of all slaves arriving in the Americas directly from Africa—just over 4.8 million people—disembarked on Brazilian shores.[34] The scale of this slave trade is even more dramatic when compared to the United States, which accounted for less than 4 percent of imports over the same period.[35] Yet the "second slavery" brought major growth in slave imports, which reached just over 1 million during the second half of the eighteenth century and another 2 million between 1801 and 1850. As in Cuba, this traffic ignored treaties banning the trade, passed in 1807 and 1831.[36] In 1850, however, the Eusébio de Queiroz Law definitively ended the trade to Brazil, giving rise to a massive internal trade in slaves to feed the burgeoning coffee plantations of the southeast.[37] While the largest Caribbean island fought a long battle for independence from the 1860s, imperial Brazil experienced a conflict of its own during the same decade: a dispute over territory and regional influence with the small nation of Paraguay on its troublesome southern border. The war dragged on much longer and proved far more costly than anticipated, and in the process it intensified political fissures and the irritations of particular sectors, especially among the military. The "shameful" need to recruit slave conscripts for the war helped place the issue of slavery firmly on the political agenda.

By the end of the 1860s, slavery had been abolished almost everywhere else in the Americas. Along with this shared international isolation, a complex cocktail of specific factors had helped to concentrate political minds on the slavery question in both Madrid and Rio. Yet slave labor and the principle of property-holding in human beings was still of central political and economic importance in each case. In response to this contradiction, and watching each other closely, the Spanish and Brazilian governments each sought a similar solution: gradual emancipation.[38] In July 1870, the Spanish government passed the Moret Law, a "free womb" law, which declared that children subsequently born to enslaved women would be free—albeit with a series of important limitations to that freedom in practice.[39] In September 1871 the Brazilian parliament passed a similar law, the Rio Branco Law. Subsequently, the 1880 *patronato* (apprenticeship) law was passed for Cuba, which set an end date of 1888 for slavery, although in the end the date was brought forward by two years and slavery was abolished in 1886. The *patronato* law renamed slaves *patrocinados*, or apprentices, and provided a series of measures for effecting gradual emancipation. The 1885 Saraiva-Cotegipe Law in Brazil emancipated the elderly and established sliding scales for gradual self-purchase. All the while, however, it was the "free womb" principle that underpinned gradual legal emancipation more than any other. The wombs of enslaved women, previously vessels for transmitting enslavement, became spaces in which freedom was, literally, conceived. Yet the contradictions and restrictions inherent in these laws, and the many outright violations of them that occurred, meant that conceiving freedom was contested terrain. In practice it was often up to women themselves to try to translate the laws' promises into lived reality for their children.

Josepha Gonçalves de Moraes had arrived in Rio as a slave around the year 1880, from Ceará in the Brazilian northeast. Her "free womb" daughter Maria, born in 1873, came with her. The whereabouts or identity of Maria's father—to whom Josepha was not married—was not discussed within Josepha's case. Josepha, an ironess, had worked in the Gonçalves de Pinho household as well as being hired out to work at another local household, headed by Joaquim Monteiro dos Santos. By the time she made her 1884 claim for custody of Maria, now ten years old, Josepha had already had experience of such legal battles. She herself had gained freedom recently, not as a generous bequest from her owners, but by taking her claim to the courts. Now, approaching a first-instance court in Rio, Josepha argued through her lawyer that she should be granted custody of her daughter because José Gonçalves de Pinho had abused and neglected the girl. Thus, the Gonçalves de Pinho family had forfeited their right, stipulated by the 1871 law, to keep Maria and use her "services" until she reached age twenty-one. Josepha's case was passed between several local judges in Rio, taking two years to reach its final conclusion and drawing in a wide range of local people—neighbors, friends, fellow ex-slaves—as witnesses.[40]

Ramona Oliva, who made her claim in Havana in 1883, had also recently gained freedom using the changed circumstances offered by gradual emancipation. Unlike Josepha, she does not appear to have resorted to litigation but rather was able to purchase her freedom from her owner,

Don Manuel Oliva, under the terms of the 1880 *patronato* law. Yet her children remained under her former owner's control, and she alleged that, even though "it is more than a year since I ceased to be a slave, I have four young children who remain in the power of my former *patrono* and I have not been able in all this time to see them, as the mother that I am." Her petition alleged that two of the children, Luis and María de las Nieves, had been born of a "free womb" under the 1870 Moret Law. Like Josepha, she thought she had a legal right to take them with her having gained full freedom herself. The other two children had been born before the 1870 law. Nonetheless, making an argument similar to Josepha's in Rio, Ramona alleged that they had the right to be free, because their *patrono* had not fulfilled the obligations, stipulated by the 1880 law, to provide them with "education." Unlike Josepha, Ramona's decision to file a claim in the capital city was not because she actually lived there herself. Rather, she alleged that she had not been listened to by the local authorities and thus had traveled to Havana to lodge a claim with the Gobierno General (General Government), one of the highest colonial offices on the island.[41]

Although Ramona and Josepha were pursuing a similar set of demands with quite comparable legal tools, they did so under very different dynamics of gradual abolition in each country. By 1880, frustration with the slow progress of the 1871 Rio Branco Law in Brazil led to the development of a broad-based, vocal abolitionist movement, which established high-profile campaigns in cities across the country, becoming most visible in Rio de Janeiro.[42] As the movement's best-known spokesman, Joaquim Nabuco, reminded the Spanish Abolitionist Society on a visit to Madrid in January 1881, "When your speakers asked the Cortes to abolish slavery, they addressed men who had no connection to slavery[;] when we addressed our Parliament, we requested abolition from slaveholders."[43] Abolition in Brazil would have to occur from *inside* a slave society where many powerful people retained deeply vested interests in the institution.[44] It would take an explosive, complex combination of forces, including continuing abolitionist pressure from a broad cross-section of society, widespread resistance from the enslaved, the breakdown of control on plantations, and a last-minute volte-face by the planters of São Paulo, to push Princess Isabel (acting as regent during the absence of her father, Pedro II) into signing a final abolition decree on 13 May 1888.[45] Despite the political impact of 1871, this course of events was not experienced by contemporaries as a given, but rather as a series of struggles whose outcome was unpredictable. As abolitionists had pointed out, under the terms of the Rio Branco Law, slavery would still have existed in Brazil well into the twentieth century.[46] In many parts of Brazil, unlike in Cuba, abolition took many planters and their former slaves completely by surprise.[47]

While in Brazil slavery was abolished from within a slave society, for Cuba, legislation was enacted by the metropolis. Politically, the complex relationship between metropolis and colonies meant that the motors of change were both stronger in some ways and weaker in others. On the one hand, because the slavery issue was so closely tied to the wider question of Spanish rule, Spanish censorship on the island prevented abolitionist mobilizing on anything like a Brazilian scale.[48] On the other, events in Cuba influenced, and were influenced by, significant abolitionist activity in Madrid and other Spanish cities, as well as in Puerto Rico.[49] Legally, while many of the provisions enacted in Brazil were also passed for Cuba, the pace of change was different. While it took two years and three different administrations in Brazil to free sexagenarians by 1885, and only then with the "compensation" to owners that they would work for another three years for free, uncompensated freedom for sexagenarians was decreed for Cuba along with the freeing of the womb in 1870. While the whip was banned in Brazil only at the end of 1886, this was declared initially for Cuba as part of the 1870 Moret Law, although in practice Cuban planters managed to reinstate various forms of physical punishment.

In each context, nonetheless, the combination of a long tradition in which enslaved people were at least theoretically able to claim freedom through the law, and the experience of gradual womb-based legal emancipation, made for some similar dynamics. On the one hand, legal change—which both reflected and helped produce social and political change—expanded the spaces for the enslaved and their relatives to seek freedom and craft their own definitions of what that "freedom" promised. On the other, the gradualist strategy and the profound resistance to change among powerful sectors of each society severely limited those spaces.[50] Owners, courts, or officials frequently ignored the laws altogether. The laws were silent on many issues that were of crucial importance to the daily lives of the enslaved, leaving it to the long, protracted struggles of individuals and families to carve out lived meaning from words on paper. Enslaved people faced huge challenges in making a claim in the first place. Yet ultimately, both on and off the record, their cumulative struggles had a significant impact on the transition process in each country.

The broader international context within which emancipation occurred was also significant for each. Lawyers, slave representatives or petitioners themselves might draw rhetorically upon a long Atlantic legacy of abolitionist discourse that aimed to convince elite readers that they shared fundamentals of the human condition with enslaved men and women and thus elicit empathy for slaves. At the same time, by the 1870s, a new vocabulary was arriving in Latin America, drawn from "scientific" racial theories, some of which disputed the very premise of humanity's shared roots.[51] Each set of ideas drew on gendered language for its effectiveness. Ideas about a shared humanity might be most effectively conveyed by appealing to a notion of universal mother-love, notionally shared by slave and elite women alike. Conversely, one of the best ways to destroy a former slave's case was to exclude her from definitions of "womanliness" as construed by elite observers.

Women like Josepha and Ramona stood at this crossroads between enslavement and freedom, rhetoric and law. It was from their wombs that the much-debated new "free" generations would spring. Yet, in practice, what that freedom might mean for them and for their children would be determined through a series of unequal but important struggles. Both enslaved men and women negotiated to attain and define the terms of freedom. Yet the new womb-based laws and the long-standing relationship between women and manumission helped to place women at the front line in the struggle for legal and social change. In the process of that struggle, old ideas about what "womanhood" and "motherhood" meant and to whom they applied were reconfigured in a new political context, while newly gendered notions about freedom and national belonging were being conceived.

SOURCES AND APPROACHES

The legal claims made by enslaved people and their freed relatives like Josepha and Ramona during the gradual legal abolition of slavery are at the heart of this study. These documents exist for both Cuba and Brazil, and they make for a fascinating opportunity to compare and analyze enslaved people's struggles with the law in each case. Nonetheless, their nature is different in each country—as we would expect, given that they were generated in two different legal and political systems, not to speak of two different languages. For Rio, the principal avenue for slaves' claims-making was through the courts: both the first-instance courts and Rio de Janeiro's appeals court. Legal claims-making, especially when it reached the appeal stage, tended to produce very lengthy cases, often running to hundreds of manuscript pages. For Cuba, while some slaves' claims might reach the courts, in practice most of the demands of the enslaved and their relatives were channeled by a variety of colonial government institutions in the nineteenth century. To these were added the boards set up to oversee the gradual emancipation process, called *juntas de libertos* from 1870, and *juntas de patronato* from 1880. This made for a relatively plural situation, in which slaves might make claims to a number of different bodies, whether at the local level or bypassing the local authorities to end up in the capital itself. Their claims were usually passed back and forth between these bodies and acted on fairly quickly, although the final decision was not always filed away with the initial claim, making it difficult to assess the "success" rate of such petitions. Beyond these standard procedures, in each city there were also some other ways in which the enslaved could make an official claim for legal freedom. There were more avenues for this in Rio, where, as abolitionist fervor took off during the 1880s, some slaves and former slaves approached private and municipal emancipation funds and societies, appeared at the offices of abolitionist newspapers, or followed a time-honored tradition of making an appeal to members of the imperial family, based in the capital and increasingly associating themselves with emancipationist, even stridently abolitionist, events and initiatives.

Analyzing these kinds of claims quantitatively is fraught with difficulties, and the results can only be very tentative. The difficulties enslaved people had in making them at all mean that those who did file a claim certainly represented a small minority. Although more of these documents are constantly coming to light, the numbers we have to go on are quite small, and we do not know what percentage of those originally made have survived. Nonetheless, for both Rio de Janeiro and Havana in the 1870s and 1880s, the figures we do have suggest women played at least a very significant, and probably dominant, role in legal and official claims-making in each city, and one that increased during the period of gradual abolition. For example, for Rio de Janeiro, a database of second-instance court cases compiled by Keila Grinberg contains 30 cases for or against the freedom of individuals, or same-sex groups identifiable by sex, made between 1871 and 1888. Of these, 27 (90 percent) concerned female slaves. Between 1850 and 1870, although their presence is smaller, second-instance appeals by or about enslaved women in Rio made up just under half the total of claimants identifiable by sex (16 of 34).[52] For Havana, where the numbers we have to go on are rather larger, they point in the same direction. A survey of 710 appeals made from 1870 to 1886, held in the Miscelánea de Expedientes collection of Havana's National Archive, 452 (64 percent) were made by women.[53] Like in Brazil, such numbers contrast significantly with pre-1870 figures, as the analyses and further statistical examples in Chapter 2 will show. However, following the approach adopted by other historians who have used these documents, I draw on them mainly as a qualitative source: as a way of getting inside claims-making as a process and understanding the specific ways in which women, in particular, used it in negotiating over the condition of enslavement. The many stories woven into this book have been selected from the close reading of several hundred legal and official claims for freedom from this period.

How to go about interpreting these kinds of documents? Because the enslaved were systematically denied access to literacy, neither Josepha nor Ramona, nor almost any of the other enslaved or ex-slave litigants discussed in this book, knew how to read or write.[54] Their spoken words were reported and reworked, whether by official legal representatives for slaves and others considered legal minors (*curadores* in Brazil, *síndicos* in Cuba), or whether by a heterogeneous array of scribes and literate acquaintances. The resulting documents range from formulaic legal statements, to flowery rhetorical arguments, to clumsily worded texts full of grammatical and spelling errors, couched in simple, direct language that often read tantalizingly like a transcription of the claimant's spoken words.

Yet certainly, we should not assume that such documents can provide us with direct access to the "voices" of petitioners. Rather, their words were "translated" by—and for—elite pens and minds. Like any translation, slave petitions were the product of a creative, syncretic act, fusing distinct voices and worldviews to craft a new text. They were molded by profoundly unequal power relations, with the petitioner almost inevitably exercising less influence on the final text than did the writer or the petitioned. The results are interesting for historians not because they can provide any unmitigated access to the minds or lives of the enslaved, but precisely because of their complex fusing of very different worlds, incorporating different groups of people who lived cheek-by-jowl in the crowded urban spaces of Havana and Rio de Janeiro but who generally achieved little real understanding of one another. In the process, they do at least provide rare, fascinating glimpses of the actions and motivations of enslaved and free(d) people.

Paying attention to these actions and motivations—or to "agency"—is not the same as declaring them triumphs for the enslaved. It does not give away anything about the specific outcomes of the stories contained in this book to say that they do not—indeed, they *could* not—have "happy endings" in any straightforward sense. Life for most enslaved people was harsh, short, and physically and emotionally painful. Former slaves continued to experience punishing labor regimes, whether before or after abolition. Re-enslavement was a common threat for those with darker skins.[55] The ending of slavery was closely entwined with the advent of "scientific" racist thought, with nefarious and durable consequences for former slaves. So while each of our protagonists tried to shape her own path, the terrain was certainly not of her making.

Nonetheless, the task of trying to understand the lives and aims of enslaved and ex-slave women remains important and interesting—both in its own right and because it can reveal much about the broader abolition processes to which their struggles were connected. This connectedness means that the purpose of telling stories like those of Josepha and Ramona is about much more than simply asserting the existence of slaves' "agency." It is certainly less interesting to debate which social group—"heroic" slaves versus "saintly" white abolitionists, for example—was most important in shaping routes toward abolition than it is to trace the complicated ways in which individuals and groups interacted.[56] This task becomes especially important in the context of the large, cosmopolitan, diverse "Atlantic port cities" that are the setting for this study.[57] Researching the lives of women of color, in particular, allows us a privileged window onto intimate connections. As nursemaids and domestic servants to slaveholding families, and as the providers of sex—whether coerced or "consenting"—to slaveholding men, they performed a biological and social bridging function between cultures and worldviews.[58]

In the same way, the stories contained in this book are about the law, but they are not separable from many other political and social aspects of urban life. They are stories about women who approached legal representatives, but then went home to crowded dwellings filled with other women of color like themselves as well as their families and children. Thus, to interpret the legal documents that are at the book's core, I have drawn on a much broader universe of sources. Understanding how Atlantic abolitionist discourse was shaped by gender at many stages and sites in its history has taken me not just to Havana and Rio but also to Madrid, London, and San Juan. It has led me to wonder how a local councilor's flattering speech to Princess Isabel of Brazil might be connected to the quest of a freedwoman to free her daughter; or to ponder the similarities between an illiterate woman's petition in 1880s Cuba and the language of *Uncle Tom's Cabin*. In order to understand legal documents and official petitions, then, I have ended up drawing on sources ranging from newspapers to postmortem inventories; from consular reports to poems and novels; and from the records of abolitionist societies to census materials and criminal court cases.

This interest in connectedness, in a set of broader overlapping frameworks that linked each of our cities, means that this is not primarily a work of "comparative" history. Nonetheless, like most studies of slavery in the Americas, it has been profoundly shaped by a venerable comparative history tradition. Even when classic comparative works have been thoroughly critiqued, they continue to spark important new insights. Frank Tannenbaum's classic 1947 thesis, for example, argued that Iberian American legal cultures recognized slaves' humanity and offered greater possibilities for manumission than in his main comparative case study, the United States.[59] His conclusions have been thoroughly critiqued by generations of scholars, who have disputed the degree of difference between slave laws in different parts of the Americas and the extent to which the codes were really put into practice.[60] Nonetheless, as Alejandro de la Fuente has recently reminded us, the Tannenbaum thesis still has a lot to tell us about slavery and the law in Cuba if, rather than seeing the law as an agent of social change per se, we follow more recent historiography and consider the law as a set of opportunities that were shaped and mobilized by the enslaved themselves.[61] This dynamic relationship between slave law and slave agency, as well as the relatively high levels of manumission noted by Tannenbaum for Iberian societies, formed the context for the struggles of the women litigants who appear in the pages of this book.[62] Building on such broader comparative insights, this book follows recent scholarship in focusing on two Iberian societies, rather than—as hitherto was common in comparative histories—an Iberian case and a non-Iberian one.[63] Thus, we find a series of important *differences* between Brazil and Cuba that emerge at the level of legal traditions, languages, or regional and political histories.

However, "formal" comparative history—a term recently used by Márcia Berbel, Rafael Marquese, and Tâmis Parron to describe the examination of two or more "case studies" by "essentially seeking an inventory of their similarities and differences and treating them as discrete units independent of each other"—can tell us only so much.[64] "Formal" comparative history often tends to be more interested in the differences between two "cases" than in exploring the connections that bound them together. Josepha and Ramona never met, but if they had, they would have had a lot to say to one another. They would undoubtedly have felt and noticed these differences between their two societies; yet given those major differences, they would perhaps have remarked particularly on the comparable nature of their struggles. As they talked, perhaps they might have wondered about the reasons for these connections. In order to understand these linkages, we need an approach whose scale is sometimes broader and sometimes much narrower than the boundaries of each particular city or its national or colonial context. Havana and Rio were connected by the economic and political resurgence of both Atlantic slavery and Atlantic antislavery, shaped over time and space during the nineteenth century. Their enslaved and freed inhabitants were also deeply connected to one another by the personal memories and the shared cultural experiences of West Africa and Central Africa. Rosalyn Terborg-Penn long ago observed the importance of studying women of African descent across societies and historical moments.[65] Exploring the connected aspects of their histories can help shed light on why women in two different cities, four thousand miles apart, came to play a major, specific, and remarkably similar role in shaping and speeding the abolition of slavery in each case.

At the same time, enslaved and freed women's trajectories were also influenced by elements that do not so easily lend themselves to either a structured comparative perspective or a broad-brush "Atlantic" approach. The everyday, the commonplace, and, indeed, the frankly parochial weighed heavily in the lives of the people in this book. A good gossip with a neighbor; the scandalous discovery of the theft of a prize chicken; or a rebellious daughter's poor choice of boyfriend: these episodes are neither reducible to neat comparative schemas, nor always visible from the lofty heights of "Atlantic" history, yet they are no less significant for being messy and mundane.[66] Such incidents were part of a broader urban social fabric. Rather than simply relating a series of isolated, individual quests for manumission, this book builds up layers of stories, aiming to create a sense of the intimate intersections that operated within a particular neighborhood and helped make claims-making a collective, social process. In so doing, I have tried to emulate what Rebecca Scott has described as a "zoom lens," focusing both in on microhistorical detail and out again at the broader horizons that shaped—but were also shaped by—such daily details.[67] Whatever the particular historical approach being employed at any given moment—or, to stick with the metaphor, whatever the zoom setting on the lens—I have struggled to ensure that the camera remains firmly focused on the human stories that sparked my nosy historian's interest in the first place, rather than on the operating manual, with its strict instructions about following a particular approach or technique.

The term "women of color" potentially refers to a very diverse group of people in nineteenth-century Brazil and Cuba. The rich complexity, and the geographical and historical mutability, of significances attached to skin color in these Iberian American societies have been well rehearsed.[68] A vast world potentially separated different "people of color," whose status and lifestyle also depended on whether they were poor or wealthy, urban or rural dwellers, born in the Americas or associated with one of multiple African identities, as well as on whether they were enslaved, freed within their lifetime, or freeborn. While this book refers to "women of color," its main interest is in women who had directly experienced enslavement, whether they remained enslaved or were struggling to maintain a precarious legal freedom. There was a tremendous social difference between such women and wealthy, lighter-skinned women from freeborn families. Among enslaved and ex-slave women, too, significant differences of status and position also existed, marked among other indicators by their place on a color spectrum. It is significant, for example, that Josepha in Rio was described as *parda*—light-skinned—while Ramona, in Havana, was referred to as *morena*—dark-skinned. Nonetheless, in societies where dark skin was at least potentially associated with slavery, people of color as a group also faced common challenges and obstacles.[69] Meanwhile, in any case, slavery's ending both invoked specific new forms of "racialization" and, as an integral part of this process, involved renegotiating the meanings of "manhood" and "womanhood"—for white men and women as well for those of color.[70] The enslaved and freed women who people the pages of this book grappled with notions of race and gender that were as slippery as they were intertwined.

CHAPTER OUTLINE

The first part of this book traces historical connections between slavery, freedom, law, and gender in the cities of Havana and Rio de Janeiro. Chapter 1 sketches the cities and labor regimes that formed the context for the lives and struggles of generations of enslaved people. The chapter also discusses how, in each country, a set of very different political developments helped usher in gradual emancipation by the 1870s. That process, however, would offer a set of quite similar opportunities to the cities' large populations of enslaved and free(d) women. Chapter 2 traces some of these legal opportunities, particularly the "free womb" laws and other emancipation legislation of the 1870s and 1880s. It explores further the legal and official petitions for freedom that enslaved people made in Rio and Havana during the 1870s and 1880s, suggesting women's particular prominence among claimants. It also considers how slavery as a legal institution, as well as legal routes out of it, worked upon men and women differently, although they shared lives and families.

Part Two of the book probes the practices of claiming legal freedom for enslaved women and their free(d) relatives. Chapter 3 analyzes how and why the theme of maternity recurred constantly within women's legal claims-making. Women historically played a significant role in claims-making and in the quest for manumission, but from the 1870s this prominence took on new significance in an altered social and legal context. As well as simply responding to legal change, their petitions also became one of the motors for further change, influencing jurisprudential decisions and, in turn, the way new legislation was drafted.

Before and after the 1870s, documents that we might expect to contain only dry, strictly "legal" arguments often deployed emotive, rhetorical language about maternity or womanhood that had no basis in the laws themselves; they both reflected, and helped produce, a combination of legal and social change. Where had such notions come from, and why did those who drafted legal claims think they might influence readers? Chapter 4 explores the discursive Atlantic World that helped engender antislavery arguments in Brazil and in the Spanish empire. In these Atlantic port cities, the rolling tides carried ideas and images as well as coffee, sugar or tobacco. Harrowing accounts of children torn from their mothers' breasts, or analyses of how slavery perverted "natural" gender roles, were familiar to previous generations of Atlantic antislavery campaigners. They were reworked, however, in new contexts, shaping the vocabulary with which slavery and antislavery were discussed in Brazil and in Cuba.

Moving away from such lofty rhetoric, Chapter 5 descends to the level of the streets of Havana and Rio de Janeiro. This was the daily social context that helped inform individual women's decisions to seek the help of the law. The chapter explores the often hidden role of fathers and other family members in seeking children's freedom, asking why their participation is not more apparent in the records. The chapter also frames slaves' struggles in the cities within a picture of constant human movement between city and countryside, which inextricably linked the urban and rural worlds.

Part 3 analyzes how gender helped fashion the meanings of freedom. Chapter 6 discusses elites' strategies for shaping the first fully "free" generation, whether in parliamentary debates on gradualism in Rio and Madrid or through a series of social and educational projects. At times sternly emphasizing hardworking obedience, and at other times grandly extolling the virtues of "manly" citizenship or "enlightened motherhood" for the free children of enslaved women, elites sought to mold the destinies of ex-slaves in newly gendered ways, with specific consequences for freedwomen and freedmen of color.

Chapter 7 contrasts such discussions with the broader and richer ways in which enslaved and freed women in Havana and Rio de Janeiro sought to give lived meaning to freedom. They sought material wealth but also greater control over their bodies and reproductive capacities. They established links of support and cohabitation, often with other women, which helped assuage ongoing poverty and dependence; yet they also fought viciously over urban space and territory in ways that complicate any easy assumptions of harmony or solidarity. In particular, as Chapter 8 explores, they wove sinuous new connections between the meanings of freedom and the meanings of motherhood. While this book's cast of central characters surely shared some notions about mothering with the elite men who wrote or received their petitions, they also sought to practice motherhood on their own cultural and social terms, derived from West and Central Africa, as well as from European models and their New World refashionings. In defining the significances of freedom for themselves and their children, they also helped shape the broader trajectories of these two postemancipation societies.

PART ONE

Gender, Law, and Urban Slavery

CHAPTER ONE

Sites of Enslavement, Spaces of Freedom

Slavery and Abolition in the Atlantic Cities of Havana and Rio de Janeiro

He knows by listening to people in the neighborhood that both the defendant's slaves and [Josepha's daughter Maria] are ill-treated . . . and he . . . has heard that this has been published in the daily newspapers.
—José Antônio Alves Rodrigues, witness for Josepha Gonçalves de Moraes,
Rio de Janeiro, 23 July 1884

Neither Josepha Gonçalves de Moraes, in Rio de Janeiro, nor Ramona Oliva, in Havana, had been born in the city where her claim was filed. Yet for each woman, these "Atlantic port cities" were not merely the backdrop to her actions, but a significant part of her story, shaping her relationship to law and labor, slavery and freedom. In turn, such women would also influence the cities in which they arrived. They joined the vast ebb and flow of humanity that made Havana and Rio de Janeiro fast-growing, cosmopolitan places, crowded with newcomers from far-flung provinces and from across the seas. Women of color were part of each city's visual landscape, vividly depicted by foreign visitors as they walked the streets selling foodstuffs or gathered at water fountains to wash clothes and chat in many tongues.[1] In the 1870s and 1880s, as Brazil and Cuba each witnessed sweeping political, economic, legal, and social change leading eventually to abolition, the long road from enslavement to freedom led through the cities of Rio de Janeiro and Havana.

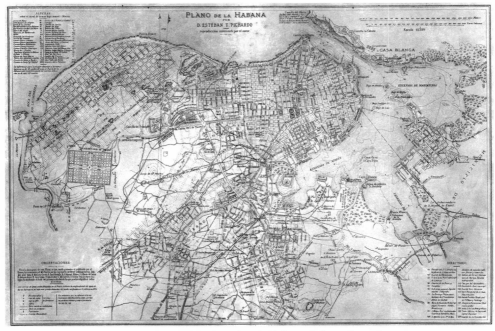

*Havana, 1881. Esteban T. Pichardo, "Plano de la Habana," 1881.
Archivo de la Oficina del Historiador de la Ciudad, Havana.*

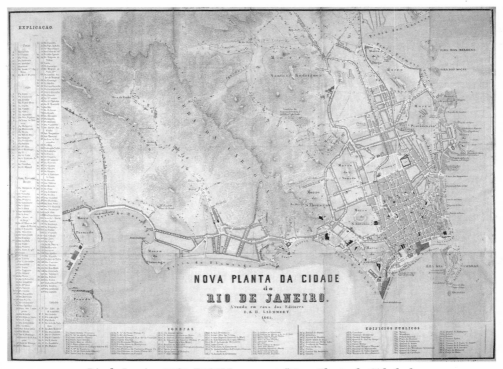

*Rio de Janeiro, 1864. E & H Laemmert, "Nova Planta da Cidade do
Rio de Janeiro," 1864. The British Library Board.*

The first and often most abiding image that greeted most travelers arriving in each city was that of the docks. Generations of visitors described bustling, lively scenes of slave porters carrying luggage and cargo, streams of passengers disembarking from across the world, and the cries of vendors peddling their wares.[2] The docks, from which goods were exported for European and North American consumption, provided the crucial link between the wealth and prestige of these Atlantic cities and the rural, plantation economies on which each country's fortunes were built. Among the many goods shipped across the world from each port, one in particular marked each city's nineteenth-century "second slavery" story: sugar in Cuba, and coffee in Brazil. Produced through the sweat and toil of countless enslaved plantation laborers, each product's growth was partly stimulated by the very abolition of the slave trade and then slavery itself in other American territories.[3]

In Cuba, sugar plantations fanned out from Havana province from the late eighteenth century. The region's population quadrupled between 1777 and 1817 as towns close to the capital that functioned as sugar and tobacco outposts—San Antonio de los Baños, Güines, Guanajay, Jaruco—mushroomed.[4] Sugar exports grew staggeringly by the mid-nineteenth century, almost doubling between 1841 and 1859.[5] By the mid-1850s, Havana's docks were officially among the busiest in the world.[6] As the lands around Havana became gradually exhausted, the sugar frontier expanded eastwards, to Matanzas and Cienfuegos.[7] Nonetheless, Havana province still contained 130 sugar estates in 1862, worked by 19,404 slaves.[8]

In Brazil, meanwhile, coffee plantations gradually conquered the southeastern provinces of Minas Gerais, Espírito Santo and Rio de Janeiro, spreading west and south along the Paraíba valley. The middle of the nineteenth century was the heyday of Vassouras, a coffee town in the province of Rio de Janeiro that became flooded with the wealth of the plantations and maintained close links to the imperial capital.[9] As with sugar in Cuba, soil exhaustion and constant expansion of production meant that coffee had a moving frontier. By the 1870s and 1880s, the most thriving and modern plantations were to be found in São Paulo, where coffee boomed as prices almost doubled over the second half of the nineteenth century.[10] National production doubled from 1850 to 1880 and would triple in the 1890s.[11]

It was in these rural worlds where the fortunes were made that helped transform Havana and Rio de Janeiro into two of the Americas' largest and wealthiest nineteenth-century metropolises. The connections between each city and its rural surroundings were intimate and quotidian. Successful planters used their wealth to construct elegant city residences where they spent much of the year. Coffee and sugar stimulated a raft of urban sectors, from banking and insurance to commerce and shipbuilding. Meanwhile, even as they were fed by imports of dried beef from Rio Grande do Sul to Rio de Janeiro, or exported boatloads of Cuban pineapples from Havana to New York, the cities' expanding urban populations also consumed the produce of their rural hinterlands.[12] On the cities' outskirts, urban neighborhoods gradually petered out into small farms, often worked by enslaved or free people of color, who also acted as muleteers and cart-drivers, daily transporting goods but also news and information into and out of the cities.[13] These rural fringes also harbored communities of fugitive slaves, who established furtive, symbiotic links of trade and communication with city residents.[14] As well as these daily connections, the rural context also played an important *symbolic* role in urban life. Even for slaves who had lived their whole lives in the city, the threat of sale to plantation labor was always in the back of their minds, and it was used by owners to maintain obedience and to discipline transgressors.

Intimately linked to the surrounding countryside, Havana and Rio nonetheless each had a long tradition of specifically urban slavery.[15] Slaves made up a staggering one-half of Rio de Janeiro's growing population for much of the first half of the nineteenth century.[16] The end of the African trade in 1850, manumission, and a significant drain of urban slaves to plantation labor meant that by the 1870s, as Josepha arrived in the city, the enslaved population had fallen considerably. Yet there were still almost 50,000 slaves in Rio by 1872—around one fifth of the city's total population.[17] Havana's slaves never reached the proportions that Rio's had done earlier in the century, but Havana had long contained significant numbers of enslaved people, who made up over a third of its population in 1791.[18] Across the nineteenth century, while the city grew, the enslaved proportion of its population fell, reaching one fifth by 1846.[19] By 1861, Havana contained 24,381 slaves, who comprised 14 percent of the city's population of 179,996.[20] As the "free womb" laws were introduced, then, the numbers of remaining slaves in each city had fallen from their peak but remained significant.

Exposed to poor living conditions, diets, and standards of hygiene, the lives of most urban slaves were harsh and short. They were pitifully vulnerable to disease and infant mortality.[21] Their work was often physically exhausting, although most perceived it as preferable to the grueling labors of field slaves, who cut cane or picked coffee in the burning sun. They were subject to brutal physical punishments, carried out by owners or by urban authorities seeking to impose public discipline.[22] And while slaves on large, stable plantations had a reasonable chance of forming families and communities away from the vigilant eyes of slaveholders, this was harder to achieve for domestic slaves, who most often lived in their owners' households.[23] Such conditions continued for many who managed to achieve freedom, since their poverty and lack of autonomy helped ex-owners to continue exercising seigneurial "rights" over them.

Despite all these hardships, Rio de Janeiro and Havana each held a compelling attraction for enslaved people. Just as the imaginary of the plantation shaped urban slave life, so slaves on distant plantations imagined cities they had never seen as places that offered greater access to autonomy and to the cash that might help them purchase freedom. In each city, for example, some slaves had long worked to earn a daily wage, a practice referred to in Cuba as earning *jornal por su cuenta* and in Brazil as *trabalhar ao ganho*.[24] As long as the enslaved person paid the owner the required daily amount, the way they earned the money and how they used any surplus was up to them. Although only a minority earned *jornal*, urban slavery also presented other opportunities to earn money. While most slaves in Cuba and Brazil would not manage to buy freedom in their lifetime, relatively high manumission rates meant they often at least knew others who had done so, keeping alight a small flicker of hope of following in their footsteps.[25] And as slaves knew, the chances of this were much higher in the cities than in the countryside.[26]

Beyond the distant hope of manumission, urban living offered some chances of greater daily autonomy, which was valuable in itself. Although prized domestic servants might be kept indoors, others were sent out to the street to perform errands, providing precious moments of social and leisure time, whether to chat with a neighbor or *parente* or to attend a dance, associational meeting, or religious festival.[27] Other slaves spent almost all their time on the street.[28] In Rio, some managed to rent private rooms to sleep away from owners' houses.[29]

Both cities also housed large numbers of free people of color, often crowded into poorer areas.[30] In Havana, they might live in *solares* (subdivided houses) in the fast-growing neighborhoods beyond the city walls. In Rio, the urban poor increasingly inhabited the rapidly expanding slum tenements known as *estalagens* or *cortiços*—this latter term meaning "beehives"—which, by the 1880s, jostled for space with wealthy residences and provoked fear and outrage among the city's elites.[31] Among the itinerant, amorphous urban population, it was difficult to tell slave from free. Urban fugitive slaves often avoided recapture for long periods, blending into what Sidney Chalhoub has termed the *cidade esconderijo*, or city hideout.[32]

Enslaved and free(d) people of color built a rich cultural and social life in the cities. Havana and Rio were home to important, longstanding religious brotherhoods—*irmandades, cofradías, cabildos de nación*—organized around African "nations," or ethnic identities recast in the New World. Brotherhoods and other associations offered their members limited manumission funds, credit, and insurance and helped with the all-important business of dying, helping pay for a "good death" through the funeral rites that both marked the deceased's social position and facilitated that person's passage to the afterlife.[33] Cities offered the best chances for such organizations to flourish, although their roots reached out into the rural peripheries and beyond, deep into the countryside.[34] The cities reverberated with African-derived religious and cultural life, whether the *calundú* divination ceremonies brought by Central Africans, the *orixá* (*orisha*) worship of the Yoruba, the cults to the *voduns* whose home was Dahomey (today's Benin), or a rich array of African Catholic practices.[35]

Other large cities—Santiago de Cuba, Salvador da Bahia—shared many of these features of urban slavery. In fact, across the Americas, as Keila Grinberg has suggested, "despite different legal traditions, the destinies of discrete groups of Africans and their descendants in cities . . . were remarkably similar."[36] Yet Havana and Rio de Janeiro also stand out from other urban centers in Brazil or Cuba. The hearts of these two Atlantic slave-based economies throbbed not just with the giddy wealth of coffee and sugar, or with the aching muscles and the dreams of freedom of enslaved urban laborers, but with the heady rush of political power. Rio was the seat of Brazilian national government—in Jeffrey Needell's words, "the beachhead of all the political tides that ran."[37] Havana was the center of Spanish military and political power in Cuba, answerable only to Madrid. As enslaved people in Rio left their cramped dwelling-places and went on their day's business, they passed the grandiose buildings of the Imperial Palace, seat of the imperial family who would play an important role in their destinies. The high-profile decisions of Rio's appeals court regarding slavery or freedom would have a disproportionate effect on the course of national legislation and jurisprudence. Meanwhile, Cuban slaves and their freed relatives like Ramona traveled long, weary miles to reach Havana, hoping to petition the highest government offices in the land. José Ferrer de Couto, writing in the late 1860s, described how "The steps of the palace of Havana, on the very frequent days when an audience is given, are always full of people of color who go to the Captain General in person to present him with their business."[38] Ferrer de Couto, a Spanish government agent who published a pro-Spanish newspaper in New York, was one of the best-known racist defenders of slavery of the period. It suited his argument to exaggerate significantly the access enslaved people had to the law and to manumission. Nonetheless, the picture he paints of the scene at the steps of the palace is compelling. Sometimes—as in the case of an 1872 freedom appeal by morena Felipa Galuzo—appeals made in Havana reached as far as Madrid itself.[39] Both cities housed British consuls, mired in the slippery international politics of slavery and abolition, with whom some litigating slaves also sought leverage.[40]

With powerful institutions came powerful men, who, from the capital cities, wielded disproportionate influence on national and colonial laws, policies, and social mores. Like most nineteenth-century Latin American elites, they drew many of their ideas from Europe. Yet as they debated slavery or emancipation, they were also inevitably influenced by their daily dealings with slaves and former slaves all around them—whether on the street, in their houses, in the nurseries where their children grew up, or, often, in their beds. Spaces for social, cultural, and political exchange were greater in these cities than anywhere else.

Of course, any resident of today's Rio de Janeiro, where luxurious gated condominiums rub shoulders with sprawling *favelas*, can attest that urban living in itself hardly guarantees any meaningful exchanges between a city's residents. In each of our cities in the nineteenth century, extreme social inequality was enforced through the vigorous and continual repression of the poor and marginal. Although wealthy families mingled with Africans and their descendants in the most intimate of daily ways, a tremendous cultural disconnect was part of the very means by which such unequal relations of power were maintained. Yet despite these carefully enforced segregations, large cities did offer more ways than small towns or rural areas in which the lines could be crossed, complicated, or even blurred. By the last decades of the nineteenth century, each city contained fewer slaves and more free(d) people. In Rio, during slavery's last years, slaveholders were typically of quite modest means, often owning only one slave, while middling urban sectors became more politically visible.[41] Printers, students at the military academies, journalists, public schoolteachers, and railway workers participated in urban riots about specific issues and joined burgeoning abolitionist movements.[42] In Havana, despite colonial repression, a variety of voices were raised against slavery, whether among burgeoning labor movements or new political parties, even as the enslaved themselves sought legal freedom in increasing numbers.[43] The capital cities, then, offered spaces where slaves' quest for freedom might connect with the broader political and social changes of slavery's final years.

WOMEN AND URBAN SLAVERY

For Ramona, arriving from rural Matanzas, Havana must have looked and felt very different from what she was used to. During the day, she perhaps walked the city's wide, elegant boulevards; if she ventured out at night, she might marvel at the gas lighting that illuminated the wealthier areas. Perhaps she wandered past the expensive shops selling imported products that clustered on glamorous shopping streets like San Rafael. But surely more striking still were the people she encountered.

Havana was home to generations of enslaved women of color, who consistently made up at least half the city's enslaved population.[44] By contrast, across Cuba as a whole, women were only 38 percent of the slave population at midcentury.[45] Enslaved women lived alongside a large population of free(d) women of color. While their numbers were around even with free(d) men across the island, women represented 57 percent of the free people of color in the *jurisdicción* of Havana.[46] Working on the streets, they were much more visible than white women, who were greatly outnumbered by white men and were often cloistered indoors.[47] For the Italian-born British journalist Antonio Gallenga, writing in 1861, "Looked at from a social point of view, what immediately strikes a stranger is that Havannah, like the Rome of Romulus, is a city without women. . . . Hardly any other women than negresses are to be seen about."[48] Far from seeing, as Gallenga did, Havana as a "city without women," it was probably precisely these "negresses" that Ramona noticed on her arrival. The streets and marketplaces she passed on her way to lodge her appeal with the Gobierno General, and the *solares* where perhaps a friend or relative put her up during her stay in the capital, were full of freedwomen like her. Like her, many of them were struggling to wrest custody of their young children, born "free" since the early 1870s, from their former owners. Struggling to assuage poverty and marginality, many cohabited with other women who did the same job or were of the same ethnic group. Perhaps they told Ramona where to go, chatted about their own experiences with the law, or told her about family members who remained enslaved across central and western Cuba.

Rio de Janeiro historically had a smaller white population and a larger free population of color than Havana, where, especially after the 1840s Escalera conspiracy, the free population of color came under increasing pressure.[49] Yet Rio, like Havana, had long been a city where women of color were a central part of the urban landscape. The city's enslaved population contained around 40 percent women in the 1830s and 1840s, unlike the plantations, whose slaves were often 70–80 percent male.[50] By the 1870s and 1880s, women represented around half of Rio's population of color, both enslaved and free.[51] Women were even scarcer among Rio's white population than Havana's, outnumbered by white men by two to one in 1872.[52]

Although African-descended men and women lived alongside one another, sharing families and communities, their daily experiences of urban labor were different. The cities' houses were built by enslaved and free(d) carpenters and masons, and their wealthy residents were driven from place to place by enslaved carriage-drivers. Their avenues were gradually widened and improved throughout the nineteenth century by gangs of enslaved or convict laborers. The cities were home, too, to enslaved water-carriers, porters, dockworkers, and latrine-emptiers, and to freed tailors, musicians, and shipbuilders. While these workers might be enslaved or free(d) depending on the period and their own circumstances, they were almost always men.[53]

Meanwhile, the residents of Havana and Rio depended on Africans and their descendants to perform another set of essential tasks. Household tables were provisioned at markets where enslaved and freed vendors loudly promoted their wares and jealously guarded their turf. The noisy, winding streets were peopled by itinerant sellers bearing fruits, sweets, and foodstuffs balanced on their heads on trays, perhaps carrying small, sleepy children on their backs. The young *moças* and stately *senhoras* of Rio de Janeiro went off to watch fashionable European opera singers— or perhaps, by the 1880s, to attend charitable events for emancipation— flaunting beautiful dresses lovingly embroidered by skilled seamstresses. As Havana's lawyers sat in their offices in the somnolent heat of long Caribbean afternoons, scribbling out the pleas of enslaved claimants who came to them seeking freedom, they sweated into clothes which had been laboriously washed and ironed by African-descended workers. Food was prepared, beds were made, and floors were washed by an army of enslaved and freed people that was overwhelmingly female.[54] Domestic work of one kind or another was the lot of most enslaved women.[55] With the exception of seamstresses, most of the occupations available to women of color, enslaved and free, did not involve high status or earning potential, unlike some of the skilled artisan occupations open to some enslaved and freed men.[56] On the other hand, many women, especially those of West African origin, successfully worked as traders and marketers.[57]

The work performed by poor women, whether enslaved or free, did not end with these tasks. For them, unlike most of their male friends and relatives, slavery and economic and social dependence meant their bodies were subjected, routinely and with little recourse, to sex with owners and other men in positions of power.[58] Such encounters ranged from untold casual rapes to lasting affective relationships. Although their very ubiquity and acceptability has helped to hide the specifics of these encounters from the historical record, they constitute the countless building-blocks, painfully stacked up over the centuries, of the racial and cultural mixtures for which Cuba and Brazil have each become known.[59] Female bodies were put to work in other intimate ways, too. Enslaved wet nurses breast-fed and cared for slaveholders' children and were often forced to give up their own children in the process.[60] In each city, meanwhile, sex was for sale. In the narrow streets of the Rio de Janeiro neighborhood of Sacramento, or in the well-known *casas de citas* along Havana's Teniente Rey street, enslaved women were coerced by owners into lucrative prostitution and free women sold their bodies to improve their precarious economic position.[61]

If gender was fundamental to urban slave life and labor, it also shaped urban routes to freedom. Women played a central part in broader struggles for manumission across most American slaveholding societies, even though overall manumission rates in those societies varied hugely. There were many reasons why. Male owners might sometimes free women, or their children, following sexual relations. Yet, as women knew only too well, this was by no means guaranteed. Instead, like most slaves who eventually achieved manumission, women would have to actively seek to make such encounters yield freedom, or at least better conditions, for themselves or their children.[62] Women who worked as street vendors, marketers, and traders were well-placed to save money to purchase freedom. On the other hand, most of the more skilled professions and formal opportunities to earn *jornal* were dominated by male slaves. And in any case, purchasing freedom did not only involve literally having enough money to do so. Self-purchase legally also required the owner's consent until 1871 in Brazil and 1842 in Cuba. Even after these dates, the owner could either facilitate or seriously obstruct self-purchase. Mary Karasch suggested that women, as domestic servants, had closer relationships with

"Female fruit seller," Cuba, 1871. Samuel Hazard, Cuba with Pen and Pencil *(Hartford, Conn., 1871), 89. The British Library Board.*

"The Quitandeira" (enslaved or free street vendor of food items), Brazil, 1857. Daniel P. Kidder, Brazil and the Brazilians, portrayed in historical and descriptive sketches *(Philadelphia, 1857), 167. The British Library Board.*

and greater influence over owners than did other slaves. She also pointed out that around half the owners who manumitted their slaves in her study of Rio de Janeiro between 1808 and 1850 were in fact women.[63] In other words, although historians have sometimes assumed that sexual relations between enslaved women and slaveholding men necessarily explain the connection between women and manumission, in fact the explanations are more complex and multiple than this.[64] Rather than understanding manumission as the straightforward product of either sex or money, it may be more helpful to consider women's own attitudes and initiatives toward securing legal freedom.

For many enslaved women, this process was entwined with the urban environments in which it most often occurred. Across the Americas, the groups most likely to access manumission were women slaves and slaves who lived in cities. Indeed, contemporaries discussing female slaves, urban slaves, and domestic slaves often assumed a certain overlap between these categories in practice. Historians, too, have noted that both women and urban slaves were more likely to be freed as discrete categories, but also that these categories also reinforced each other: city slaves gained manumission at higher rates because more of them were women, while women's high levels of manumission can partly be explained in terms of their access to urban environments.[65] Again, though, the connections were less straightforward than they appear from the statistics. A complex, gendered relationship between slavery and urban life underpinned the quests for freedom of the women whose legal struggles this book follows. As they could surely have told us, though, neither being female nor living in a city offered any particular guarantee of freedom. At least in part, freedom through legal means was born out of the aims and strategies of the enslaved person in question and of the people around him or her.

ON THE MOVE IN ATLANTIC PORT CITIES

Rio and Havana were places that housed populations on the move, whose residents' own lives and memories connected the cities to far-flung places across the ocean that lapped at each of their shores. Central to these lives and memories was Africa. Brazil had both a longer history as a fully fledged slave society and a larger free African-descended population, while Cuba had imported slaves en masse only since the late eighteenth century. This contrast has led Christopher Schmidt-Nowara to observe that, in the nineteenth century, "The tension between slavery and freedom was perhaps greater in the Spanish Antilles than it was in Brazil."[66] Yet despite these different historical trajectories, the African diaspora also created striking cultural connections between nineteenth-century Havana and Rio. The "second slavery" in each coincided with the collapse of the Oyo Empire in today's Nigeria, helping to fill the slave ships with defeated Yoruba who broadly became known as *nagô* or *mina* in Brazil and as *lucumí* in Cuba.[67] They brought a wealth of distinctive linguistic, cultural, and religious traditions, which remain evident in Afro-Cuban and Afro-Brazilian culture today. Meanwhile, theirs was only one of a cacophony of voices in each of these profoundly cosmopolitan cities, where the Ewe-Fon, Igbo, Kimbundu, and Mande languages were spoken daily on the streets.[68]

The Middle Passage was only the first of many journeys undergone by Africans and their descendants in the New World. While Ramona apparently made a deliberate choice to go to Havana, Josepha was still enslaved when she was brought to Rio. Her daughter Maria had been born in the northeastern province of Ceará in 1873. Somewhere in the following decade, as drought swept the arid northeast, mother and daughter were moved or sold down to Rio—a distance of over one and a half thousand miles. Their journey was just one in a vast exodus which gathered momentum in Brazil from the 1850s after the tide of new arrivals from Africa was stemmed. As the poorer northeastern provinces declined and the coffee plantations of the southeast boomed, hundreds of thousands were sold south.[69] From 1852 to 1862, an average of 3,370 slaves per year arrived in the port of Rio from elsewhere in Brazil.[70] The trade accelerated from the 1870s, with 10,000 per year reaching the center-south between 1873 and 1881.[71] By the 1880s, Brazil's remaining enslaved population was overwhelmingly concentrated in the southeastern provinces, creating divergent political positions on the slavery question among the vast country's different regions. The new influx of West African slaves from the northeast altered the ethnic mix of Rio de Janeiro's African-descended population, previously dominated by people from Congo-Angola.[72] The sparse records of these thousands of sales hint at untold personal tragedies. Who was Maria's father, for example? Did he also make the journey south, or was he left behind? For hundreds of thousands like Josepha and her family, sale south meant separation from kin, as well as from cultures and ways of life established in the northeast.[73] Even if they arrived together, the fortunes of men and women who were sold to Rio also often diverged. Men, who were more likely to be sold in the internal trade in the first place, were also more likely to be sold out of the city to coffee plantations. Women were often bought for domestic work—Josepha worked as an ironess, for example—or indeed, among young lighter-skinned women, for prostitution.[74] Either way, they were more likely to remain in the city.

In Cuba, too, slaves experienced constant geographical movement, not just across the sea but across the island, which has yet to be traced in depth by historians. While for some purposes, owners and the colonial state tried to prevent enslaved people from moving around, owners also had to transfer slaves from city to plantation or between their rural properties as economic needs required. Although they knew that mobility might help feed the flames of insurrection, they needed people of color as drivers, messengers, and transporters of goods for sale.[75] The enslaved themselves, meanwhile, became adept at making legal arguments based on their own geographical locations or their status as "urban" or "rural." In fact, movement and mobility became one of the most contentious legal issues that slaves and their owners in Cuba wrangled over as the nineteenth century wore on.[76]

The gradual ending of slavery during the 1870s and 1880s also saw movement of a new kind in the cities of Havana and Rio de Janeiro. The enslaved population of each city fell faster than in the surrounding rural areas.[77] Historians have suggested a process of "ruralization" of slavery, as urban slaves were transferred to plantation labor where their prices were highest.[78] If more men than women were being sold to plantations, how can we account for the fact that the female enslaved population also fell at about the same rate? At least part of the answer is presumably that women in the cities were finding ways out of slavery. In any case, as Rebecca Scott long ago pointed out for Cuba, "The causes of emancipation cannot be found solely within the sugar plantations, for as emancipation proceeded, these plantations held proportionately more, not fewer, of Cuba's slaves."[79]

Africans and their descendants in the cities mingled with influxes of other migrants. Havana was home to large numbers of peninsular Spaniards—whether poorer manual workers from Galicia or the Canary Islands, or the Basques and Catalans who often became wealthy traders.[80] Rio, despite independence from Portugal and waves of Lusophobia, remained home to large Portuguese communities.[81] The cities of Rio de Janeiro and São Paulo experienced a population explosion from the 1870s, fuelled by the arrival of almost 80,000 European immigrants between 1870 and 1890.[82] Around 125,000 indentured Chinese laborers arrived in Cuba between 1847 and 1874.[83] Each city played host to a steady stream of European and North American visitors. Marveling at local customs in the "tropics" and publishing their "discoveries" for European audiences, travelers helped shape local people's own imaginaries of their countries and cities.[84]

The arrival of so many human beings fuelled each city's rapid, uneven expansion. By the 1870s, Rio de Janeiro had expanded north and south, incorporating new, leafier suburbs where residences for the wealthy grew up, while the poor crowded together in the filth and stench of the Old City. The city had boasted gas lighting and underground sewerage since the 1850s, yet squalor and poverty continued to jostle with the elegant cafés and shops lining central streets like the Rua do Ouvidor.[85] Indeed, until the turn of the century, the city's "reputation as a pesthole flourished. Travelers at best described Rio as exotic. . . . More often, one notes fear of yellow fever's seasonal slaughter and disdain for Rio's crowded streets, tawdry public places, and stench of filth, perfumes and sweat."[86] The *Revista Illustrada* newspaper mercilessly mocked the dreadful state of the city's streets in November 1885, depicting the risks encountered by residents who ventured out on the streets, from falling into potholes to suffocating from the stench of the filth littering the city's streets.[87] Nonetheless, Rio's increasingly urban character contrasted with Brazil as a whole, where, by 1890, 90 percent of the population still lived in rural areas.[88]

Havana also grew enormously over the nineteenth century. The city's 51,307 inhabitants in 1791 became 179,966 by 1861.[89] By the year after the abolition of slavery, the population was 200,448.[90] This number was not so far behind Rio's 1872 population of 274,972, especially considering Cuba's much smaller size than Brazil's. The original walled city (today's Old Havana) was gradually dwarfed by the areas that had grown up outside the walls, whether poor and squalid neighborhoods like Jesús María, or wealthy suburbs like El Cerro, with gardens and large houses where the rich escaped the noise and smells of the old city's narrow streets.[91] Boats crisscrossed the bay many times a day, ferrying passengers back and forth between the main city and the settlements of Regla and Casablanca. In 1863, the walls began to be demolished, making way for lucrative new building works.[92]

Meanwhile, Rio and Havana were each connected to their rural hinterlands and to the wider Atlantic World by the advanced transport infrastructure that facilitated the "second slavery." In Cuba, the first train had left Havana for the sugar-producing town of Bejucal, 27 kilometers away, in 1837. By 1870, when most Latin American nations were just developing their rail networks, Cuba already possessed 1,255 lines.[93] Railroads transported goods for export to Havana's docks and passengers to stations

Cartoon depicting the conditions of Rio de Janeiro's streets in 1885.
"Coisas da atualidade" ("Current events"), Revista Illustrada, *16 November 1885, 4–5.*
Fundação Casa Rui Barbosa, Rio de Janeiro.

on the city's outskirts.[94] In Rio, railroads appeared from the 1850s, and a regular system of coaches and trams ferried passengers between the city center and its newer suburbs.[95]

Thus Havana and Rio de Janeiro were cities on the move, in many senses. From the beginning of the 1870s, however, each witnessed changes and movements of a new kind, becoming the centers from which two parallel, if very different, processes of gradual abolition would unfold.

WARS, LAWS, AND CHANGING MORES:
GRADUAL EMANCIPATION IN BRAZIL AND CUBA

By the end of the 1860s, Cuba and Brazil were the only remaining slaveholding territories in the Americas, except for Spain's smaller and less lucrative colony of Puerto Rico. The paths to emancipation trodden by each over the subsequent two decades were carved out of very different political contexts.

In Cuba, the slavery issue was inseparable from the broader question of the island's colonial status. The Spanish government was acutely aware of the threat posed by the United States, looming only ninety miles to the north and well positioned to annex Spain's remaining colonies.[96] Spain needed allies and could not afford a reputation as a backward, repressive, slaveholding colonial power. On the other hand, however, Spain could not afford to alienate Cuban planters through any sudden declaration of abolition. At the same time, Spanish liberals embraced abolitionism, and the Spanish Abolitionist Society (founded in 1865) began to put pressure on the Spanish Cortes.[97]

In 1867, the Spanish called a meeting in Madrid to discuss colonial political reform. The Junta de Información, as it was called, was composed of sixteen Cuban and four Puerto Rican deputies. The latter, with little vested interest in maintaining slavery, forced the question of abolition onto the agenda. Cuban delegates' responses were ambivalent. While they were much more conservative than the Puerto Ricans, advocating a long-term, gradual emancipation plan rather than immediate abolition, their willingness to actually discuss the matter at all surprised and angered conservative elements back in Havana.[98]

The *junta* episode proved a major disappointment for Cuban elites, who chafed at heavy taxation and the favoring of peninsular Spaniards for coveted positions.[99] After raising hopes by calling the *junta* in the first place, the Spanish government failed to take action, driving many who had previously favored reform within the Spanish empire to embrace full independence.[100] In October 1868, rebellion broke out in the east of the island, sparked in the first instance by local creole planters. The rebellion, which became the Ten Years' War (1868–78), was not a cohesive movement, even after the various provinces that rose up were unified under the leadership of *hacendado* Carlos Manuel de Céspedes. He and other leaders did not immediately or unequivocally abolish slavery. Over the course of the war, rebel leaders on the ground became much more radically pro-independence and pro-abolition, yet the movement's wealthy supporters in Havana and abroad remained tied to slavery and fearful of the prospect of "race war," never supported a full invasion of western Cuba. Nonetheless, it was the Cuban rebels on the ground, not the Spanish government in Madrid, who were the first to declare full abolition.[101]

Linked to the developments on the island, radical change had meanwhile also swept into Madrid, in the guise of the September 1868 Liberal

Revolution. The new Cortes announced broad reform for Cuba and Puerto Rico, including reform on the slavery question. Fears that the United States would back the Cuban rebels finally prompted Spain to pass the Moret Law, a "free womb" law for gradual emancipation, on 4 July 1870. The law notionally freed children subsequently born to enslaved mothers. Segismundo Moret y Prendergast, the foreign minister, was a liberal abolitionist, but also a pragmatic politician. His 1870 law aimed to placate international opinion while preventing radical change.[102]

In February 1878, the exhausted and divided Cuban rebels gave in, signing the Pact of Zanjón with the Spanish, although one group continued fighting, waging the unsuccessful Guerra Chiquita (Little War) in 1879–80. The eastern part of the island, then, had seen twelve virtually continuous years of war. The war had a massive impact across the island, radicalizing and polarizing political positions. Economically, its effects were devastating, and these, combined with falling sugar prices and rising prices for slaves, forced a series of structural changes to Cuba's sugar sector.[103] Small *ingenios* (sugar plantations with their own mill) gave way to large *centrales* (central sugar mills) as smaller and less efficient producers went bankrupt. Cuba faced economic depression by the mid-1880s.[104] Economic dependence on the United States, which received 94 percent of Cuban sugar by the late 1880s, increased sharply.[105] For enslaved people in eastern Cuba, the war's results were even more dramatic: many who had fought gained freedom during or after the war.[106]

However, the fighting had never reached the prosperous western half of the island, which contained 86 percent of the 1862 slave population.[107] Here, routes out of slavery would primarily be through law, not through war. Although planter resistance ensured a very slow response to the Moret Law, the law nonetheless initiated a gradual process of change. The state entered the private relationship between slave and owner in new ways, while the enslaved themselves sought legal routes toward freedom at a rate that had not been anticipated. Meanwhile, abolition in Puerto Rico in 1873 led to calls from Spanish abolitionists to do the same for Cuba. Decreasing slave numbers and international pressure led Spain to pass the *patronato* law of 13 February 1880, which nominally abolished slavery and introduced an eight-year apprenticeship period. Slaves, now officially *patrocinados*, were to be paid a minimal but symbolically significant monthly stipend. As "loss of authority led to further loss of authority, *patrocinado* initiatives created their own momentum, . . . and the decreasing importance of slavery made government enforcements of *patrocinado* rights less difficult." The *patronato* was ended on 7 October 1886, two years earlier than planned.[108]

In Brazil, as emancipationist sentiment gradually grew over the 1860s, a war of a different kind helped set the political scene for emancipation. After Paraguayan dictator Francisco Solano López sent his troops across Argentina into Uruguay in March 1865, Brazil declared war on Paraguay, in October that year. Although Brazil, Argentina, and Uruguay allied against the small nation, the fight proved much longer and harder than expected. Brazil's dilapidated, underfunded army was unable to recruit enough volunteers, and the slave conscripts that took their place caused embarrassment at the spectacle of a large but militarily weak power forced to depend on enslaved soldiers. This proved particularly poignant when the Conde d'Eu, husband of Princess Isabel, the heir to the throne, encouraged the newly formed provisional Paraguayan government to abolish slavery there, making it impossible not to address the issue at home. The war's consequences in terms of slavery were, in some ways, similar to those of the Ten Years' War in Cuba: it delayed legal action on slavery in the short term, but helped ensure it would be a political priority once the war was finally won by March 1870. Brazilian politicians watched closely as the Moret Law was passed in Madrid a few months later, handing Brazil the embarrassing role of being the last American slaveholding power to take action on emancipation.[109]

The building momentum for emancipation did not mean that the passage of the 1871 Rio Branco Law, Brazil's "free womb" law, was simple or straightforward. Rather, it was hugely contentious in a country whose most influential legislators and politicians were slaveholders, and where the "free womb" concept struck at the very foundations of the principle of property in human beings. Nonetheless, after almost a year of stormy debate in Parliament, and conscious of the Spanish move the year before, the bill finally passed into law on 28 September 1871.[110] Like in Cuba, the results of the law were both greater and smaller than had been intended: smaller in that owners routinely flouted it, but greater in that it eroded the personal power of owners over their human property and widened the routes by which the enslaved could seek legal freedom.

After the law's passage, the process we now see as a gradual "transition" was also far from smooth or obvious to most Brazilians.[111] Emancipation legislation was made possible only by broader political and social struggles. In response to the slow pace of change under the Rio Branco Law, broad-based abolitionist campaigns took off in urban centers around the country in the 1880s. Changes and concessions were battled over at every step. In fact, the position of the national government hardened against further legislative change from the mid-1880s. A reform ministry headed by Liberal senator Manoel Pinto de Souza Dantas came to power in 1884, endorsing a bill for uncompensated emancipation of sexagenarian slaves that outraged slaveholders. A series of political crises saw Dantas's cabinet replaced by the much more conservative administrations of José Antônio Saraiva and, in turn, João Maurício Wanderley, Baron of Cotegipe. Cotegipe's ministry eventually passed a much more conservative version of Dantas's original bill, known as the Saraiva-Cotegipe Law, in September 1885, which "freed" sexagenarians but required them to work another three years as "compensation" to owners.[112] The developments infuriated abolitionists, and the movement regained momentum in opposition to the conservative turn in national politics.

Meanwhile, regional differences played an important part in creating a political consensus against slavery in Brazil. Thanks to the internal trade, it was no longer in the interest of the elites of most regions outside Minas, Rio, and São Paulo to support slavery.[113] Indeed, strong abolitionist pressure and dwindling slave numbers brought an official declaration of abolition in the province of Ceará—Josepha's northeastern birthplace—by March 1883, as well as in Amazonas the following year.[114] Strong abolitionist pressure, dwindling slave numbers, and mass slave flight from plantations in the southeast helped finally hasten abolition by May 1888.[115] As rural fugitives sought freedom outside the law's provisions, their urban counterparts often sought it *within* the law, challenging its very definition and application.

Thus, the decision to embrace gradual emancipation emerged within two very different political and historical contexts. Nonetheless, each path led to the adoption of a comparable set of womb-based laws that helped position women at the center of the legal emancipation process. It was in the capital cities—sites that were both comparable and interconnected within a broader Atlantic setting—where their actions would have particular resonance.

HAVANA, RIO DE JANEIRO, AND ATLANTIC ABOLITIONISMS

The cities in which Ramona and Josepha each found herself were places where eddies of proslavery and antislavery opinion met and mingled. Movements or ideas formed at local, national, or provincial level took on new significance in the cities; antislavery perspectives flowed in and out with the daily tides. The actions of our two protagonists and others like them make more sense when understood in this context.

By the time Josepha took her daughter's case to court in the mid-1880s, a popular abolitionist movement was conquering the streets and squares of Rio de Janeiro. Local societies and clubs sprang up, coalescing from 1883 under the umbrella of the Abolitionist Confederation.[116] Like urban abolition movements across the country, Rio's movement helped refashion the "practice of politics" in late-nineteenth-century Brazil.[117] Large public rallies, concerts, theatres, and bazaars helped mobilize the energies of sectors of the population who had previously been excluded from the formal political arena—including, in significant numbers, women from different social spheres. The high-profile campaigns of abolitionist newspapers showcased broader political developments.[118] Rio's movement was uniquely placed to impact national politics, receiving maximum visibility at the very heart of the Brazilian empire.

A combination of very different influences and agendas helped shape antislavery politics in the capital. The city's Livro de Ouro slave emancipation fund is an example of this dynamic. The fund was established by the municipal council in 1885 with the conservative aim of containing popular fervor and ensuring a gradual, controlled transition. However, as Cotegipe's government came into office and national politics hardened against abolitionism, the fund ended up taking on a more radical significance.[119] Drawing in the abolitionist press to some degree, as well as the many local people who raised or donated funds or manumitted slaves, the decisions about which slaves to manumit also depended on the initiatives of enslaved people themselves—especially women, at whom, like many other private and municipal emancipation funds operating in Brazil at the time, the fund was primarily targeted. The presence of the imperial family, especially the Princess Isabel, at the showy emancipation ceremonies held periodically in the city from 1885 to 1887 helped link the family to a broad antislavery agenda in a very public way, which was noted by enslaved people and their relatives and, at times, caused significant friction between national and municipal politicians.[120]

In the city of Rio, it was not the 1885 Saraiva-Cotegipe Law that proved the last straw for the abolitionist movement but the June 1886 regulations for it, which became known as the "Black Regulation." Although the law had banned the interprovincial slave trade, the regulation reversed the normal protocol and defined the imperial capital as part of the surrounding province of Rio de Janeiro. This effectively reopened the slave traffic between the city and the "slaveocrat" province, exposing the slaves of the Corte (as the court city was known) to sale to coffee plantations—a threat that, as we have seen, was one of urban slaves' own greatest fears.[121] In the resulting furor, long-standing tensions between the municipal council and the national government to which it had long been subjected reached the boiling point. Fervent abolitionist José do Patrocinio ran a high-profile campaign for local office on the strength of the issue and was elected councilor in June 1886.[122] That July, at the fifth municipal emancipation ceremony, in front of the imperial family and government ministers, the president of the municipal council openly condemned the regulation and asked the emperor to overturn it.[123] The politics of the fund, reaching figures from the imperial family to slaves themselves, reflected the nature of abolitionist forces in the city more broadly. Enslaved people turned to abolitionist newspaper offices for help with their struggles with owners; the press regularly published the twists and turns of slaves' legal cases. There were intimate connections between campaigners in the city and fugitive slaves living in communities like the Leblon *quilombo*; and illiterate slaves learned quickly about changes to the law or the political landscape and sought to apply them to their own lives.[124]

When Ramona arrived in Havana in 1883, a very different atmosphere greeted her. This fortress city, the seat of a weakened but intransigent colonial power, saw none of the public abolitionist ferment that surely touched Josepha's life and helped inform her actions in Rio. For the first ten years after the Moret Law was passed, Spain had struggled to put down the uprising in the east. The need to repress popular mobilization around any political issue meant that spaces for developing abolitionist views were severely limited. Radical abolitionist sentiment was expressed much more openly, then, by the rebels in the east than was ever possible in Havana.

In the capital, however, some stirrings of opposition to slavery were publicly felt, especially in the postwar years. The newly constituted Liberal Party embraced gradual abolitionism by the 1880s, as did the small Democratic Party from 1881 and, from 1882, the Autonomist Party.[125] Following a longer tradition of antislavery literature, Antonio Zambrana's abolitionist novel *El negro Francisco*, inspired by literary *tertulias* (social gatherings) held at the Havana house of lawyer and erstwhile legal slave representative (*síndico*), Nicolás Azcárate, was published in 1873. Significantly, however, it was not published in Havana but in Santiago de Chile, where its pro-independence author was representing the Cuban revolutionaries.[126] Meanwhile, developments in the city were influenced by those of the broader Spanish imperial world. A liberal abolitionist movement had developed in the metropolis since the 1860s, while abolitionist sentiment in Puerto Rico also played a significant role in shaping events in Cuba. Whether Spanish or Cuban-born, the lawyers and officials who would channel Ramona's appeal were woven into the intellectual fabric of the Spanish empire. The actions of enslaved people in the capital, then, both responded to and influenced the broader politics of slavery and abolition far beyond the island's shores.[127]

The atmosphere in each city, then, presented both significant differences and striking similarities in terms of the opportunities and limitations they presented for enslaved and freed people who came there to make legal claims. Studying the two cities in tandem, meanwhile, also encourages us to notice the broader context that connected them. In both Brazil and Cuba, activists and writers conceived of themselves and their struggles, and their governments enacted legislation, with reference to each other.[128] In January 1881, for example, Brazil's best-known transatlantic abolitionist, Joaquim Nabuco, visited the Spanish Anti-Slavery Society in Madrid. After Spanish abolitionists enthusiastically welcomed him as part of "the Latin race" and "the great Liberal family", Nabuco described their common aims, reminding the audience that the abolitionist struggle was an "international" one.[129] The task was also inherently comparative, and the comparisons ranged across a much wider frame of reference than that of Cuba and Brazil.[130] Antislavery thinkers drew on a corpus of ideas and imagery developed by earlier Atlantic antislavery campaigns, just as proslavery thinkers had long done.[131] Nabuco spent much of his time building international antislavery contacts, especially in London.[132] Rio's Abolitionist Confederation had links with international antislavery figures including Antonio Maceo, Frederick Douglass, and Victor Schoelcher.[133] The Spanish Abolitionist Society's official emblem was "a black man with one knee on the ground, his hands bound in a chain, in a supplicating attitude"—the same iconic image that had been popularized in Britain by Josiah Wedgewood's abolitionist cameos in the 1780s.[134] The United States, looming only ninety miles from the Cuban coast and home to significant émigré communities in Florida and New York, played an ever-larger role in Cuban cultural life, while U.S. abolitionism would have a significant impact on both Spanish imperial and Brazilian approaches to antislavery.[135] While migrants and returnees, coffee and sugar, and rum and tobacco flowed into and out of Havana and Rio de Janeiro, so the cities also functioned as cultural and intellectual Atlantic crucibles, importing, reworking, and exporting ideas. Individuals' particular struggles, then, were part of the shifting, contested politics of slavery and antislavery that, albeit in different ways, were engulfing the Atlantic cities to which each woman, like so many others before her, had arrived.

The gradual emancipation laws that helped chart slaves' legal struggles thus emerged from two very different political contexts. Cuba experienced a revolution that presented radical alternatives to Spanish rule and slavery. The colonial setting helped produce a complex interplay between disparate forces, whether the Spanish government, abolitionists in Spain and Puerto Rico, the rebel movement in eastern Cuba, or the entrenched positions of Cuban slaveholders. Brazil certainly did not see a revolution but did undergo a national war with important consequences for the slavery issue, while dramatic political and social change, pushed on by a vibrant abolitionist movement, helped drive abolition forward from within this oldest and best-established of American slave societies.

Despite the differences, Havana and Rio de Janeiro were also connected. The dynamics of slavery and abolition in each were shaped by the broader framework they shared. The African diaspora linked their populations' individual histories and collective cultures; ways of thinking and talking about slavery flowed back and forth across the Atlantic into and out of their newspapers and literary circles. Within each city itself, enslaved activity, elite actions, and broader political and social developments connected and clashed in unpredictable, complicated ways. In these fertile urban spaces, enslaved and freed claimants—especially the women who had historically made up a significant part of their populations—grappled with slavery's legal consequences for their lives. The next chapter will map out this shifting legal context in which they did so, charting its gendered implications and exploring women's connections to the pursuit of legal freedom.

CHAPTER TWO

The Law Is Final, Excellent Sir

Slave Law, Gender, and Gradual Emancipation

*The law is final, Excellent Sir, and it must be obeyed, and for he
who refuses[,] may the punishment indicated for offenders fall upon him[;]
may he be obedient and respectful.*
—Ramona Oliva to Gobernador General, Havana, 9 August 1883

With these words, Ramona Oliva's petition claimed freedom for her five children from her former owner, Manuel Oliva. The unusually passionate wording of the document vividly evoked the efforts of countless other ex-slaves to bring their understandings of the law's new provisions to bear on their former owners. In small towns, like the one where Ramona initially made her claim, powerful individuals found it particularly easy to use their personal sway to ignore such initiatives. Convinced that existing local mechanisms of access to law would not give her a fair hearing, Ramona had undertaken a journey of some sixty miles to the colonial capital, filing her claim at the office of the governor general.

Given the extremely unequal power relations between former owners and former slaves captured so well by Ramona's petition, why should she think she had any chance of success? Who drafted this document in the name of a woman who explicitly discussed in it her own illiteracy, and can we consider any of these words to be "hers"? Why did so many women like her make claims like this one? This chapter traces the gendered evolution of the law of slavery and emancipation in Cuba and Brazil. The law's development was marked, in each case, by the collective impact of struggles by the enslaved themselves, in which women had played an important, specific part. As their wombs became the instruments through which gradual emancipation would occur, women sought to uphold the new laws and influence their interpretation.

ENSLAVED PEOPLE AND THE LAW

In the early 1990s, delving into the collections in the basement of the Brazilian national archive, Brazilian historian Keila Grinberg began to work with a collection of legal cases of enslaved people who, throughout the nineteenth century, had made claims for freedom that reached Rio de Janeiro's appeals court. Although their existence was known about by other historians of slavery at the time, they had not been systematically analyzed before. On working with them, Grinberg found some surprising results. In this largest and oldest of slave societies, not only had these appeals been heard, but almost half had been decided in favor of the slave.[1] This realization echoed the notion, analyzed by other Brazilian historians who had already worked with first-instance legal cases, of the law as an arena for social and political struggle that could be accessed by the enslaved or their freed relatives—even if only by a minority and on unequal terms.[2] The legal claims also suggested that enslaved people did not simply participate in the ways the laws were *implemented*. Their tendency to seek legal redress meant that—although gradually and in limited ways—their demands and priorities filtered into the very process through which legislation was drafted in the first place.[3] These discoveries have prompted an ongoing wave of interest in the relationship between law and slave agency across Brazil, as scholars unearth still more *ações de liberdade* (legal suits for freedom), as they are collectively termed, filed at diverse local and regional courts across this vast country.[4] The Brazilian developments have fascinating parallels with research for Cuba, where Rebecca Scott's groundbreaking work revealed how enslaved people's initiatives collectively helped speed the emancipation process itself.[5] Other scholars of Cuba have delved back across the nineteenth century, revealing how the evolution of law and jurisprudence in the colony was influenced by the engagement of the enslaved with the legal arena.[6]

In each setting, a series of official provisions anticipated at least some access to the law for the enslaved, although the usual means of doing so differed. A slave with a grievance could approach the courts, usually through an official representative, called a *síndico procurador* (or simply *síndico*) in Cuba, and a *curador* in Brazil. In Brazil, the surviving evidence we have of these struggles mostly comes from court records themselves.

These include local first-instance courts, as well as the country's various appeals courts—one of which was situated in Rio.[7] Meanwhile, in colonial Cuba, although some slave claims reached local courts and justices of the peace, colonial government institutions often assumed these functions in practice. Throughout the nineteenth century, slave claims were directed to government divisions like the Gobierno Superior Civil, later re-formed as the Gobierno General, in Havana. During the 1840s, for example, enslaved people in Havana might make claims through any one of five different channels.[8] From the 1870s, a series of local and provincial boards, called *juntas de libertos* in the 1870s and *juntas de patronato* in the 1880s, were set up to oversee the transition process. Their functions included hearing and settling claims by the enslaved.[9] Yet the higher government authorities and central *juntas* in Havana continued to receive multiple slave claims, since many enslaved people or their relatives appealed the decisions of the local *juntas*, or bypassed them altogether in favor of the authorities in the capital city.[10] There were thus various potential avenues for official petition-making, arranged in a hierarchical structure with the cities, and especially the capital city, at the top. Indeed, as Claudia Varella has shown, "the *síndico* and the city were linked": the office of the *síndico* had grown up in the first place as part of the institution of the *ayuntamiento*, or municipal council, which was implemented by the Spanish as they founded towns and cities across the New World.[11] These different and often competing avenues for claims-making in the Spanish colonial context in Cuba made for a rather more plural, fluid situation than the Brazilian case. The Cuban process of claims-making generated a large number of fairly brief documents of a handful of pages each. Instead of reaching the courts, claims were passed between different colonial authorities and dealt with quite quickly, although they did not always file away the final decision along with the original appeal. This was different from the Brazilian context, where the legal cases generated by enslaved claims-making might run on for several years and generate hundreds of pages of proceedings—especially when they reached the appeals stage.

Regardless of the exact means by which claims came to official attention, Cuba and Brazil were nonetheless similar to one another (and different from many other slave societies) in that there existed a long-held *assumption* that enslaved people would, to some degree, participate in the law's implementation. It was this assumption that led to an 1863 ruling by the Cuban Gobierno Superior Civil about the case of a enslaved man named Domingo, who argued that his self-purchase price had had been set too high. The Gobierno Superior Civil concluded that the price had indeed been "not entirely fair for the slave." However, "as he had not made any complaint either before or after the decision," the petition was turned down "unless Domingo makes a complaint in the meantime."[12] In other words, it was up to the slaves—illiterate and in an extremely unequal power relationship with owners—to find out about the laws and push to have them implemented.

BEFORE THE 1870S: WOMEN, MANUMISSION,
AND CLAIMS-MAKING IN BRAZIL AND CUBA

Scattered liberally across the pages of works on nineteenth-century slave claims-making in both Cuba and Brazil are the names of many enslaved women. Although few specifically gendered studies exist, this suggests that long before the period of the 1870s and 1880s that are the focus of this book, women played an important role in enslaved people's quest to use the law to gain legal freedom. In order to understand women's legal activities, then, we need to understand the new political and legal context of emancipation in which they were operating, but we also need, first, to consider how each woman's decision to approach the law was rooted in an older relationship between women and legal freedom.

Women's presence is difficult to track quantitatively with any real accuracy, given the small and scattered numbers of surviving claims. Some figures we do have are nonetheless suggestive of this presence of women within slave claims-making, long before the advent of the 1870s "free womb" laws. In Cuba, among 348 records of slave claims made to the Gobierno Superior Civil from across the island over the nineteenth century, women's presence was initially quite small when compared to women's numbers in the enslaved population as a whole, but it grew substantially over time.[13] Only 10 percent of the 70 cases the collection contains for 1800–1849 refer to women, but among the 248 cases made between 1850 and 1866, their proportion grew to 27 percent.[14] Meanwhile, as briefly sketched in the Introduction, figures from Keila Grinberg's database of Brazilian *ações de liberdade* that reached Rio's appeals court are also suggestive of the significant role women had long had in this process. Between 1850 and 1870, second-instance appeals by enslaved women in Rio made up just under half the total of claimants identifiable by sex (16 of 34).[15] This was in a society where enslaved men outnumbered enslaved women significantly overall, although the balance was more even in the cities.[16] This gendered difference between urban and rural environments is probably what explains the lower representation of women among the

Cuban figures, which are drawn from across the island, whereas the Brazilian figure discusses Rio only.

The numbers are small but striking, especially if we compare them with women's presence in *criminal* cases. For Brazil, a survey of criminal appeals cases with slave defendants that reached Rio's courts in the period 1851–79 contained women defendants in only 8 percent of cases.[17] This much smaller female presence reflects what we find among works that discuss *extra*legal responses to the condition of enslavement across the Americas. Whether marronage, violent crime, or violent uprisings are the focus, we tend to find fewer women mentioned.[18] Gendered studies of these phenomena might in the future help explain why women appear so much less often in historical documents and historians' analyses. For now, the discrepancy between women's appearance in civil versus criminal cases suggests differences between the strategies enslaved men and women tended to adopt to cope with, or find ways out of, slavery. Discussing such differences for early-nineteenth-century Rio, Mary Karasch suggested that "many rebellious male slaves never even sought to use the manumission process but sought to 'liberate' themselves by running away. They found their freedom in the forests, while more dependent women had to seek it in the city."[19]

Karasch's words remind us that seeking freedom through legal means involved a conscious *choice* by enslaved individuals (albeit within very constrained circumstances) to pursue a specific set of activities toward freedom. These activities did not only, or even principally, play out in the courts. Legal claims-making occurred where other routes to manumission had been unsuccessful, and where the claimant also had sufficient resources and determination to seek legal redress. Nonetheless, this minority of cases provides us with a small but fascinating window onto the much broader social universe of manumission. In Brazil, women—especially women living in urban environments—were particularly prominent within the country's long history of relatively high attainment of manumission. Nineteenth-century Cuba was different in that it was a much newer slave society, but it was similar in that access to manumission was also quite broad and was dominated by urban women. Women's relative prominence among legal claimants for freedom in each country throughout the nineteenth century suggests that manumission was not just something that was *done to* them, but that this process was at least partly shaped by women's own actions and aspirations.

In nineteenth-century Cuba, one arena in which women became particularly prominent was *coartación*. This was a practice whereby an enslaved person made a down-payment toward freedom, which fixed his or her price and in the meantime afforded a series of specific guarantees.[20] A similar practice, *coartação*, also existed quite widely in Brazil from the eighteenth century, particularly in Minas Gerais, but, like self-purchase in general, it depended on the owner's consent.[21] The Cuban 1842 slave code, on the other hand, made *coartación* and self-purchase a *right* for those who could produce the necessary sum of money.[22] Particularly important was the right not to be sold without first being given a license—called *papel*—to seek a new owner. This allowed slaves living in cities—with whom, over time, many of the rights of *coartación* gradually became associated—a small glimmer of hope that they might avoid the threat of sale to the isolation and hard labor of plantation slavery. *Coartados* only ever represented a minority of the enslaved population in Cuba and, among them, only a much smaller percentage still would ever attain full self-purchase.[23] Yet this did not prevent *coartación*'s existence from being a thorn in the side of slaveholders.[24] Meanwhile, enslaved people were usually less interested in the distant hope of full self-purchase than they were in *coartación*'s much more attainable promise of greater control over their own geographical location.

Like manumission more broadly, *coartación* was an activity in which women, and particularly women living in cities, were overrepresented. In their survey of 23,045 Cuban slave sales between 1790 and 1880, Laird Bergad, Fe Iglesias, and María del Carmen Barcia found that although women represented around 50 percent of those sold, they made up 68 percent of those who were *coartados*.[25] By 1871, according to Rebecca Scott, less than 1 percent of the overall Cuban slave population had achieved *coartado* status, but women slaves had a significantly higher chance of doing so: 58 percent of the *coartados* were women.[26] Over 40 percent of these *coartados* lived in the mainly urban *jurisdicción* of Havana.[27]

Even more than manumission in general, *coartación* depended not just on the owner's will but on the enslaved person's ability to save money, their knowledge of slave law and customary practice, and their ability to put that knowledge to good effect. Women's significant participation in *coartación*, then, confirms that in order to understand the broader dynamics of manumission, we need to understand the part played by gender in shaping enslaved people's particular activities and aspirations. Why did women apparently have this long-standing tendency to seek legal routes toward freedom? Part of the answer surely lies with the fact that the very institution of slavery that shaped their lives and actions had different effects upon men and women, actively shaping gendered relations of power in both enslaved and free society.

GENDER AND SLAVE LAW

From its Roman foundations onwards, Iberian slave law did not conceive of slaves as gender-neutral subjects: their sex mattered.[28] There are many examples of this. Centuries-old provisions anticipated that masters might manumit certain slaves, including the women who had breast-fed or cared for them when they were children; such ancient notions, as we will see, were not infrequently reflected in women's freedom claims in the late nineteenth century.[29] Slave law both anticipated and sometimes tried to prevent prostitution of women slaves by their owners.[30] Such long-standing legal stipulations might acquire new relevance at new historical junctures or in the hands of particular individuals. In Rio de Janeiro in the 1870s, for example, police commissioner and local judge Miguel José Tavares Bastos initiated a major campaign to rid some of the seedier central city streets of enslaved prostitutes by bringing over two hundred of these women's cases to court in the space of a few months. The women's lawyers based their arguments on Roman law principles that a master who abused his dominion over a slave should lose ownership.[31] For Cuba, nineteenth-century laws intended to ameliorate slaves' conditions tended to equate "milder" treatment with the protection of women and children, assumed to be weaker and more vulnerable.[32] Protection, of course, went hand in hand with subservience: slave families gradually acquired greater legal protection in ways that assumed male dominance within those families.[33] In Brazil, legal scholarly opinion gradually converged during the nineteenth century against the idea of allowing sex between masters and enslaved women on moral grounds, with lawyers often suggesting freeing the children who resulted from such encounters and, sometimes, their mothers too.[34]

The sex of the owner, as well as the slave, also mattered in law, since slavery also worked to shore up gendered relations of power more broadly.[35] The most important example of this is the way in which slave status was legally passed on from one generation to another. In both Cuba and Brazil, as well as across the Americas, the Roman-derived principle of *partus sequitur ventrem*, meaning that the child's status followed the womb, governed this genealogical inheritance of enslavement. Passing, literally, through the womb, slave status was passed through the mother's line.

Regardless of the father's status, if the mother was a slave, then so was her child.[36] Indeed, wombs had long been central to legal definitions of slaves as property rather than persons. The thirteenth-century Castilian Siete Partidas legal code explained it thus: "Slaves are considered more as commercial items than as people; hence property rights are acquired in the same way as they are with objects. . . . thus, he who is born of a slave mother is also a slave, even if his father is free, . . . so the mother's owner also owns her child, just as the sheep's owner also owns her lamb."[37]

This, of course, was the exact opposite of what occurred in free society, where it was the father, not the mother, who bestowed his child with status and "legitimacy." There was a clear and deliberate connection between the two different rules. Male slaveholders were conceived of as the *paterfamilias*, playing the role of family head to their own wives and children but also to dependents, servants, and slaves of both sexes.[38] It was *partus sequitur ventrem* that allowed for the untold sexual encounters between enslaved women and their male owners on which American slave societies were built. *Partus sequitur ventrem* ensured that these encounters would not undermine property-holding in slaves, because the resulting children followed the mother's status and remained enslaved—unless, of course, the slaveholder exercised his patriarchal rights and chose to free the child or the mother. By the same token, slaveholding men were thus largely free to rape without losing their property rights over the children born to their slave women, while enslaved fathers were systematically denied authority over their children. Through the wombs of women, *partus sequitur ventrem* ultimately reinforced the patriarchal power of slaveholding men over enslaved men.

This gendered legal context meant that enslaved men and women, even though they lived and worked alongside one another or had families together, also had different relationships with the law. Slave fathers could, and did, love, nurture, or help to buy the manumission of their children; yet most were not tied to those children through any official link.[39] Instead, it was usually only the mother's status that was documented when the child was born. Partly for this same reason, it was mothers who most often took on the formal world in seeking legal freedom for them. Indeed, making an argument that would also be valid for Brazil, Joseph Dorsey suggested that "the Spanish legal system deemed slave women, especially slave mothers, more acceptable plaintiffs in struggles of this type."[40]

The gendered ways in which slave law underpinned masters' domination of slaves are not specific to Cuba and Brazil—many of the basic tenets were shared across the different American slave societies. What was broadly different about Iberian societies was the degree to which manumission was permitted, which made women's tendency to pursue legal freedom particularly significant. From the start of the 1870s, however, this ancient relationship between the womb and slavery was fundamentally recast.

FROM *PARTUS SEQUITUR VENTREM* TO "FREE WOMB" LAWS

How might slavery be ended gradually and peacefully, ensuring a steady labor supply, some notion of "compensation" for slaveholders, and the continuation of a hierarchical social order? Isolated on the world stage by the late 1860s as the last slaveholding powers in the Americas, and mindful of the twin specters of recent civil war in the United States and the longer shadow of slave rebellion in late-eighteenth-century Saint Domingue, Brazil and Spain had each begun to ask this question. Watching each other, they each found the solution in "free womb" laws, technically freeing children born to enslaved women while their mothers remained enslaved. If slaves had long occupied a tricky legal status somewhere between property and personhood, the new laws created the even more bizarre legal concept of an enslaved woman whose womb was free. The ominous implications of breaking the ancient link between the womb and property rights over human beings were not lost on slaveholders. Heated discussions raged in the Brazilian Parliament, for example, about whether, while the fruit of a tree legally belonged to its owner, the "fruits" of enslaved women's wombs would be considered free.[41]

The thinking that led contemporaries to propose this particular method of abolishing slavery—which we can call "free womb logic"—had a venerable trajectory.[42] There were various Atlantic precedents: "free womb" measures had previously been adopted by, for example, Gran Colombia, Chile, and Portugal and had been discussed by Abraham Lincoln in the United States.[43] Cuban priest Felix Varela had suggested a "free womb" law to the Spanish Cortes in 1822.[44] In Brazil, influential lawyer Perdigão Malheiro proposed freeing the womb in 1863. The idea was taken up in a study about the best means of ending slavery that was commissioned by the emperor in 1865 and carried out by José Antônio Pimenta Bueno, future viscount of São Vicente, by 1868.[45] Other commentators considered simply freeing all women, so that their children would be born free.[46] Meanwhile, thanks to *partus sequitur ventrem*, free womb logic had historically operated from the bottom up as well as from the top down, with enslaved families purchasing the freedom of women members first in order to ensure that future offspring would be born free.[47]

The Spanish Moret Law of 1870 and the Brazilian Rio Branco Law of 1871 had various differences, but each "freed" children subsequently born to enslaved mothers.[48] It was freedom in name only: in Cuba, such children were obliged to serve their mothers' masters until they were eighteen. In Brazil, meanwhile, children were to remain with the mothers' owners until age eight, whereupon owners could decide whether to continue using their "services" until age twenty-one, or whether to hand them over to government protection, in exchange for 600 *mil-réis* in "compensation" for the expense incurred in raising them. In practice, there was very little difference between the Cuban and Brazilian stipulations, since only 113 children in Brazil were ever handed over to the state by Brazilian slaveholders.[49] Both laws also made provisions not just to "free" these children, but to shore up and alter the family structures into which they were born. Thus, the Brazilian Rio Branco Law prohibited the separate sale of children under age twelve from their mothers or fathers, or of married couples from one another.[50] The Spanish Moret Law similarly prohibited the separate sale of married couples, as well as the sale of children under age fourteen from their mothers.

There were important differences, too, partly as a result of the law's different prior evolution in each context. While in Cuba, self-purchase and *coartación* were legal rights for slaves since 1842, enslaved people in Brazil did not have the right to self-purchase without their owner's consent before 1871, and the *pecúlio* (the Roman-derived term for slaves' savings, used in both Brazil and Cuba) that they had long generated in practice was not legally protected. The Brazilian Rio Branco Law thus represented a major watershed, since it recognized enslaved people's ownership of their *pecúlio*, as well as their right to use it to purchase freedom regardless of the owner's wishes. This led to a widespread push for self-purchase among the enslaved, often through the courts, from 1871.[51]

Unlike in Cuba, the Brazilian law introduced a national emancipation fund, intended to gradually free slaves across the country. Adopting free womb logic, the fund prioritized enslaved families for manumission; *partus sequitur ventrem* ensured that, in practice, this meant freeing mainly women and their children.[52] Poorly administered, it freed insignificant numbers in itself.[53] However, the fund's existence and its gendered priorities helped inform the policies of many private or municipal emancipation funds that sprang up across the country during the abolition campaigns of the 1880s, providing, in the process, another route toward manumission that enslaved women and their children sought to access.[54] Such policies had a political significance far beyond the small numbers freed, helping foment and give focus to broader abolitionist sentiment. Spanish abolitionists complained, for example, that the Brazilian 1871 law had provided for both national and private initiatives toward gradual emancipation, while "in the Antilles, the existence of emancipation societies is prohibited."[55] These complaints were echoed in 1881 when Joaquim Nabuco visited the Spanish Abolitionist Society in Madrid. When Nabuco complained that the provisions of the Rio Branco Law were more limited than those of the Moret Law, Spanish abolitionist Rafael de Labra countered him by arguing the opposite, asking wistfully: "Would it not be legitimate to ask the powers of the State to permit, in Cuba, . . . the formation of societies that could contribute to the great work of redeeming the slave, whether by exciting abolitionist opinion, [or] fomenting partial manumissions?"[56]

Each law provided for the creation of a national slave register, with slaves not registered after a certain date to be deemed free.[57] While widespread fraud occurred, the registers did signal a new willingness on the part of the state to monitor, and encroach on, the private property rights that had long allowed some human beings to enslave others with very little formal regulation. Interference by an outside authority in their "private" relationship with owners was also, of course, something enslaved had long sought as a weapon in their unequal struggles.[58]

Meanwhile, the Spanish Moret Law went much further than the Rio Branco Law on two more points. First, the Spanish law "freed" sexagenarian slaves without compensating owners. This would prove far more controversial in Brazil, where even compensated emancipation for sexagenarians would come only 15 years later with the Saraiva-Cotegipe law. Second, the Moret Law banned the use of whippings to punish slaves, theoretically undermining owners' very ability to control enslaved workers. Appreciating the loss of "moral authority" they would suffer as a result, owners pushed hard against such measures. The 1872 Cuban-drafted regulation of the Moret Law re-introduced various corporal punishments, and stocks and chains were definitively banned only in 1883 after considerable struggle over the issue between Cuban slaveholders and Spanish abolitionists.[59] Yet even this was unthinkable in Brazil until late 1886, by which point many had accepted that slavery was, in any case, nearing a complete end.[60]

On 13 February 1880, a decade after the Moret Law was passed, the Spanish government enacted the *patronato* law, officially abolishing slavery in Cuba.[61] *Patrocinados* were to be paid a small but symbolically important stipend of 1–3 *pesos* per month (less for women than for men) and, as under the Moret Law, *patronos* were obliged to provide them with food, clothing and a vaguely defined basic "education." As the 1885 Saraiva-Cotegipe Law would later do in Brazil, the *patronato* established price scales for self-purchase. *Patronos* were also obliged to free one quarter of their *patrocinados* annually from 1884, so that slavery would end by 1888. In the meantime, however, for the remaining *patrocinados*, the law's stipulations were a change in name only: they remained under the control of their masters, working in similar conditions. Nonetheless, the *patronato* law fundamentally set Cuba apart from Brazil in the sense that it came with an established end date; in Brazil, during discussions of the Rio Branco Law, the possibility of setting an end date for slavery had been explicitly discarded, and only a fierce political struggle would finally force final abolition onto the government agenda.[62] In Cuba, although major struggles around the implementation of the *patronato* law helped bring the date of final abolition forward by two years, nonetheless the idea of an end date had been accepted.

Cuba's colonial relationship with Spain also made for important contrasts between each state's willingness to intervene in the owner-slave relationship. In Brazil, abolition would have to come from inside a slave society; in Cuba, legal change was enacted by a distant metropolitan government that was anxious to control the island in the face of sustained uprisings that had helped force the question of abolition onto the agenda in the first place. For Maria Lúcia Lamounier, Cuba's colonial status meant that the differences with the Brazilian transition process definitively outweighed the similarities.[63]

Yet if Cuba's colonial relationship with Spain made for a greater willingness to pass legislative measures, it also helped complicate the actual application of the laws on the island. Passed in Madrid in early July 1870, the Moret Law was not published in Havana until September. It could not be implemented without an accompanying *reglamento*, which the Cubans did not produce until November 1872. Drafted by slave-owners, the *reglamento* reinstated some forms of corporal punishment and emphasized control over and obedience of *libertos* (freedpeople).[64] A similar process occurred after the passage of the 1880 *patronato* law.[65] At the same time, the barefaced fraudulent use, on the one hand, and avoidance, on the other, of the new laws at every level in Brazil remind us that a colonial relationship was not required in order for there to be a vast gulf between the letter and the practice of the law.

As we have seen, the colonial relationship in Cuba also created differ-ent routes by which the enslaved might go about negotiating their status. In the 1870s and 1880s, the new *juntas* gave enslaved people a whole new channel for their grievances. While the mechanism of *juntas* was denied to Brazilian slaves, they turned to the medium of the courts. Meanwhile, precisely the kind of ferment in civil society from the 1880s that the Span-ish abolitionists had lamented a relative lack of in Cuba meant that there were also many other avenues through which Brazilian slaves might nego-tiate or petition for legal freedom. These ranged from the multiple private emancipation and abolition societies to municipal and state government initiatives, to the imperial family, which slaves in Brazil had a long tradi-tion of petitioning for clemency or changes in their conditions.[66] The Bra-zilian imperial family was based in Rio itself, in contrast with the Spanish Crown, which remained a distant—if symbolically important—force on the other side of the Atlantic.

Whether in Brazil or in Cuba, the degree to which slaveholders and officials flouted legal change means any study of slaves' relationship with the law needs, first, to ask whether this is even worth studying at all. In both countries, British pressure to end the slave trade while governments and slaveholding elites remained deeply invested in it economically and politically had created a decades-old tradition of passing laws only to ignore them systematically. Culturally, this tradition went deep enough to coin the expression *para inglês ver*—for the English to see, meaning the pretence of doing one thing while actually doing something completely different—which is still commonly used in Brazil today. Judging by such precedents, there was no guarantee that the emancipation laws of the 1870s or 1880s would actually be implemented at all.[67]

Yet in each case, the very passage of the laws represented an undeni-able rupture with the past, of which slaveholders were acutely aware. The new possibilities opened up by the laws were not lost on enslaved people, who, in seeking to apply them to the realities of their own lives, helped hasten and alter the transition process.[68] In each context, women were propelled to the forefront of this groundswell of enslaved activity in spe-cific new ways.

GRADUAL EMANCIPATION AND ENSLAVED WOMEN'S QUEST FOR FREEDOM

The legal framework of emancipation, just like the apparatus of slav-ery that it modified, had specific implications for women. In particular, the legal metaphor of a "free womb" presented the notion of a separation between the unborn child and the womb that gave it life: the former was "free," the latter remained enslaved.[69] Following hundreds of years in which the "fruit" of women's wombs legally belonged to their owners, these children were now nominally "free," even as the law gave owners considerable scope to continue exercising rights over them. In the spaces opened up by the ambiguities in the law, it was mothers who were best placed to seek to apply the laws on their children's behalf. In the process, they rearticulated their own bond with their children and staked a new claim to custody of them.

In both Rio de Janeiro and Havana, existing statistics imply the 1870s and 1880s saw enslaved people making claims about their legal status in increasing numbers. For Brazil as a whole, the available evidence from the city's appeals court at first seems to belie this, since Keila Grinberg found *fewer* appeals cases from 1871 onwards than in 1850–70. However, as she pointed out, the 1871 Rio Branco Law provided for more *ações de liberdade* to be resolved by first-instance courts, so fewer claims would reach the appeals court.[70] For cases originating in Rio, though, the annual average reaching the appeals court from 1871 to 1888 was about the same as before 1871.[71] In other words, either the city's slaves continued to litigate at the same rate as before 1871 (in practice, at a higher rate relative to their dwindling numbers in the city's population), or—assuming many appeals were now being resolved at first instance—they were making so many that despite the 1871 ruling, similar numbers were still getting through to the appeals court as before. For Cuba, too, the main collections of the National Archive, where slave claims to the colonial authorities are to be found, clearly contain more such cases as the nineteenth century progresses, with a particular surge of hundreds of appeals, held mainly in the vast Miscelánea de Expedientes collection, from the 1870s onwards.[72] Even assuming that this partly reflects the increased survival or preservation rate of such documentation over time, the difference is very striking, suggesting that more claims were simply being made over the years, and especially from the 1870s.

Among this growth in legal activity by enslaved people, women's involvement seems to have increased significantly after the passage of the "free womb" laws in each setting. For Rio de Janeiro, Grinberg's database of appeals court cases contains 30 cases for or against the freedom of individuals, or same-sex groups identifiable by sex, made in Rio between 1871 and 1888. Of these, 27 (90 percent) concerned female slaves. This represents a marked difference from the 1850–70 period. Of course, the numbers are too tiny to be anything more than suggestive, but they do imply a shift in terms of women's litigation activity.[73]

For Havana, the numbers we have to go on are rather larger, and they point in the same direction. Of a survey of 710 appeals made from 1870 to 1886, held in the Miscelánea de Expedientes collection, 452 (64 percent) were made by women.[74] In the Consejo de Administración collection, women made up 67 percent of 43 individual appeals made by people explicitly from Havana and 65 percent of the 104 appeals from elsewhere or whose origin was not stated.[75] Like in Brazil, such numbers contrast significantly with pre-1870 figures.

Women did not only increase numerically among enslaved claimants in the 1870s and 1880s. As more women claimants appeared, the *kinds* of claims also changed. Cuban claims made before 1870, for example, were frequently complaints about ill treatment; these feature much less prominently after 1870. This shift is clearly attributable to the greater numbers of women claimants. Even before the laws of the 1870s that "freed" their wombs, women were more likely than were men to seek freedom through courts and official means for their children and for other relatives; such claims appear much more frequently from the 1870s.[76] Within the Miscelánea sample, 130 claims were made explicitly on behalf of another person, of which 81 percent (105) were filed by women. In the Consejo de Administración collection, 12 appeals made explicitly on others' behalf were all made by women.

These figures both confirm and help explain other features of the emancipation process in Cuba. We know that, once the Moret Law came into effect, *coartaciones* rose hugely: they increased by 25 percent by 1877, while the slave population had decreased by 25 percent nationally. Forty-two percent of the new *coartaciones* took place in the *jurisdicción* of Havana, which contained only 8 percent of the country's slaves in 1871. Women, once again, made up 58 percent of this *coartado* population.[77] Yet the study of claims-making, with its ability to help us get "inside" *coartación* as a process, implies that even these high numbers may underestimate women's overall involvement in that process. As they did in claims for freedom more generally, women frequently took the lead in securing *coartación* on behalf of others, particularly their children.[78]

Scant as they are, the numbers we have available suggest that in each country—at least in the capital cities—women moved, or were propelled, to the forefront of a newfound impetus among the enslaved to apply the new laws to the realities of their own lives. The numbers, however, have little to tell us about the motives, processes, or understandings of the law that brought these people into the offices of scribes and legal representatives. What did they hope to get out of litigation? How did they think their own lives and those of their families might change as a result? Before delving into the documents their initiatives left behind, it is worth taking a moment to consider the people who turned their spoken words into formal, written documents. Scribes, laywers, *síndicos*, *curadores*—it was these men who captured, in scrawled lines of faded ink, faint echoes of the hopes and aspirations of Brazil's and Cuba's "free womb" generations.

REPRESENTING SLAVES

In both Brazil and Cuba, legal representatives were provided for enslaved petitioners, as for all those deemed legal minors—whether women, children, or, in Cuba, Chinese indentured laborers.[79] These professional lawyers might, at other moments, provide legal defense for slave *owners* as well as for slaves, and they often owned slaves themselves. Most, then, did not see themselves as championing liberty in any general sense, but as exercising a professional role, with varying degrees of dedication. It was common for slaves in Cuba to complain about *síndicos*, accusing them of "indifference and apathy," or, worse, of being in league with their owners, jeopardizing their claims thanks to self-interest or personal connections.[80] *Síndicos* were not paid, and were thus particularly susceptible to bribery and fraud.[81] *Síndicos*, meanwhile, complained back: they were overworked, and there were far too many enslaved people to deal with at any one time, so that "unless the interested parties press for it, it is impossible for a *síndico* to keep in mind the many complaints which are constantly being made to him."[82] Meanwhile, they were commonly accused of taking advantage of supposedly ignorant slave claimants to serve their own ends. One Brazilian lawyer defending a slaveholder railed about "the greed for profit, the depraved behavior . . . of those who, under the cloak of philanthropy, take away other people's slaves in order to take advantage of their services!"[83] The accusations were partly the result of the procedure, common to both Brazil and Cuba, whereby a slave claimant was "deposited" away from their owner's custody for the duration of the litigation process. Slaves were generally *depositados* at public institutions like Havana's Asilo de San José or Casa de Beneficencia, but were also often placed in private homes, including those of *síndicos* and *curadores* themselves, leading to accusations by owners that the representative had "seduced" their slaves into leaving.[84] In the case of women claimants, this "seduction" might be literal as well as figurative. In one 1880 Havana case, for example, a *síndico* defending a young *mulata* woman was accused of "inappropriate usages and dealings" with her, thanks to "the particular interest of his fiery youth" towards her.[85] The *depósito* process often proved a flashpoint of conflict between slave representatives and owners, who stood to lose considerable earnings during long absences by litigating slaves.

For the enslaved litigant, being in *depósito* might provide a useful means of escaping the direct control of their owner and their normal living and working conditions, even if the claim itself was eventually unsuccessful.[86] It could also, though, cause new tensions. In Havana in June 1863, in the Paula neighborhood near the port on the east side of the city, a fight broke out in a subdivided house on Calle de la Habana. The house functioned as a *depósito* for both enslaved Africans and Chinese indentured laborers, but was also home to free people. José, a Chinese worker whom his companions called Lechuza (owl), tried to put a bundle of clothing belonging to a deposited enslaved African, Ciriaco Sánchez, in the room of Magdalena García, a free washerwoman who had recently arrived. Ciriaco objected on the grounds that Magdalena was "a *negra* who had only moved in last Saturday and he did not know her." An official from the *sindicatura*, who had been at the house earlier that day—presumably to oversee the process of *depósito* or to discuss their cases with enslaved and indentured residents—had just left and so did not witness what happened. The case provides a glimpse of how *depósitos* might throw a constantly changing mix of different people together, creating tensions but also, surely, new solidarities and chances to exchange information about the litigation process.[87]

Most *síndicos* and *curadores* were certainly not unequivocal champions of the interests of the slaves they represented. On the other hand, they also resist easy characterization as a group.[88] Trained and steeped in the law, their actions were undoubtedly shaped by its stipulations to a large extent.[89] Yet, like the judges or colonial officials who would decide upon the cases they constructed, these men lived in the world, as well as in the offices and courts of law. They read newspapers as well as legal tomes, ran for election, and exercised other administrative or political functions. Over the course of their lifetimes and often long careers, they watched— and helped shape—changes to the broader political and social meaning of slavery as an institution. In the process, their own perceptions of their roles, and the kinds of arguments that they might make or be swayed by, also evolved.[90]

Cuban lawyer Nicolás Azcárate and *hacendado* and Cuban patriot José Morales Lemus both provide examples of men whose opinions shifted dramatically over the course of their lives in response to the events unfolding around them, both on the island and in the Spanish metropolis.[91] Each acted as a *síndico* in Havana in the early 1860s, aiming to smooth over disputes between masters and slaves, rather than prioritizing liberty for the enslaved. In 1866, each man joined the deputies representing Cuba at the Spanish Junta de Información. Along with their baggage, they thus arrived in Madrid bearing firsthand experience of dealing with slaves' legal claims on the island, which would become relevant as their Puerto Rican colleagues raised the issue of slavery at the meeting. As revolution broke out in both Cuba and Spain, each would change their views on slavery. As Christopher Schmidt-Nowara has pointed out, if "Azcárate, like Saco and Arango before him, recoiled in horror from the prospect of slave emancipation" before 1868, "by the end of the [Spanish and Cuban] revolutions, he was actively advocating abolition."[92] Indeed, in 1881, Azcárate co-founded the Democratic Party in Cuba, among whose main causes was the abolition of the *patronato*. He had also become a member of Madrid's Spanish Abolitionist Society.[93] Meanwhile, however, Azcárate also sat on Cuba's Consejo de Administración—hardly a radical or pro-slave body.[94] Morales Lemus, meanwhile, freed his own slaves—although he continued to fear social disorder and race war—and joined the rebellion against Spain, ending up advocating the patriots' cause from exile in New York.[95] Cuban *síndicos*, then, espoused political notions that differed greatly both between one another and over time. Whatever their views, though, it is unlikely that they could ever completely divorce the practice of law from its broader political and social context.

Unlike their Cuban counterparts, Brazilian *curadores* did not experience a revolution. Nonetheless, they too stood on rapidly shifting political sands. Their actions as lawyers assumed new significances as they lived through the Paraguay War and the gradual growth of antislavery opinion over the 1860s, the political and legal watershed of 1871, and then the more radical abolitionist campaigns that coalesced from 1880 onward. The best-known, if not the most typical, example of a slave legal representative is Afro-Brazilian lawyer Luiz Gama, who learned to read and write while enslaved, used his legal knowledge to prove his own freeborn status, and went on to provide legal defense for numerous enslaved people in the city of São Paulo. An active writer and journalist, Gama ensured the cases he dealt with remained firmly in the public eye, commenting on them in newspapers and thus intimately connecting the law and the broader political movement for abolition. Although Gama was an exceptional figure in almost every sense, he collaborated with a number of other less high-profile figures who also took on slaves' causes, drawn particularly from the Freemason movement. He also forged connections between the worlds of enslaved people, who sought his house for help and refuge, and the men of letters and politics among whom he moved with ease.[96]

In Rio de Janeiro, the imperial capital, legal battles over enslavement and freedom also became more visible and more political thanks to the abolitionist movement of the 1880s. The mulatto lawyer Domingos Gomes dos Santos, nicknamed "The Radical," was one of the founding members of the Abolitionist Confederation and was close to the strident abolitionist José do Patrocinio.[97] Like Gama in São Paulo, Patrocinio and his colleagues used the *Gazeta da Tarde* newspaper to bring enslaved people's court cases into the public eye, connecting law and broader politics. Meanwhile, though, even by the 1880s, abolitionist activists represented a minority among lawyers. Indeed, plenty of their colleagues could be accused of being actively antiabolition. In November 1886, the *Gazeta da Tarde* published a scathing series of letters about *bacharel* José Ferreira Nobre, Patrocinio's arch-rival in the turbulent world of municipal politics. Nobre, a municipal councilor, had created the *Livro de Ouro* municipal slave emancipation fund in 1884. As a politician, he raised funds for grandiose emancipation ceremonies being held in the city, yet as a lawyer he continued to provide legal defense for slaveholders—a contradiction that Patrocinio delighted in pointing up.[98]

Meanwhile, *curadores* and *síndicos* were not the only means by which the words of the enslaved filtered through into written records. Freedpeople sometimes found private lawyers to draft their petitions, rather than the representatives to which slaves had access. One of Josepha Gonçalves de Moraes' claims was drafted by a lawyer, Alexandre Cardoso Fontes. At other times, a literate relative or acquaintance might draft documents on the litigant's behalf, like Joaquim Monteiro dos Santos, who wrote several of Josepha's petitions for her. Josepha knew Santos because she had been hired out, while still enslaved, to work in his house, and had possibly continued living there after she was freed. Like others who penned such documents, Santos evidently had an interest in the case in one way or another.[99] In Cuba too, a variety of literate acquaintances might draft documents—we do not know who wrote Ramona's petitions to the Gobierno General, for example, but we do know that such scribes varied considerably in their knowledge of spelling and grammar. Sometimes literate relatives, or perhaps someone making an informal living as a scribe, might write such petitions. The variegated documents that were generated by all this activity present us with all sorts of interpretive challenges. While their attitudes might have varied, those who did the writing were usually privileged, educated, white men, whose lives and viewpoints were far removed from those of the people whose search for freedom they recorded. Their writings represent neither unmitigated expressions of slaves' "agency," nor direct transcriptions of their words. They were not drafted for the eyes and ears of the enslaved people they claimed to represent, and much less for those of historians who, today, are so curious to learn about their lives. Instead, they were written in accordance with specific protocols and formalities and were intended to produce very specific responses from other men—judges or colonial officials—who occupied positions of power.

Yet to dismiss their use as sources would surely also be to dismiss the long-standing creative relationship that enslaved people had established with the law in each of these slave societies. If Cuba and Brazil were both societies where access to written culture was central to civil status and property-holding, they were also places where the majority of people were illiterate. Thus, *most* people, whether enslaved or free, had recourse at many points in their lives to the pens of others—in this sense enslaved people were no exception. One way to think about the function of *síndicos*, *curadores*, and scribes is as translators, engaged in a creative process by which one person's aims and worldviews were filtered, modified, or explained in order to become comprehensible to another, very different group. These occurred in the context of highly unequal relations of power, yet they were not one-way encounters. This rich, syncretic quality to claims-making documents has much to tell us about how, through the law and officialdom, very different conceptions of slavery and freedom met and mingled.

Although more slave claims for freedom are being discovered all the time, those who could marshal the necessary economic resources and personal connections to make them were in the minority. Thus, this book can directly tell the story of only a quite select group. Among them, a smaller number still actually had their claims met.[100] Even with the advent of social and legislative change from the 1870s, the majority of enslaved people left no written record of their hopes, fears, or actions, while the long shadows of slavery still hung over the lives of those who did achieve a precious letter of freedom. Yet the minority whose distorted voices did reach the written record still have a lot to tell us about the broader process by which enslaved people conceived of and sought freedom. This condition, however precarious and however little it did to alter the daily conditions of their lives, was something enslaved people consistently valued and worked toward. Ultimately, this book follows them in assuming that achieving and defining freedom was something that was worth a great deal of time and effort.

This chapter has examined the gendered legal context in which, historically, women took on a particularly prominent place in performing the daily legal work of seeking freedom, often for different reasons and under different circumstances than men. Slavery and manumission had contrasting historical trajectories in Brazil and Cuba, but women's connection to manumission and to claims-making had deep roots in each. During the 1870s and 1880s, and especially in the capital cities, womb-based emancipation in each setting brought this historical connection particularly to the fore, although the tools at women's disposal and the circumstances under which they would go about using them were often different. In order to understand their motivations and actions, we as historians need to follow them into the offices of *curadores*, wait with them on the steps of the governor general's palace in Havana, and try to peek over their shoulders as they sit with a *síndico* for a precious fifteen minutes to dictate their petitions.[101] Yet we also need to accompany them as they step back out onto the hot, dusty streets of these two Atlantic cities where their conceptions of freedom were formulated. Meanwhile, as the tired lawyers close the door on the last pesky claimant of the day, and the scribes throw down their pens and wipe their inky fingers with a sigh of relief, we also need to probe the changing social and political worlds that helped these men craft their "translations" of enslaved people's voices. The remainder of this book will attempt all these tasks.

PART TWO

Seeking Freedom

CHAPTER THREE

As a Slave Woman and as a Mother

Law, Jurisprudence, and Rhetoric in Stories from Women's Claims-Making

> *The mother having left slavery, those children who do not belong to*
> *another are rightfully hers: de facto, because she gave birth to them, and de jure,*
> *because the Law authorizes her for this.*
> —*Ramona Oliva to Gobernador General, Havana, 9 August 1883*

With these words, three years before the end of the Cuban *patronato*, Ramona Oliva's petition staked a claim to custody over her children. Behind the petition's apparently simple words lie many of the complex questions that are the subject of this book. As this chapter will show, this language about the rightful claims of maternity appears again and again in women's claims-making in both Brazil and Cuba. Why did Ramona's claim emphasize not just a legal, "de jure" claim for custody, but also a "de facto" one, which implied a broader, socially recognized set of "rights" about ex-slave women's maternity?

In fact, changing notions about motherhood became a focal point that brought together many aspects of legal, social, and political change within the gradual emancipation processes occurring in both Brazil and Cuba. In these two very different contexts, which were nonetheless both comparable and connected, these processes threw up a series of questions. What did mothering mean? What did a "good" or appropriate mother look like? Perhaps most importantly, who could be a mother? Was motherhood universal, or did its significance and legitimacy rest upon legal and social status? Such questions were not new, but they were now being posed within a fast-changing legal and social context. In making appeals about freedom, women and their representatives both reflected and made important contributions to these broader legal and social changes. This chapter tries to get inside individual women's quest for freedom as they approached courts, slave representatives, and government bodies, during as well as before the advent of the 1870s "free womb" laws. Women in Brazil and Cuba approached the law in different ways, and they had different petition-making tools at their disposal, yet their aims were similar. In establishing the legal metaphor of a free womb in the body of an enslaved mother, transition legislation was designed to address the issue of property rights in human beings. Women's petitioning brought a much more complex set of concerns about changing perceptions of their own roles as mothers to bear on this legal process.

CHANGE AND CONTINUITY: NOTIONS OF MATERNITY IN CLAIMS FOR FREEDOM

Both before and after the passage of "free womb" laws in Cuba and in Brazil, claims for freedom employed a combination of legal arguments and extralegal, rhetorical appeals to socially constructed ideas about motherhood. Yet gradual emancipation brought a set of interconnected shifts in both the legal and the social significance of these terms for slave and ex-slave women. Examining claims-making before and after the advent of legal change can help us chart women's contributions to these shifting parameters.

In October 1867, Quitéria Maria da Piedade, a freed former slave of Rio de Janeiro's Carmelite Order, gave 600 *mil-réis* to one of the Order's friars, Luiz de Santa Bárbara Pereira, in exchange for the freedom of her *parda* daughter, Laudelina. Laudelina had been rented by the Order to a third party, José da Costa e Souza, along with one of the Carmelites' *fazendas* in Magé, about twenty miles northeast of the capital. One of the potential implications of achieving her freedom would thus be the chance for mother and daughter to be reunited in Rio, where Quitéria had deposited the money. She had been lent the 600 *mil-réis* by a "benefactor," one Tenente Fonseca, whose relationship to her was not discussed— he may have been an employer or patron, her lover, or the father of her *parda* child.

Despite the signing of the document and the alleged exchange of the money, Laudelina's freedom did not materialize. Quitéria then tried "all amicable means" to persuade the Order to keep its side of the bargain, engaging in the kinds of complex negotiations that we can assume preceded the filing of many official claims, ensuring that many disputes were resolved without ever arriving at the office of a *curador* or leaving a paper trail for historians to follow. When the "amicable means" failed, she commenced a legal suit for Laudelina's freedom.

The Order, represented by Friar Francisco Fausto do Monte Carmello, admitted that Friar Luiz had signed a document agreeing to the transaction, but argued that he had had no authorization for this, being "weak-spirited and easily tricked." Monte Carmello insisted the Order could not break its rental agreement with José da Costa e Souza. The latter, in his turn, argued that while he might consider freeing Laudelina, she was worth 1 *conto* and 500 *mil-réis*—almost triple the 600 given to Friar Luiz by Quitéria.

In arguing that the Carmelites should be made to keep their word, the *curador* who defended Laudelina, Manoel Jorge Rodrigues, sought the moral high ground for the slave girl and her mother, using emotive appeals to pity and charity. He highlighted the fact that the friars were not upholding their own professed religious values: "the freedom contract is not a game that anyone should play with, particularly not a Religious Order, where only acts of charity and justice should be found." He added that Laudelina "is a poor little *parda* in very ill health . . . for which reason her mother wished to pluck her from the claws of slavery." His legal case essentially rested on proving that a contract for freedom had been entered into, and that the amount that originally changed hands was reasonable, given Laudelina's ill-health. Yet the *curador* also employed arguments that had no strictly legal basis. There was no law stipulating that slaves should be freed because their mothers wanted them to be, or because they were poor or pitiable, or even because they were ill. In pre-1871 Brazil, as the Order's defense lawyer pointed out, "It is a generally acknowledged principle, based on the Constitution of the Empire, that the Owner cannot be forced to confer freedom upon his slave, and much less so for a price set by the slave himself."[1] Despite this clear legal practice, the *curador* also invoked ideas that carried long-standing social currency—increasingly influential in this period of discussions about slave emancipation—about how a "good master" ought to behave toward slaves.[2]

The experienced, professional lawyers who defended slaves would surely not have made such arguments, speaking beyond the law to the "new humanitarian winds" blowing across imperial Brazil, had they not thought they would have some influence on judges.[3] Souza, at least, took them seriously in his response: "It is not true that the slave Laudelina is ill . . . but if by chance it were true, I would have her treated with due care, as I do with the many slaves I possess, who are well fed and dressed and treated humanely in their sicknesses." Rather than simply denying that Laudelina was ill as part of an argument about her value, he addressed what he would have done for her if she *had* been, justifying his rights to her labor on the moral grounds of treating his slaves humanely and indirectly responding to the rhetoric employed about mother and sick daughter by the *curador*. Indeed, the Carmelites elected to free all their slaves by December 1871, implying that by the late 1860s they were finding their moral position as slaveholders increasingly difficult to defend, and that after the passing of the 1871 law soon after Laudelina's case, that position would become untenable.[4]

At both the first-instance and appeals court levels in Rio, the suit was resolved in Laudelina's favor. Judges were convinced of the legal arguments of the case: a contract had been made and broken by the Order; that the girl was sick and hence the initial value placed on her had been reasonable. Yet the arguments about pity and charity were also significant. As the next chapter will explore, debates about slavery and abolition both in Brazil and across the broader Atlantic World invoked not just economic or political practicalities, but also a new language of emotion and sympathy for slaves. This language found its best expression in evoking the plight of enslaved women and their children. Judges and lawyers were not removed from these wider sea-changes, but were themselves woven into the political and social fabric of the Brazilian empire. They were members of the influential Instituto de Advogados Brasileiros or sat in parliament; they were landholders, businessmen, and often, of course, slaveholders.[5]

Quitéria performed a dual function in her daughter's legal case. At a practical level, it was she who paid Laudelina's freedom price and appealed when purchase alone failed. At a rhetorical level, however, her quest also allowed the *curador* to make an emotive reference to her maternal desire to free her daughter. Even before the passing of the "free womb" law a few years later, the emotive bond between slave mothers and their children was recognized, in rhetoric if not in law, by slave owners, lawyers, and judges and was bound up with changing understandings about what constituted humane treatment of slaves.[6]

In Cuba as well as Brazil, the passage of the "free womb" laws saw a combination of change and continuity in the practice of women's legal petitioning. While much of the language about the claims of motherhood can be recognized from appeals made before the changes to the law, the discursive context in which it was being received was changing. Meanwhile, the laws gave new tools to women in their long-standing quest for freedom on behalf of themselves and their children.

In March 1873, Luisa, a black enslaved woman who lived in Havana with her owner, Doña Cándida Vidal, made a trip to see one of the city's *síndicos*, D. José Alamo. From her mistress's house, she would have had to walk only a few minutes before arriving at her destination. Wending her way along Concordia, the long, narrow central Havana street where she and Doña Cándida lived at number 116, she turned a corner onto the busy Galiano Avenue and deposited 600 *pesos* with the *síndico*.[7] Her aim was twofold. The money was intended to secure her own immediate freedom for the price of 550 *pesos*, and also the *coartación* of her young son, Santiago, with the remaining 50. Santiago was described as *pardo*, implying his father was white, although the logic of *partus sequitur ventrem* meant his father's status was irrelevant to the legal niceties of the case. Nor do we know where the money had come from—perhaps from Luisa's own savings during hours snatched from her labors for her owner; perhaps with the help of Santiago's father, friends, extended kin networks, or one of the associations to which living in Havana provided access.

Lacking the resources to free herself and Santiago outright, Luisa had strategized to make use of the money at her disposal. By freeing herself, she would increase her ability to earn money, helping her save for Santiago's complete freedom. *Coartación*, meanwhile, would give her some control over his destiny. Crucially, it would reduce the risk of being separated from her son by making it more difficult for Doña Cándida to sell him to someone outside the city. Luisa requested that once her own freedom had been issued, "the *coartación* of my aforementioned son be undertaken and . . . he be entrusted to me, on the understanding that I will pay his *jornales* either daily or monthly." To all intents and purposes, then, Santiago would be "free," and this freedom would bring her custody of him, as long as Luisa could pay his *jornal*. Luisa's strategy was surely informed by the paths trodden toward manumission by generations of women before her, who had used *coartación* as a means of expanding their rights over their children and preventing separation from them.

Yet over a month after she had paid the money, Luisa had not received the freedom and *coartación* documents she expected from the *síndico*. What was an enslaved person to do when failed by the very representative allotted by the colonial state to defend their interests? Despite her illiteracy, Luisa knew the answer. She did what many others in the city around her had done and paid 50 cents to have a petition drafted by a scribe, complaining about Alamo's neglect of her case to the Gobierno Superior Político. The appeal also alleged that Doña Cándida had refused to cooperate. Indeed, "far from carrying out such sacred duties" as freeing a mother and guaranteeing her son's future, she had responded by "disregarding the Supplicant and attempting to have her deposited at the Paula Hospital," a women's hospital in Havana where, since 1863, it was standard practice to deposit enslaved women involved in disputes with their owners.[8] Luisa's petition painted this as a strategy by Doña Cándida to keep her quiet.

The official at the Gobierno Superior who dealt with the plea, Vicente González de Valés, took Luisa's part. "The *negra* Luisa," he wrote, "is worthy of consideration as a slave woman and as a mother; she has given the 600 *pesos* to the *síndico*, and there is nothing more just than to carry out what she requests, because it is very just." It was certainly "just" for Alamo to take notice of Luisa as a slave—upholding the claims of slaves who had made payments for freedom and *coartación* was part of his job. However, there was no official stipulation that he should take particular notice of her as a mother.[9] Yet González de Valés assumed that her petition, as a mother, was "just." Although the final outcome to Luisa's petitioning was not recorded in her file, the Gobierno Superior Político did instruct Alamo to explain why no action had been taken. Describing her both "as a slave woman and as a mother," her petition had evoked a response that was based both on the letter of the law and on notions about maternity that were not to be found among its provisions.[10] The language about the "sacred" nature of the mother-child bond appeared not only in the petitions of mothers like Luisa who were trying to free children, but vice-versa. In the case of Juana Romero, a Cuban-born freedwoman who attempted to free her *lucumí* mother the year after Luisa's appeal, her appeal argued that she had a "sacred right" to see her mother and that the owner's violation of this right was "offending nature itself."[11]

Those who drafted petitions on women's behalf, and perhaps also the claimants themselves, assumed that such rhetoric might enhance the hard-headed legal arguments being put forward. As we have seen, the rhetoric of motherhood was a constant before and after the "free womb" legislation of the 1870s. Yet as the legal and social significance of motherhood shifted, so did the significance of the rhetoric within the appeals. Thus, Quitéria's appeal in Brazil dated from just before 1871, yet in seeking pity and charity for an enslaved mother and her sick child, it appealed to the "new humanitarian winds" blowing across Brazil—winds which would themselves have an impact on discussions about legal change. Luisa's petition in Cuba a few years later used the notion of a "sacred right" of motherhood, which we can find in appeals long before the 1870s, but it did so in a new legal context in which the words held a new meaning. One of the new uses of this rhetoric about motherhood was its capacity to "level" the petitioner and the petitioned.

"PUT YOURSELF IN MY PLACE": MATERNITY AND LEVELING RHETORIC

Rhetoric about maternity could be especially effective to signify universality and thus appeal to a notion of basic human equality. As subsequent chapters will explore, the rhetoric had a long history beyond as well as inside the courts, on both sides of the Atlantic; but by the 1870s and 1880s, it also chimed with the growing influence of strong abolitionist arguments being made in Brazil and the Spanish imperial world.

In Havana on 8 September 1882, as the effects of the Spanish 1880 *patronato* law were starting to be felt, an aging black woman initiated a legal battle on behalf of her child. María Forbes's appeal aimed, if not to free her son, José, from the *patronato* itself, then at least from the ill-treatment to which his *patrono* was allegedly subjecting him. Forbes's petition was signed with a cross to indicate her illiteracy and sufficiently badly written to indicate fairly poor education on the part of whoever penned it for her. It described her as a slave, although she was now technically a *patrocinada*, speaking volumes about how little the law had changed the lives of many in her position. Along with the majority of the island's remaining *patrocinados*, María and José labored in sugar production in Lagunillas, Matanzas, one of Cuba's most intensive sugar producing regions. María had, she said, failed in her several attempts to help her son locally. Hence, she followed the route that Ramona would take two years later, seeking justice from the highest authority—the Gobierno General in Havana. We should not be surprised at María's ability, like many other enslaved and freed people, to move quickly and effectively across the island when necessary. Lagunillas was close to the port of Cárdenas, which boasted excellent shipping and rail links to Matanzas City and Havana.

Once in the capital, María's petition explained that she was the "mother of many of the same condition and class," all on the same plantation. "But

Sir," it continued, "of my said children the most unfortunate is one named José, and it is for his sake that I implore at the feet of Your Excellency." Since 1875, said the petition, José had been receiving ill-treatment at the hands of his *patrono*. A complaint made to a *síndico* in the city of Cárdenas had failed when the *patrono* denied the charges. Despite legal change, former slaveholders—especially in rural areas far from the center of the colonial bureaucracy that provided more tools for petition-minded *patrocinados*—continued to act as if they were beyond the reach of the law, and indeed, they often were. Following the incident, "despite the appeal of the Señor Síndico, he [the *patrono*] set upon my son as he came out [of the *sindicatura*], taking him to the *finca* where in addition to a severe physical punishment he was thrown into shackles . . . a spirit of vengeance always possessed our owner."[12] Eventually, "given that the pleas of the *Mayoral* [slave overseer] were useless and the cruelty toward [my son] continued, I advised him as a mother that he should present himself to the Señor Síndico of Lagunillas." In a grim example of the potential dangers of claims-making for *patrocinados*, especially in rural contexts, the *patrono* not only failed to put in an appearance at the *sindicatura*, but also "waited for [José] to come out and ordered him to be handcuffed, striking him and wounding him with sticks and shots from firearms as if he meant to kill him." For some "mysterious reason," he refused to allow José to seek a new *patrono*, refusing perhaps to relinquish his authority or the power to punish him. At he end of her missive María returned to the theme of maternity:

> So then, Your Excellency, who is the father of the people[,] the protector of the unfortunate[,] and the first authority in these provinces[,] take pity on a mother who daily witnesses an outrage against a being of her own flesh and blood and remembering your Lady and mother put yourself in my place . . . I continue to plead that Your Excellency will . . . be so kind as to clarify and administer justice for this unfortunate mother.

Notions of motherhood and fatherhood, protection and pity, were long-standing ideas used by petitioners in Cuba as well as in Brazil, which "humble" women—free as well enslaved—often found especially effective.[13] As María, a helpless mother, humbly sought justice for her unprotected son, so the governor, as a powerful "father," should feel pity and therefore provide justice for vulnerable *patrocinados*. The idea that the governor of Cuba, the most powerful man on the island, should "put himself in the place" of an old, black former slave woman was certainly audacious. Nonetheless—as María pointed out—the governor had a mother too. The notion that motherhood was a shared, fundamentally human trait was, as the next chapter will show, becoming a central trope in abolitionist rhetoric. Such language, which aimed to "level" the petitioner and petitioned, was not new, but it took on a new resonance in an altered historical and legal context, in which María's children would form part of the island's first fully free generation.

The complaint was heeded. The governor at the time may have been particularly disposed to take action in favor of appealing slaves: "English Consul General Crowe could say of the new governor, Luis Prendergast, that he had since his arrival impartially enforced the laws relating to slavery, 'and whenever they left a doubt he declared in favor of the slave.'"[14] The Gobierno General wrote to the Matanzas Junta Provincial de Patronato the day after María's petition was made, requesting clarification. The *junta*, responding over two months later, told a different story: José, they said, had not been being ill-treated on the plantation, but had been put by his *patrono* to labor on public works in the city of Cárdenas due to his bad behavior, "it having been suspected that he was harboring other *patrocinados* who were runaways from the *finca*." The *junta* said María was now satisfied with the knowledge that José was working in Cárdenas and he was no longer in the *patrono*'s clutches. Was José the hapless victim of his *patrono*'s cruelty, as painted by his mother's appeal? Or was he a rebellious *patrocinado* helping runaway slaves, as argued by the *junta*? When the truth was so difficult to discern, perhaps the rhetoric—an old technique lent a new resonance by the altered legal context—was particularly helpful in swaying opinions.

It was also a sign of the times that after a long struggle to be heard, María's petition had consequences she had not sought. Another appeal, possibly made by José himself, alleged that in addition to everything else, he was not receiving the stipend owed to him by the *patrono*, and in January 1883 the Gobierno General therefore ordered the *junta* in Matanzas to free him. In irritated tones, the communication reported that the *gobierno* "had also been pleased to make it known to the Junta de Patronato of Lagunillas that in future, it should remember the bases for the present decision, and carry out the necessary measures on its own, without limiting itself to simply reporting on events." The communication signaled the real differences between the reception of claims regionally and in the capital. To boot, the Gobierno General also ordered the Matanzas *junta* to confirm María's own age—her petition had stated she was 62. If this was correct, she must be freed too. María's appeal on José's behalf now promised to bring not only his freedom but her own as well.[15]

While Havana presented the possibility of appealing to one set of colonial authorities over another, in Rio de Janeiro there were other authorities whom slave women and their relatives could petition for mercy and sympathy for their plight. One possibility, traditionally used by slaves as well as, for example, prisoners and their families appealing for clemency, was the imperial family. Here, again, old traditions took on new significance, as the women of the imperial family embraced a more public commitment to emancipation over the 1880s, presiding over grandiose municipal emancipation ceremonies held through the municipal "Livro de Ouro" emancipation fund. The fund mainly freed women and children, and although it was thought of by town councilors as a "beneficent" initiative on their own part and that of slaveholders, a closer look at its functioning reveals that the city's slave women were aware of the fund and used it to achieve freedom. One such woman was Maria Rosa. Like María Forbes in Havana, she used the language of motherhood to ask that her reader "put yourself in my place."

Maria Rosa's chosen recipient for her March 1886 petition was none other than the Empress Teresa Cristina, who was due to hand out letters of freedom to slaves at a forthcoming emancipation ceremony, which would be held on Teresa Cristina's own birthday, later that month. The petition commenced by humbly stressing the vast distance between petitioner and petitioned: "It is a poor black freedwoman who dares today to humbly petition, at the feet of Your throne, for the Imperial Clemency of Your Majesty." Having heard about the birthday emancipation ceremony, Maria Rosa was sure that "this must make your magnanimous heart tremble with joy, because you have already given so many demonstrations of your love and of charity towards the unfortunate class of the enslaved." Having painted the empress as a great but charitable lady and herself as a helpless ex-slave, the appeal continued: "Well, *senhora*: I am the mother of an unfortunate creature who is almost always ill and on the point of coughing up blood, with three young children, and who is still under the yoke of captivity." She asked that Teresa Cristina help to have this "unfortunate creature," her daughter Ludovina, emancipated at the forthcoming ceremony. Maria Rosa's petition closed with a return to the motherhood theme: "This is what this poor mother implores of the Magnanimity of Your Majesty, as she also hopes that this great occasion will be repeated for many long years, always accompanied by the happiness that you so greatly deserve, together with Your August Family."[16]

Although less direct than the appeal of María Forbes, the point was nonetheless clear: while one "poor mother" watched her sick daughter and three grandchildren languish in slavery, another was celebrating her birthday surrounded by her "August Family." The final word of this letter, addressed to a woman frequently called "the mother of the Brazilians," was "family." Flattering rhetoric aside, Teresa Cristina, who had watched two of her own sons die in childhood and brought up two daughters, had certainly felt the pain of watching her children suffer.[17] Like María Forbes in Cuba four years previously, Maria Rosa's appeal underlined how she and her family, as much as any other, were people, not "things." The leveling implications of her arguments, carefully softened by the emphasis on humility and social distance, had a particularly direct impact when made from one mother to another.

Aside from the rhetoric, Maria Rosa's claim was also aided by a much more practical consideration: Ludovina, it turned out, was the slave of Dr. José Pereira Peixoto, himself a municipal councilor. Since local councilors were supposed to be freeing their slaves as part of their emancipation drive, it was surely not lost on Maria Rosa that this put him in an awkward position. Peixoto conceded Ludovina's freedom on 13 March, supposedly "to commemorate the great birthday of our . . . Empress."[18] Had the empress actually intervened? Quite possibly she never even read the letter herself. Or had the missive simply shamed Peixoto into action? One way or another, the appeal had an immediate effect. On 14 March 1886, a week after it was made, Ludovina received her freedom letter from the hands of the woman to whom the letter had been directed.[19] The gendered language of humility, and women's desire to use it in order to free their children, echoed the Cuban context. The tools and strategies used by women in Rio to achieve their goals, though, were necessarily quite different. Maria Rosa and women like her, for example, embraced the Brazilian fashion for public emancipation ceremonies, which aimed to enact the gratitude of slaves and the beneficence of owners, emancipation societies, or public bodies in "generously" bestowing freedom. Yet they did so with their own purposes in mind, and surely took their own meanings from such events. These meanings would surely have been quite familiar to their Cuban counterparts, who used the different tools of petition-making at their disposal in order to try to achieve them.

*Satirical depiction of emancipation ceremony held through "Livro de Ouro"
emancipation fund, Rio de Janeiro, 2 December 1886.* Revista Illustrada,
8 December 1886, 8. Fundação Casa Rui Barbosa, Rio de Janeiro.

*Official portrait of first emancipation ceremony held through "Livro de Ouro"
municipal slave emancipation fund, Rio de Janeiro, 1885. "Primeira emancipação
municipal" ("First municipal emancipation"), by Pedro José Pinto Peres, Rio de
Janeiro, 1885. Câmara Municipal, Rio de Janeiro.*

There were other ways, too, in which women's petitions could have particular rhetorical effect. One of these was by playing on the intimate intersections between slavery and the family life of slaveholders. This was another very old trope—as Chapter 2 explored, such arguments dated back to Roman times. Yet such arguments also took on new meanings by the last decades of the nineteenth century, as a deep discomfort grew up about the ties of blood, sex, and maternal milk that, via enslaved women's bodies, bound slaveholders to their slaves and white families to those of color. This racialized discomfort—which coexisted with more liberal humanitarian arguments about the "equality" of all humans through motherhood—became another reason to argue for abolition. Neither the legal nor the moral implications of this discomfort were lost on enslaved women and those who represented them.

In Havana in August 1862, for example, an enslaved *mulata* woman, Juana Sánchez y Sánchez, appealed to the Captain General for her own freedom and that of her daughter Ángela. Juana's claim said she could prove that Ángela's father was Juana's owner, D. Gregorio Masá, a Havana military man with a public reputation to uphold. The case was passed to Nicolás Azcárate, then Havana's second *síndico*. He reported later that month that although Juana "lacks proof to back up her position," and her owner "roundly denies the allegation," Masá nonetheless had elected to "avoid the scandal of a lawsuit." Despite Juana's legal case being weak, Masa agreed to free Ángela and grant *coartación* to Juana. As Juana Sánchez y Sánchez, Gregorio Masá, and Nicolás Azcárate all knew, the social stigma associated with "leaving one's blood in slavery" might prove strong enough to give the slave a significant hold over her owner.[20]

That same year, another *mulata* woman, Paula, made a similar claim for her own on the grounds of having had a child with her owner. Her claim's verisimilitude rested on tropes that were common in nineteenth-century slave society. It alleged that not only had her master "seduced" her, but he now "punishes her to satisfy the jealousy of a woman with whom he lives." As subsequent chapters will explore, the image of the sadistic mistress who was jealous of her husband's lust for slave women was repeated with striking frequency in abolitionist writings and would have had clear resonance for those processing and judging Paula's petition.[21] Others followed the same route as Juana and Paula: In March 1870, a *morena* slave woman, Dolores Chacón, claimed to the Gobierno Superior Político in Havana that she "had conceived a child with [her owner, D. Joaquín Chacón] and afterward he had offered her freedom, [but] he now refuses to keep his word." Meanwhile in 1879, Caridad Olazabal alleged that her owner had not only fathered her son, but then kept the son while separating him from his mother by selling her into prostitution.[22]

If on the one hand, claims by these women could invoke the social stigma of family connections with slaves, they were effective only to the extent that owners cared about their reputation, because they lacked a strong *legal* justification. The Spanish 1784 Código Negro Carolino prohibited fathers from becoming the owners of their own children, and although the code was not adopted, the principle was sometimes upheld by courts when they freed these children. Yet this code was never fully put into practice. Moreover, the rule explicitly prohibited the manumission of the enslaved mothers themselves in such circumstances.[23] Had it not done so, this would have provided a massive exit strategy for countless women subject to sexual relations with owners that ranged from "consenting" sex to rape. On the other hand, older legal provisions had provided some precedents for manumission of slaves with whom a "family" relationship existed. Since the thirteenth-century Siete Partidas, owners were *permitted* (although certainly not obliged) to manumit slaves in such cases. This included slave wet nurses who had breast-fed the children who would grow up to become their owners, as well as the slave women's own children whom they had suckled at the same breast (*hermanos de leche*).[24]

Thus, both before and after 1870, women attempted to employ either weak legal precepts or slippery and shifting social conventions to work in their favor. Usually the best way forward was by stressing the bond between mother and child. One of slave mothers' most important legal quests was to ensure that they were not separated from their children— whether or not those children had been fathered by their owners. Partly thanks to such legal activity, the law gradually evolved toward at least some recognition of the bond between mothers and young children. The 1842 Código Negro, for example, banned separations of mothers from children under three years old.[25] The 1870 Moret Law took this process much further, raising the minimum age at which children could be separated from mothers to fourteen.[26] Thus women at different points—Juana and Paula in the 1860s, Dolores on the eve of the passage of the Moret Law, or Caridad some years after it—were increasingly likely to be able not only to claim freedom for children sired by owners, but to tie their own future to that of those children. A kind of symbiotic relationship existed, then, between the legal and social claims of enslaved motherhood. The productive tension between the law's evolution and its wider social resonance was something that women's claims-making, before and after the 1870s, sustained and helped to develop.

This kind of tension can be traced in a Brazilian case, brought on behalf of a group of enslaved people who lived on a *fazenda* in Guaratiba on Rio's rural fringes, that reached the capital's appeals court in 1878. The slaves had belonged to Francisco d'Albuquerque Muniz Tello, who had now died, leaving them to be claimed by his heir, Antonio José da Silva Ribeiro. Ribeiro produced registration documents to prove that Tello had registered these people as slaves before his death. The *curador*, well-known lawyer Carlos Busch e Varella, argued that these were fakes, and that many slaves had not been registered.[27] The requirement to register them was new, resulting from the Rio Branco Law. Failure to do so led, according to the law, to the slaves' freedom.

Beyond simply stating that Tello failed to register some of the slaves, Varella added some extralegal spice to his argument. He evoked practices that were common to the experience and increasingly to the critique of slavery with which his peers—themselves products of Brazilian slave society—were certainly familiar. Among the slaves, he said,

> there were many whose color, along with certain practices which are unfortunately frequent in the monotonous life of a bachelor, especially on an isolated *fazenda* . . . , makes their paternity very suspect; and hence, they were never registered. Francisco d'Albuquerque Muniz Tello recognized some of his natural children, almost all of them born to his servant Ludovina, but he recoiled at the fear of making brothers into the slaves of their own brothers.

To do so, he added, would have been an "atrocity." According to Varella, the trigger for the case had been Ribeiro's attempt to reenslave a freed *parda* from the *fazenda*, Mathilde, and her children. Mathilde had resisted, showing her freedom document and demanding a reexamination of the registration documents: it was thus discovered that they were fakes. The relationship between Mathilde and the deceased Tello is not clear. Strikingly, however, various enslaved and freed women were the ones who, at different moments during this long legal case, appeared to be spearheading the slaves' demands, implying that they had had a particularly intimate relationship with Tello. As the mothers of slaveholders' children, women bridged the gap between one family and another in physical terms, but they attempted to make this work in legal terms also, making claims for freedom for family members.

Although the initial judgment had found in favor of the owners, the appeals court in Rio freed the group. The judge did not explain his reasoning, and there were many factors in this complex case; however, the *curador*'s explanation of why Tello had not registered them was surely plausible for judges familiar with Brazilian slave society. In the climate of late 1870s Rio, though, such relations between slaves and owners were also beginning to spur a new set of ideas about the moral and biological corruption that slavery—through the bodies of enslaved women—posed to free families and to Brazilian society as a whole. These ideas, which will be explored later in this book, had important implications for enslaved women as they sought to gain and give meaning to freedom.[28]

As well as claims about sex between enslaved women and their owners, claims by women on the grounds of having been *symbolically* absorbed into owners' families as maternal figures were potentially quite effective. The intimate act of suckling a child was often seen as generating a family link of sorts, with attendant ties of obligation. In Havana in August 1878, Don Antonio Gassie freed his *coartada, criolla* domestic servant Catalina González "in recompense for her good services as the nurse of the child Doña Margarita de la Soledad Portocarrero y Gassie y Valdés," his grand-daughter.[29] And in Rio in July 1884, as abolitionist fervor hit the Corte, "Sr. Dr. Ferreira Vianna, on the grounds that the *parda* Inésia, . . . had suckled his granddaughter Maria da Glória, restored her to freedom for the sum of 450$."[30] These women did not make legal claims but perhaps were able to use social convention and personal ties to secure "beneficent" manumission.

Other owners allegedly reneged on promises made on the grounds of symbolic maternal ties. In Havana on 11 October 1872, Isabel Casas, *morena*, appealed to the Gobernador Superior Civil, explaining that "she was bought by Don José Lopes Robert . . . with the object of breast-feeding his son." Perhaps as a way of securing her full compliance in performing this essential task, Lopes promised he would free her after sixteen months on the job. Yet, she alleged, at the end of this period she was told that she must first continue to nurse the child for another seven months. Because the owners lived in Marianao on the outskirts of the city, this left Isabel separated by quite a distance from her own son, who was in central Havana, "in custody of the *morena* Leocadia García, who lives at Calle del Trocadero no. 72." Leocadia's role was, of course, fundamental, looking after Isabel's son and perhaps even breast-feeding him, something that slave wet nurses were frequently denied the chance to do for their own children. Perhaps thanks to her own frustration with the situation, Isabel's relationship with her owners apparently worsened; her petition alleged that, eventually, they expelled her from the house. Yet when Lopes Robert was contacted by the Fourth Síndico, he acknowledged that "it is true that he offered her freedom and he is willing to honor the offer, and if he has not already done it, it has been because he did not know the slave's whereabouts." Evidently it had been accepted by both parties that nursing the child would lead to freedom. The social weight of such ideas, and Isabel's willingness to turn theory into concrete practice through the mechanism of appeal, allowed her to forge a bridge between two very different families that led from enslavement to legal freedom. Yet, as in many other examples, it was only Isabel's claim that ensured the promise would be kept.[31] Appeals like Isabel's thus evoked much older legal and customary traditions that sought to avoid the "family" connections between owners and slaves that were generated through enslaved women's bodies. Yet such relationships also took on a set of newer significances in the context of gradual emancipation, symbolizing, for some, the inherent injustice of slavery and its effects on mothers, and, for others, its morally corrupting influence upon society as a whole.

MOTHERS AND JURISPRUDENCE

Isabel Casas's claim, made in the early 1870s, might easily have been made before the legal changes of that decade. Indeed, as we have seen, women's legal aims and strategies before and during gradual emancipation displayed at least as much continuity as change: these women and their representatives made appeals on the available legal grounds as well as attempting to evoke social obligation or gendered notions about pity or motherhood that had a long history.

At the same time, the legal context and the opportunities it presented also shifted in important ways after the passage of the "free womb" laws of the 1870s and over the following two decades. Mothers' newfound ability to make claims for their own freedom and that of their children was a radical departure, since slavery had systematically denied enslaved men and women the right to custody of their own children, positioning slaveholders as "parents." Yet the laws only painted these new principles in broad brush-strokes and left out many finer details about the ways the law would be implemented. It was in the legal disputes that were fought on a daily basis that the workings of the law in practice would be established.

The Cuban Moret Law: The Spirit or the Letter?

One of the most important contradictions the Moret Law left unresolved was that it prohibited the separation of enslaved mothers and children, but not the separation of a child from a *freed* mother. The issue was especially problematic with *liberto* children (the term used to refer to children born "free" under the 1870 law's provisions). If their freed mothers were allowed to take their children without paying compensation, then the principle that such children must serve time working for owners in "compensation" for eventual full freedom would not be respected. Yet if they were not allowed to go with their mothers, the principle—established by the same law—that mother-child ties must be respected would be violated. The inconsistency caused consternation: "Both parents and sympathetic observers were indignant at the *de facto* requirement that parents ransom their free children from former slave masters."[32] Faced with such contradictions, slaves and free(d) people and their representatives used the intimate relationship between law and socially accepted notions of justice and morality to appeal to what they understood as the *spirit* of the Moret Law. Although the Madrid government in its communications on the issue often referred to "parents," the law on separation referred to mothers only, again placing women on the front line of this particular legal tangle.

On 4 September 1876, Inés Gangá, *morena libre*, made an appeal through the Third Síndico in Havana, Joaquín Fabré, to the Gobierno General. She was seeking either *coartación* or freedom for her twelve-year-old enslaved son, Faustino.[33] For this purpose, she had deposited 227 *pesos* in notes in December of the previous year at the *sindicatura*, and later deposited another 150.[34] Yet, thanks to a change of *síndico* after the initial deposit had been made, over eight months later no action had been taken. In the intervening time, Faustino was sold. A charade similar to that suffered by Juana Romero two years before ensued: the young boy was sold another three times, and finally ended up on the remote Isla de Pinos (now Isla de la Juventud). Inés's appeal requested that Faustino's new owner bring him back to Havana, so that he could be *coartado* there as she had intended, and reunited with her. Yet, unsurprisingly, once his new owner, Don Victoriano Calero Lorenzo, had been tracked down by the resourceful *síndico*, he argued that it would be too expensive and difficult for him to bring Faustino back, requesting that Inés go to the Isla de Pinos instead, for the *coartación* to be carried out there. Standard practice was that transactions and claims would be carried out at the place of residence of the owner, not the slave.

The Third Síndico's indignant response sought pity for Inés along lines we are now familiar with: she was an elderly, impoverished woman and mother. It was harder, he said, for Inés to travel than for Calero, "not only because of her sex and age, being over sixty, but also because she is an unfortunate *jornalera* [day laborer] who lives off the product of her own work, while her son's owner owns at least this one slave, and has other resources which the unhappy mother lacks."[35] He also pointed out that Faustino had been purchased long after his mother had paid for his *coartación* in Havana, so the sale should never have occurred. The *síndico's* clinching argument, however, was based on the Moret Law. Even though Inés was free, not enslaved, the *síndico* argued that the *spirit* of the law still favored her claim:

> The said little black boy was taken from this Capital without his mother's knowledge and sold to the Countryside being under twelve years of age, and . . . although the letter of the law refers to slaves, its elevated, humanitarian and philosophical spirit also includes slave children whose mothers are free, because the latter condition does not deprive them of, but rather promotes, the means of attending to, caring for and protecting their young children, with the present case being an obvious example in which maternal longing and desire seek out the little, helpless son to aid and protect him, seeking his *coartación* which is the first step toward freedom.

Thus, argued the *síndico*, Faustino should be brought to the capital so that his mother could find an alternative buyer for her son, who lived nearer to her.

Inés's case ruffled some feathers at the Consejo de Administración. In the face of several dissenters, the majority eventually ruled that "the Law [of 1870] does not prohibit the transmission of control over slaves under fourteen separately from their mothers, except when the mothers are slaves." Inés was free, not enslaved, so the owner should not be "subject to the extralegal demands" being made. On the other hand, they also acknowledged her "maternal affection," age, and poverty. Thus, the ruling compromised: rather than Inés having to travel herself to the Isla de Pinos, the *coartación* money should be sent by the *síndico*, so that Faustino could be *coartado* there. The decision was passed to the Gobierno General for ratification.

This was apparently a difficult question for the Gobierno General. After six weeks, it elected to take the Consejo de Administración's concession to Inés a step further. The Gobierno General confirmed that the matter should be dealt with by the *síndico* nearest to the owner. However, the Havana *síndico* should meanwhile attempt to gain the owner's consent for a price evaluation and *coartación* of the boy back in Havana, "so that the elderly mother involved does not experience the pain of being separated from her son, which she would never have had to fear if the sale had been carried out with her consent." Inés's "extralegal demands," as the Consejo de Administración had called them—which were based on the principle that mothers and young children should not be forcibly separated, *regardless of their legal status*—held considerable weight for the Gobierno General. The bizarre decision to send the money to the Isla de Pinos, only for Faustino to be recorded as *coartado* in Havana and sent back to the capital, was apparently an attempt to compromise between the "letter" and the "spirit" of the law. On 27 April 1877, the Third Síndico (Fabré) confirmed that Faustino's owner had agreed to the proposal, as long as he did not have to make the journey to Havana himself.

It was apparently Inés herself who refused what might have seemed a good arrangement for her. In August of the same year, the Third Síndico of Havana informed the Gobierno General that she had refused to allow her money to be sent to the Isla de Pinos, "since she was not unaware of the excessive price which slaves are given in the countryside." Like many other claimants, she knew that negotiations for freedom with owners, unequal as they were in the capital, were much more so outside of it: she could not afford for them to take place without her being present.[36] With the accumulated bitterness of a long, unequal struggle, she explained that

> since she had not achieved . . . her proposed object of relieving her son's enslavement . . . but rather his situation had worsened, as had that of the claimant herself, since the deposited sum was raised through taking a loan with interest and she found herself having to return it all, without having achieved her purpose in making the sacrifice of taking out the said loan; she requests that the deposited sum be returned . . . so that she can return it to its owner and free herself from the interest that she is paying.

Credit was scarce and interest high in war-torn 1870s Cuba, even for those with reasonable purchasing power.[37] Inés's loan might have come via one of the *gangá cabildos* operating in Havana. Yet the late 1870s were a time of decline and challenge for the *cabildos*, with prominent *gangá* members complaining of fragmentation and an aging membership.[38] Inés was old, frail and repeatedly described as poor. One can imagine her frustration as the money sat uselessly in the Havana *sindicatura* for a year and a half, while she heard nothing from her son and continued paying the interest. On 13 September, she made a final request to the Gobierno General for her money to be returned. Apparently Calero, Faustino's owner, had named a freedom price of 3,000 *pesos* in notes. Inés, "because of my many aches and pains and my advanced age," could not possibly afford this, and she did not even dispute the price. With the same kind of appeal to charity on the grounds of motherhood made by many other women before her, she hoped that the "affectionate sentiments of Your Excellency as a father" and the Gobernador's understanding of "the affliction of a mother in this unfortunate case" would persuade him to permit the return of her money. In a final demonstration of the lengths to which women went for their children, she explained that she would use it to go personally to the Isla de Pinos and *coartar* Faustino, "since it is not possible for me to free him." The request for the return of the money was granted, but whether Inés would really ever see Faustino again is not revealed, since the document ends here.[39]

Yet Inés's quest had nonetheless obliged the colonial administration to ponder the silences of the Moret Law and the predicaments in which women were left as they tried to negotiate over them. The Consejo de Administración took Ines's case more seriously, for example, than a comparable consultation by a Havana *síndico* made a few months earlier, in May 1876, about whether the owner of Plácida, a slave girl under fourteen whose freed mother lived in Güines (in southeastern Havana province) had the right to sell the girl to someone resident in Guanabacoa (across the bay from the capital). In this instance, the Consejo had simply ruled that the sale could go ahead, since "the Law was intended to safeguard the natural bonds between mothers and children *within relations of slavery* with their respective owners," which did not extend to freed mothers.[40] Even so, they recommended that Plácida's mother be informed of the decision, recognizing her right to consideration and implying it was probably she who had brought the case to the attention of the *síndico* in the first place.[41] Petitions like those of Inés and Plácida, then, may not have been successful in themselves, but they were significant as part of a gradual evolution of jurisprudence toward recognizing some of the claims of freed mothers over their children. There were certainly plenty of ways in which the "spirit" of the law was routinely violated. Owners frequently moved children under fourteen back and forth between their rural and urban properties without any mention of moving their mothers, which presumably separated mothers from their children.[42] Yet mothers' appeals helped keep the "spirit" of the law in the minds of decision-makers in Havana and Madrid. In 1882, after the introduction of the new *patronato* law, the Consejo de Administración received a request from the Gobernador Civil of Santiago de Cuba. The communication asked that women who had been declared exempt from the *patronato* (i.e., freed) be allowed to take along their *liberto* children (those born after September 1868) with them, without paying compensation to *patronos*.

Again, controversy ensued. A report by one Consejo member, José Bolívar, made the very points that the Third Síndico had made a few years earlier during Inés's case, pointing out that the request was in the spirit, if not the letter, of the 1870 law: "The mother was a slave; on the birth of the child, it follows her condition. If the mother becomes free, it seems natural that the child should also obtain this favorable condition." Although it was important to stick to the letter of law, the report said, there also existed "extremely high moral interests, which cannot be ignored."

Despite such views—expressed by at least two of its members in different reports—the Consejo finally ruled against the proposal from Santiago. Yet the tone of its final statement suggests that this was now a harder decision than it had been in Inés's case a few years before. Perhaps this was because, unlike Faustino, this case referred specifically to children who had supposedly been born "free." Or perhaps the council simply found itself forced to uphold, on legal grounds, a decision that it found difficult to justify morally. The ruling accepted that it was "against humanity" that

> children under 12 should be ripped from their mother in order to hand them to their *patrono*, since although he may educate them, treat them well and feed them, such a transfer . . . has no other object than to compensate, with their labor, the expenses of rearing them, while . . . the mother loses the person or persons who could help her to support herself.

Also, said the Consejo, the 1880 law had not improved the condition of children under twelve—mothers were still required to pay "a compensation price generally far superior to the resources at their disposal." The problematic nature of the issue was highlighted by another Consejo member who complained that, in the absence of proper regulation, the provincial *juntas* were all resolving such questions differently, as they saw fit. Nonetheless, the Consejo could not bring itself to let go of the property principle. Ultimately, it upheld what it saw as *patronos'* legal right to compensation for the expenses of raising these children.[43]

Eventually, the amount of legal wrangling caused by mothers did yield results: a year after this decision, the issue was partially resolved by a royal decree from Madrid, which stated that "parents who are free or who in the future become free can take charge immediately of their children, born from 17 September 1868 onwards, without being obliged to . . . [pay] compensation."[44] This would not have helped Inés, because Faustino was born before this date, but it would certainly facilitate freedom and the maintenance of family ties for many other mothers and their children.

In fact, Ramona Oliva had done the same as other women like her in anticipating the decree's logic—in her case, by only a few months—when she filed for custody of her children in Havana in August 1883. The poorly written but passionate first-person appeal, sent in her name to the Gobernador General, argued that her free womb children "are kept unjustly by the aforementioned *patrono*, because since their mother has left captivity, her children are rightfully hers *de facto* and *de jure*; *de facto*, because she has given birth to them, and *de jure*, because the Law authorizes it." Unfortunately for Ramona, as we have seen, the law did not in fact authorize it at the time she made her petition. Yet, through the claims of mothers like her, it would very soon do so.[45] Ramona, then, was part of this broader push for maternal rights that drove the evolution of jurisprudence even though individual claims were not successful.

Owners themselves were perhaps beginning to cede such claims. On 10 July 1884, Don Jorge Méndez, *patrono* of two young brothers, Gavino and Vicente, appeared at his local Junta de Patronato in Regla and renounced his rights over both of them. The renunciation was made explicitly "in recompense for the good services of their mother," and "he cedes all rights in favor of the mother of the *patrocinados* for her to make the use [of them] that she wishes." Gavino and Vicente were informed of the "obligation they are under to contract their labor and live according to the precepts of their mother." It was standard practice to remind *patrocinados*, on being freed, of their duty under the 1880 law to make a labor contract or risk punishment for vagrancy. However, there was no legal provision that they had to obey their mothers! Apparently, the assumption that freed slaves should remain under someone's "guidance" or control had, in this case, fused with increasing social and legal positioning of mothers as having some rights to keep their children and prepare them for the postemancipation world.[46]

Over the 1870s and 1880s, the claims of Cuban mothers to keep their children with them and to have a say in their destiny were increasingly recognized, gradually if very imperfectly eroding the status quo in which such rights and responsibilities had been understood as belonging principally to children's owners.

Born Conditionally Free?
The Rio Branco Law and Womb Politics in Brazil

While the Cuban Moret Law created new legal controversy over wombs and birth, such debates had a long history already in Brazil by the time the Rio Branco law was passed on 28 September 1871. A question unresolved in Brazilian law was this: if, as commonly happened, a slave woman was *conditionally* freed, but had to first serve out a number of years before being entitled to enjoy full freedom, would any children born to her in the meantime be considered free or enslaved?[47] The Rio Branco Law clarified the situation for children born from September 1871 onwards, but it did not resolve the question about children born before that. However, as in Cuba, the "spirit" of the law and of the times, along with the actions of women who helped bring their children's cases to court, helped set a general, if contested, trend toward such cases being resolved in favor of freedom.[48] Indeed, for one *curador*, making a case in 1870 for upholding the freedom of Henrique, the nineteen-year-old *preto* (black) son of a *preta* woman named Marianna, who had been conditionally freed when he was born, "today . . . the constant practice" had become to rule that he was free.[49] As Martha Abreu has noted, during the Brazilian parliamentary debates on the "free womb" law in 1870–71, "both the government and the opposition used the defense of slaves' maternal rights to justify and legitimate their analyses."[50] The legal cases brought by women about their wombs' status helped shape this broader political context.

For example, black freedwoman Basília initiated a freedom suit in April 1870 in Cabo Frio, Rio de Janeiro province, on behalf of her four children: Ismael, Domiciano, Lauriano, and Basília. Her appeal fed directly into the legal and political debates of the day. Basília, who took her children's claim to a *curador*, Manoel Martins Torres, said she had received conditional freedom from her original owner, José da Costa Guimarães, but despite this she had since been sold twice, and was now "owned" by Francisco Gomes da Rocha Guimarães, along with her children. The initial judgment in Cabo Frio ruled that the four children were free.

As the appeal of the case moved to Rio by early 1871, to be decided at the same time as Henrique's, the great political debates taking place in the capital came more explicitly into play. The owner's lawyer specified that "We are not apologists for slavery; on the contrary, we deplore that it is still a fact among us, which is linked to the right of property." Rather than focusing on the specific issue of *this* woman's children, the discussion of wombs and status thus quickly spilled over into the general issue of how—given that (supposedly) no one was now an "apologist for slavery"—the institution could be phased out without damage to the principle of property.[51] Showing how controversial these cases remained, the appeals court overturned the initial ruling, declaring on 25 April 1871 that Basília's children remained enslaved. After another appeal, on 12 September 1871, just days before the passage of the Rio Branco bill, the original decision was reinstated, confirming their freedom.

The argument made by the owner's lawyer, that Basília's original owner had not intended to free her children too, may well have been correct. Complaining about how the current political context had shifted the way the law was being read on this point, Guimarães's lawyer alleged that Basília's children "always lived as slaves, resigned to their fate, until they were inspired by those propagandists for the freedom of other people's slaves." He made the common assumption that ignorant, powerless, enslaved litigants must have been induced by outside influence into taking legal action. Certainly, he did not consider that the initiative in the case might have come from the children's mother, who, in so doing, helped shape broader shifts in the politics and law of enslaved wombs.[52]

In both Brazil and Cuba, "free womb" legislation brought changing notions about the significance of motherhood to the forefront of debates about slavery and emancipation. Claiming that their children were "rightfully theirs," women placed maternity at the heart of their legal struggles for freedom. In so doing, they capitalized on legal and jurisprudential changes, but they also collectively helped to shape them. The available tools for claims-making differed in each case. Enslaved claimants and their relatives in Cuba potentially approached multiple *juntas*, *síndicos*, and colonial authorities. In Brazil, the principal route remained the local and appeals courts, although enslaved people might also petition various public figures—including, as we have seen, the Rio-based imperial family. The kinds of legal opportunities and openings available also differed across the two contexts. Despite these different settings, women pursued similar aims and strategies in each country, hinging their claims upon notions about motherhood that were being rethought in the context of gradual emancipation.

In each case, their claims made use not only of de jure legal arguments, but of rhetoric about slavery and freedom as de facto, socially defined terms. In order to understand why these kinds of extralegal arguments were seen as potentially effective, we need to look outside the legal world of the courts, *juntas*, and *síndicos* to the newspaper stands and the bookshops, the streets and the squares, of each city. The next chapter, then, will consider the broader social and discursive worlds within which legal claims were made and interpreted.

Exaggerated and Sentimental?

Engendering Abolitionism in the Atlantic World

The money he gave to the aforementioned ingênua [child born "free" after the 1871 Rio Branco law] was solely because he took pity on the misery she was suffering, considering his humanitarian principles [. . .] the minor Maria never received clothing from the Defendant but instead lived off the Plaintiff herself.
—José Fernandes Braga Rodrigues, witness statement in support of Josepha Gonçalves de Moraes, Rio de Janeiro, 22 September 1884.

With these words, one of the neighbors of freedwoman Josepha Gonçalves de Moraes, who was seeking custody of her daughter Maria through the courts of Rio de Janeiro, explained why he had helped Josepha care for Maria when Josepha's ex-owners allegedly neglected her. In so doing, José Braga Rodrigues helped Josepha make a moral case, as well as a legal one, that Maria should be handed over to her mother's care. Josepha's case, like those of many other women we have met as they approached courts and *juntas* in 1870s and 1880s Rio and Havana, made use of and helped expand new legal openings that had specific resonance for women and their children. Yet, as we saw in Chapter 3, their petitions also often invoked changing ideas about pity, charity, or maternity that were not simply legal but cultural and social.

Where did these ideas come from? Why should the women making them, or the legal representatives who "translated" their demands for elite male consumption, think they would have any effect? This chapter explores how a changing set of ideas about women—enslaved and free— helped frame public imaginaries of slavery and antislavery in Brazil, Cuba,

97

and the broader Atlantic World by the 1870s and 1880s. Slavery's shocking separation of mothers and children, the link between femininity and emotion, or the question of whether all women were equally "maternal" or whether some were more motherly than others were all hotly debated topics within arguments about slavery and abolition. In the process, gendered imaginaries of what manhood and womanhood meant—whether for enslaved or free men and women—were debated and recast.

The local circumstances of each city led to very different levels of antislavery mobilization. In Brazil, what Seymour Drescher has called an "Anglo-American variant" of antislavery developed in the 1880s, as a broad-based abolition campaign sprang up across the country in response to the national government's increasing recalcitrance on the slavery question.[1] Havana was too much under colonial control for such overt or organized activity, but there were certainly limited spaces for abolitionist discussions—whether in some sectors of the press, among liberal intellectuals, or within the budding labor union movement. Beyond the island itself, Madrid was home to a lively abolition campaign since the 1860s, which drew its vitality from Puerto Rican as well as Spanish members via profound interconnections between metropolis and colonies. Meanwhile, whether in Cuba or in émigré groupings in New York or Florida, separatist voices presented a radical alternative to Spanish rule and gradual abolition.

Yet the very different contexts of Brazil and Cuba were also linked in important ways. Discussions of slavery and abolition held in each were forged in an Atlantic intellectual crucible of which each was a part. Brazilian abolitionists and their counterparts in the Spanish imperial world drew much of their campaigning style from earlier Atlantic abolition campaigns, looking especially to the British.[2] They also dialogued to a considerable degree with each other. At the same time, as they took cautious steps toward emancipation, the Brazilian and Spanish governments, as well as public commentators generally in each setting, looked toward one another, comparing and imitating.[3]

Antislavery commentators formulated their arguments within two broad, overlapping Atlantic intellectual matrices. The first led them to employ the language of equality, painting enslaved people as comparable or similar to their elite readers. The second led them to express deep fears about biological and moral corruption from nonwhite people in general and Africans in particular, drawn both from an older corpus of racist thought and the new "scientific" intellectual currents that reached Latin America by the 1870s. Although these two tendencies might appear contradictory today, they were each part of the intellectual toolkit of most educated thinkers of the day and can each be found in the work of most contemporary commentators, even though individuals took up different positions along a broad spectrum. Each tendency, in turn, drew on a set of tropes and images with which to talk about slavery and abolition. This language helped fashion the discursive spaces in which women like Josepha operated. To appreciate such women's own conceptions of freedom, we need to consider the ways in which other people conceived of these women.

THE SEPARATION OF MOTHERS AND CHILDREN

One ever-present theme within debates about slavery and abolition was the separation of enslaved mothers from their children. These debates echoed, and also helped propel, enslaved women's own legal demands, even though these women would not necessarily have shared the definitions and concepts of motherhood that were assumed by elite commentators.

In June 1870, prominent Republican abolitionist Emilio Castelar made an impassioned speech to the Spanish Cortes as it debated Foreign Minister Segismundo Moret's proposals for a "free womb" law. Speaking from his "heart" and his "conscience," he argued that Moret's proposals did not go far enough and advocated immediate abolition. Reaching one of the most dramatic parts of his long address, he stirred his hearers by describing advertisements in the Cuban newspapers:

> Would the Foreign Minister give these newspapers to his children to read? I cannot believe he would. . . . They say: "For sale: two mares . . . ; two black females, mother and daughter; the mares together or separately; the blacks, mother and daughter, together or separately." (*Sensation!*) The poor black woman . . . has conceived her child in moral suffering, and . . . has given birth in physical pain, [and] although this child could be her consolation, a playing card or a billiard-ball will decide their fate. The blacks are gambled on, and, often, one man wins the mother and the other the daughter, and the bet separates what God and nature have united. On seeing this, we seek—and Oh! we cannot find—human justice and divine justice. Heaven and conscience seem empty."[4]

Such statements were firmly anchored in recent Cuban realities. In a survey of advertisements for rent or sale of slaves in the cities of Havana and Matanzas from the 1830s and 1840s, Sarah Franklin found 56 advertisements that listed a wet nurse for sale, rent, or trade. Only 33 of these addressed the issue of whether the woman's child would accompany her.

Of these 33, 16 women were explicitly offered for sale or rent without their children.[5] Although his speech made lengthy economic and political arguments for abolishing slavery, Castelar also sought and achieved an emotional response—a "Sensation!"—from his audience, by referring to the pain of enslaved mothers separated from their children. In so doing, he invoked an already-familiar image that would continue to help raise the temperature of debates on abolition across the Atlantic over the next two decades.

The mother-child separation image recurred again and again in abolitionist rhetoric, and both responded to and helped shape processes of legal change. Even before it was passed, the Moret Law was denounced by the liberal Spanish press on the grounds that it would not prevent such separations. *La Revolución* called Moret's proposals "a project which, after proclaiming the freedom of the womb," allowed "the separation of mothers and children and the splitting-up of families."[6] The Republican *La Igualdad* took a similar line: "we shudder to think of the future reserved by the project for those two-year-old children who will be bought by the State . . . taking them from their mothers' laps only to . . . give them in tutelage . . . to private individuals or to some organization more appropriate than the State to care for the poor things."[7]

In due course, the law was passed and, as we have seen, it banned the separate sale of enslaved mothers and children under fourteen. Yet the image continued to be useful: antislavery commentators now argued that the law was not being complied with. Mother-child separation provided a flexible, immediately recognizable trope that could be used for very different political ends. In 1872, for example, in drafting a set of reports for discussion of the Cuban rebellion by the U.S. Congress, Cuban patriots Francisco Vicente Aguilera and Ramón Céspedes argued that the rebels were much more ready to abolish slavery than were the Spanish. To this end, they stressed the ineffectiveness of Spain's 1870 law, citing, as Castelar had done, advertisements from the pro-Spanish Havana newspaper, the *Diario de la Marina*, for mothers to be sold separately from young children. They asked, "Can any further proof be wanted of the shamelessness with which Spain violates her most solemn obligations, and laughs at the opinion of civilized nations, passing apparently humane laws without enforcing them?"[8]

The rhetoric of mother-child separation also loomed large in Brazilian abolition struggles in a similarly symbiotic relationship with legal change. Arguments about this question were a major part of the heated debates about the 1871 law—itself passed with an eye to the Spanish law of the previous year.[9] Once passed, the Brazilian law prohibited the separate sale of children under twelve from enslaved parents (usually, in practice, mothers). As the previous chapter explored, both legislative and jurisprudential reforms were partly informed by the protracted legal struggles of enslaved women themselves, who resisted separation from their children. Meanwhile, outside the courts, the abolitionist movement coalesced around the argument that the Rio Branco Law was both insufficient and not being complied with. The first number of *O Abolicionista*, the organ of the Brazilian Anti-Slavery Society, cited "advertisements for the buying and selling of human creatures . . . the hiring of mothers, separated from their children, as the wet nurses of other children, a speculation as vile as it is lucrative . . . ; the mortality of the *ingênuos* . . . [as] sources of humiliation for every Brazilian."[10] Thus, *O Abolicionista* combined two major tendencies in the Brazilian abolitionist movement that have sometimes been seen as mutually exclusive, but which in fact often worked in tandem: the use of emotive appeals aiming at sympathy for slaves' plight, and the argument that slavery made Brazil economically and socially "backward" and was thus a source of shame.[11] In this sense, sympathy for enslaved mothers and families was a "modern" emotion.[12]

Throughout the increasingly heated campaigns of the 1880s, the issue remained a constant theme for Rio's abolitionist press. In January 1884, the *Gazeta da Tarde* ran an emotive item about a "miserable woman named Leocádia," a "supposed slave" who had just given birth, yet "she perhaps did not even have time to read in her child's calm gaze that poem of love and hope that can only be spelled out by a mother's heart. The child was taken from her and, surely, the *roda* opened once again to receive another poor unfortunate. In a few days, as soon as she has left her bed, she will go to nurse someone else's child." The newspaper then proclaimed: "Let us put an end to this infamy; the right to motherhood is the most sacred of all rights."[13] The *Gazeta da Tarde*'s frequent references to the "sacred rights" of slave mothers would have been familiar to Havana's *síndicos* as they conducted legal defenses for such women. It was this kind of denunciation, perhaps, that helped spur Rio's city council into opening the city's first municipal maternity hospital by 1880, catering mainly to enslaved and free *parda* women.[14]

Slavery's defenders, meanwhile, also found the mother-child-separation argument hard to ignore (at least in public discourse, as opposed to private practice). Instead, they tended to accept that the notion held social currency, and tried to engage with it on its own terms. The Cuban deputies at the Madrid Junta de Información in 1866–67, for example,

Political cartoon depicting the sale and potential separation of slave families in Brazil in 1885, despite the proposed new law being discussed at the time. "Coisas da atualidade! O ministro fazendeiro explicando o seu projeto aos lavradores." ("Current events! The landowning minister explaining his project to the [enslaved] workers.") Revista Illustrada, 30 June 1885, 4–5. Fundação Casa Rui Barbosa, Rio de Janeiro.

had been caught out by their Puerto Rican colleagues' proposal to abolish slavery. Countering with proposals for only gradual emancipation, as was to be expected of some of Cuba's most prominent slaveholders, they were careful to incorporate a nod to slave families and mother-child separation in their report:

> The family does not exist for the slave; the Church will bless his love, but the will of the master . . . will create obstacles [to it] . . . separating the husband from his wife, the children from their parents. And unfortunately for them, their degradation and brutalization will never be so complete as to extinguish in their breasts the sensibilities of the natural instincts. Thus we have seen . . . a mother kill her four children, and then attempt to take her own life, on being unable to resign herself to separation from the eldest, who had just been sold.[15]

On the one hand, the deputies charged enslaved people with "degradation" and "brutalization"—burdens that (ex)slaves would carry into freedom as far as many commentators were concerned, whether they attributed them to inherent inferiority or to the experiences of slavery. On the other hand, the deputies nonetheless marshaled the familiar denunciation of family separation, perhaps hoping that in so demonstrating their sensibilities, they could defuse more radical abolitionist demands.

Other conservative commentators met abolitionists' claims about the abuse of the law by countering that mothers and children were well treated. Reporters for the English language publication *The Anglo-Brazilian Times* were, on several occasions, taken to plantations in Rio de Janeiro province, owned by men who were careful to show them not just how efficiently their plantations were run, but how humane their treatment of slaves was. In particular, visitors were shown how well children and mothers were treated. Following a visit to the Paraíso Plantation owned by the Baron of Rio Preto, one reporter waxed enthusiastic in October 1874:

> [T]hough slavery is an evil of great magnitude, its evils to the slave seem to vanish into nothingness upon estates like that of Baron do Rio Preto, and we believe that the most ardent antislaverist of England, were he to visit . . . , would confess that under such a rule . . . slaves can be content, even happy . . . There he would see . . . children freeborn by virtue of the act of September 1871 treated with paternal solicitude, and looked to not only by their mothers but by nurses specially detailed to their charge.[16]

On the other hand, the family separation issue could also be addressed by negating enslaved people's ability to form families at all. British journalist Antonio Gallenga, for example, argued that although the Moret Law in Cuba was encouraging enslaved women to have children, "in the case of really free negroes, and in countries where liberty has ceased to be merely prospective, family ties are as utterly disregarded, and infants as shockingly neglected, as they were in the worst days of bondage."[17] Such allegations, rooted both in centuries-old European notions about "uncivilized" Africans and in newer, scientific racist ideas, made abolitionists' quest for sympathy for slaves an urgent task.

SLAVE WOMEN AND SYMPATHY

As he addressed the Cortes in his June 1870 speech, Castelar asked the following question:

Now, groups of this Chamber, do you not all share the sentiment of humanity? And of what does this great sentiment, which distinguishes modern peoples from those of antiquity, consist? It consists of putting oneself in the place of those who are weeping, of those who are suffering. May we who have homes remember those who do not; may we who have families remember those who have no family; may we who have freedom remember those who groan under the yoke of slavery.[18]

Here, Castelar staked out his broader aim in evoking the image of mothers and children being sold separately like animals: he hoped to arouse feelings of sympathy for enslaved people in his hearers. Because sympathy relies on a sense of fellow-feeling, listeners needed to be persuaded that the enslaved were, in some fundamental sense, like themselves. African slaves and their descendants were entitled to freedom, said Castelar, whether "as sons of God, as sovereigns in nature, [or] as members of humanity."[19] Legal and philosophical arguments about how man's natural state was freedom were familiar terrain; they were employed often by *curadores* in Brazilian *ações de liberdade*, for example.[20] Yet in practice, this theoretically egalitarian viewpoint was usually tinged—if not profoundly underscored—by racist beliefs in nonwhite inferiority.[21] In Europe, men of science debated whether humanity stemmed from one root, or from multiple ones—debates that would be absorbed and reworked by Latin American intellectuals in the decades after Castelar made his speech.[22] Castelar's assertion about the "sentiment of humanity" contrasted significantly with such thinking.

The task facing abolitionists was different from inside a slave society, as in the Brazilian case, than it was for someone like Castelar, whose challenge was to awaken metropolitan Spaniards to the implications of slavery in the distant Antilles. Despite the different contexts, Spanish and Brazilian abolitionists each aimed to bolster their pragmatic economic and political arguments for ending slavery with an emotive, sympathetic response toward enslaved people. One of their most frequent strategies was the portrayal of the suffering of enslaved women. The denial to them of the "sacred" rights of motherhood, their exposure to sexual abuse by masters, and the denial to them of the protection granted white women from such abuse that was part of elite masculine self-imaginings, all made them particularly poignant examples of slavery's cruelty. This was a trans-Atlantic phenomenon. British and North American abolitionists in previous decades had used images of suffering enslaved women to encapsulate both the fellow humanity and the cultural inferiority of enslaved people, adapting the classic slogan "Am I not a man and a brother?" to "Am I not a woman and a sister?" and replacing the image—originally produced by Josiah Wedgewood—of a kneeling enslaved man in a supplicating gesture with that of a kneeling woman.[23]

In Cuba, literary portrayals of slavery's excesses dated back to the Havana literary circle that formed around planter and intellectual Domingo del Monte from the 1820s and received impetus from the presence of British abolitionist Richard Madden in the late 1830s. Influenced by Romanticism, these works embraced emotive depictions of slavery's worst effects, although they were written long before the coalescence of political views explicitly challenging the institution. Largely written by slaveholders, published abroad or appearing on the island only later in the century, these works nonetheless helped create discursive spaces in which sympathy for the enslaved could be expressed. The plight of women featured prominently in works from Félix Tanco y Bosmoniel's *Petrona y Rosalía* (1825), to *Francisco* by Anselmo Suárez y Romero (1839), to Cirilo Villaverde's *Cecilia Valdés* (1839).[24] Gertrudis Gómez de Avellaneda's 1839 novel, *Sab*, produced outside the Del Monte circle, contained an unusually explicit denunciation of slavery.[25]

Later on, these traditions of sentiment began to reach broader audiences. In 1860s Havana, tobacco workers—black, white, free, and enslaved—listened to the traditional *lectura* (reading aloud) as they worked. The *lectura* exposed tobacco workers to varied genres of writing—including the declarations of the Spanish Abolitionist Society. Among the offerings were the popular "sentimental readings," portrayed by caricaturists as leaving listeners in floods of tears as they worked.[26] The use of sentiment as a call to political action spilled over from slavery into other issues, as workers also heard denunciations of how tobacco workers were treated like slaves, with children being whipped and shackled.[27]

In Brazil, meanwhile, nineteenth-century audiences and readerships were accustomed to consuming images of the sufferings of the enslaved and, particularly, of enslaved women. Bernardo Guimarães' novel *A escrava Isaura*, written in the mid-1850s although published in 1875, narrated the sorrows of the enslaved Isaura, persecuted by the sexual advances of her owner's young son Leôncio.[28] Stage versions of *Uncle Tom's Cabin*—which became an Atlantic abolitionist phenomenon, performed from Madrid and London to Port-au-Prince and Lima and which appealed especially to women—proved popular among Brazilian audiences from the 1850s.[29] José Alencar's play *Mãe*, which portrayed an enslaved mother making the ultimate sacrifice for her son, was a hit with Rio audiences since it was first performed in 1860. Alencar, a member of the Conservative Party, did not write the play with abolitionist intent or at a time when an abolitionist movement yet existed in the country—indeed, he would later oppose the Rio Branco law.[30] The play's flowery rhetoric and tear-jerking powers fitted the broader Romantic tastes of nineteenth-century audiences and readers.[31] Yet as the political context shifted by the 1880s, the familiar rhetorical style of dramas like *Mãe* took on new significance.[32] Theatres, by this decade, were no longer merely about entertainment; they became recruiting-grounds and showcases for abolitionist mobilization.[33] In November 1886, for example, Rio's *Phoenix Dramática* theatre staged a play called "The Mother of the Slaves," "modeled . . . on *Uncle Tom's Cabin*." The *Revista Illustrada* newspaper applauded not just the production's artistic merit but how it conveyed "the anguishes of the miserable slaves" to impassioned audiences. Such plays were systematically reviewed by the abolitionist press, with broader political intent.[34]

This new political intent meant that reviews of artistic manifestations of antislavery in Rio papers were now also interspersed with reports of real slaves' sufferings. Here, as in fiction, editors seemed to view stories about women and children as making particularly good reading. In January 1884, for example, the *Gazeta* emotively described an *ingênuo* who had been beaten because he tried to defend his enslaved mother from physical punishment. This punishment, in turn, was inflicted because she had "possessed the modesty to refuse to sate the libidinous desires of her tyrant" (the owner).[35] The suffering of mother and son aimed at a sympathetic emotional response from readers. This, in turn, was facilitated by emphasis on the woman's "modesty," implying that she too "deserved" the protection from sexual violence that, in theory, was afforded to elite women.[36] In other words, it helped break down the vast gulf assumed to exist between "modest" elite women and European-derived notions of licentious, animal-like women of color. Such a strategy would have been familiar to earlier British campaigners, who had highlighted enslaved women's "moral degradation" at the hands of slaveholding men and, in the process, replaced stereotypes about licentious black women with notions of those women as innocent, passive victims of male lust. British women campaigners asked that their enslaved "sisters be granted the same "privileges" of male protection that they enjoyed as middle-class white women.[37]

Motherhood, assumed to be at the core of gender identity for elite women, was a powerful tool for generating this kind of sympathetic emotional response on behalf of enslaved women. In Madrid in 1872,

D. Salvador Torres Aguilar, professor at the recently founded Madrid University, spoke to a packed auditorium of the Spanish Abolitionist Society. Addressing "ladies" as well as "gentlemen," he argued that the merits of the Brazilian "free womb" law outweighed those of the Spanish equivalent, because the Brazilian law specifically allowed women who gained freedom to take their children under eight with them—thus preventing the problems this very issue was causing for the freedwomen in Cuba whom we met in the last chapter. Switching to the feminine of the second person plural (*vosotras*), Torres Aguilar then specifically addressed the women in the audience: "And I ask you now: what mother will accept her freedom if, along with it, she is forbidden from returning to the place where her children suffer the torments of servitude? Would you not prefer slavery, with the right to see and be able to care for your children, to freedom with complete separation from them?" He was answered with lively cries of *Bien* from his audience, which rose to a *sensación* when, a few minutes later, he described an enslaved woman in Cuba who, "blind with maternal love," cast her three children off a rooftop and then jumped to her death, rather than be separated from them.[38]

Despite what Torres Aguilar saw as the advantages of the Brazilian law, abolitionists in Brazil argued it was not being complied with, as we have seen. Like Torres Aguilar, they drew parallels between enslaved and free women, using maternity as a focal point. In January 1881, *O Abolicionista* reproduced extracts from a speech made at the festival of Nossa Senhora do Rosário, in the town of Pelotas in Rio Grande do Sul, Brazil's southernmost province, by local cleric Dr Augusto Joaquim de Siqueira Canabarro:

> Do you hear the wail of a child? It is a creature which in vain waits for the moment when it can rest its lips on the maternal breast . . . in vain, yes, because not far away, some tears, which offend our eyes, tell us that a loving mother, just like all other mothers but for the fact that the mark of slavery weighs upon her, cannot reach her child, because an alien power gave her a child which was also alien to her, towards which, however, she, ignoring the fruit of her own body, is obliged to lavish all her care, all her affection! Do your ears not hear the sobs and laments that seem to challenge the most hardened of hearts?[39]

Canabarro not only detailed the enslaved woman's plight, but explicitly equated her maternal role to that of "all other mothers." Thus he aimed to create sympathy in even "the most hardened of hearts." Nossa Senhora do Rosário was a well-known Afro-Brazilian religious brotherhood and festival.[40] Canabarro's audience probably included many people of color, female and male, enslaved and free.

Rhetorically addressing women—even notional women in mainly male audiences or readerships—was useful when making these kinds of appeals. Women functioned as important receptors for appeals to the emotions. It was socially acceptable—indeed, essential to their gender identity—for women to be influenced by "impulse," understood to spring from sentiment rather than from the assumed male preserve of "reason."[41] Indeed, abolitionist language was often as much about shoring up participants' gender identities as about freeing slaves.[42] In this sense it followed a Brazilian tradition in which masculinity and rhetoric had long been intertwined, as young male law students embraced Romantic styles and sentimental writings as part of a rite of passage into adult male, elite life. While their poems might address women, the production of poetry and oratory helped to define them as a class of future rulers, excluding women and non-elites through language itself.[43] Abolitionist men praised women who freed slaves for their feeling and impetuosity, and for acting from family-based identities as wives, sisters, mothers, or daughters, thus putting older notions about women's roles to new political purpose. Men who freed slaves, on the other hand, were described as noble, strong, resolute, and bold. They might be described as "family fathers," but, unlike women's family descriptions, this term in nineteenth-century Brazil conveyed patriarchal power, prestige, and authority.[44]

In the process, notions about what femininity meant for elite women—as well as for slave women—were rethought as part of antislavery mobilization. The topic aroused great interest and debate among antislavery writers—who were mainly, if not exclusively, men. In early 1884, for example, the *Gazeta da Tarde* asked for readers' responses to the following question: "Is the Brazilian woman proslavery?" The question generated varied responses and weeks of newsprint. Commentators—mainly male readers—provided indications that women were participating in antislavery movements to quite a significant extent. "On one side or the other," said one unknown author, women were always "casting themselves into the most heated part of the fray, with [the] heroic and reckless impetus that comes from sentiment, and which is born of the blind impulses of the heart." He gave an example of a recent abolitionist festival, where he had witnessed "a moving spectacle" which "made tears well up in every eye." The speaker, Dr José Agostinho dos Reis, a member of Rio's Escola Polytécnica, had discussed "the retrograde tendencies of the better half of the human species," without there being much protest from the theatre boxes, which were "all full of ladies." Reis then said he could not believe that, "because of having been born a slave, any of his countrywomen could see in that a motive to despise him." The passage continued:

His voice tremulous with emotion, and his eyes moist with tears, [Reis] exclaimed that if any of his countrywomen thought that this was a reason to despise him that they should say so . . . At that moment, one of those spectacles was witnessed which the roughness of masculine hearts cannot resist. The ladies stood up in the boxes and, with their faces bathed in tears, waved their handkerchiefs at the orator, exclaiming:—No, no![45]

Women were useful as a symbolic receptacle for the emotions orators like Reis wished to arouse. After all, abolitionist men could hardly have been depicted weeping copiously and waving their handkerchiefs without forfeiting the masculine image required to maintain political credibility.[46] Indeed, they needed to defend themselves from accusations like that of prominent proslavery planter Antônio Prado, who declared cuttingly in July 1885 that "the slogan of the abolitionist movement is exaggerated and sentimental."[47] In other words, by evoking sentiment and emotion, abolitionists were drawing up new gendered codes of conduct for elite men and women as well as repositioning gender roles for the enslaved. The process was intertwined: enslaved mothers became suitable receptors for the charitableness that came to be understood as underpinning free women's involvement in antislavery. Such arguments had direct practical consequences. A Brazilian legal case initiated on the eve of the passage of the Rio Branco Law, for example, revolved around the question of whether a young child, Francelina, who had been freed at birth by her mistress while the mistress's husband was away on business, ought to have her freedom upheld. The *curador* stressed that the mistress had taken pity on the baby, who was sick at the time, and had accepted her enslaved mother's payment for freedom. Thus she had "practiced two actions permitted in law: one of humanity and the other of economy." The judge, ruling for Francelina's freedom to be upheld, argued that "Woman . . . because of her weakness and susceptibility, errs when the slave needs her aid in order to achieve freedom."[48]

ABOLITIONIST WOMEN

The rhetoric of sympathy and emotion had a practical corollary. Across the Atlantic World, where abolitionist momentum developed, women tended to participate in significant numbers.[49] Abolitionists exchanged, read, and corresponded internationally, cultivating links with and perspectives from Britain, in particular.[50] Thus, some of the rhetorical and organizational style of abolition movements that developed in Spain and Brazil, and of antislavery commentators in Cuba, followed those seen in Britain, as well as the United States, where women had long been prominent participants.[51] At least some of these transnational links were cultivated by women themselves. The Birmingham-based Ladies' Negro's Friend Society, one of the longest-running British women's antislavery societies, published a letter in the Madrid newspaper *El Abolicionista Español* in 1865, asking Spanish women to embrace abolitionism; in 1871 they wrote to the deposed Spanish Queen Isabel II regarding Cuban and Puerto Rican slavery; and by 1880 they were still going strong, publishing a letter to Brazilian women in *O Abolicionista*.[52]

Women's potential to bolster Atlantic abolition movements was enhanced by a specific nineteenth-century vision—particularly well-developed in Iberian societies, perhaps, but present in Anglophone ones as well—that women brought moral authority to society.[53] As Christopher Schmidt-Nowara has shown, the implications of this can be seen in metropolitan Spain even before the Spanish Abolitionist Society was formed, as liberal social reformers of the 1850s and 1860s "sought to open the public sphere to women," hoping their presence would "civilize the harsh male public world."[54] This concern then fed into Spanish abolitionism, with a short-lived women's chapter within the Spanish Abolitionist Society. Advocating a role for women in public life, abolitionist Joaquín María Sanromá later took up the question of morality in the late 1860s, evoking the dichotomy of men as rational, women as emotional and compassionate: "You are . . . the great moral force brought into the political world. Your mission is to light the fire of sentiment in those icy atmospheres. Oh! for too long politics have been a snowy region!"[55]

The rhetoric of morality, emotion, and sympathy, in turn, could be powerfully appropriated by women themselves. In 1866, the newly founded Spanish Abolitionist Society held a poetry competition. Winning first place was well-known Spanish social reformer Concepción Arenal with a poem that posited charity and moral virtue as being particularly feminine strengths.[56] Meanwhile the poem "Charity for the Slave! To the Mothers of Families" was entered by moral reformer Joaquina Balmaseda, author of several very popular manuals on "proper" behavior for women. The poem emphasized that charity began through the home and maternity:

Mother, if within your home,
a temple of chaste loves,
Where the Lord made the flowers
of your affection grow, . . .

. . . .

You remember those who, immobilized
By the torment of chains,
Suffer terrible anguish
And have their children stolen
Who are the blood of their veins,

How tenderly, loving mother,
Trembling with emotion,
You will kiss your tender child!
How, seeing him still in front of you,
Your heart will tremble!"[57]

Reflecting contemporary reformers' belief in separate spheres of action for men and women, García Balmaseda urged women to act as moral guardians, exercising their "charitable" influence on men not by direct public action but by "weeping and imploring."[58] Her advice to women on the abolition question fitted the general admonitions of her ladies' manuals: "Never try to usurp the rights of the man, for then you would have to cede your own rights to him; and all the applause of a parliament, all the honors of a ministerial chair, are not worth the smile of your son when he wakes and holds out his arms to you, or the pleasure of sweetening, for your life's companion, the bitterness that public life brings him."[59]

In Brazil, like in Spain, elite women had long been involved in public beneficent and charitable activities, particularly through their considerable mobilization for the Paraguay War effort.[60] There were already precedents, then, for their "charitable" activities—perceived as occurring outside the political sphere, but in fact now mobilized in the deeply political cause of antislavery.[61] In August 1886, Italian opera singer Nadina Bulicioff, who was visiting Rio de Janeiro, publicly freed six enslaved women after one of her performances. Using donations she had made to the Abolitionist Confederation, she shared the stage with abolitionist José do Patrocinio and a "ladies' commission" as she handed letters of freedom to the six women. The *Gazeta da Tarde* praised Nadina's "great womanly generosity",[62] while the *Revista Illustrada* gushed:

We believe Bulicioff was extraordinarily moved on seeing in front of her the poor women for whom she represented a redeemer, and so, handing out the letters of liberty, she embraced and kissed the women being freed, with such a fraternal effusiveness . . . that everyone trembled and, with tears in their eyes, acclaimed the sublime woman, who identified with our sentiments. The stage was full of ladies, who had brought [Bulicioff] presents . . . Everyone rose to congratulate the humanitarian benefactress . . . Her Majesty the Empress was crying, and on the benches, the handkerchiefs, after waving enthusiastically, were dampened with spontaneous tears which the slaves' sufferings drew from the audience.[63]

High-profile women provoked public outpourings of sentiment in other Brazilian cities too: in the northeastern city of Recife, home to a vigorous abolition campaign, opera singer Giuseppina de Senespleda Battaglia delighted audiences by freeing women slaves.[64] Women's abolitionist contributions, however, were not limited to the few individuals who gained public notoriety. Abolitionist men in Brazil were acutely aware of women's potential contributions to a movement that sought to open the sphere of popular political mobilization to new sectors of the population.[65] Rio's Abolitionist Confederation held separate women's meetings.[66] Women made donations and organized events like bazaars and charity functions. Planning an auction in March 1884 to raise funds and celebrate the first anniversary of abolition in Ceará, the Confederation specifically targeted "ladies, Brazilian and foreign" to donate items.[67] One of the most prominent donors, Olympia Guimarães Catta Pretta, "distinguished abolitionist and the wife of noted medical doctor Councilor Dr. Catta Pretta," rounded up her friends to donate their valuables, explaining that "The religious sentiments I profess teach me to combat slavery, and, despite the limitations of women's sphere, I will work always on behalf of the oppressed."[68] Taking care not to be seen to step outside their "women's sphere" by emphasizing values seen as "womanly"—charity, religiosity—women like Olympia nonetheless lent financial support and social respectability to a movement with increasingly radical political implications.[69]

If a small cohort of women took the lead, frequent references to large cohorts of "ladies" at Brazilian abolitionist events like the one headed by Nadina Bulicioff indicate a much broader female consumption of antislavery ideas. Luiza Regadas organized two Abolitionist Confederation events staged at Rio's Polytheama Fluminense Theatre in January 1884,

Image depicting benefit concert of Nadina Bulicioff in Rio de Janeiro, August 1886. "A distincta abolicionista Nadina Bulicioff" ("The distinguished abolitionist Nadina Bulicioff"), Revista Illustrada, 20 August 1886, 8. Fundação Casa Rui Barbosa, Rio de Janeiro.

attracting "a numerous attendance of ladies, always ready to attend wherever liberty takes another step forward."[70] At the second, the speaker who set them to waving their handkerchiefs was Mercedes de Oliveira, a native of the northeastern province of Pernambuco. Oliveira was a pioneer in many ways, not only in agreeing to give this public antislavery speech, but as a medical student who had raised a storm in Pernambuco's provincial assembly by requesting a scholarship. She would later co-edit a New York-based Portuguese-language newspaper that promoted women's rights.[71]

In her speech, Oliveira responded to the controversial question asked of readers by the *Gazeta da Tarde* in January 1884: "Is the Brazilian woman a slaveocrat?" Oliveira roundly refuted many readers' opinion that women were indeed "slaveocrats," arguing instead that the Brazilian woman was "the enemy of slavery, that vile institution that makes a rational being into a vile merchandise, which destroys the maternal heart because it takes a poor woman's child from her arms to throw him on the *roda dos expostos* . . . Show me: where is the educated woman . . . who does not feel tears well up in her eyes and whose face does not blush with shame every time she sees the whip cut the slave's flesh, or lucre and misery separate mothers from children, husbands from wives?"[72]

The fact that the newspaper raised this question confirms that there was considerable interest among Rio's abolitionist leaders in how women might contribute to their cause, and they soon had occasion to put the theory into practice. Later that same year, in June 1884, Manoel Dantas's Liberal ministry came to power, endorsing uncompensated freedom for sexagenarian slaves. The bill caused outrage in Parliament and a crisis for the Dantas government, which the emperor was forced to dissolve, with elections to be held in December. The elections, then, would be crucial to the fortunes of the bill and to abolitionist hopes in general. In this context, in September 1884, an anonymous piece addressed "To the ladies of Brazil," appeared in the *Gazeta da Tarde*. Explaining in detail the recent events in Parliament and the importance of the forthcoming elections, it urged women to persuade men to vote for "sincerely abolitionist candidates": "You, ladies, can do a great deal—you can unite, not through words or through platonic intentions, but through deeds, through tenacious and serious pleas to abolitionist campaigners. Ask your husband, your son, your brother . . . all those whom you love . . . to work for abolitionism." Using the maternal arguments now familiar to us when addressing "ladies," it continued: "Be the protector of the oppressed, especially of those old people, many of whom are the parents or grandparents of the devoted women who nursed you or your children with as much love and affection as if they had borne you!"[73]

In Brazil, women's participation in abolitionist campaigning did not lead to the kinds of calls for women's rights that developed in Britain and the United States.[74] Yet mobilizing women for abolition did generate broader discussions of women's social roles in society, tapping into an increasing, transnational interest in the question of women's education over the second half of the nineteenth century whose repercussions were felt in Brazil, in colonial Cuba, and far beyond.[75] The proabolition *Revista Illustrada* newspaper, which ran its own series about women, *O Eterno Feminino*, in 1886, commented: "Across the press, both in the Court and the provinces, the beginnings of propaganda about the vindications of the fair sex can be seen."[76] While the column went on to mock the notion of women entering politics or other "masculine" spheres, "O eterno feminino" also provided, at other moments, a space for critiques of the domestic roles to which elite women were condemned.[77] These new ideas about free women went hand in hand with the rethinking of womanhood among the enslaved.

"TRAFFICKING IN THEIR OWN BLOOD": SLAVERY'S CORRUPTION OF FAMILIES AND GENDER ROLES

If women slaves were often invoked by antislavery discourse in order to seek pity for slaves in general, they also became central to another set of arguments, which emphasized slavery's corruption of society and the family. Border crossings between enslaved and enslaver, or white and nonwhite—described by Joanne Nagel as "ethnosexual" encounters— occurred through the bodies of women of color via sexual relationships and the suckling and rearing of white children.[78] Such encounters in the heart of elite families provoked considerable anxiety among contemporaries, who, in expressing their fears, tended to focus particularly on gender roles in general, and on women in particular.[79] Drinking from both the liberal and scientific racist wells of thought, antislavery commentators trod a fine line between lamenting the fate of slaves whose families or gender roles had been corrupted by slavery and expressing fear and shame about the "pollution" caused by the institution or, by extension or implication, by nonwhites generally. The boundaries between describing the "degradation" caused by the experience of slavery and ascribing this "degradation" to nonwhiteness itself, were subtle and porous.

As well as pointing out the separations and distortions that slavery caused to *enslaved* families, antislavery discourse also argued that the institution corrupted *slaveholding* families.[80] The "unnatural" relations between the two groups, and their consequences for women, helped emphasize the barbarity of the institution. Spanish Abolitionist Society member Enrique Vera y González, in an 1881 history of slavery, pointed out that the situation of women slaves was especially cruel, "subjected to the same cruel treatment as the black man, beaten barbarically . . . by the same people whom she has suckled at her breast."[81] Vera y González quoted the following passage from American journalist James O'Kelly's picture of Cuban slavery:

> View slavery from whichever side we may, we shall be able to perceive nothing but moral turpitude as its immediate result. Trampling all laws human and divine underfoot, we shall see the slave-master and his assistants handing over their own flesh and blood to this terrible life of degradation, and exposing their own children to the lash of the

master . . . A system capable of so deadening the best feelings of our nature as to change human beings into monsters, must be regarded by all honorable men as accursed.[82]

O'Kelly's words, first published in 1874 and cited by Vera y González seven years later, themselves echoed an older abolitionist argument that slavery produced "unnatural" family relations. In 1865, a pamphlet published in New York by "several Cuban and Puerto Rican abolitionists" calling for annexation of the island by the United States had argued that:

> to apply the epithet of barbarous and bloodthirsty to the negroes is the height of impudence in men so destitute of moral sense . . . who traffic in their own blood, as there are a great many among the slave dealers who sell in bondage their own children; who forget in their blind lust of gold that the majority of them drank the liquor of life at the breast of a negro woman, because their mothers would rather neglect their most sacred obligations than spoil their carnal beauty.[83]

Such accusations implicated both male and female slave-owners. Both were violating codes of behavior regarding their families which "civilization" demanded. Men sired, and then sold, children. In so doing they violated slave women's "natural" maternal role as well as their own paternal one. Women, meanwhile, neglected their "sacred" maternal obligations in favor of sensuousness and vanity.

Similarly, a poem published in Rio de Janeiro in 1886 depicted a group of slaves who were being sold. After describing one woman among them as having just had her child taken from her as part of the process of sale, the poem turned to describe one of her companions:

> This one has provided, poor thing,
> The vile satisfactions of the sensual slave-trader.
> Laughing, he bade her farewell,
> The unhappy woman leaves, but he keeps the money.[84]

The sufferings of enslaved women, then, presented a useful way to criticize the nefarious consequences of "ethnosexual" relations between slaveholder and enslaved.

As well as corrupting families, it was common to argue that slavery warped "natural" gender roles, among both owners and slaves themselves. An 1860 piece by Cuban poet and novelist Anselmo Suárez y Romero, who was from a wealthy slaveholding family, described the narrator's return to the family plantation after a six-year absence. Among the generally shocking conditions he finds among the slaves, he is particularly moved by the women: "still girls, already given over to concubinage and prostitution; . . . the fathers and husbands, selling their daughters and their wives." In prostituting "their" women, fathers and husbands inverted elite patriarchal masculine norms, which revolved precisely around controlling women's sexuality. Thus slavery undermined slave men's masculinity by denying them proper control and protection of "their" women.[85]

As men were prevented from performing their "natural" masculine role as provider and head of the family, so women were denied the protection from work and the seclusion in the home that were part of definitions of womanliness for elite observers:

> . . . those young women who a little over half a decade ago exhibited all the splendor of . . . their race, how are they now? Prematurely mothers, their children scarcely know who is their father; the cares of breast-feeding, together with field work, have exhausted them . . . The curvaceous female figures have assumed the rigid muscles of men . . . Ah! It is the woman who suffers the worst effects of slavery! Thus she can be neither mother, nor daughter, nor wife, nor sister, nor friend![86]

Hard physical work in the fields was "man's work." Women who were forced into working in the fields were thus described as becoming physically degendered, and hence—since a genderless humanity was difficult to conceive of—degraded and dehumanised.[87] Part of the Domingo del Monte circle in Havana that, from the 1830s, produced literary criticisms of slavery's worst excesses (which they could not hope to publish on the island) while continuing to own slaves themselves, Suárez y Romero was not necessarily attacking the institution of slavery in this piece. Nonetheless, his line of reasoning correlated closely with an 1861 statement by Spanish liberal reformer Segismundo Moret, who, a decade later, would put his name to Spain's "free womb" law. For Moret, referring to Spanish metropolitan society, "The female worker is no longer a woman."[88]

Slavery also, it was argued, warped gender roles among slave owners as well as among their slaves. The Cuban deputies at the Junta de Información observed:

> The sentiment of shame, that delicate flower of education, and of the purity of habits, receives early blows from the gusts of slavery. A slave is not a man, and frequently the most innocent girl, the most bashful young lady, will see him without shock or embarrassment, semi-naked as he performs field or domestic work.[89]

The notion that slavery defeminized slaveholding women had a long, transatlantic history. As Suely Gomes Costa has explored for Brazil, it was constructed in part over the course of the nineteenth century by European travel writers, shocked at the "brutalizing" effects of slaveholding on Brazilian women.[90] New ideals of charitable, merciful elite womanhood gained ground in Brazil over the nineteenth century, even as the well-rehearsed images of women barbarically punishing their slaves continued to provide rich material for abolitionist campaigners by the 1880s. Thus, like in the case of women's participation in abolitionist campaigns, a shifting transatlantic set of models of femininity helped to mold antislavery discourse. In Rio, in February 1886, a fifteen-year-old slave girl named Eduarda escaped from the house where, for three years, she and her companion Joana had allegedly suffered savage beatings from her owner, Dona Francisca da Silva Castro. On escaping, Eduarda was taken by two women she met to the offices of the *Gazeta da Tarde*, where she related the tale of her tortures "in front of innumerable people, who listened to her in stupefaction" before taking her before a local magistrate.[91] Joana died the following day; Eduarda survived, but had been left nearly blind. Despite this, D. Francisca was later absolved. The grisly details of the case were widely publicized by the abolitionist press.[92] For Evaristo de Moraes, recounting in 1924 the history of abolition through which he had lived, Dona Francisca personified "female criminality, exceeding, in its cruelty, male criminality"; from then on, "the masses saw in every mistress of slave women another Da Francisca de Castro."[93]

Depictions of women like D. Francisca raised a difficult contradiction for antislavery writers. Were women the compassionate, charitable, and sentimental beings they loved to describe at such lyrical length? Or were they vicious fiends and slave-torturers? It was just such a contradiction between conflicting popular stereotypes that prompted the *Gazeta da Tarde*'s 1884 column, since "At our political rallies, in abolitionist societies' discussions, in the press, in conversations, this has been a point of constant controversy, dividing opinions completely . . . Even in the law courts, orators' opinions have been now on one side, now on the other."[94] The column acted as a useful snapshot of this broader debate.

For one contributor, who signed simply "Delia," women's jealousy meant they were indeed cruel mistresses, punishing their women slaves for their husbands' sexual pursuit of slaves: "The white woman cruelly avenges herself for this *humiliating* rivalry . . . instead of despising her husband . . . Who is the real criminal—the slave woman who bears abjection because she fears the whip, or the *master*, who ought to be humane

Image depicting the slaves Joana and Eduarda, owned by D. Francisca de Castro. Revista Illustrada, *18 February 1886, 8.* Fundação Casa Rui Barbosa, Rio de Janeiro.

and dignified under the roof where his children sleep?"[95] This roundly refuted the notion of "lascivious" slave women who were complicit in their own sexual abuse.

Maranhão-born novelist Aluízio Azevedo argued vociferously that women were especially cruel, describing a wealthy old woman he knew in Maranhão who went to pray at mass every day leaving her slave being physically punished. Such examples provided him with material for several similar characters in his 1881 novel, *O Mulato.* Dona Maria Bárbara tortured slaves; Dona Quitéria Inocência Santiago was "a rich, Brazilian widow, very religious and particular about purity of blood, for whom a slave was not a man, and nonwhiteness was, in itself, a crime"; while Dona Amância Sousellas thought slaves needed "The whip, the whip! until they cry 'enough'!"[96]

For others, women slaveholders had simply become corrupted by slavery; they were not inherently cruel. Abolitionist João Clapp argued: "The Brazilian woman was born among slaves, and was fed with the milk of a slave woman. Her cradle was rocked to the sound of the painful songs of slavery! . . . And today she judges slavery to be her legitimate right. Can the Brazilian woman, in these conditions, be free of the leprosy that corrupts our social body? Is she perhaps responsible for this evil of ours? No." The remedy was education and reform of the family: "in the family home that is not completely contaminated" by slavery, "the saving of souls through the abolition of the slaves should be injected into the spirit of the woman as a religious idea."[97] Luis Gonzaga Duque Estrada also argued that women were not inevitable or natural "slaveocrats"; their behavior was the result of the lack of education. Thus, discussions of slavery again led back to questions of women's education and social roles.[98] For Azevedo, women were "sixty years behind" in educational terms. And an unsigned piece, written in the first person as if by a woman, blamed women's subjugation for their proslavery behavior: "We ask for a book and they give us a theatre seat; we ask for a pen and they give us a crotchet needle."[99]

SLAVERY, SOCIAL SICKNESS, AND FEMALE BODIES

As an extension of notions about the warping of families and gender roles, the idea of sickness in the social body in general was also common among slavery's critics. In March 1876 Rio's Municipal Council president, Adolpho Bezerra de Menezes, praised the Brazilian army for "liberating" Paraguay from slavery: "It is well worth being vanquished, when the conqueror, putting his hand on the heart of the second Lazarus, speaks the words of life, liberty, and progress: *Surge et ambula* [stand up and walk]."[100] As abolition was declared, the Paraguayan nation, like Lazarus, was miraculously cured of its sickness. Almost exactly a decade later, at Rio's fourth municipal emancipation ceremony in 1886, council president João Pereira Lopes used the word "abolition" for the first time at one of these public events. He described it as a "national ideal . . . which convulses the country[;] it is . . . a question of life or death for Brazilians who love from their hearts this beloved homeland."[101] The changes produced in the nation by abolition would be like the convulsions of a sick person; abolition would bring life, and its neglect, death, to all patriotic Brazilians. Back in 1866 in Madrid, Emilio Castelar had lamented "the moral death of a society, if such a name can be given to something that carries the corpse of slavery within its body."[102]

Often, the cause or the symptom of the disease was portrayed as sexual immorality. The "Several Cuban and Puerto Rican abolitionists" writing in New York the previous year argued: "Slavery has proved to be, at all times and places, a social leprosy. Concubinage, adultery, and impurity of life, are vices inherent in it."[103] Because "contamination" from slavery's vices occurred via women's physical and social roles as reproducers, they were again in the spotlight when its effects were discussed. Fear of midwives and nurses of color in Havana dated back to at least the 1830s.[104] It persisted into the 1870s, as Puerto Príncipe (Camagüey)-born writer and journalist Aurelia Castillo de González, discussing enslaved women who raised their mistresses' daughters in Cuba, condemned the "horrible mixing of slave and mother which is so common there!" Castillo de González called slavery "that error that all Cubans suckle on," which "filters into the veins of our moral organism and corrupts it."[105] Brazilian writer Nísia Floresta had expressed similar sentiments in the 1850s, seeing breast-feeding as a patriotic duty for white women even as she saw slave wet nurses as a threat to domestic and national stability.[106]

Long-standing gendered concerns about morality, family life, and the "health" of the nation in slavery fed into specific new anxieties about postemancipation social control. In Rio, such preoccupations prompted municipal debates during the 1880s about the regulation of domestic servants and wet nurses—women who crossed racial, social, and public-private divisions in disquieting ways, spreading moral corruption and biological pollution.[107] At the same time, efforts were being made in Havana, Rio, and beyond to regulate prostitution, another proponent of infection, whose effects were analyzed in terms closely linked to discussions of slavery.[108] The areas of Rio where it occurred were "focal points of infection, recognized as damaging to the social body," while prostituted women were bought and sold "like slaves."[109] In the famous words of novelist Joaquim Manoel de Macedo, Brazilian slave society was like an "unfortunate woman who, forming the habit of prostitution, abandons herself to it with indecent folly."[110] All these anxieties, then, had a strong component of unease regarding the bodies of poor women and women of color—an unease that coexisted with the ideas about sympathy and fellow-feeling among women, and particularly mothers, that have been the main focus of this chapter. They had important implications not only for the process by which slavery was abolished, but also for elites' conceptions of the roles of women of color in postabolition societies, as Chapter 6 of this book will explore.

This chapter has traced the discursive toolkit for which literate men reached when writing down and evaluating legal claims. Whenever such men looked outside the law's stipulations to persuade their hearer with an apt example or metaphor, they mined a rich seam of (anti)slavery imagery in which women and womanhood figured prominently.[111] Judges, scribes, and officials were steeped in the law, but they were also woven into a social and political fabric, whether they owned slaves themselves, were persuaded into buying trinkets for their wives at bazaars run by abolitionist "ladies," or happened to be reading an engrossing novel that recycled familiar gendered tropes to denote the suffering of the enslaved or slavery's pernicious corruption of society. The rhetoric that molded their conscious and unconscious cognitive processes had both a long history and a broad Atlantic reach. The intense public abolitionist campaigns organized in Rio, of course, could not remotely be replicated in colonial Havana. Nonetheless, abolitionism in Spain itself and in Puerto Rico created an Atlantic space for discussions of slavery and abolition, where ideas ebbed and flowed between colonies and metropolis. Beyond this ran a still broader set of currents, as commentators in Brazil, Spain, and Cuba drew ideas and comparisons both from one another as well as from earlier Atlantic precedents. These notions were profoundly shaped by changing ideas about masculinity and femininity. As part of this process, elite women were marshaled into supporting a political cause whose best expression was found in emotive images of slave women separated from their children or forced into sex with slaveholders. Thus, when a lawyer asked for compassion for an enslaved mother threatened with separation from her child, pleaded for her exemption from harsh rural work, mentioned that she had nursed her master's children, or hinted at physical intimacy between master and slave, he pushed specific gendered buttons for his readers, invoking not just changing legal stipulations but new cultural and social developments. Changing images of enslaved and free femininity at times limited, and at others helped expand, the spaces in which female litigants maneuvered.

At the same time, claims-making women brought with them their own very clear notions about how they hoped to gain freedom. These women were, of course, themselves Atlantic subjects, drawing not only on the European-derived cultural images described in this chapter, but on African cultural norms about slavery, freedom, and gender. They, too, were participants in the construction of the political, social, and legal life of the cities, taking their grievances to the courtrooms but also bargaining with emancipation societies, complaining to sympathetic journalists, or mobilizing their families or neighbors. As such, their own gendered conceptions of freedom were not just constrained by, but also helped influence and expand, the kinds of elite notions that have been discussed in this chapter. One key arena where these struggles played out was the very landscapes of the cities themselves, to which Chapter 5 turns.

CHAPTER FIVE

I Wish to Be in This City

Mapping Women's Quest for Urban Freedom

I beg Your Excellency that, since the Junta where I reside expelled me,
denying me my rights, taking advantage of the ignorance in which I have been
raised, and presuming I do not know the Law, which is true, you will allow [. . .]
the case [. . .] to be opened at the Junta de Patronato in Havana.
—Ramona Oliva to Gobernador General, Havana, 9 August 1883

With these words, Ramona Oliva's appeal argued that, although she did not live in Havana, she ought to be able to make her claim for her children's freedom in the colonial capital. Ramona had traveled some sixty miles from the small settlement of Bolondrón in Matanzas. Her appeal reminds us that both the legal struggles over slavery and the public wrangling over emancipation that have been the subject of previous chapters were framed by a specific context. It was in the cities, and above all the capital cities, where these processes found their most fervent expression. Yet Ramona's life and struggle do not fit neatly into divisions between "urban" and "rural" slavery. Instead, individuals' struggles for freedom were underscored by movement. The threat of being moved against their will, or the determination to move of their own volition, underpinned the urban strategies of many others who arrived in the cities of Havana and Rio de Janeiro. This chapter maps both their journeys to the cities, and, once they arrived, the close connections between urban living and the quest for freedom.

Ramona's complaint about the difficulty of gaining a fair hearing in her small town would have been familiar to her contemporaries, in Brazil as well as in Cuba, as the case of Mathilde and other *fazenda* slaves in Guaratiba near Rio de Janeiro, discussed in Chapter 3, reveals. As the case unfolded, the lawyer for the owner's heirs made a common argument. The group, he said, had not made the claim themselves, but had been "incited by the philanthropy of someone who wished to exploit their services." The *curador*, Carlos Busch e Varella, countered what he called this "malign insinuation" thus:

> Who can be unaware that poor oppressed people, isolated in a rural parish, with no means or resources, would never reach the gate of the august temple of Justice, if someone, taking pity on their misfortune, did not help them, bringing them by the hand to the authorities which can and should protect them, hearing their laments, and upholding their contested rights?[1]

The fact that the claimants had had outside help was legitimate, in other words, because it was common knowledge that their isolation would otherwise prevent them from accessing the "august temple of Justice." Indeed, the fates of rural and urban slaves were often conceived of as being worlds apart. In November 1885, regulations were issued for the registration of slaves provided for by the Saraiva-Cotegipe Law passed earlier that year. Outraged by a provision that slaveholders did not need to register slaves' family origins, urbanite mulatto abolitionist José do Patrocinio blustered in his Rio newspaper:

> If a mulatto slave of Mr. Antônio Prado [minister of agriculture in the new Conservative government and inveterate slaveholder] were to die—a slave more or less of the age of the mulatto who writes these lines—and I should have the misfortune to pass by the plantation of the illustrious minister . . . I would have no means of proving that I am not the slave of that great lord . . . The official would look at me, and comparing me with the register, would say: mulatto, thirty-odd years old, born wherever you like, son of whoever you like![2]

Writing from a city that, like other Brazilian cities, was pulsating with abolitionist fervor, Patrocinio imagined a scene on a rural plantation. Thus he highlighted the centrality of geography to the relative power of enslaved and enslaver. Once away from the city, with its greater access to the mechanisms of law, identity frauds were far easier to commit.

Enslaved and enslavers alike had long conceived of transferal from urban to plantation labor as a form of punishment. Cuban writer Antonio Zambrana, in his 1873 novel *El negro Francisco*, described an *ingenio* as "a separate empire," "a den with no escape, a dreadful tomb."[3] When the enslaved did move from one milieu to another, their movements were often against their will. With the 1850 ending of the Atlantic traffic in Brazil—and despite its continuation in Cuba—internal trades became a defining feature of the lives of enslaved people in each context, the threat of enforced movement hanging over them and their families whether or not they themselves were moved.[4]

Yet even as they were denied mobility or moved against their will, enslaved people's journeys could sometimes also subvert, as well as uphold, the conditions of their enslavement. While accepting the stark contrast between slaves' lives and litigation possibilities in urban and rural environments, historians of both Brazil and Cuba have also begun to recognize the sheer scale of the mobility of both enslaved and free(d) people of color.[5] The port cities of Havana and Rio de Janeiro were each well-connected to distant plantations and towns by the fast-growing transport and communication networks that were crucial to the growth of the "second slavery." Yet such connections were also forged by moving human beings, who transported not only goods or their labor but information, gossip and rumor, in muffled voices and multiple tongues. Human movement underpinned slavery, but also helped shape its gradual demise. In both Brazil and Cuba, gradual abolition was marked by major wars that displaced large numbers of enslaved and free people, whether as troops recruited to fight in distant areas, freed returnees seeking a new life in a different place, or refugees from the battlefields.[6] The Brazilian abolition movement was underscored by the movement of both ideas and people—including abolitionists and slaves—between the cities of the southeast and the surrounding provinces, or between slaveholding provinces of the north and the provinces where abolition had already been declared.[7] Among this mass of humanity on the move were countless individual journeys—undertaken despite hazards and hardships—by enslaved people and their freed relatives seeking the "august temple of Justice."

Ramona Oliva was already a free woman by the time she arrived in Havana. To reach the capital city, she had surely had to overcome multiple obstacles, funding her journey from Matanzas, finding a means of transport or enduring physical hardship by walking, and obtaining both lodging along the way and information about the route. Even so, she had more control over her own mobility than the many enslaved people in Cuba who, despite great odds, also reached the colonial capital. Paulino Criollo arrived in Havana in February 1862 from an *ingenio* "in the *jurisdicción* of Colón, or Cárdenas"—he was not sure which—having "come, on foot and penniless, to Havana."[8] Enslaved black *criolla* Severina Hernández returned to Havana in early 1878 from a *potrero* in Havana province to which her owner, Bernardo Lastra, had recently transferred her.[9] She made an appeal to the Gobierno General only three days after her absence was noted.[10] This feat of coordination, transport, and avoidance of recapture achieved by an illiterate, enslaved person may seem surprising today, yet it was such a frequent occurrence in Cuba that it was not thought worthy of comment by *síndicos*.

This picture of considerable mobility in the claims-making process in colonial Cuba was partly a result of the enslaved claimants and their relatives approaching a range of different administrative bodies, whether local *síndicos*, *juntas*, or colonial officials. They sometimes bypassed the local *juntas*, journeying directly to the center of the colonial administration in Havana. In both Brazil and Cuba, the enslaved were surprisingly mobile and usually intended to stay in the cities once they arrived. But the colonial Cuban picture contrasts with Brazil, where struggles over geography as a very part of the development of the jurisprudence on slavery are less apparent than for Cuba. In Brazil, the main space for official slave claims-making was the courts, rather than the diverse, hierarchically structured administrative bodies in Cuba.[11]

In Cuba, this mobility of enslaved people around the capital city was noted in 1873 by the Conde de Cañongo, president of Havana's recently created *junta de libertos*. Arguing that his *junta* should be upgraded from "second-class" to "first-class" status, he wrote:

> Although Cienfuegos, Colón or Cárdenas . . . may contain a greater number of slaves than this *jurisdicción*, is it possible to hide . . . the fact that the large *dotaciones* on their *fincas* spend years and years in ignorance of their duties and rights and hence of the means of upholding them? In the *jurisdicción* of Havana this is not the case. There is a constant movement, and as the center of operations of all kinds, one notices . . . this natural movement that the rest of the Island does not experience.[12]

Seeking to aggrandize his own *junta*, the Conde ignored an inconvenient fact: much of the "constant movement" in Havana involved people like

Ramona or Paulino, coming from precisely the sugar-intensive regions of western and central Cuba whose slaves he portrayed as too isolated and ignorant to pursue their rights. Seeing Havana as the best base from which to make their petitions, these people created "rival geographies," challenging owners' and authorities' understandings of their place.[13]

Indeed, in May 1871 the Gobierno Superior Político in Cuba took specific measures to resolve a common problem for local *juntas* across the island: enslaved people often presented their claims in different *jurisdicciones* from the ones where they or their owners lived.[14] Legally, owners were entitled to make slaves present their claims in the owner's town of residence, helping owners wield local power and influence to stifle slaves' complaints. Claimants, however, applied "rival geography" here too. Paulino Criollo's *síndico*, Nicolás Azcárate, pointed out that his owner had relatives in Havana, so there were grounds for the claim to be made there. Other enslaved claimants, like the *morena* Juliana, who made a claim on behalf of herself and her daughter in 1871, stated that their owners resided in Havana for at least part of the year, as was customary among many *ingenio* owners.[15] Within the capital itself, the existence of different authorities was an important tool for enslaved people: the Gobierno Superior Civil had already observed how "many slaves present themselves in hearings to [this body], without having done so first to the respective *Síndico* . . . some of them coming from distant points in the capital which, in essence, is nothing more than running away."[16] Slaves and owners used different geographical vocabularies, with enslaved people referring to "unavoidable" absences or to "accidentally finding themselves" in the city while owners—and often authorities—simply viewed unauthorized slave movement as flight.

In Cuba, this struggle to reach and make use of the "august temple of Justice" took on particular significance during the gradual emancipation period. Rebecca Scott, in her study of slave emancipation in Cuba found that not only did the number of slaves and *patrocinados* fall faster in Havana province (dominated by the city of Havana) than elsewhere, but that the *kinds* of routes out of slavery also differed by province. Havana *patronos* were more likely voluntarily to renounce their rights over *patrocinados*, but their *patrocinados* were also the most likely to gain freedom by legally proving *patrono* violations of the law, making for a dynamic of "abandonment and attack."[17] The large numbers of women in Havana may help to explain this. Their role as domestic servants in *patronos'* houses surely facilitated some leverage to press for freedom privately; when this failed, women might make formal claims against them. Once again, women found themselves at the forefront of legal struggles, this time over geography and the urban living that were bound up with the quest for legal freedom.

"I WISH TO BE IN THIS CITY": WOMEN AND THE JURISPRUDENCE OF GEOGRAPHY IN CUBA

Severina Hernández, who came back to Havana from the *potrero* to which she had been sent, did not only make her journey because she thought she would have a better chance of attaining justice there. She also wanted to live in the city:

> Severina Hernández . . . has been transferred to the *Potrero* Santa Rosa, against her will . . . And . . . I am *coartada* at $550 in gold, and I am not willing to work in the countryside, but [wish to be] in this City, giving *jornal* to my owner, . . . for which I have legal grounds, and since, despite this, I have been refused the permission I requested to come to this City, . . . I found myself obliged to absent myself, . . . in order to present myself to Your Excellency, requesting justice.

Severina was one of a multitude of enslaved claimants who had achieved *coartación* in Cuba. *Coartación*—which, as we have seen, was the act of making a down-payment toward freedom that fixed one's price and afforded the linked right of *papel* to seek a new owner if threatened with sale—"resulted from practice, not from official intervention or royal legislation."[18] However, it had undergone a process of absorption into law, partly as a result of enslaved people's insistence on having their understandings of customary rights legally upheld. Yet there remained considerable ambiguity. During the 1870s, the total number of *coartados* grew rapidly, and 42 percent of the new *coartaciones* were granted in the city of Havana.[19] This rise in numbers, and the many legal ambiguities, made for constant negotiation about this issue during the 1870s, before the 1880 *patronato* law introduced a sliding scale to formalize and facilitate self-purchase.[20]

Although *coartación* led to full self-purchase for only a small minority, Severina's petition and countless others like it suggest that for the enslaved, the most important aspect of *coartación* was its promise of increased control over one's own sale or movement. *Coartado* petitioners wished to remain in cities, where, in turn, *coartación* and self-purchase were easier to achieve; thus, gradually over the nineteenth century, *coartación* became associated with urban living.[21] Meanwhile, both customary and legal distinctions between "urban" and "rural" slaves gradually developed. This process was fuelled, in part, by the colonial state's interest in keeping as many enslaved laborers in sugar production as possible. Since at least midcentury, a tax was levied on "domestic" slaves—often conflated with "urban" slaves. A special wartime tax was also levied on urban slaves in 1872.[22] Whether *coartados*, urban slaves, or domestic slaves were being discussed, women like Severina were disproportionately represented among them all. In the shifting spaces between law and customary understanding, they jostled for the right to stay in Havana.

Because of the customary links between *coartación* and urban living, Severina believed her *coartada* status gave her the right to stay in the city. What she did not perhaps know was that precisely because so many *coartados* had been making this argument, the Gobierno Superior Político had declared in 1871 that the right to seek a new owner applied only to urban *coartados*—those who had made their down-payment in a city.[23] Thus her owner, Don Bernardo Lastra, successfully argued that since she had been registered in Pinar del Río province and brought to Havana only a few months previously, she was a "rural" slave whom he could transfer at will.

The Moret Law and its social context gave women new weapons in this geographical struggle. In Havana in June 1873, *coartada* Justa Morales made an appeal to the Gobernador Superior Civil. Justa lived in the small town of Bejucal, around twenty miles south of Havana, where her owner, Don Cayetano Rosich, was planning to sell her to an *ingenio*. Arguing that her *coartada* status meant she had the right not to be transferred without her consent, her representative also used language now familiar to readers. Justa had a five-year old daughter, and "the humanity, nature and feelings of the Supremo Gobierno . . . must oppose the separation of the mother and daughter, if the former is not completely a slave and the latter is of such a tender age." Although Justa's original desire was simply to remain in Bejucal, her quest led her to Havana. She declared she had been "ignored" by the local *síndico*, and thus "today she finds herself in the unfortunate necessity of disturbing Your Excellency." Again, the argument about geography arose: the local *síndico* denied this, alleging that in fact Justa's owner had given her ten days to seek a new owner in Bejucal for herself and her daughter, but she had failed to find one. She had then, he said, run away to Havana, without ever having appeared at the Bejucal *sindicatura*. Whatever the truth of the matter, Havana clearly offered Justa enhanced legal and practical opportunities. In the city, she hoped to gain the rights she thought she had as a *coartada*: the chance to remain in an urban environment and the security of not being sold away from it.

She requested that, while the case was resolved, she should be deposited not in Bejucal but in Havana. This might allow her time to make contacts in the city, or to earn money to use toward eventual full self-purchase.[24]

Enslaved women also pressed for the right to remain even when they had *not* achieved *coartación*. On 13 October 1875, a *síndico* in Regla, across the bay from Havana, consulted the Gobierno General about the case of black enslaved woman Juana Pérez. Juana was officially listed as part of the *dotación* of a coffee plantation belonging to her owner, Don Juan Muro. Yet she had been working in Regla for one of Muro's sons for around a year. Muro was now planning on selling the plantation and had listed Juana among the assets that would go along with the sale. As in the case of Justa, Juana's *síndico* argued that selling her would separate her from her three children, who were in Regla.

The main issue around which this case came to revolve, however, was owners' habit of avoiding the tax on urban slaves by transferring those listed as "rural" slaves to work in urban labor, often for long periods. Owners sought total control over enslaved people's mobility, putting them to work in urban centers when it suited them and later selling them as "rural" laborers, disregarding the new family and community links the person had built up in the city. Seeking to discourage this tax evasion, the Consejo de Administración concluded that given the amount of time Juana had spent in the city, her de facto "urban" status should be made official, and she should be given a license to seek a new owner in Regla instead of being sent back to the countryside. The implications would extend beyond Juana's case, however. The Consejo ruled that in future, "Any slave belonging to the *dotación* of a rural *finca*, who can prove . . . that he has been put for a period of four months to any . . . work or occupation in a town, will be considered as a domestic slave, with the benefits which the law concedes to this group."[25]

The ruling established by Juana Pérez's case was almost immediately of benefit to another woman making a similar appeal. On 30 March 1876, María de Regla, whose owner, D. Lorenzo del Toro, lived in San Antonio de los Baños in Havana province, made an emotive appeal in Havana to the Gobierno Superior Político:

For years she has been established in this City paying [Del Toro] *jornal* or rent earned through her labor; a few days ago her master demanded that she return to his service in the countryside and since she is by now old and in pain and she is hired out she has pleaded that she should not be deprived in her old age of this small relief to her miserable state and condition, since she is no longer able to perform the hard labor which [Del Toro] wishes her to undertake in the countryside, forgetting her many years of loyal service and the fact that she has suckled all his children at her own breasts.

The petition then alleged that she was possibly older than sixty and that sending her to the countryside would be "shortening the few remaining days of her life." It thus applied all the possible kinds of arguments that might make her listeners sympathize with her plight. María was old; she was ill; and she had "mothered" the children of her ungrateful owner, who still wanted to put her to field work. There were other strategies at play too. María had deposited 51 *pesos*—just over the minimum amount required—in Havana for her *coartación*; but this measure was only "in case she is not covered" by the Moret Law as a sexagenarian. Not only might she gain sympathy, but she had made a down-payment for *coartación*; not only did she claim rights as a *coartada*, but if she was over sixty she was covered by the Moret Law. Interestingly, it was only when threatened with sale that María, who presumably could have sought *coartación* or legal freedom on age grounds before, mobilized these tools in her defense. Her priority, it seems, was less about her exact legal status than about avoiding sale and the destruction of her life in Havana.

The struggle over geography continued, however. María's owner demanded his right for the case to be heard in San Antonio, where he lived. María objected, arguing she was "hired out in the custody of her owner's son, who receives her *jornales*" in Havana. The son argued back: he was not her legal owner, so the claim should be made in San Antonio. Owners thus mobilized their own network of family relations, spread between urban and rural Cuba, to capitalize illegally on the income they could generate from their slaves. Hired slaves' daily earnings in towns could be considerable, with an average washerwoman earning her owner at least 50 *pesos* per month.[26] When the slaves, whose lives and families hung in the balance, attempted to stay in their newfound urban locations, owners tried to turn the tables and send them to seek justice in the provinces, where both parties knew it would be less attainable. María's petition described "the lack of confidence inspired in her by the *síndico* of San Antonio."

Ruling on the case, the Gobierno Superior Político declared that "since a ruling exists which gives rural slaves who have remained more than four months in this City the right to enjoy the benefits of domestic slaves," María, who had been "in this City far longer than the minimum time," should be considered as *coartada* in Havana, not San Antonio, and allowed to seek a new owner in the capital. The ruling that resulted from Juana Pérez's appeal thus shaped María's destiny, allowing her the chance to cross the divide between urban and rural slavery and remain in Havana.[27]

FAMILIES ON THE MOVE IN RIO AND HAVANA

While specific struggles over the jurisprudence of slavery in Brazil were less focused than in Cuba on the issue of rural versus urban slavery, Brazilian slaves also often aimed to travel to the cities and make lives for themselves there. In each case, women's tendency to seek freedom on behalf of their families gave them a vital, specific role to play in this geographical quest for freedom.

On 13 January 1888, two judicial officials arrived at the house of Antônio Pedro Jardim, on Rua Miguel de Frias in Rio de Janeiro, and apprehended a young boy, Aleixo. Their actions resulted from an allegation by Tenente João Cândido Teixeira Chaves, who lived in Magé, some twenty miles northeast of the city. Chaves alleged that Aleixo belonged to him and had run away. Finding Aleixo was not difficult: he was the son of a freed *parda* woman, Anna, who was working for Jardim. After her former owner in Magé had died, she had gained freedom and left for the capital, either bringing Aleixo with her or perhaps having him follow her later. Jardim said he had hired Anna without knowing her son's status, perhaps simply assuming that a mother would bring her child with her. Anna had made the same assumption. Her journey from enslavement to freedom, from Magé to Rio, would not be complete unless she took Aleixo with her.[28]

Women like Anna in Brazil saw their own quest for freedom as part of broader family strategies. Their legal actions in cities created links to much broader networks of people in rural areas. In Cuba, women played a similar role and had similar priorities, but the even greater importance of mobility within the process of negotiating legal freedom meant that their actions in Havana might produce particularly striking results. In 1883, for example, *patrocinada* Margarita Pedroso complained to Havana's Junta Provincial de Patronato of severe physical abuse by an overseer on the *potrero* "Baco," in Arroyo Naranjo on Havana's southern outskirts. She was brought to Havana, where her *patrono*, the wealthy Don Ignacio Peñalver, also resided, and deposited in the Asilo de San José.[29] There she spent eight months, meanwhile making a series of petitions about how, while in deposit, she had not been paid the stipend owed her. Meanwhile, she was able to mobilize other family members, although they lived outside the capital. In May 1884, her daughter's husband, *moreno libre* Pedro Peñalver, made an appeal on her behalf. Pedro lived in Bejucal, but had "accidentally" found himself in Havana. Eventually, Margarita gained both freedom and a license to *trabajar por su cuenta* (work on her own account) while remaining in Havana—an enormous change from her alleged situation less than a year previously, enduring physical punishment on a rural *potrero*.

However, Margarita harbored further ambitions. From her new base in the capital, she also sought freedom for no fewer than six of her children. In this, she benefited from the October 1883 ruling that freed women could take their children without paying compensation—a right that, as we saw in Chapter 3, was the direct result of other women's struggles with the law. All her children were *patrocinados* of Ignacio Peñalver, some living in Havana and others scattered across his possessions in Havana and Pinar del Río provinces. Reaching far beyond the city where it was initiated, then, Margarita's strategy freed and united in the capital city not just one, but seven people.[30]

THE GENDERED GEOGRAPHIES OF SLAVE TRADING

Just as they did not express surprise at the numbers of mobile litigants, so contemporaries were not surprised that so many of them were women. This is interesting for historians, given that studies of slave mobility usually suggest that women were less mobile than their men. Women were kept in domestic servitude or assigned other work on plantations that granted less access to travel and geographical knowledge; they were less able or willing than men to undertake flight alone because hampered by small children or by the fear of rape or other violence along the way.[31] Yet it may be that in the case of movements toward and around cities, women were more mobile than we have given them credit for. Indeed, female mobility may also simply have passed unremarked as a result of a set of gendered assumptions about the nature of rural and urban slavery, which can be seen in both Brazil and Cuba, of which individual enslaved and freed women were sometimes able to take advantage.[32]

In November 1866, delegates at the Madrid Junta de Información considered the following question:

> It being apparent from statistics that in the towns there are more than 100 slave women for every 100 males, while in the countryside there are only 59 women per 100 males, what measures could be adopted,

without injuring owners' rights or clashing with established customs, to take some of these women, currently employed in domestic service in the cities, to the rural plantations?

The committee of eleven Cubans and two Puerto Ricans that considered this question concluded that, in fact, owners should *not* be obliged to send their female domestic slaves to rural areas. Their reasons stemmed from a mix of social customs and pragmatism. First, the proposal "goes against the sentiments of affection among the *Masters* [and] veneration and respect among the *slaves*, that generally exist between owners and domestic servants."[33] Second, if enslaved women were sent away from cities there would be no one to perform their important functions. Third, these women would be unable to cope with hard field labor, because they were used to a "very different kind of occupation."[34]

The deputies were responding to specific circumstances of the ending of the transatlantic trade to Cuba, which, like in Brazil since the 1850s, was leading to an increasing concentration of slaves in plantation labor.[35] The clandestine international trade continued apace in Cuba until at least the end of the 1860s, in contrast with Brazil where it had come to a definitive end in 1850. Perhaps for this reason, the process of sale and transfer of slaves within Cuba has not yet been fully mapped by historians, either in its quantitative proportions or in terms of the lived experiences of enslaved people. Yet this accelerating internal trade clearly increased the threat that hung over urban slaves of enforced sale, hire, or simply transfer between the properties of a single owner.[36] It was particularly male slaves, however, who were threatened with this transfer. The deputies' assumptions suggest that the women we have been discussing might hope to appeal to socially constructed notions about the city as the best "place" for women.[37] María de Regla was old and weak and deserved gratitude for acting as her owner's wet nurse; Juana Pérez feared separation from her children; and so on. Perhaps making use of her light skin as well as her sex, a petition on behalf of enslaved Cuban *mulata* Dorotea Herrera simply said that her "weak constitution" would not be able to cope with "extremely hard" rural work with which she was threatened when her owner wished to transfer her to the countryside.[38] Such entreaties might strike a chord with readers familiar with ideas like those of Suárez y Romero, discussed in the previous chapter, about how hard work in the fields defeminized women.[39]

In Rio, individual enslaved women gained sympathetic publicity from the press when they were threatened with sale outside of the capital, especially after the "Black Regulation" fanned the flames of abolitionist anger with its threat to remove the city's slaves to plantations.[40] Gendered geographical assumptions of this kind were marshaled to back up broader Brazilian arguments for ending slavery. The abolitionist newspaper *A Revista Illustrada* noted in April 1886 : "According to the figures from the Ministry of Agriculture, the number of enslaved people is under five hundred thousand. Remove the women . . . remove the slaves in cities, who do not produce anything, and it will be evident that what remains for national production is such a risible figure, that we can proudly affirm that our country's production is already based on free labor."[41] In making an argument about slavery's economic irrelevance, the article also unconsciously employed a gendered binary: male slaves in "productive" agricultural work, women in urban labor. Although it only partially reflected the complex realities of national slaveholding patterns, this assumption nonetheless came naturally to writers and readers. Enslaved people themselves shared at least some of the same assumptions. Across the Anglophone Caribbean after emancipation, for example, women left field labor wherever they could.[42] In Cuba, a "geographically gendered division of labor" often separated free couples of color, the husband working on a plantation and the wife in the city.[43]

In Brazil, the massive internal slave trade had, since the 1850s, been a gendered affair. Males outnumbered females by around two to one among the generally young slaves brought south for plantation labor.[44] The women who were sold in Rio—around 3,500 per year in the 1870s— were also more likely to be kept in the city, with its voracious appetite for female domestic labor and enslaved prostitutes.[45] Although the journey was equally painful, arrival in the city thus held different meanings for male and female slaves.

The lists of thousands of enslaved women who were categorized for potential manumission through the national emancipation fund in Rio provide glimpses of lengthy journeys and untold sorrows. Theresa, *preta*, had come to the Corte after being registered in Cabo Frio, Rio de Janeiro province, along with her three children. There was no mention of the children's father, nor was it clear whether the children had been able to accompany her to the capital. Gertrudes, a forty-nine-year-old *preta* working in agriculture, had been registered along with her two children in Sergipe in the northeast. She had a husband, Anselmo, but "the name of his owner, his registration number and other details are unknown; it is only known that this slave lives in Bahia."[46] Josepha Gonçalves de Moraes, too, had been sold to Rio with her daughter Maria, very possibly separating them from Maria's father. This enforced migration surely caused a

Image of "Slavery," painted as an enslaved woman being transported through the countryside by "the Saraiva Cotegipe Law." "A lei Saraiva e Cotegipe e o trem abolicionista" ("The Saraiva-Cotegipe law and the abolitionist train"), Revista Illustrada, *13 August 1887, 4–5. Fundação Casa Rui Barbosa, Rio de Janeiro.*

rupture in Josepha's life similar to that faced by men who were sold south. Yet like many other women in her situation, Josepha was not sold on to plantation labor, but remained in the city, and this had probably helped her in gaining her own freedom and initiating her suit for custody of her daughter.[47] Together, the journeys made by women like Josepha made the capital city swell with new female lives, which for better or worse would be rebuilt there. Having arrived in the cities, women might use their new location in order to purchase legal freedom.

RIO DE JANEIRO AND WOMEN'S
QUEST FOR SELF-PURCHASE

Unlike in Cuba, in Brazil it was only with the 1871 Rio Branco Law that slaves' right to use their savings for self-purchase was legally confirmed. As a customary practice, however, savings and self-purchase predated the law's passage. Since early colonial times, urban slaves had been best placed to attain manumission both "gratis" and through self-purchase, and women had been prominent among them.[48] After 1871, the strategies they could employ expanded. Firmina, a black enslaved woman, deposited 150 *mil-réis* in a savings fund, the Caixa Econômica Perseverança, which had accumulated an interest of 12$50. In August 1883 she applied for authorization from a first-instance court in Rio to get the money out. It was not enough in itself to buy her freedom from her owner, but she planned to use it towards a *sortéio de emancipação*—an emancipation lottery—being held, perhaps, by an abolitionist society, or an *irmandade* or mutual aid association.[49] Emília, *crioula*, got a loan from João Antônio Mendes Sota of 700 *mil-réis* in May 1882 in order to buy her freedom, but had to serve him for another two years in exchange.[50] In a sense, of course, Emília had simply changed owners. Yet she had also attained a legal guarantee of her freedom after two years, and been able to leave her previous owner, Carolina Umbelina de Sá.[51] Carolina, it turned out, was growing old and perhaps infirm; she died in early 1884. This suggests a canny use of timing on Emília's part, since the death of their owners threatened slaves with instability, and particularly with the possibility of being sold away from the cities.[52]

Women, who were prioritized for freedom through both the national Emancipation Fund and Rio's Livro de Ouro fund, knew they were more likely to be freed if they could show they had their own savings, which often made up a considerable part of the overall price paid to owners. Indeed, women's considerable contributions—here and elsewhere in Brazil—meant these manumissions were due at least as much to their own efforts as to the emancipation funds themselves. In a private emancipation fund established in the northeastern city of Recife in the 1880s, for example, women's savings accounted on average for 71 percent of their total compensation price.[53] Six people listed to be considered for freedom through the national fund in August 1880 included five women, who had saved an average of 450 *mil-réis* each.[54] This was almost equal to the average cost of slave emancipations through the national emancipation fund in Rio.[55] A few years later, in drawing up lists of slaves to be freed through the Livro de Ouro fund, the municipal council stated that "those women who have their own savings should be preferred" for selection.[56] Women learned quickly of the opportunities presented. In November 1887, a young enslaved woman named Josepha offered the council a deal: she requested 200 *mil-réis* from them to contribute to her freedom, which could be added to 100 *mil-réis* she had already saved, making up her 300 *mil-réis* freedom price. After an apparent bargaining process, she was freed for only 150 *mil-réis*, of which her own 100 *mil-réis* would thus represent two-thirds.[57]

Savings were also part of broader strategies for urban autonomy. In late 1882 an enslaved black woman, Monica Maria da Conceição, was brought with her owners from Vassouras, in Rio de Janeiro province, to the capital to serve as their child's wet nurse. Yet once in Rio, Monica lost no time in disappearing into the "city hideout," resurfacing four years later in 1886 with a suit for *manutenção* (official recognition of her freedom).[58] Acting as her *curador* was the abolitionist mulatto lawyer Domingos Gomes dos Santos, nicknamed "O Radical," who was close to radical journalist José do Patrocinio. He alleged she had been abandoned by her owner, Henrique Gaspar de Lahmeyer, and as such had been living in Rio, "feeding herself at her own cost, living . . . at her home on the Rua General Cabrita no. 9, when she is not hiring herself out." Soon after her appeal, she was declared free by a first-instance court in Rio.

Appealing against this judgment, Lahmeyer gave his side of the story. According to his lawyer, Monica had simply run away and had resurfaced in Rio a year later, in July 1883, in an attempt to use her savings to purchase her freedom. Like many Cuban owners we have met, Lahmeyer tried to ensure the case would be heard in Vassouras, depositing her there; but by April 1884, Monica fled again—back to the capital. Struggles over urban and rural geographies, with owners trying to keep slaves in the countryside and slaves aiming for the cities, were not written into the legal framework of slavery in the same way as in Cuba, but they were clearly still an important part of many enslaved people's quest for freedom. Attempts to recapture Monica were "always fruitless." Another ruling overturned the first, the case dragged on, and it was still running in 1888 when final abolition was declared. Litigation in Rio, although lengthy and uncertain, had allowed Monica a significant degree of autonomy. Meanwhile, she had accumulated savings that, since the self-purchase had not gone ahead, would remain hers to use in her new life in freedom in the city.[59]

WOMEN AND FAMILIES IN THE CITIES

We have seen how women were more likely than were men to seek the freedom of their relatives—particularly their children—as a fundamental part of their own struggles with the law. Yet by the same token, women did not act alone. Rather, within the cities and in the family networks that stretched far beyond them, their claims-making drew on the wide circle of people, especially family members, who were fundamental to their lives.

One important group of people were, of course, the fathers of enslaved children. Enslaved fathers were less likely than mothers to appear as the principal claimants for their children's freedom, for a number of reasons. Fathers were even more likely than mothers to have been separated from children by sale. Slavery threatened all the connections in a slave family, often regardless of laws to the contrary; yet *partus sequitur ventrem* meant that mothers' relationship to children was at least established in written records, while legislation and social norms prioritizing motherhood had begun to offer at least some theoretical protection from separation to mothers, though paying less attention to enslaved fathers. Meanwhile, maternalist emancipation legislation and feminized abolitionist rhetoric sharpened women's legal and discursive tools more than they did men's. If we want to understand the implications of legal and discursive change, it makes sense to focus on women's relationship with the law. Yet this does not mean women claimants acted without the help of the fathers of their children. Enslaved families, as units, often prioritized women's freedom over men's in the first place, in order to ensure that children would be born free. The legal and bureaucratic structures within which appeals were made helped silence the role of appellants' families and friends, leaving a picture of atomized, individual manumission struggles. Filing them away for historians to "discover," scribes and functionaries exercised what Michel-Rolph Trouillot has called "archival power."[60] Rarely, for example, is the source of the money offered by enslaved women for their children's freedom discussed. As well as women's labor and savings, we know much of it was contributed by relatives.[61]

The fact that at least some fathers could, and did, make claims on behalf of children suggests that that many more might have done so if legal, discursive, and practical conditions had permitted.[62] Some stepped into this role, for example, when the children's mother was less able to do so. In Rio de Janeiro, in July 1885, black freedman Manoel Vicente responded to the municipal council's calls for recommendations for slaves to set free at their ceremonies by putting forward his three children. He had authorization for this from his ex-owner, who owned the children as well as their mother, Mathilde.[63] Freed Manoel was in a stronger position to make this case than was enslaved Mathilde.

Appeals by men might use emotional language to describe the condition of fatherhood just as women's did for motherhood. In Havana, free *moreno* Juan Vázquez, an unmarried dock worker, asked the Gobierno Superior Político in 1873 to lower his nine-year-old daughter's freedom price. His petition described him as "a poor father who has consecrated . . . the fruits of his labor and all, absolutely all his savings . . . to manumitting his only daughter." He hoped that, "redeemed from the yoke of slavery, he can keep her with him and provide her with a more adequate education than that . . . which she can receive in slavery," adding, "how many, how very many are the bitternesses and sufferings of the father who pleads." However, his appeal was not successful.[64]

Some claims specifically involved both parents. The woman's role, however, tended to receive greater emphasis. In June 1885, a freed couple sent a letter from the municipality of Rezende, in Rio de Janeiro province, to Rio's municipal council, asking for help in freeing their daughter, Paulina. Paulina was in Taubaté, in the Vale do Paraíba coffee zone in neighboring São Paulo province. Having heard, even from so far away, that the municipal council was preparing to free slaves through the Livro de Ouro fund, they requested that the council help them make up her freedom price by adding to the amount they had already saved. The petition opened by discussing their joint efforts to free Paulina: "Manoel Caetano Alves d'Oliveira and Benedicta Caetana, both old and rheumatic . . . , freed years ago by their ex-owners, declare that through their savings earned with hard work . . . they have managed to amass the quantity of 150 *mil-réis*, in order to free their daughter named Paulina." However, Manoel then faded from the picture, and the rest of the petition focused exclusively on the mother: "the *liberta* Benedicta, seeing that her last embittered days are ending without the hope . . . of achieving her just aim[,] comes with a tortured heart to try a last effort, begging on her knees." Benedicta, the petition said, would pray for "all those who take an interest in the anguish of the poor old woman," and the missive asked for the readers' "commiseration for the pain and desperation of an unfortunate mother." The petition does not, of course, tell us whether the case was really being pushed more by the "unfortunate mother," or whether the peculiar power of language that evoked maternity meant that the parents or scribe simply thought that an emphasis on Benedicta's plight would have more influence on their readers.[65]

In Cuba in April 1878, a family effort was commenced to free three siblings, José Ernesto, José Casimiro and Manuela, owned by Doña Luisa Fernández of San Miguel de Padrón on Havana's rural outskirts. Their mother, black freedwoman Antonia Fernández, her free(d) black husband Cecilio Guillermí, and the three children all acted in the case.[66] The couple had acquired 1,800 *pesos* in notes, which they had hoped to use to free all three siblings. Yet a price evaluation, carried out under the supervision of Bráulio de Vivano, *síndico* of Guanabacoa, evaluated the three at a far higher price than the family could afford. In protest, the couple petitioned the Gobierno General, via one Enrique Girand, who penned the document. The letter alleged that Vivano was in league with the owner and requested a reevaluation outside Guanabacoa.

Irritated, the *síndico* wrote to the governor defending his actions. In the process, he left us an unusually detailed description of the daily interactions between *síndicos* and the people whose claims they dealt with. Vivano said that a few days before the evaluation, Antonia had appeared at his office bearing the 1,800 *pesos*. She was then joined by Cecilio, who confused matters by declaring that he had won 5,000 *pesos* on the lottery, of which he had given 2,800 to one "Señor Riquelme" for them to be passed to the *síndico*, and he "insist[ed] on this although the 1,800 *pesos* brought had been counted three times, until it was observed that Antonia, who was behind Cecilio, pulled at his trousers, and understanding the signal he said that it was all right." Cecilio's blustering insistence was apparently calmed by his wife, and the day of the evaluation was set without further incident.

However, said Vivano, on the day of the evaluation, Cecilio returned to see him to make another demand: that he name a price evaluator recommended by Cecilio's allies or patrons, Riquelme and Girand. Vivano refused.[67] The next day, angry at the large amount stipulated, Cecilio returned to the *sindicatura*, demanding his money back: "in a haughty tone he told me that the price evaluation was incorrect and that Señor Riquelme had advised him to appeal to . . . Your Excellency, hence the undersigned was expecting this complaint." The *síndico*'s diagnosis echoed what elites often assumed about petitions by enslaved or freed people of color: they were being manipulated by outside agents.

After his alleged attempt to force the *síndico* into doing what he wanted, Cecilio then dropped out of the surviving records of the case. Antonia, however, continued the long, slow process of the claim on behalf of her children. When other arguments failed, she played the "motherhood card," stressing that "A helpless mother humbly petitions Your Excellency," and pointing out her past services as wet nurse to Luisa Fernández's children. The case hints intriguingly at gendered responses to perceived injustice. Cecilio used threats and marshaled local allies; Antonia calmed him down and then attempted, using emotive "maternal" rhetoric, to circumvent the *síndico* through humble petitions to an outside authority. On the other hand, perhaps the document tells us more about the *síndico*'s own responses to male and female claimants, seeing Cecilio as more threatening than "humble" women petitioners. In any case, Antonia was either able or willing to persist in petitioning long after Cecilio dropped out of the picture, remaining the driving-force behind the process.[68]

"Family" relations in both Brazil and Cuba also extended far beyond blood ties to broad adoptive family networks.[69] Among them, godmothers were the most likely to take legal action on behalf of godchildren, standing in for mothers who were not able to do so themselves. Free black woman Josefa Achondo, in Havana, saved 51 *pesos* to have her god-daughter Francisca, the daughter of her enslaved *comadre* Genoveva, baptized as free.[70] Enslaved Isabel Casas, as we saw in Chapter 3, was able to leave her child with a free woman of color in central Havana while she nursed her owners' child in Marianao. Such women drew on the support and experience of other women.

Religious brotherhoods helped speed the manumission quest of some of their members. Occasionally, they also interceded with authorities on their behalf. In 1854, enslaved *congo* woman María Luisa fell out with her owner and was punished by being sent to work in the countryside.[71] She was a member of a *cabildo congo* (a religious brotherhood for *congos*) in the capital, whose free black head, Pedro Real, made a complaint to the colonial authorities on her behalf.[72]

Women's legal activity, then, was often only one part of the story: although they tended to appear as the key litigants on behalf of family members, at the same time these family and associational networks helped them in their quest. Fundamental, too, in shaping women's routes to the law and their expectations of it, were the other women who lived all around them.

STREETS OF WOMEN

In order to understand the conditions under which women approached the law, we need to imagine them not just as they presented their petitions, but as they walked the crowded, noisy streets of the Atlantic port cities that were the context in which their claims were made. On those streets, they had conversations—in Spanish, Portuguese, Yoruba, or Bantu—that gave them important information; perhaps they compared notes with other women who were planning on presenting the *síndicos* or *curadores* with their own petitions, stopped on a street corner to gossip with a freedwoman selling sweets, or haggled with the black women traders who dominated the marketplace with their noisy cries. We also need to follow them into the small rented rooms they perhaps called home, where they may have lived with a male partner but also with other women of the same occupation, and wander by their side through city neighborhoods where every house contained a female domestic slave, hearing the news of the day as it spread like wildfire down the streets, borne not on paper but on the tongues of women.

In both Rio and Havana, women made up about half the enslaved population—a higher figure than that which they normally reached outside the cities. The continuing demand for female labor meant that women slaves were particularly concentrated in some central areas. In Havana, women made up 63 percent of the enslaved population of the Third District in 1853–54. Within this, their numbers rose in particular neighborhoods, reaching 81 percent of the slaves in San Leopoldo neighborhood and 75 percent in Dragones.[73] Although more women than men found their way out of slavery through manumission, the proportions of enslaved women were still high into the 1880s, probably because men were more likely to be sold outside of the city while women were more likely to be brought in. By 1882, the proportion of women among the Third District's *patrocinados* was 69 percent. These women's owners were often other women: 57 percent of the area's *patronos* were female.[74] In Rio in 1872, the enslaved population similarly comprised roughly half women, with higher concentrations of women in particular parishes, although not on the same scale as some of the Havana neighborhoods. Women represented almost 60 percent of the enslaved population, for example, in affluent areas with a high demand for domestic labor like São Cristóvão and Glória.[75]

How did these numbers look on a particular city street? Take Havana's Calle San Nicolás, for example, in 1853–54. Between house numbers 70 and 136, there were 22 adult women slaves, spread between 22 different houses, but only 4 adult male slaves. Nearby streets presented similarly high numbers of slave women—usually with women owners. On San Rafael 104 lived Doña Isabel Fernández and her slave Mónica; at number 108 lived Doña María Josefa Oliva with her slave Margarita, and so on.[76] By 1882, at San Nicolás 33 lived Doña Dolores Ortiz, a widow, with 5 women *patrocinadas*; around the corner at San Rafael 53 was Doña Valentina de los Dolores Balsa with *patrocinadas* Merced and Amalia. The 1882 count also, however, reflected these women's involvement in the changing times: Amalia, like many others recorded in the survey, was in fact in deposit, involved in legal proceedings for freedom.[77] Surely the other *patrocinadas* living close by would learn about their neighbors' involvement in such activities.

The streets of central Rio de Janeiro became the focus of attention of abolitionist societies and clubs in the 1880s, which aimed to emancipate all slaves living on a particular street or block. The way in which slaves were classified for manumission through the national Emancipation

Fund, as well as the municipal council's Livro de Ouro fund, was similarly local in focus. On the Rua do Lavradio, for example, fifteen people were classified to be freed by the national fund between 1880 and 1883. Only one was a man; the rest were women and their children.[78] In the freedom ceremony of the Livro de Ouro of March 1886 a few years later, a further four women on Lavradio were freed, receiving their freedom letters from Empress Teresa Cristina, along with the daughter of Maria Rosa, whom we met in Chapter 3. And meanwhile Lavradio became the focus of a campaign by the Associação Abolicionista Joaquim Carrão, which aimed to free specific parts of the street.[79] The pattern repeated on streets nearby. The numbers emancipated in this way were, of course, very small. Yet their local impact on the hopes and strategies of enslaved people, particularly women, was surely very great, in a city where abolitionist campaigning touched the lives of the enslaved along with almost everyone else.

How might this picture affect the life of one woman? Brazilia, a young *parda*, had been brought by her mistress to Rio de Janeiro from Bahia. In 1871, she was among the scores of young women who appeared before judge Tavares Bastos on the grounds of having been prostituted by her owner. However, the prostitution allegations soon took a back seat in her case, her *curador* emphasizing instead that Brazilia had been brought to Rio by ship as a "free person," and that since then she had *lived* as one. She lived separately from her mistress with her mother, a Bahia-born *quitandeira* (itinerant street vendor of food items) who was registered as the household head. With them lived a twenty-year-old woman from Maranhão in northern Brazil, who, like Brazilia, worked as a seamstress. As part of the case, the *curador* built up a detailed picture of Brazilia's life "as free" in Rio, paying her own rent on the women's home on the Travessa de Santa Rita. She was surrounded by other women from all over Brazil who did the same, free(d) but also sometimes enslaved, who were seeking the greatest possible autonomy in their living conditions.[80]

When they could manage to live separately from owners or employers, the urban poor typically rented rooms in cramped, subdivided buildings.[81] In each city, free(d) women assuaged their poverty and marginalization by cohabiting with other women of color. What was it like, for example, to live on Alambique Street in Jesús María, one of Havana's poorer neighborhoods beyond the city walls? In 1861, its mainly free residents were racially mixed: 50 percent were declared white, 45 percent were free people of color, and the remaining 5 percent were slaves and Chinese. While the street as a whole was mixed, individual households generally were not: people of color lived separately from whites. Twenty-five percent of households on the street were female-headed.[82] Nine years later, the street was still full of households made up of women of color, who often lived with others of the same occupation.[83] With them lived children who did not share their surnames, perhaps the children of enslaved or absent *comadres* or other family members.[84] Similar patterns emerged on streets nearby, grouping free(d)women of color together and ensuring a constant flow of news and information.

GOSSIP AND INFORMATION

In October 1884, a judicial official arrived at a Havana house on Calle San Miguel to deliver the results of a hearing about a quarrel that had taken place between two of the residents. Talking to "a black woman who said she lived in the house and that her name was Luisa Sánchez," he discovered both the interested parties were out and left the documents containing the result of the case for her to give them when they returned. We can assume Luisa already knew all about the quarrel—it had probably drawn in other people living in the house as witnesses, allies, or simply gossipers. It would also be her job to communicate the outcome of a judicial case that, as well as being a dispute between two individuals, was a profoundly social event.[85]

A single city street was the site of a thousand conversations taking place every hour, shaping illiterate people's strategies for dealing with the law. Black *patrocinada* Lucía Collazo, seeking freedom from her *patrona* for noncompliance with the 1880 law, complained in September 1883 that "For several Saturdays in a row she has gone to the Junta [Provincial de Patronato], with the number of her file, and she is always told to come back next Saturday." Why Saturdays? Perhaps the *junta* opened its doors to *patrocinados* only on Saturdays, echoing an older Spanish colonial tradition in which the complaints of the poor at the *audiencias* of Lima and Mexico City were made on this day.[86] Or perhaps this was the only day when busy working women could get there—although Lucía, a *jornalera*, had more control over her time than many others. Either way, her phrase is suggestive of claims-making as a quotidian practice, a routine stop on her weekly round. On Saturdays, she would wait outside the *junta*, almost certainly along with others, perhaps seeking a good spot in the shade to stand or sit. As she waited with her fellow claimants, surely they chatted about the progress of their cases. If the documents left to us by their actions are anything to go by, the majority of those waiting with her were other women. Perhaps it was they who suggested, after seeing her return week after week to no avail, that she take her complaint to the *junta*'s superior, the Gobierno General. Eventually, this is precisely what she did.[87]

Josepha Gonçalves de Moraes, in Rio, was on the other side of the free/enslaved divide from Lucía in Havana by the time she litigated for custody of her daughter Maria in August 1884. Yet her legal case, like her life more generally, was intimately shaped by social connections with free and enslaved people living and working around her. Josepha's former owners, who claimed custody of Maria, lived in Catete, on Rua Dois de Dezembro 20, where Josepha had also lived until being freed. While enslaved, Josepha had also lived for a time on the Rua dos Barbeiros, where she had been rented out. Her witnesses were people who lived or worked on or near these streets. As her case went on, it perhaps resonated for other women living close by. Rita, a thirty-eight-year-old black woman who lived with her mistress two doors down from Josepha's ex-owners, gained freedom via the Livro de Ouro fund in March 1886, a few months before the final conclusion of Josepha's own case.[88] Sebastiana, a twenty-two-year-old black woman living on the same street, did the same in July.[89] At number 11 was forty-six-year-old Rachel, a seamstress, and her fourteen-year-old *parda* daughter Josepha. They were classified for freedom through the national Emancipation Fund in 1880.[90] Judicial officials filed Josepha's case away separately from anything related to the lives of her neighbors; yet surely, others close by who might also be seeking custody of children were aware of her example.

Women's participation in the culture of urban claims-making had long roots, but its potential impact on a given street or neighborhood increased during slavery's final years. In August 1882, a fifty-three-year old black washerwoman, Teresa Baez, appeared before the Junta Local de Patronato in Regla, across the bay from Havana. Teresa, who lived on Calle Santuario 7, declared that she had previously been the *patrocinada* of the heirs of Don Benito Mateos y Mendo. Yet since Don Benito's death, she had been living independently. She now wished to formalize this "free" status.[91] Although her petition mentioned only Teresa herself, a glance at the activities of some her neighbors leaves us with little doubt about the social context that must have shaped her understandings of how to achieve freedom. Not long afterwards, in March 1883, a neighbor on Santuario, the *moreno* Anselmo, successfully made the same claim as Teresa.[92] In July that year, at Santuario 26, a protracted struggle commenced between two young *pardas*, Francisca and Guadalupe, and their *patrona*. Like Teresa and Anselmo, their *patrono* had died and the girls were unwilling to accept the transfer of his rights over them to his wife.[93] Exasperated, their *patrona* complained that the girls had even defied her orders by walking around the streets with their mother, who lived locally and had recently attained freedom through self-purchase. They thus lent local visibility to their claim to freedom.[94] One person who perhaps took note was Don Jorge Méndez, who, as we saw in Chapter 3, turned the young *patrocinados* Gavino and Vicente over to their freed mother's care in July 1884.

Sometimes, the links between one suit and another were more direct, with potentially drastic consequences for owners. One Havana slave-holder, Don Bernardo Lastra, may have begun to regret his various purchases of women slaves when they all began claims almost simultaneously. His troubles began with Severina Hernández, whom we met earlier in this chapter, refusing to accept transfer to the countryside and returning to Havana to make a claim in 1878. In September 1880, another of his *patrocinadas*, Ceferina, ran away and began filing legal claims to different authorities in the capital. During a two-year struggle, Ceferina spent a long period in the Asilo San José, depriving Lastra of her labor, before eventually winning freedom. In the meantime, two more of his *patrocinadas* also sued for freedom and were placed, along with Ceferina, in the Asilo. One, Felicia, even gave birth to a child while in deposit. Because of this, she was moved to the women's hospital, the Hospital de Paula, and Lastra complained that "I had to pay two *onzas* in gold for her stay." Beyond the women's claims in themselves, Lastra also became involved in litigation over them on at least two occasions with other owners, making a total of at least six different sets of legal proceedings in eight years, all of which cost him time and at least some money.[95] One of these owners had himself had recent troubles with litigating slave women.[96] Slaveholders, of course, assumed a certain amount of inconvenience and expense as a normal part of the profitable business of slaveholding, but such concerted action on the part of one's *patrocinadas* during these final years might make owning them start to feel more like a liability than an asset. For owners who were less well off, or being squeezed by the economic recession in Cuba, several suits at once might become a real burden on their finances or time.

Women like Severina, Felicia, and Ceferina blurred the lines between individual and collective action, with consequences for the broad emancipation process that were greater than the sum of their "individual" appeals. For Joseli Mendonça, while slaves who made freedom claims may only have been thinking of their own freedom as they went to litigate,

"in thinking of themselves, they also thought of others close to them."
They were also "encouraging in other slaves the idea that this attitude
was a concrete possibility, . . . sowing worries and fears among the masters themselves, questioning the continuance of their dominion."[97] Acting
from the cities, women like Monica Maria da Conceição had an important impact well beyond their boundaries. As Monica continued to make
her way in Rio, her owner's lawyer accused her of being a "runaway and
litigious slave" whose "behavior demoralized the slaves on the appellant's
fazenda and induced dangerous indiscipline among them."[98]

The quest for freedom of the women whose lives this book follows, then,
was inextricably bound up with urban living. Claims made in the cities,
however, were part of much broader networks that stretched out into the
rural environments in which their relatives labored. The links between
mobility, women's agency, and family networks within claims-making
were common to both Brazil and Cuba, although in Cuba they became
written into the changing jurisprudence itself, as slaves and owners each
tried to make use of legal distinctions between rural and urban slavery
to suit their own ends. Making claims in cities, women might draw on
many allies: male and female relatives; information about others' experiences that flowed from house to house in the mouths of neighbors and
workmates; and the gendered geographical assumptions of slaveholders
and authorities, who increasingly construed urban slavery as female while
attempting to keep male slaves in plantation labor.

The cities, though, were not just the places where freedom was sought.
For women like Monica, they also became an important part of defining
what that freedom would come to mean. These conceptions of freedom
are the subject of Part III of this book.

PART THREE

Conceiving Freedom

CHAPTER SIX

Enlightened Mothers of Families or Competent Domestic Servants?

Elites Imagine the Meanings of Freedom

The minor Maria, daughter of Josepha Gonçalves, lives contentedly, and is treated
with devotion by José Gonçalves de Pinho and his wife; the minor's mother, recently
freed and living with a lover, is certainly not able to give her good education and care.
—*Judge Joaquim José de Oliveira Andrade, Rio de Janeiro, 7 August 1886.*

With these words, Judge Oliveira Andrade ended Josepha Gonçalves de Moraes's two-year custody battle. In so doing, he also crushed the hope, vaunted by abolitionists and clearly shared by Josepha herself at some level, that freedom promised the "sacred rights of motherhood." Throwing out the various witness statements Josepha had brought to demonstrate that her former owners were neglecting and abusing Maria, Oliveira Andrade concluded that her legal case against them had not been proven. Adding insult to injury, and social significance to the legal ruling, he went on to justify his decision by painting Josepha as an unsuitable mother, "recently-freed and living with a lover."

Oliveira de Andrade's statement does not negate the importance of studying the struggles and goals of women like Josepha—indeed, in a sense it makes the task all the more urgent. However, it does remind us how seriously we must take the extremely unequal power relations that were the context for such struggles. Oliveira de Andrade's conceptions of freedom and of womanhood would have an immense and immediate impact upon Josepha's ability to turn her own "visions of freedom" into reality.[1] It also reminds us of the chasm that often existed between the impassioned rhetoric of sympathy for enslaved women, examined in earlier chapters of this book, and the gendered and racialized boundaries that sharply delineated most elite commentators' notions of the limits of freedom. Discussing Brazilian writer Joaquim Manoel Macedo's fictional portrait of Lucinda, an enslaved woman, Sidney Chalhoub notes: "Although Macedo attributes Lucinda's moral defects to the institution of slavery [rather than to innate defects], his description of slaves is so viciously unfavorable that it becomes difficult to imagine that such people, once freed, could exercise the rights of citizenship and participate in political life."[2]

Not everyone thought or expressed themselves like the judge. Emancipation opened up a series of gendered debates about ex-slaves' future—debates that would not be resolved by the time formal abolition was declared. Ideas about ex-slave men tended to veer between notions of "citizenship" (often idealistic in expression but qualified in practice or intent) and the desire for social order and hard work. Although women were, in a sense, secondary to this focus on men as citizens or workers, elites nonetheless relied heavily on them to turn their visions of postemancipation society into reality. Could women help construct newly "moralized" ex-slave families, educating and socializing their children for lives in freedom? Or were they to be feared as a source of social and biological "contagion" for their own and others' children, and best treated only as an ongoing source of domestic labor? This chapter explores how elites' discussion of these questions helped stake out the ground upon which women like Josepha would chart their own understandings of freedom.

"MORALIZING" EX-SLAVE FAMILIES

One reason why ex-slave women were a regular discussion topic was that, like their peers elsewhere in the Atlantic World, elites contemplating the ending of slavery in both Brazil and Cuba focused on the family as a channel for social reform.[3] Individuals with widely differing views about how, when, and why to end slavery nonetheless shared a concern with "moralizing" slave families as part of the process. Even in the mouths or pens of strongly antislavery figures, ideas about "moralization" often veered between blaming ex-slaves' "immorality" on slavery, and, in practice, blaming or punishing ex-slaves themselves for it. Enslaved women's role as the vessels through which emancipation would occur, and the notion of women as the guardians of morality, ensured ex-slave women's "morals" received particular scrutiny as part of gradual emancipation processes, whether before, as part of, or following legal change.

Don Lorenzo Allo Bermúdez, one of a group of Cuban exiles who mobilized in 1850s New York against Spanish rule, made a speech at the New York Cuban Democratic Atheneum on New Year's Day, 1854. A close friend of Cuban antislavery writer Gertrudis Gómez de Avellaneda, Allo collaborated with a New York-based newspaper, *El Mulato*, which broke away from mainstream exile opinion by advocating the abolition of slavery in Cuba.[4] His speech argued for abolition and universal rights for ex-slaves, on the grounds both of economics and Christian morality. He then turned to the question of slavery's effects on women:

> In connection with slavery, virtue is no longer virtue. For a slave woman to marry a slave and to preserve her conjugal fidelity, is to condemn herself and her children to slavery; and for that slave woman to surrender herself to a libertine, is to aspire to her own freedom and to the freedom of her children. This . . . is confirmed by the extraordinary number of children born of slave women out of the bonds of matrimony. And these slave women, for whom virtue is not virtue, nurse their masters' children, and have a large share in the formation of their first ideas. How deplorable for children are these two schools! The conduct of their fathers as masters, and the example of the nurses who attend on them from their cradle.[5]

While Allo thus laid the blame for women's conduct at the door of the institution of slavery, his explanation also blended subtly into a damning portrait of all such women as immoral, whatever the reasons. The solution he proposed was a "free womb" law, which

> would be for slave fathers the greatest of benefits; and that new generation would not abhor labor, since it would see in industry its subsistence, its well-being, and its future. These children would form a new tie between the master and his slaves. The master in treating them well would have the best means of stimulating their parents to work; and the latter in their turn would endeavor to merit this kindness toward their children by persevering in work.[6]

Some sixteen years before the advent of the Moret Law, Allo hoped to mold slave families according to his own ideals as a means of ensuring harmonious but subservient labor relations. Others would subsequently follow his thinking.

A decade later, in 1866, as Cuban and Puerto Rican deputies were being elected to the Madrid Junta de Información, Cuban lawyer Francisco de Armas y Céspedes published an influential book, *La esclavitud en Cuba*, in which he rejected government-led measures to end slavery, including "free womb" proposals. Armas y Céspedes, in fact, used very similar liberal language to that employed by, for example, Republican abolitionist Emilio Castelar, but did so for very different political ends. Thus he argued that slavery was un-Christian, asking, for example, "Would it seem just and fair that white men were reduced to slavery . . . ? The idea is contrary to all human sentiments. Then why is this not the case for the blacks?"[7] Yet whatever the reasons he gave for it, ultimately his view of the condition of Cuba's slaves was damning indeed, citing their "ignorance, stupidity, and laziness" as reasons why, in practice, they could not be immediately freed.[8] Before freedom could be given—and for Armas it was a gift, not a right— the task of "moralizing the black" needed to be undertaken. The means of doing this was the (ex-)slave family in general, and mothers in particular.

Rejecting the idea of a "free womb" law, Armas y Céspedes then considered another possibility: freeing only the girls born to enslaved mothers. Rejecting this too, however, he argued that it would undermine "moral" family relations. The "female" [*hembra*], he predicted, "despising the male [*varón*]," would

> look outside her own race for the union to which she is by nature inclined; which would . . . encourage . . . illicit unions, against Christian morality and social convenience . . . [H]ow will those children be brought up, fed, and educated, if they are born of slave fathers and free mothers? If each of the latter only had one child, the difficulty would not be so great, because the mother could work for herself and her child; but given the well-known fecundity of the African woman, it is rational to suppose that many would have a great number of children.[9]

Invoking an array of well-worn notions about African-descended women, Armas y Céspedes went on to argue that although ex-slave women would have numerous children, they would not care for them properly, exposing them to a welter of dangers from infanticide and destitution to "immorality" and crime.[10]

Armas y Céspedes used these concerns about promoting "moral" families to argue that Cuban planters themselves should be left to deal with the business of slave emancipation. He went on to describe his vision of what this should entail. As well as advocating that the state should pay for religious missions to minister to the enslaved, he emphasized above all that slaves' "family sentiments" should be stimulated. Families, which he defined specifically as a married man and woman and their children, should be provided with separate dwellings, and their relationship should be free from the owner's authority "except in serious cases, and then only to avoid the abuses of the father or the husband." Contrasting with the specter he had raised of morally errant, destitute, single, freed mothers that would result from a "free womb" law, Armas y Céspedes thus painted a happy picture of male-headed family relations among slaves as a basis for a broader patriarchal social order.[11] It was this same logic that led the Cuban deputies at the Madrid Junta de Información to advocate "strengthening the links of the slave family, as an extremely important preparation for its transition to the state of freedom." They stressed that "the members of a family, understood as the parents with their children, whatever the age of the latter, may never be separated . . . under any circumstances, or for any reason."[12] For Allo, Armas y Céspedes, and the *junta* deputies alike, the goal of "strengthening" and "moralizing" families was ultimately a hardworking and obedient workforce.

Elite preoccupations with the family did not end with the passage of the Moret Law three years after the Cuban deputies made their recommendations. Similar language appears, for example, in Pedro Gutiérrez y Salazar's 1879 text, *Reformas de Cuba*. Salazar argued that the presence of the wives and mothers of male slaveholders had historically made for a comparatively mild form of slavery in Cuba, since "the Christian woman" had "moralized" both slaves themselves and slaveholders. This, he assured his readers, promised harmonious postemancipation relations.[13] In turn, slave family structures would ensure ex-slaves remained on plantations and worked for their former masters after abolition, since "if they already have freedom, what will there be for them to seek outside the *conuco*, far from their companions, perhaps from their father, their wife, [or] from their own children?"[14] Salazar was an active member of Madrid's Sociedad Matritense de Amigos del País (founded 1775), among whose principal goals was the promulgation, in Spain, of industry, agriculture, and education.[15] Meanwhile, he had also served in the Spanish colonial administration in Manila and Havana, and, like other Spanish liberal reformers, his concern to establish harmonious and productive labor relations spanned both metropolis and empire.[16] For these reformers, "The strengthened family stabilized the male worker, protected the honor of women, and provided children with a loving environment and opportunity for education, all of which ensured the reproduction of healthy and industrious workers. In short, the family . . . complemented, rather than antagonized, capital."[17] Segismundo Moret invoked similar visions in 1870, during debates about the law that would bear his name:

> Imagine in a picturesque landscape a modest house lit by the rays of the setting sun. Inside, a black mother embraces her child. As the father returns from work he lovingly greets his son. The planter, the former master, passes by on horseback through the beautiful farm where hordes of slaves once lived; the planter waves in friendship to the former slave, who affectionately returns the greeting.[18]

Cozy visions, then, of "moral" black families—modeled, of course, on white, elite, patriarchal ideals—could potentially be harnessed in the service of very different political ends, whether by the essentially proslavery Cuban deputies or by Moret to advance his argument for womb-based gradual emancipation. Such notions often underpinned, for example, the passionate rhetoric employed by the advocates of immediate abolition, examined earlier in this book, who criticized slavery because it separated "loving mothers" from their children or forced them into "men's" work. Yet it was also a particular notion about what constituted a "moral" family that led Judge Oliveira Andrade to deny custody of her child to Josepha.

In Brazil, discussions of families dominated the parliamentary debates over the 1871 "free womb" law. The law's opponents raised the specter of slaveholders neglecting *ingênuos*, state intervention breaking down the bonds of gratitude that had held mothers and their children on plantations, and as a result ex-slave families breaking up. Its advocates, in turn, argued that it would do the opposite, strengthening family ties and hence maintaining a compliant workforce.[19] Senator Fernandes da Cunha envisioned that "the children will become workers on a soil where they were born, where their mothers live, to which all their feelings are tied. . . . It is where they fall in love, where they get married, where they learn to work and serve. That is where they prepare themselves for the future production of what Brazil needs."[20] Competing visions of postemancipation society placed ex-slave women under particular scrutiny in the debates. Baron Villa da Barra proposed freeing *all* enslaved women as a means of ending slavery, thus avoiding undermining the property principle by severing the connection between the legal status of the mother and that of the "fruits" of her womb. He was met with similar objections to those voiced by Armas y Céspedes for Cuba only a few years previously: these women, it was argued, would leave their masters and resort to prostitution. To refute this idea, Villa da Barra fell back on family sentiment. Freed women, he retorted, "will remain among their relatives . . . Slave women have hearts, they have blood ties, ties of love—of friendship—which must be respected because it would be barbarous to separate the people who make up a slave family."[21]

Like in Cuba, Brazilian elites thought "moral" families were, ideally, male-headed. The final text of the Rio Branco Law made provisions, for example, for a national Emancipation Fund, which aimed at strengthening a particular kind of family structure among the enslaved. Thus the fund prioritized particularly married couples, with some, like Bahian deputy João Mendes de Almeida, arguing that the man should be prioritized over the woman because "the male . . . everywhere and at all times has been the head of the family because he has primacy, and as such he should be the first to enjoin the inherent rights of human beings."[22] Only after the married couples came unmarried mothers with children. Wiebke Ipsen has suggested that such policies were concerned with instilling patriarchy among ex-slave families.[23]

On the other hand, as those who designed and implemented the laws well knew, there was a vast gulf between the theory and the practice. Low marriage rates among the enslaved and free population alike, as well as the long-standing practice in slave societies of *partus sequitur ventrem*, ensured that the vast majority of those actually freed by the fund were unmarried enslaved women with their children, who did not fit the ideal model at all.[24] Fabiano Dauwe's study of the emancipation fund's operations in Desterro, Santa Catarina (southern Brazil) observes that minors freed by the fund were frequently allotted *tutores* (guardians), especially "when the emancipations were . . . made up exclusively of mothers and their children. Apparently, it was believed that the mother would not have the ability or power to take responsibility for her children on her own."[25]

Meanwhile, beyond the operations of the state, the private act of emancipating slaves was commonly used in Brazil as a means of shoring up family structures, among slaveholders as well as among slaves, and of cementing the ties between each. In November 1871, just after the passage of the Rio Branco Law, the newspaper *A Republica* announced that "Mr. João Pereira Monteiro, father of the distinguished academic from São Paulo, João Pereira Monteiro Jr., celebrated yesterday the return of his son to this city by granting freedom during dinner to one of his slaves, aged six, named Virginia." The emancipation of a young female slave celebrated and upheld the patriarchal slaveholding family, winning the comment from the newspaper that "The act of such a respectable *pai de família* is greatly to be praised."[26]

In both societies, then, elites dreamed that emancipation would shore up family "morality" among ex-slaves—defined, if they paused to define it at all, by marriage and by male-headed households. There were differences in emphasis: Brazilian slaveholders, undergoing the tortuous process of abolishing slavery from within a slave society, would prove particularly obsessed with enforcing gratitude and social control, adopting visual representations of ongoing hierarchy through emancipation ceremonies, for example.[27] Cuban elites had similar goals but had to contend both with the generally more liberal concepts of what freedom might bring to ex-slaves espoused by metropolitan commentators, and with more radical visions posed by the rebellion in the east. Yet in both cases, *partus sequitur ventrem* and the free womb logic that succeeded it ensured that discussions of emancipation ended up focusing on women and their children. The contradictions helped create, restrict, and complicate women's relationship to their "free" children. Meanwhile, the contradictions also gave elites other thorny issues to ponder. What would be the role of these children in postemancipation societies, and how might they be persuaded to perform it? The solution proposed was education.

EDUCATING "NEW CITIZENS"

In neither Brazil nor Cuba during or after abolition was there any sustained state-led attempt to address the education and welfare of ex-slaves and their descendants. Thirty-six years after abolition in Brazil, Evaristo de Moraes estimated the level of illiteracy to be 80 percent and berated the lack of education for *libertos* and their descendants; Afro-Cubans struggled during and after abolition to have their children educated in schools that often closed their doors to nonwhites, sometimes resorting to segregated schools.[28] Nonetheless, the perceived need for education of ex-slaves and their children occupied an important space in discussions about abolition.

In Cuba, both the Spanish Moret Law and the *patronato* law charged owners with providing free womb children with "the primary teaching and education necessary to exercise a skill or trade."[29] As the parents of these children often knew, if they could prove that education was not being provided, the children were legally entitled to freedom.[30] In Brazil, by contrast, the Rio Branco Law did not discuss education of *ingênuos*. In private consultations, the Ministry of Agriculture and the Council of State concluded that owners had no obligation to educate them.[31] However, since 1824, the constitution stipulated education as both a right pertaining to "citizens" and a duty to be discharged by the state.[32] Slaves, excluded from the definition of "citizens," were explicitly barred from the doors of public schools from 1854.[33] Yet for almost everyone else, the term "citizen" was in practice a contested and often fluid concept in nineteenth-century Brazil.[34] While there was no coordinated government effort to educate ex-slaves, 1871 did provoke a number of initiatives for educating *libertos* and especially *ingênuos* by education professionals, abolitionists, and others.[35]

What was the purpose of such education? Views swung between, on the one hand, discussing its potential for controlling ex-slaves, cementing ties of gratitude and dependence, and ensuring a ready supply of labor and, on the other, seeing it as a way of helping freedpeople to take up a meaningful place in society as what many commentators described as "citizens." The two tendencies were different in degree rather than in kind, representing points along a scale that ranged from fear and control to "benign" paternalism.

For Cuba, as with discussions of ex-slave families, metropolitan observers took a noticeably different stance on education from those based on the island, although each referred to a notion of "citizenship" (by which they meant within Spain and the empire).[36] Abolitionist Spaniards were more likely to use lofty liberal language in imagining the purposes of education. In his 1881 history of slavery, Spanish Abolitionist Society member Enrique Vera y González optimistically discussed the situation of ex-slaves in the United States:

> And the blacks? Those beings *born to be slaves* and those *half-men* . . . are today citizens, they enjoy every right, they practice universal suffrage, they create large numbers of schools . . . , they sit in the chambers as representatives of the country . . . and in sum, they contribute in every way . . . to prosperity and progress . . . because they have been given the light and morality of enlightenment, justice, and freedom.[37]

Despite such exalted visions, even Vera y González assumed that "enlightenment, justice, and freedom" would have to be *given* to people who had not previously possessed them.[38] Others, meanwhile, discussed education precisely as a justification for *postponing* citizenship. Gutiérrez y Salazar, while stressing that ex-slaves had the human potential to become "citizens" and "equals," argued that their civil rights must be limited and their political ones delayed until they had become sufficiently "educated" to exercise them.[39]

Cuban-drafted regulations were considerably less romantic than Vera y González about the purpose of "education." The 1872 Regulation of the 1870 Moret Law retained the notion stipulated in the Spanish law that free womb children must be taught a "skill or trade." The regulation went further than the law, however, emphasizing also the need for "moralization." *Patronos* were to "instruct [free womb children] in the principles of religion and morality, inculcating in them a love of work, respect for the laws and love of their neighbor."[40] The logic behind such stipulations was explored in the 1877 Cuban regulations for *juntas de libertos*: "Since . . . the children of slave mothers . . . will make up the next generation of men of color, the *juntas* will . . . ensure the children are educated . . . so that they may become moral citizens who are useful to society."[41]

Even here, while the tenor of the Cuban regulations was clearly about education as a means for disciplining and controlling future "free" generations, there were hints at small but significant shifts in how these children were conceived of. Not only did the 1877 regulations refer to them as "citizens," but they also called them *niños*. This standard Spanish term for "child" had, in the past, very rarely if ever been used to describe the children of slaves, who were referred to as *párvulos* (or, from 1870, as *libertos* if freed).[42] Indeed, in Francisco Calcagno's antislavery novel, *Romualdo, uno de tantos*, set in 1830s Cuba, a Spanish priest who has recently arrived in a Cuban village incenses local slaveholders who attend his Sunday sermon by referring to slaves' children as *niños*.[43] The use of the term in the 1877 regulations hinted at an admittance of these free womb children to the ranks of childhood in the present, as well as to those of "citizens" in the future.

Although in practice most *patronos* did not take the legal stipulations about education seriously, colonial administrative bodies did appear to think it important in terms of access for the first "free" generation to some broadly defined sense of rights and social entitlement. In 1884, the Junta de Patronato of Matanzas consulted the Havana Consejo de Administración about owners who were failing to educate free womb children. In its response, the Consejo stressed the seriousness of this part of the law. It described the children as "unfortunate souls to whom, by freeing them, Society, the State, and even their own owners have made the most important and honorable commitment to give them, through . . . instruction, sufficient means for addressing, in their new state of life, the necessities that this will bring." This would ensure that "on fully entering into their rights they will not find them still more hateful than servitude itself . . . because they lack enlightenment and instruction."[44] The language of the future "rights" of these children, and of the state's and society's "commitment" to them, rubbed shoulders with the description of them as "unfortunate souls," invoking charity, pity, and freedom as generously given.

In practice, as the Matanzas *junta's* question implied, many Cuban owners apparently ignored the stipulations of the laws altogether. Antonio Gallenga noted in 1873 that "To educate and discipline the negro, or even to find out to what extent he is capable of improvement, is a problem about which few persons have as yet troubled themselves in Cuba."[45] Probably for this reason, while education was theoretically extolled and legally required, it is rare to find references to what, if anything, it involved in practice.

In Rio, the abolitionist press extolled various private and municipal initiatives toward educating *ingênuos*. In December 1885, the *Gazeta da Tarde* newspaper praised a school that had opened its doors to *ingênuos*, describing how "Senhor Felipe Pereira de Andrada, director of the Felipe Nery School, celebrated the anniversary of the law that freed slave women's wombs by inaugurating classes in which the *ingênuos* could be educated, in order to understand the duties of free men." Despite the celebratory tone, the writer evidently conceived of the *ingênuos'* future in terms of "duties," not of "rights."[46]

Education for work was, in practice, usually the top priority. That same month, journalists from several of the city's newspapers, including abolitionist José do Patrocinio, went to visit an asylum for poor children at the invitation of its director, Daniel de Almeida. Impressed, the *Gazeta* reported that the asylum was "one of the best of its kind," a place where poor children were trained to become skilled workers. Here, "a poor unfortunate child" could find "the light of reason, the truth of things." The pupils learned reading, writing, and other academic subjects, which (for boys) might eventually grant them suffrage in a country whose vast illiterate population had recently been excluded from voting.[47] Yet the main priority was that the "poor unfortunate child" should "develop a love of work and learn . . . to earn his daily bread without sin." Almost ecstatically, the paper depicted "those hundreds of children, working continuously and eternally happy. The beads of sweat running down their frank and rosy little faces amid their smiles of purity. . . . Work seems to be like a cherished toy . . . which they all enjoy."[48]

As the children at the asylum worked, portraits of Viscount Rio Branco and Carlos Gomes (an opera composer who supported abolitionist campaigns in the city) looked down at them from the walls—reminding children to whom they "owed" their freedom and reminding historians of elites' obsessions with gratitude. Time and again, the "emancipators" aimed to ensure that ex-slaves and their children should remember, in the future, those who had "granted" them freedom. As we have seen, the visual imagery of gratitude spawned by other Atlantic emancipation processes was adopted and adapted with especial enthusiasm in Brazil.[49] Like the love of work, gratitude was also something that might be achieved through education. As municipal councilor Oliveira Rosário reminded his colleagues on 14 May 1888, the day after final abolition was declared in Brazil, "the Council . . . must understand that after the emancipation of the slaves, the absolute necessity of educating their children increases, so that they may one day appreciate the heroic sacrifices made by those who . . . contributed to the redemption of their nation."[50] He proposed that two new schools be founded, bearing the names of Princess Isabel and José do Patrocinio, reminding ex-slaves' children of the "benefactors" who had helped bring them freedom.

Nonetheless, Oliveira Rosário did implicitly include *ingênuos* in a national imaginary, referring to the "redemption" of "their nation." Brazilian elites often went further, describing freedpeople as future "citizens." Yet unlike Vera y González in Spain, they did not usually assume ex-slaves would take up the kinds of political—or even civil—rights that they themselves enjoyed. In a very old slave society that was, in Robert Cottroll's words, "comfortable with status and hierarchy," it was perhaps this very assumption of inequality that allowed elites to refer to "citizenship" without needing to state that it would have clear limits.[51] Through emancipation, they aimed to cement ties of patronage that would leave an indelible stamp upon the quality of that "citizenship."

In December 1885, at the third emancipation ceremony sponsored by Rio's municipal council, interim president Cláudio da Silva gave an unusually conservative speech, sounding a note of caution in contrast with the more openly antislavery speeches that his colleagues increasingly made on such occasions. Da Silva described the slaves being freed as "new citizens," thus finding an effective means of both expressing and qualifying citizenship. He went on to extol the virtues of education, arguing, "We should not only concern ourselves with freeing the slave; we should also confront . . . the extremely difficult problems of . . . the use and moralization of the element which is today being emancipated . . . Guiding the new citizen through the sumptuous gateway of social freedom into the communion of free men is essential." He then offered a warning to the enslaved people standing in front of him: "If, however, any of them should stray from the path of honor and duty, blinded by the moral degradation of the environment in which he has hitherto lived, this Illustrious Council will still be able to exercise its power to make him understand that those who were recently humble must not subsequently become troublemakers."[52] Such outright threats of reprisals against ex-slaves were rare at these ceremonies, which usually concentrated on celebrating the occasion and anticipating full abolition. Yet even in more upbeat speeches, councilors betrayed their assumptions about the limits to the roles that ex-slaves were to be educated into performing.

The following year, on 29 July 1886, a municipal emancipation ceremony held on Princess Isabel's birthday freed sixty slaves in Rio. The next day, on 30 July, the municipal council opened a school in the outlying rural parish of Santa Cruz, aimed specifically at educating the children of workers at the recently founded city slaughterhouse there. The school was named Santa Isabel after the princess, who, along with the councilors and other members of the imperial family, including her father the emperor, traveled out to inaugurate it. The imperial family had a long relationship with Santa Cruz, where they had retained a palace and summer residence since the arrival of the court in Rio in 1808. There had been a train link since 1878, and Pedro II attended the opening of the new slaughterhouse there in 1881. The slaves of the imperial family, who were freed by the Rio Branco Law, would have included those of Santa Cruz. Thus, the family's visit inaugurated a school that potentially would educate the children of their own former slaves. The speeches made on the occasion portrayed education as a subtle blend of benevolence and control.

Extolling the benefits of educating the slaughterhouse workers' children, Councilor Thomas Rabello noted that "the benefit of the child leads to the gratitude of the parent." If his children were educated there, "the slaughterhouse laborer will become a zealous worker; because his future life will be linked to his children's fate and if he severs the links which tie him to this establishment, he will destroy forever the guarantees which accompany his offspring and constitute the treasures of his old age."[53] Education, then, provided the link between social control and family structure, tying family members to one another as well as to a labor regime. Rabello had a very specific practical outcome in mind. The school would, he declared, help prevent the "continual turnover of workers" at the slaughterhouse, allowing it to supply the growing needs of the capital for fresh meat—an ever-present concern that occupied many pages of Rio's press as well as enormous amounts of the council's time.[54]

As well as hoping it would secure the slaughterhouse's postemancipation labor supply, councilors drew broader connections between the opening of the school and the ending of slavery. Presenting the previous day's emancipation ceremony and the school inauguration as part of the same initiative, Councilor Luiz de Moura flattered Princess Isabel for her charitable, "womanly" support of each cause:

> The Council has taken two measures to commemorate the glorious birthday of [the Princess]: founding a school and distributing 60 letters of freedom. The complementary nature of these measures is evident . . . because if freeing slaves means smashing the fetters that bind their arms, educating children means freeing them from a slavery perhaps heavier and more fatal—the slavery of ignorance. The harmony between these measures and the magnanimous tendencies of Your Highness is striking, because with your angelic hand you broke, in 1871, the iron cuffs that would have bound a whole generation of unfortunates; and your heart . . . responds to the wails of unprotected children, of whom you have become the affectionate mother.

Moura neatly linked education for "disadvantaged children" with the freeing of *adult* ex-slaves, with Isabel acting as a "mother" to them all. He thus implied an indefinite state of infancy, and concomitant tutelage, for ex-slaves.[55] In so doing, he echoed a broad tendency among private emancipation societies, donors, and abolitionists, who conceived of emancipation and education as interrelated and "generously" bestowed.[56]

Whether education aimed at "morality," "citizenship," hard work, or family life, its purpose and meaning varied for boys and girls. The asylum for poor boys, set up in Rio in 1875, aimed to "receive boys of six to twelve years of age and to educate and teach them a trade." The boys would then undergo a period of "apprenticeship" where they would "work three years in the workshops, at half wages."[57] Another school trained boys to be tailors, supposedly combining academic study with training in their trade.[58] Girls, meanwhile, were trained for domestic work.[59] The notion of educating for "citizenship," too, was assumed to apply directly only to boys. These long-standing gendered approaches to education gained new stridency in the views of Brazilian Republicans, who were keen proponents of education. Prominent Republican Ennes de Souza argued in December 1885 that a good Republican education "educates a man to be a man, to be the head of a family and to be a useful citizen. . . . What more could we ask for in educating a Republican?"[60] Girls were explicitly excluded from such visions. Yet, as they considered the roles ex-slaves would play in postabolition society, elites could not avoid discussing women's contributions, whether as domestic laborers or as future mothers of citizens.

As we saw in Chapter 4, the second half of the nineteenth century saw a growing transnational interest in educating women—seen as the guardians of morality—so they could educate their children.[61] This burgeoning interest had ramifications for both Brazil and Cuba. Women's education gradually expanded, while teaching became one of the few professional activities that, in both Havana and Rio, women—including those of color—began to exercise in growing numbers.[62] Although discussions most often focused on the education of elite women, many contemporary observers applied the same logic to the education of poor women, and, from the 1870s, to the "freeborn" daughters of slave women, who in the future would give birth to "citizens." The abolition process thus saw considerable discussion of how enslaved and freed women might contribute to the education and preparation of their children for freedom. In Rio, during the 1880s, a number of municipal projects specifically addressed poor women's or girls' education as well as broader welfare. A maternity hospital, catering mainly to *parda* enslaved and free women, was founded in 1880; a school for girls was opened in the outlying suburb of Jacarepaguá in 1886; and, once elected to the municipal council from 1886, José do Patrocinio successfully proposed that an asylum for poor girls be opened, on the model of the boys' asylum founded over a decade previously.[63] In the Spanish empire, Gutiérrez y Salazar, discussing poor and ex-slave families in Cuba, Spain, and the Philippines, stated that education "begins in the arms of the mother, in the breast of the home."[64] Of course, in a sense his position echoed the claims of enslaved and freed mothers. In Havana in 1882, black woman Francisca García sought custody of her child; her appeal asked, "Who could be in a better position than a mother to provide for her child's nurture, education, and happiness?"[65]

Yet there was no fixed answer to Francisca's question. Other commentators suggested a possibility that would not have been to her liking: that in fact many others—whether owners or educational and welfare establishments—were much more competent than she to educate her children. Meanwhile, regardless of their views on the maternal qualities of women of color, elites rarely lost sight of the need for their domestic labor.

One municipal school set up in Rio for *ingênua* girls created stormy debates among municipal councilors that revealed their profound uncertainties about these girls' role in postemancipation Brazil. The proposal to found and run the school, made in February 1884, came from a woman teacher, Dona Teresa Pizarro Filha.[66] The council approved the school, named after Princess Isabel, which ended up taking in sixty girls aged between four and fifteen. From the outset, training the domestic servants that continued to be in demand in the city was a key part of many councilors' aims, as Councilor Torquato Fernandes Couto emphasized in March 1884:

> To the numerous problems of public education which in Europe are demanding solutions, we must add one more that for us is particularly pressing. In Europe there are families which from one generation to the next have worked in domestic service, the parents passing their experience to the children; for us, domestic service has been undertaken by slaves. It must be understood that, although I hope there will be many exceptions, freedpeople and above all *ingênuos* are destined to become domestic servants.[67]

The planned curriculum included reading, writing, arithmetic, religious education, and Brazilian history. However, the main focus would be on "notions of personal hygiene" and "domestic economy." The girls would do needlework, make sweets and drinks for sale, take in washing and ironing, and be given prizes for the best domestic work.[68] According to the school regulations, "as well as elementary education, the *ingênuas* will be taught to perform properly their functions in the domestic household."[69]

In order for this to happen, Fernandes Couto returned to the need to educate children to work. Echoing his peers' fear of vagrancy, he argued that "It is necessary . . . to prepare them to live in society, instructing them, teaching them to work, instilling in them good morals and the habit of industry," since "otherwise the *liberto* and the *ingênuo* will become a social danger." While in Europe, Couto argued, a love of work and practical domestic service skills were passed on from parents to children, in Brazil the children of slaves "are naturally in contact with their parents, who transmit to them imperfect habits and ways of thinking." Thus discounting *ingênuas*' parents from playing a useful role, he argued that the girls should be removed from their influence. Ironically, of course, these girls were ultimately being trained to perform exactly the same kinds of labor as their enslaved mothers and grandmothers had done before them. Surely, these women could have taught their daughters to wash clothes or make sweets—and perhaps many had already done so. What might these mothers, as they sought to have their children's "free" status recognized or to retain custody of them, make of their daughters' removal to the care of Teresa Pizarro Filha? Aiming to stamp their mark on the nature of ex-slave families, Couto and others who thought like him helped set the stage for the struggles that ex-slave women faced over the very definitions of freedom, maternity, and womanhood.

The notion that ultimately, other women would be needed in order to instill the kinds of "morals" in children that their ex-slave mothers were unable to provide was echoed by Cuban journalist and reformer Aurelia Castillo y González, who had dedicated considerable time and ink to mobilizing Cuban elite women to help in the antislavery cause. In 1882, writing of "a race which is raising itself up," she acknowledged slaves' historical efforts to free themselves, "forming families of honorable artisans, which maintained from parents to children and from children to grandchildren, with a certain modest pride, the good opinion and appreciation of the society in which they lived." Nonetheless,

> It is up to us, the most advanced element of society, to help them on and guide them . . . passing on to them the moral and civilizing doctrines that we have accumulated over centuries in printed volumes and in family traditions; it is up to us to direct their faltering gaze upon the book, their trembling hand upon the paper, their clouded intelligence upon the wide horizons which are opening up to them.[70]

Despite their best efforts, former slaves would need the input of former masters in order to achieve education and "morality." Elsewhere, Castillo y González returned to her notion of elite women as central to such tasks and hence in need of education themselves. She advised that such women should stop entrusting their children to nursemaids, who were "ignorant and almost always immoral," taking direct responsibility for their own children's moral education.[71] These nursemaids, of course, were very often enslaved or free(d) women of color. As we saw in Chapter 4, fears that women who nursed and reared the children of the elite or performed sexual services as prostitutes threatened to corrupt elite families—physically or morally—grew in both Cuba and Brazil during slavery's final years. All these notions raised serious questions about the capacity of ex-slave women to raise or educate children—whether other people's or their own. Indeed, Castillo's words had been anticipated decades previously by prestigious lawyer Antonio Bachiller y Morales, who, advocating white immigration in 1863, stressed the need to avoid importing "hostile" African women, since "a generation that is the product of barbarous and idolatrous mothers cannot bear the fruit of morality and progress."[72]

For Brazil, Wiebke Ipsen noted that gradual emancipation coincided with the extolling of "Republican Motherhood" by abolitionist Republicans. Yet the notion was increasingly applied only to some women, not to others. Images of nonwhite mothers gradually disappeared from the pages of the *Revista Illustrada* over the 1880s and 1890s, to be replaced by white women who were depicted not on the streets but, more and more, in the home. This points at a gradual exclusion of nonwhite women from the very definition of motherhood, and hence from one of the main ways in which most people conceived of womanhood itself.[73]

Of course, all this had tremendous consequences for the struggles of enslaved and freed women around the issue of motherhood during the transition years, providing a heavy counterweight to the kinds of abolitionist rhetoric we saw in Chapter 4 that sought fellow-feeling for enslaved mothers from free women. Hierarchical visions of who could and could not be a "good" mother informed Judge Oliveira de Andrade's decision that Josepha was unsuitable to raise her daughter Maria. The same logic also allowed Josepha's former owners successfully to portray themselves as more suitable "parents" for Maria than Josepha herself. Slaveholders had long held "paternal" notions of themselves as part of their very self-identifications. As emancipation unfolded, they continued to cast themselves in this role, seeking, with considerable success, to retain "parental" control over other people's children. This, of course, does not mean their actions were not, in many cases, kindly meant. The patronage instinct frequently combined the desire to retain these children's labor and subservience with genuine concern and affection for them or their mothers. Indeed, in Brazil today it is common to hear affectionate assertions that one's domestic servants are "almost part of the family."

Bernadino José de Oliveira Bastos was the owner of a *parda* domestic slave, Eduwiges, whose daughter Leonor was born in Rio in March 1872, soon after the Rio Branco Law was passed, and baptized as an *ingênua*. In July 1885, when Leonor was thirteen, Bastos formally renounced his rights over her, leaving her "completely free." However, "since the child requires support and assistance," she would continue "in his house and under his care." Oliveira Bastos thus sought to substitute his finite statutory rights over Leonor with the far more insidious ties of personal patronage.[74]

In Havana, a similar situation occurred some years previously in 1873, when Doña Elvira Perovany applied for custodial rights over Salvador Miguel Pérez, a young boy. Perovany explained "that she is the mistress of the black woman Matilde Criolla who, due to her impeccable conduct, is worthy of the consideration of the undersigned, and she cannot be indifferent to her sorrows, watching her weep for her son who is under fourteen, and free." The tears, said Doña Elvira, were because "his father, who is now deceased, having freed him, . . . placed him as an apprentice [*contratado*] domestic servant in the house of Don José María de Flores, whence he fled last 15 January." Despite his notionally "free" status, Salvador was captured and placed in the Asilo de San José. He was then *contratado* once more, to Don José Celestino Valdés of Arroyo Naranjo, outside the city's limits, where Perovany alleged he was not being taught any trade. She emphasized that "since the little black boy Salvador has no father, he has no more protection than that of his mother, and of she who speaks, as her owner. . . . Since the minor needs to learn a trade, and someone who will care for him, no one except the exponent can do this adequately." By doing so, she would also be saving Salvador's morals: "Since he no longer has a *peseta* to his name because the Asilo charges him rent, he must necessarily give himself up to dreadful vices in order to make money." She thus begged to be granted custody, "saving the son, consoling the mother, and allowing her to carry out this work of charity." *Síndico* Vicente González de Valés subsequently backed Perovany's position, arguing that she would make Santiago "a man who is useful to society" as well as being able to support his own mother, "freeing her from slavery through his work and savings."[75]

Neither Oliveira Bastos in Rio nor Perovany in Havana apparently encountered obstacles in gaining custody of their enslaved women's children—despite the fact that each child was nominally "free"—in societies where the lines between ownership, protection, and control were still in the process of being redrawn. On the other hand, as this book has explored, many mothers were also able to invoke the "sacred rights of motherhood" to put up considerable opposition to such strategies, especially once they had gained freedom themselves. The apparent lack of maternal opposition in these two cases may, of course, simply reflect the vastly unequal power relations between these enslaved mothers and their owners. On the other hand, given such women's inability to attain fully autonomous custody of their children (or even the undesirability of such autonomy, if it meant poverty and isolation), Bastos's or Perovany's actions may alternatively have reflected initiatives taken by these enslaved mothers themselves. Like other political actors in societies where patronage held sway, they perhaps sought to mobilize the mechanisms of personal protection for their children as their best or most realistic option.[76]

Meanwhile, women like Josepha—who was free, unlike the two enslaved women in the examples above—took an alternative approach, staking their claims to motherhood through the courts and questioning the idea that they were not suitable to raise their children. As they did so, such notions were being questioned elsewhere too. By December 1884,

Rio's school for *ingênuas* was experiencing serious problems, which were brought to the municipal council's attention in a report by its education committee. The report noted that the teacher, Pizarro Filha, was also taking in other pupils, but teaching them separately from the *ingênuas*. The committee indignantly suggested that "she is repelled by the idea of erasing the divisive line that society so unjustly drew between free and enslaved, and which modern civilization aims to make disappear." The municipal councilors deemed this segregation unacceptable "in an age where equality is preached" and declared that "it is saddening, indeed disgusting, that at an educational establishment, the first temple raised and consecrated to liberty, equality, and freedom of men," a teacher would "obey outdated prejudices."[77] The committee's modernizing arguments about education echoed closely the tenor of broader debates about education among Rio's teachers and journalists.[78]

Embedded within the committee's criticism were very different ideas, then, about the part freed girls ought to play in creating these bold visions of the future. Truly modern schools, said the committee, should "educate free citizens and enlightened mothers of families." In linking mothering to modernity, the committee followed broader trends in late-nineteenth- and early-twentieth-century Brazilian medical discourse. As noted by Okezi Otovo, "maternal duties had become a widespread public concern" by the start of the twentieth century in Brazil's major cities, as "physicians, politicians, and women's charitable societies organized . . . to assert that bearing and raising healthy children was the key to a national regeneration."[79] The committee complained that in the case of the school for *ingênuas*, rather than following such notions of modernizing maternity, "the instruction which is given to the unfortunate *ingênuas* . . . is clearly intended, not to prepare future mothers of families, but competent domestic servants; not to enlighten the spirit or shape the character of the *ingênua*, but to make her feel that she should not aspire to anything beyond domestic service." The committee warned that if this state of affairs continued, the council would merely be helping to "train slaves who are educated in order better to serve their masters; it would be clarifying their intelligence, preparing their morality, opening their hearts to the noble and generous sentiments of love of family and humanity . . . in order to then suffocate them in the black and lethal atmosphere of a disguised enslavement."[80] Educating the *ingênuas* as "enlightened mothers of families" who would shape the next generation of "free citizens" was education for freedom; education for domestic service would keep them, in practice, enslaved.[81]

These stridently expressed differences between the committee's position and that of Torquato Couto could not mask some assumptions they all also shared. Whether they foresaw roles for *ingênuas* as mothers of their own families or as servants in the families of others, in neither case did these visions reach beyond the domestic realm, despite the fact that every time the councilors stepped out of their chambers into the city's noisy streets, they encountered the African-descended women who had long been a central part of the city's economy and public life. Indeed, *mina* African women traders at the marketplace would cause headaches for the councilors less than a year after these debates took place, helping stage one of the earliest strikes recorded in the city.[82] Nor, as they imagined the *ingênuas'* future roles, could they ever satisfactorily divorce mothering and domestic duties from servility, for, of course the two would continue to be intimately linked in the lives of many women of color. As nurses, domestic servants, and wet nurses in wealthy households, such women would continue to be auxiliaries to elite women's maternity as well as mothers in their own right.[83] Indeed, as Sarah Franklin has observed for nineteenth-century Cuba, "Motherhood for white women . . . was not so much concerned with the quotidian care of infants and young children, but rather with supervising their care. . . . Motherhood for black women had as its chief concern the rigors of the everyday care associated with young children."[84] The intensely *physical* aspects of mothering—the exhausting, endless labor of changing, soothing, breast-feeding—would broadly continue to be performed by women of color, whether for their own or for others' children. Nonetheless, the debate over the school for *ingênuas* did expose significantly different positions among the councilors in terms of the roles of ex-slave women, particularly in terms of the *moral* dimensions of maternity.

In the end, it was the Ministry of Empire, to which the council was subordinated in the task of providing public education, that quashed the whole debate.[85] Refusing to provide the funds requested by the council, the ministry argued that *ingênuos* could be educated in existing public schools, thus "avoiding any distinction between classes."[86] In this, the ministry followed other quiet attempts by the imperial state to impose "silence" around the matter of color, in order to avoid raising racial tensions.[87] Yet the episode had caused councilors to reflect on—and to some degree, perhaps, to modify—their visions of these *ingênua* girls' future. In April 1888, the same Torquato Couto who had previously advocated removing *ingênuas* from their parents' bad influence now proposed the

Cartoon depicting black market women's role in a strike at Rio de Janeiro's marketplace, October 1885. "Greve dos legumes" ("The vegetable strike"), Revista Illustrada, *17 October 1885, 8. Fundação Casa Rui Barbosa, Rio de Janeiro.*

creation of crèches for Rio's workers. Crèches would be "of great bene-fit to the poor classes, because they allow, above all, mothers to work for the well-being of the family, without the worries that caring for the chil-dren cause them." Couto thus acknowledged poor women's role as both workers and mothers. On the other hand, the measure also acknowledged the practical impossibility that—as the education committee had seemed to suggest—the women of the poor might somehow be able to dedicate themselves fully to being "enlightened family mothers."[88]

Whether figuratively wringing their hands about the need to "moral-ize" families or extolling the potential for ex-slaves to become "citizens," elites' "visions of freedom" invariably allotted specific roles to ex-slave women and their daughters. Abolition was a moment, then, in which not only the meanings of freedom, but the meanings of womanhood for ex-slave women, were debated and recast. Differences among elite posi-tions occurred within quite narrow limits. Ultimately, whether these women were useful only for domestic labor and—to quote Judge Oliveira

Andrade—"not able to give [their children] good education and care," or whether they ought to become "enlightened family mothers" of what some termed "new citizens," such commentators were limited by their own inability to imagine womanhood beyond the domestic associations of elite models of femininity.

These discussions also occurred upon fast-shifting historical sands. Before any firm conclusions were reached, new notions of womanhood would emerge in both Brazil and Cuba, ushered in by the social and political changes that swiftly followed abolition. In Brazil, the Republican government that took over from 1889 brought specific new notions of "Republican Motherhood" and its own gendered approach to education.[89] The Cuban independence movement inspired alternative visions of womanhood in the figure of Mariana Grajales, while, after the war, Afro-Cuban associations sought access to the "respectability" of white society by embracing "morality" and patriarchy for women of color.[90]

Elites' varying notions about the postemancipation future of women of color, then, were limited, contradictory, and forged in a fleeting historical moment. Yet for women claimants, they mattered a great deal. Oliveira Andrade's view of Josepha as an "unsuitable" mother helped shape the uneven terrain on which her struggles to conceive freedom were fought. Idealistic discussions about education's potential to forge "citizenship" or "enlightened motherhood," meanwhile, helped Ramona stake a claim to custody of her children and enhanced opportunities for them. Yet such women's conceptions of freedom and of womanhood were also much richer than those elites conceived on their behalf. It is to these conceptions that the final chapters turn.

CHAPTER SEVEN

She Was Now a Free Woman

Ex-Slave Women and the Meanings of Urban Freedom

And the Defendant was thus living from her income,
with her three children and the Claimant, enjoying general esteem . . .
and seeking to increase her assets for the good of her offspring.
—Manoel Furtado de Mendonça, administrator of
Eva Joaquina de Oliveira's estate, Rio de Janeiro, December 1868[1]

On 17 March 1886, Rio de Janeiro's police chief, João Coelho Bastos, wrote to the city's municipal council. In his letter, Bastos denounced an attempt by artisan Jeronymo José de Mello to take a young *parda* woman, Gabriella, "through violent means," to Nova Friburgo, a small city in Rio de Janeiro province. The abolitionist press daily berated Bastos and the police force over which he presided for "slaveocrat" behavior—imprisoning nonwhite people, humiliating them by forcibly shaving their heads, and packing them off to plantations outside the city with little proof of whether they were enslaved or free.[2] Yet in this communication, Bastos confirmed the police had actually prevented what he called the "criminal act" of removing Gabriella by force by her former owner.[3] Gabriella had been Mello's slave until earlier that month, when she was freed at the emancipation ceremony that had also freed Maria Rosa's daughter Ludovina, whom the reader met earlier in this book.[4] Possibly through a complaint made by Gabriella herself, the police had been notified about Mello's plans, and she was able to resist with the help of the very police that were busily catching supposed runaway slaves elsewhere in the capital.[5]

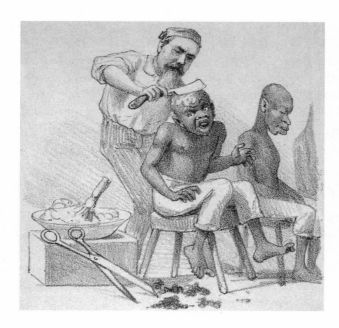

Cartoon depicting the forcible shaving of the heads of suspected fugitive slaves by the police, Rio de Janeiro, November 1885. "A nossa polícia" ("Our police"), Revista Illustrada, 30 November 1885, 4–5. Fundação Casa Rui Barbosa, Rio de Janeiro.

By using force to take a young woman away from the city, Mello attempted to exercise the rights he had held over Gabriella as her owner and which had helped define the meaning of the owner-slave relationship. He could sell or move her away from her social networks and from the working conditions and chances to accumulate savings that the city offered her. He could also commit violence against her body. For Gabriella, the letter of manumission handed her by the empress signified the end of these rights over her. Remaining in the capital offered her a possibility of greater autonomy in all these areas of her life. Bastos's brief communication affords us a glimpse of myriad gendered struggles over freedom's definitions.

Gabriella's successful galvanizing of police protection was the exception, not the rule, for most freedpeople. Ex-owners still wielded great power to enforce their own definitions of freedom for their former slaves. Only a few years previously, Mello had been able to have another slave, Martinha, incarcerated simply for "speaking obscenities," and old habits died hard.[6] In any case, ex-owners maintained control through more insidious means than outright violence, preserving the paternalistic relations with dependents that had underwritten slavery. Maintaining freedom, as well as acquiring it, was a major problem for people of color.[7] Yet the fact that the enslaved continued to seek legal freedom reminds us that it was certainly worth a great deal. The quest was shared by freed men and women, who were linked inextricably by bonds of family, neighborhood, work, and culture. Yet just as enslavement often held different meanings for the women and men who suffered it together, so the factors that shaped people's understandings of freedom included gender. This chapter addresses some of the ways in which women like Gabriella conceived freedom: what they understood by it and how they sought to weave it into their lives in the rapidly changing port cities of Rio de Janeiro and Havana.

"INCREASING HER ASSETS FOR THE GOOD OF HER OFFSPRING": PROPERTY

Freedwomen were like freedmen in that they sought wealth and property ownership as a means to put distance between themselves and slavery and to advance socially. In other words, property was a way of giving meaning to freedom. Women's wealth creation, though, was significant in the context of the debates we have examined in previous chapters. Depictions of ex-slave women's future roles swung from seeing them as domesticated mothers in male-headed, "moral" families, to negating their maternal roles altogether and seeing them as laborers in other people's domestic settings. Freedwomen's property accumulation presented a lived alternative to such visions—one that combined motherhood and work, and that also combined partnership with men and earning an income on their own account. Since colonial times, of course, work outside the home necessarily featured significantly in the lives of poor women across Latin America.[8] Yet in "African" cities like Rio and Havana, women's lives in freedom were also shaped significantly by African gendered patterns of work and family. In Rio, *mina* women dominated trading and markets, used this money to buy freedom, and then invested in other *mina* women to help in their labor, subsequently freeing them and bequeathing their property to them in a family-like arrangement.[9] Drawn from the West African practice of "woman-marriage," this strategy prevented their property from being absorbed by the state if they died intestate.[10] Other women who lived with male partners nonetheless also followed West African gender conventions in defining themselves as material providers for their families.[11] In practice, of course, different models for labor and gender roles combined in women's postemancipation lives. The search for property accumulation can be seen as being part of a broader process by which women lent their own meanings to freedom.

At the same Rio emancipation ceremony of March 1886 that freed Gabriella, another *parda* woman, nineteen-year-old Rosa, also gained freedom from her owner, D. Maria Silva Araújo. However, Rosa then became embroiled in a dispute with one Delfino Lerma, "who says he is her legal representative, has her freedom letter in his possession and demands that she pay him . . . 700 *mil-réis* in exchange for expenses he incurred for the achievement of her freedom." Lerma demanded that Rosa give him the wages she was earning as a domestic servant, which she refused to do, informing the police about the dispute. The issue over her wages was inextricably linked to the preservation of her status as a free woman. Paying them to Lerma would mean, in practice, that Rosa had merely exchanged one master for another. Claiming the wages as her own, on the other hand, gave concrete significance to her freedom. Although we do not know the outcome of the dispute, it is significant that she was able and inclined to claim police protection of this newfound "meaning" of freedom.[12] Compare this to the situation of black *patrocinada* Teresa Baez in Regla, who as we saw in Chapter 5, petitioned in 1882 to have her de facto "free" status formalized after her owner's death. According to her claim, "she enjoys complete freedom as . . . nobody has interfered with her since she pays nothing to anyone[;] nor does she receive help from anyone."

The importance Rosa or Teresa attributed to autonomous wealth accumulation was not new. In cities across the slaveholding Americas, enslaved women and their families had long been active in accumulating savings and using them as a route toward freedom. In a sense, property accumulation was a continuation of, and used the same financial and legal tools as the manumission process itself.[13] From the 1870s, the means of achieving freedom through personal savings expanded in both Cuba and Brazil.[14] For women like Rosa, money was not just a route to freedom, but a means of shoring up her new status. Money offered the possibility of freeing other family members, especially children, and of improving her own living standards and the life opportunities of the children she might have. It was also an important way of putting social distance between her slave past and the color of her skin.

The complex and contested meanings of wealth for the making of lives in freedom underpinned a Havana claim by Águeda del Rey, a black freedwoman who sought maintenance payments from Florindo del Rey, father of their three children, in July 1878. Águeda and Florindo, both described as *lucumí*, had baptized their first two children in the small town of Santa María del Rosario, southeast of Havana, in 1873 and 1874 respectively.[15] At this point in their lives, both were recorded as having the surname O'Reilly. By the time their third child, Simona, was born in 1877, the parents had not only both moved to Havana, but had each changed their surname to Del Rey. Águeda and Florindo were not married, so all three children were registered as *hijos naturales* (the children of unmarried parents), but they had been recognized by their father at birth, which helped Águeda in her quest for his economic support. Although she and Florindo appear to have moved to Havana together, by the time she filed to the first-instance judge in her neighborhood for maintenance a couple of years later, they were living separately—perhaps because they were no longer a couple, or perhaps due to one or both living with employers or patrons. In support of her application, Águeda declared that she had neither an income nor assets with which to support the children. Florindo argued that "it is true that they are his children, [but] because the claimant [Águeda] has removed two of them from the house where he had placed them in Guanabacoa, he only pays maintenance . . . for the youngest, who is breast-feeding."

The case thus presents a series of snapshots of a family's social and geographical movement away from slavery. As they sought to fashion meanings out of freedom for themselves and their children, Águeda and Florindo cooperated at some moments but disagreed at others. The two were perhaps former slaves of the O'Reilly family who, on achieving freedom in Santa María, chose to put both the surname and their rural location behind them, striking out for new opportunities in the capital.[16] Despite not cohabiting in Havana, they continued to share a social world, living across the street from one another on Calle Virtudes. Águeda thus knew that Florindo "has won on the Lottery, in the company of others, 7,500 *pesos* and also he earns two *pesos* per day for his labor" and could bring witnesses, presumably people known to both parties, to prove it. Playing the lottery, often in groups along with other enslaved companions of the same ethnic denomination, was one well-known means by which both urban and rural slaves in Cuba sometimes managed to buy their freedom.[17] Florindo and Águeda disagreed about how to bring up the two older children, now aged five and three. Seeking to exert the kind of paternal control over Águeda and the children that was denied to enslaved men, Florindo insisted they remain where he had "placed" them in Guanabacoa, on the other side of the bay, perhaps in the household of a relative or patron. His way of enforcing this decision was to withdraw financial resources when Águeda removed the children. Águeda, on the other hand, perhaps shared the logic of other freed women we have encountered in this book: that freedom, unlike slavery, promised custody of children. Perhaps a clash of gendered cultural expectations was occurring, with Florencio insisting on

Hispanic-derived assumptions of paternal control over the children's destinies, while Águeda was conscious that "Yoruba custom assigned women full responsibility, both inside and outside the household, of caring for the children, the culmination of female honour."[18] Her petition implies she was juggling a complex set of circumstances. On the one hand, in taking the children she had acted independently of Florindo, undermining his claim to authority. On the other, her petition's very success depended on making an argument about her total financial dependence on him. Being paid a monthly allowance would precisely continue this situation: living in urban poverty, separately from Florindo, but with increased chances of bringing them up according to her own beliefs about what was best for them. The issue of income thus encapsulated a struggle over divergent understandings of freedom's significances.[19]

While most women like Águeda lived in poverty, they could nonetheless look to the example of other women of color who had long attained ownership of at least some wealth or assets.[20] This included, for example, real estate. Earlier in the century, women represented the majority among Havana's real-estate owners of color.[21] They continued making very frequent appearances in records on the sale and tax of houses later in the century.[22] Real estate ownership certainly did not equate to wealth and might even become a burden. Mercedes Estévez, a sixty-nine-year-old *carabalí* widow, was refused a tax exemption on her house in 1879, despite her neighbors' testifying to her extreme poverty.[23] Others suffered expensive losses to their houses through fire.[24] Yet ownership of real estate in cities where house prices were rising rapidly constituted one of the best forms of investment and was something freedwomen might at least aspire to.[25]

In Brazil, black freedwoman Eva Joaquina de Oliveira died in 1868 after not only gaining freedom but amassing a considerable fortune. Her partner, Manoel Furtado de Mendonça, with whom she had cohabited for nine years and had three children, but whom she had never married, was left to administer her estate, valued at over 44 *contos*, until their young children reached majority age.[26] Manoel expressed Eva's purpose in accumulating wealth in maternal terms: "increasing her assets for the good of her offspring." By this definition, wealth accumulation provided a route to a particular kind of free motherhood for Eva—active economic provision for her children. Eva's had been a typical mid-nineteenth-century route to wealth in Rio de Janeiro, through real estate and slaveholding. Of the 44 *contos*, 14 represented the value of a small farm (*chácara*) she had purchased on the outskirts of the city, and most of the remainder—29 *contos*—was held in slaves.[27] A long list of expensive furniture, household items, and gold and silver was worth a little over one *conto*.

On her death, Manoel spent over one *conto* on an elaborate set of arrangements for Eva's funeral rites. In a hierarchical society deeply marked by Baroque Catholicism, death, like life, was marked by legal and socioeconomic position. One of the purposes of wealth was to ensure a suitably lavish funeral. Slaves were less likely to die a "good death." The baby son of one of Eva's enslaved women, Laurentino, died around the same time as his owner, yet Manoel recorded no funeral expenses on his behalf.[28] In death, as in life, wealth underscored the distance Eva had traveled from enslavement to freedom.

Wealth like Eva's was beyond the possibilities of most freed women of color, but they did zealously amass smaller items of property and tried to defend them from the constant threat of theft. Just as petition and legal redress had been a tool for gaining freedom, so free women made use of the police and the courts to recover stolen property. And just as in the legal struggle for freedom, their allies were often other women of color who shared their occupations and cramped living-spaces. Early one May morning in Havana 1864, black laundresses Rosario Martínez and Asunción Herrera arrived together at the police station of Guadalupe neighborhood. During the night, they said, someone had stolen the clothes they had hung out to dry on the communal patio of the shared house on Calle Manrique where each rented a room. The clothes belonged to two white men who lived close by, presumably the women's laundry customers. Asunción estimated the clothes stolen from her alone to be worth 48 *pesos*—the equivalent of several months' earnings.[29]

Defending property, like attaining manumission, was a profoundly social business. It drew in a wide spread of neighbors who were intimately familiar with the claimant's life and routines. One morning in May 1881, Rita Folles, an unmarried, sixty-year-old black woman born in New Orleans, who worked as a cook, informed the Havana police that a turkey, a hen, and a rooster had been stolen during the night. Rita had been keeping the birds on the communal rooftop terrace of the subdivided house where she rented a room. Visiting the house on Calle del Conde, inspectors confirmed that "since the terrace is within easy reach of the neighboring houses and by extension with the whole block, it would be easy to take the Turkey, Hen, and Rooster." How could she prove, Rita was asked, that the birds had been up on the roof? Rita answered simply that "all the neighbors of the house" would be able to testify—and indeed they did. The key witnesses were other women of color who lived in other rooms of the building. Adelaida Oviedo, a forty-eight-year-old African-born washerwoman who lived in a room toward the top of the house, had heard a noise up on the roof. Gregoria Urrutia, a twenty-four-year-old black Havana-born washerwoman, "had heard this morning when she woke up that the animals belonging to the *morena* Rita had been stolen but she does not know how it happened". Rumor and gossip helped build up social understandings about property ownership in the same way as they built a picture of an individual's legal status: neighbors living in the houses on either side "knew" about the theft straight away because they had heard Rita telling "all the other neighbors on the block."[30] As the case progressed, it became clear that not only the information about property was shared, but so, in fact, was the property itself. Only when Rita testified for the second time did she mention that in fact, it was only the turkey that belonged to her, while the rooster and hen belonged to Adelaida. Adelaida confirmed this when questioned, but for each woman, the issue of who individually owned the birds appeared less important than the defense of the property against theft.[31]

Just as proximity and shared working environments often led to alliances among women in the defense of property, so these same factors also caused disputes between them. Rio de Janeiro's *Gazeta da Tarde* newspaper ran a semi-humorous column in the 1880s called "Galeria Policial," summarizing the latest crimes and arrests on the city's streets. The same paper that vigorously defended freedom for slaves spent much newsprint poking fun at the tumultuous, rowdy behavior of the free men and women of the *povo* (common people), many of whom can be understood to be nonwhite because of the deliberate play on surnames associated with ex-slaves. Particularly "juicy" material was provided by frequent reports of fights between women over items that seemed trivial to middle-class readers, though important and hard-won for their owners. In August 1886, "Galeria Policial" described how Isabel Maria da Conceição, while walking past *estalagem* number 56 on the Rua Passagem, had spotted a shawl with "beautiful colors." The paper joked: "They told her it belonged to one Maria da Conceição, and this was enough for Isabel to reason that: 'Maria da Conceição . . . that's me too, so the shawl is mine.'"[32]

While such reporting trivialized these disputes, a closer look at struggles over property reveals much about its more complex significances for freed women. One August Sunday in Havana, 1878, Rosenda Valera, a freed *parda* seamstress, moved out of a room she had been renting in an *accesoria* on Calle Aguilar. On leaving, she entrusted two precious bundles of items, later valued at the large sum of 80 to 100 *pesos* in gold, to her neighbor Belén Carvallo, until she could come back for them. Belén, who rented another room in the *accesoria*, was a twenty-year-old *parda* from Santiago de Cuba who "for the last six months has worked at her occupation as a washerwoman in her own home." Like Belén, twenty-eight-year-old Rosenda was also not from Havana, but from Matanzas, reminding us of the background of constant human movement that characterized urban freedpeople's lives. Although Belén and Rosenda had lived in the same building for only six months, this had been enough time to build up the trust necessary for Rosenda to leave the bundles with her neighbor.[33] They contained large amounts of quality clothing, belonging in part to Rosenda's customers. They also included a number of personal items that Rosenda listed from memory, with the loving detail of one to whom each hard-won item held tremendous significance. Perhaps the most important among the possessions was a little box, containing her own letter of freedom and her two children's baptism documents. She had left behind not only the property that freedom had enabled her to accumulate, but the very documents that helped guarantee that freed status.

Yet when she came back for them, Belén told her that another woman had come and asked for them in Rosenda's name, describing their contents in detail, and Belén had given them to her. Here, perhaps, gossip had again played its part, this time allowing an unknown third party to trick her way into acquiring the precious bundles. Although Rosenda reported the incident to the police, she believed Belén's story, maintaining throughout that her friend "deserves the best reputation as an honorable woman and she believes her incapable of keeping something that is not her own." The case was eventually closed without Rosenda's property having been recovered, but even this devastating loss to a freed working mother of two does not seem to have dented her trust in Belén.[34] Property was valuable, but personal loyalties might be even more so. Such complexities, of course, were lost on the readers of Rio's "Galeria Policial." The meanings of property were multiple: in defending it, women defended all sorts of things that were important to them: community, friendship, reputation, autonomy, and a contested set of cultural assumptions about their ability to raise their children as they chose. In so doing, they gave lived definition to free womanhood.

URBAN SPACE

Urban women also needed to defend less tangible things than property. Both Rio and Havana were growing fast, partly as a result of the emancipation process itself, as freed migrants and European immigrants poured in. In Cuba, significant numbers of the free(d) population were dispersed by the experience of war, with women particularly likely to migrate to the capital.[35] In Rio, property prices and the cost of living were rising; the city's slum housing seemed, to elites terrified of the propagation of disease, to grow up overnight, and local authorities carried out demolitions "in a very violent manner," representing "a calamity for the poor classes."[36] Street crime was rife, but policing mainly existed in order to protect the wealthy, often leaving the poor with no choice but to defend themselves as best they could on the streets and in their cramped homes.[37] The meanings of freedom—for both men and women but in different ways—were about defense of their honor, person, and space, as well as their right to their hard-won "corner" of urban life. Women's immediate rivals were often other women.

Thus a fight that broke out between two women in Havana in May 1887, ostensibly about the theft of a dress, escalated into something more akin to a defense of territory. Asunción Castañeda accused Mercedes Romana of having stolen the dress from the shared patio of a subdivided house where Asunción lived. Receiving a tip-off from a neighbor about the culprit's identity, Asunción went out looking for Mercedes down the winding streets of central Havana, surely asking those she knew along the way about whether they had seen her. Accompanied by her lover, Eufemio Roselló, Asunción finally tracked Mercedes down on the Calzada de Belascoaín and confronted her. Mercedes denied the accusation, "insulting [Asunción] terribly." Mercedes, in turn, alleged that Asunción and Eufemio called her "very disgusting" and hit her. Mercedes, a washerwoman who lived in a *solar* on a nearby street, denied stealing the dress, saying she had gone by Asunción's house only to get washing from her customers. In her statement she painted Asunción as an aggressive woman and claimed that since that day, "whenever the declarant goes round there, Asunción tries to hit her." Asunción did not manage to bring her complaint to court: after Mercedes repeatedly failed to appear at court hearings, the case was simply closed. These women's quarrel would be resolved not by the law but by verbal and physical confrontations over territory in Havana's crowded collective living-spaces, streets, and neighborhoods.[38]

One weapon that women were particularly prone to use, and to which they were also uniquely vulnerable, was insult. In Rio, the *Gazeta da Tarde*'s "Galeria Policial" delighted in reporting examples of women who insulted those around them. Maria Luiza da Conceição was locked up for insulting a shop owner on Rua S. Pedro; Maria Meirelles dos Santos was fined 20 *réis* for "obscene words" and insults to a passer-by; Camila Maria da Conceição was arrested after insulting a guard on the Rua do Regente.[39] Such offences added another source of humor—the contrast between the portrayals of rowdy, violent, or drunk women of the *povo* with elite expectations of feminine behavior. In a sense, both the newspaper columnists and the women disputed the performance of femininity on the city's streets and squares. Indeed, racialized descriptions of disorderly women helped create a social imaginary of particular urban areas.[40] One piece described how "Maria Emília da Conceição was arguing yesterday on the Rua da Ajuda in a dreadfully inappropriate manner. What barbarities she spoke, dear God! What language! What a disgrace!" The guard, it reported, had her locked up "in order to uphold certain conveniences for public morality."[41] The paper reserved even more explicit condemnation for Maria Umbelina da Conceição, remarking of her "disorderly" behavior that "she is a leopard [*onça*], not a woman."[42]

Some women, of course, could get away with being more "unfeminine" than others. In April 1884, a fight broke out between two women on San Rafael, a central shopping street in Havana frequented by well-to-do customers. Doña María de los Ángeles Pinto Santana, a white Canary Islander washerwoman, alleged that a black woman, Agustina Briones, had insulted her and bitten her on the arm. Agustina denied the charge, but Doña María brought a witness—a male, white one, at that—while Agustina had none. In addition, the judge applied a provision of the Spanish penal code stipulating that it should be considered "an aggravating circumstance when the deed is committed against a white by a nonwhite."[43] Agustina was given eleven days in jail as well as made to pay court costs.[44]

Compare this with a much more vicious brawl between two Canary Islander women, which was nonetheless dealt with more leniently by authorities. The fight broke out in a subdivided house in Casablanca (across the bay from Havana) in April 1876. Tension had been mounting for weeks between Dolores Pérez and Felicia González over the space allocated to animals on the patio of the house. Once more, the collective spaces of these cramped dwellings provided the spark to the flames. The women's arguments, which their husbands had tried unsuccessfully to put an end to, were voiced in the vocabulary of honor and defamation. Dolores told Felicia "frequently and daily" . . . that she was a "whore," and "that she had been [a whore] in the Canaries and she was still one on this Island." The two women came to blows one day while their husbands were out working on the docks. Several witnesses saw them rolling around on the floor, biting, kicking, punching each other, and exchanging obscene insults. They were separated only when an enslaved man and his free black friend, who happened to be passing by, stopped to intervene. In court, however, each woman received only fines and proportions of the court costs.[45]

Such cases depict the daily task, for the women of the urban poor, of defending not just property and territory but honor and femininity. When their disagreements reached the courtrooms or the newspaper columns, they were interpreted by—but they also contributed to—racialized elite expectations about "feminine" behavior. Back out on the streets, they marked out the meanings of their womanhood in opposition to other women around them, using their voices, fists, and teeth.

WOMEN WHO OWNED WOMEN

Urban slaves' relationships with owners were generally much closer than those of plantation slaves with their distant or absent masters. Closeness might lead to greater conflict as well as to greater possibilities for negotiation. It might work either to enhance or to restrict the enslaved person's chances of manumission. What it undoubtedly did was to provide an example of routes toward freedom and of the concrete possibilities offered by life in freedom, especially when the owner was—like many urban slaveholders—of the middling or poor sort, or even a former slave.

In these slave societies, of course, for women as well as for men, one of the "meanings of freedom" had long been access to property in slaveholding. Large numbers of urban slaveholders in both Havana and Rio were women. Slaveholding did not necessarily imply affluence.[46] Women slaveholders were often poor, single, or widowed, struggling with economic and social marginality, dependent on the rent of a single slave for their income.[47] They used slave women to work alongside them in their low-paid "women's" occupations.[48] Not infrequently, they themselves were former slaves.[49] Such women offered an image of life in freedom to which enslaved women might aspire.

The close relationships between slaves and owners could foster cooperation between them. In Rio, one woman entered her "slave," Sabina, for freedom at the emancipation ceremony of 7 September 1887, only for the municipal council to discover later that Sabina was *already* free at the time. Sabina could hardly have been unaware of what was happening; she must have submitted to a medical examination in order to obtain her "freedom" and sat through a liberation ceremony to receive her letter from Princess Isabel. While she may have been duped or coerced in some way by her mistress, it seems unlikely given the information that Rio's enslaved women had access to about the ceremonies and their willingness to turn to the law or the police to uphold the freedom they gained at these events. It is more plausible that Sabina and her former mistress had worked out an arrangement by which both might benefit from the compensation money. This would mean Sabina's "emancipation" was neither—as successive historiographical traditions would have it—generously granted nor heroically won, but rather the result of a moment of collusion between former slave and former owner, each woman acting in her own interest.[50]

Much of the high demand for the labor of enslaved and free women came from women themselves, who purchased female slaves to help them in their work. Doña Paula and Don Santiago Chenevar, who ran a Havana laundry business, purchased seventeen young women and girls from various parts of the island to work as washerwomen in 1875–76.[51] Enriqueta, a Matanzas-born seamstress, started work at a tailor's shop, "La Moda," in Havana in 1878. She had been first bought and sold, along with her four-year-old daughter, by various women in Havana, both white and of color. "La Moda," situated on the fashionable Calle Obispo, was run by Doña Carmen Bujia de Sar, whose husband bought Enriqueta to work as "a seamstress alongside her mistress."[52] The closeness of such working relationships surely provided women like Enriqueta with a notion of how life might be in freedom.

Most women owners—especially those who were themselves freed slaves—could expect to remain poor, dependent on the labor of one or two slaves. Yet others, like Eva Joaquina de Oliveira in Rio, whom we met in the preceding pages, did achieve significant wealth. The way Manoel told it, Eva had built up her fortune directly upon the business of slaveholding. She had come to their partnership nine years earlier, he said, as the owner of three women slaves; during their time together, he "paid the expenses of the household" they shared on the Rua da Conceição, while Eva "was able, through her labor and that of her women slaves, which consisted of *aluguéis* [rental fees for day labor by slaves], sewing and washing and ironing clothes," to increase her wealth. By the time she died, she owned no fewer than twenty-nine slaves. Among the twenty-three adults, all but one were women, mainly *pretas* (both younger Brazilians and older West and Central Africans), with some *pardas*.[53] Six of the *preta* women had *pardo* children, also belonging to Eva.

Eva's enslaved women had clear ideas about how to go about gaining their own manumission. Their actions, sparked perhaps by Eva's death and certainly aided by the broader economic and social sea-changes following 1871, contributed to the slow but sure decline of the estate. In

January 1870, a year after Eva's death, her Brazilian-born slave Victorina offered Manoel 500 *mil-réis* for her baby daughter Alexandrina to be baptized officially as free. Simultaneously, her companion Zeferina made the same request for her two-year-old daughter, Galdina. Manoel agreed to both. He justified his decisions using the vocabulary of maternity. Victorina, he said, was "dominated by the impulses of maternal love," while Zeferina had nursed Manoel and Eva's own daughter Elvira after Eva's sudden death, "exercising the important functions of a mother with praiseworthy zeal."

Manoel had a practical motive, too, however. He stated repeatedly, in his lengthy explanations of his economic decisions made on behalf of the heirs, his perception of the profound economic changes occurring in Brazil. In the past, "based on the principle . . . which was generally followed, especially by those who possess only small amounts of capital, that they will gain very little profit . . . from shares," he and Eva had "consolidated our income through daily wages from our slaves." However, after Eva's death, "the day rates decreased, the slave women who had paid 40 *mil-réis* began to pay 30; those who had paid 30 began to pay 25." And the total income became insufficient to support a large family—which of course included feeding and clothing all the slaves themselves, not to mention expensive medical treatments when they became sick, as they often did. As the debates about the Rio Branco Law raged in March 1871, Manoel announced his decision to try to sell various of the slaves and employ the capital in shares, citing "the delicate circumstances in which the country finds itself, due to the preoccupations over the servile element which have depreciated the value of slaves so much, and which have turned upside down the spirits of . . . those who have invested their fortunes in this sector."

Meanwhile, Eva's slave women continued to seek routes out of enslavement for themselves and their children. Before 1871, Manoel had had the option of refusing self-purchase requests; after the law passed, self-purchase became a legal right for slaves who could provide their agreed price. Four of the women claimed this right in 1872 alone. They included Victorina, who only a year previously had secured the freedom of her baby. Others pursued different avenues toward freedom. In 1871, almost two hundred freedom suits were initiated in the space of a few months as a result of Tavares Bastos's campaign against slave prostitution. It turned out that much of Eva's fortune was probably amassed through prostituting her young, female purchases. The appeals court generally overruled the first-instance courts' decisions and returned the women to slavery, and indeed none of Eva's former slaves ultimately gained freedom in this way. Nonetheless, at least three of them filed suits, or had them filed on their behalf. This represented a major expense for Manoel, who blustered in December 1872: "As for the three women slaves whom the philanthropists wish to free *gratis* at someone else's cost, I hope that they will very soon return to the control of the heirs [the three children], whence they were removed by speculators, who have for around eighteen months been using their services, making the Supplicant spend almost two *contos de réis* on these scandalous legal suits."

By April 1885, only five slaves remained of the original twenty-nine. At least one, Theodora, gained freedom through the Livro de Ouro slave emancipation fund, receiving a letter of freedom from the hands of Princess Isabel in July 1885. Although it was Manoel that wrote letters to the council seeking this manumission, we can assume that, like other women freed through this fund, Theodora knew about it and sought manumission through it, perhaps contributing her own savings in addition to the 300 *mil-réis* that the council paid to Manoel.[54] Upon reaching majority age, Eva's son Balbino would claim that Manoel had mismanaged his mother's property. Although this may have been true, perhaps more significant was the experience of 1871, with its heady mix of economic and social change. Adding to this mix was the very clear agenda for freedom shared by Eva's enslaved women. Undoubtedly, like so many other urban enslaved people, they drew on collective knowledge about routes toward manumission before 1871 and about changes to the law after it. They were surely also influenced by the very example of their former mistress. They had watched Eva, herself a freed slave, as she purchased them and grew rich from their labor, "increasing her assets for the good of her offspring." Upon her death, they embarked on the same path, although the world in which they would attain freedom was no longer one in which slaveholding was available as a route towards wealth-creation and social distance from their own enslaved past.[55]

THE BODILY MEANINGS OF FREEDOM

In the Cuban city of Matanzas on 15 December 1868, enslaved woman Tomasa Oña dictated an official petition to one Manuel Portillo, "assistant at the store . . . since the declarant does not know how to write," and he wrote it "according to the instructions she gave him." The petition recounted a horrifying tale that her free six-year-old daughter, Candelaria, had apparently just told her. Some eight days previously, Candelaria had been raped by an adult man, Don Higinio, who worked at a neighboring house and collected water every day from the Oña household, where Candelaria had been at the time.[56] The little girl, doctors later confirmed, was severely injured and suffering from hemorrhaging. After explaining what had allegedly happened, Tomasa's statement summarized why she was justified in bringing a case, declaring that Candelaria "is free and she herself alleges that the aforementioned Señor grabbed her and had relations with her[57] and it seems that she is not yet old enough for this suffering [and] that this Señor has hurt her very badly . . . and so I hope that you will see fit to resolve the matter in the most just way . . . , God keep Your Excellency for many years, her mother, Tomasa Oña."

It is rare to find formal records of complaints by enslaved women about rape—not because they did not suffer it, but precisely because they had extremely little recourse against it.[58] Tomasa's case thus offers a precious indication of how enslaved women might have thought about what freedom promised in bodily terms. Justifying why the case should be investigated, Tomasa listed her daughter's age and Candelaria's own testimony. Her first consideration, though, was that "she is free." Candelaria, Tomasa would later explain, had been baptized as a free person in the local church. She was an *hija natural* with no stated father, but she had godparents—Agustín Congo and Rosa Fernández. Although we do not know how Candelaria's freedom was attained, the interest she and so many enslaved women took in their children's manumission, recounting the details by heart when asked, implies that Tomasa herself might have helped name these people and ensure Candelaria was baptized as a free person. While Tomasa remained enslaved herself, she was well aware that Candelaria had a different status from her own, and this status shaped Tomasa's expectations about the limits of legitimate access to her daughter's body. Uncomfortably, the implied counterpoint to her arguments about Candelaria—that she was free, and a child, and therefore off limits—was Tomasa herself. As an adult, and a slave, by this same logic she could expect little or no redress against men who forced her into sex.

Tomasa's view that freedom promised her daughter protection from unwanted sexual encounters was not shared, however, by those who determined the outcome of her suit. Although the case did reach the Audiencia (High Court) in Havana, serious measures were not taken to bring Higinio to justice. He ignored the summons to appear in court and disappeared, and there was apparently little official effort to find him. Three years later, the case was officially closed. In a society that did not protect most non-elite women from rape, Candelaria's legally free status was not enough in itself to change the outcome of the case. Yet the fact that Tomasa made it at all implies that women like her did see freedom as something that ought to increase their rights over their own bodies.[59] It provides a tiny glimpse into what Elsa Barkley Brown, writing on black women's experience in the postemancipation United States, called a "collective memory of sexual harassment," remembered by women "not as a singular experience but as part of a collective and common history."[60]

As previous chapters have shown, the abolition process saw (ex-)slave women's bodies become the focus of public scrutiny, whether in legal discourse about the womb and its "fruits," abolitionist images of the abuse of enslaved women's bodies, or "scientific" attempts to regulate wet-nursing and prostitution. When women chose, or were obliged, to open the intimacies of their lives to elite eyes via court cases or police investigations, their own complex understandings of bodily freedom had to be packaged within the very restrictive discursive spaces of elite understandings about women's bodies. On the one hand, women or their representatives might draw on the kind of rhetoric employed in abolitionist campaigning, representing slavery as subjection to violence and freedom as an end to that violence. Meanwhile, however, "scientific" knowledge tended to assume that all nonwhite, nonelite women—whether enslaved or free—were likely to be "dishonorable." Women who sought greater bodily autonomy through official channels hence charted a precarious course between different elite preconceptions, which rarely arrived at the outcome the woman was seeking. The documents generated in the process, however, provide us with clues about women's understandings of the bodily meanings of freedom.

Freedom allowed women at least to resort to the law as a possible tool for shaping the terms of sexual encounters. In September 1885, in Rio, the *Gazeta da Tarde* indignantly reported that a twelve-year-old girl had been raped[61] using "physical force, brutally and barbarically employed by the cruel despoiler of a garland which decorated the head of a twelve-year-old child." The child had allegedly been raped by a man who lived in the same house as her, on the Rua dos Arcos.[62] In a society where female honor served to shore up male power, one might expect that the girls' father had made the complaint. However, it was the child's stepmother, one Maria Carolina, who took her to the police. The proactive role this suggests for women—mothers, stepmothers, neighbors—in the "defense of honor" of deflowered or raped girls is borne out by studies of both *belle époque* Rio and nineteenth-century Cuba. Girls often lived with mothers rather than with both parents, and even when fathers featured in such cases, they tended to play a supporting role to women's active engagement in them. The women who brought such suits did not consider virginity, or "honor," irrelevant concepts, but they did have very different understandings of the relevance of these terms for their own lives from those of the elite jurists who would ultimately decide the outcome.[63]

More common than cases involving children were complaints of the abduction or deflowering of teenage daughters. Such complaints, usually made by mothers, frequently turned out to be more about a power struggle between mother and daughter over the girl's sexuality than between the young woman and her partner. In Havana, in May 1884, black nineteen-year-old Genara Carricarte spent a night away from the house where she lived with her mother, Carlota. Carlota assumed Genara had spent the night with her lover, Manuel Hernández y Herrera, described variously as a *moreno achinado* or *pardo achinado* (Chinese-looking). Although Carlota knew all about her daughter's relationship with Manuel, which "she does not oppose in any way," she objected to Genara spending a night away from the house. She took her complaint to the local inspector, accusing Manuel of *seducción*. Genara's father, black laborer Marcelino Carricarte, played only a supporting role, in part because he and Carlota, although married, did not live together. Thus, he could declare only that his wife had come to his house the previous day to tell him their daughter had run away, and that he knew nothing further. Instead, Carlota called on a neighbor or friend, "the *morena* Rita," as witness to her daughter's disobedience.

Upon being questioned, Genara and Manuel demonstrated very different interpretations of the meaning of sex for their relationship. Genara said she had left her mother's house that evening because her mother, despite consenting to her relationship of two years, had caused her daughter "displeasures" by refusing to allow Manuel into her house. Manuel, she said, had promised marriage to Genara and to her parents, and had not spent the night with her. Rather, seeing that Genara refused to return home, "he took her to an *accesoria* . . . where his mother, the *morena* Ana Herrera, lives, and left her there" until the following morning. Reflecting the intimate sharing of crowded living-spaces, fifty-one-year-old Ana Herrera and thirty-three-year-old Timotea Zalazar, both washerwomen, said they had both been sleeping at Timotea's house—probably her room in the subdivided *accesoria*—when Manuel appeared with a "morenita" they did not recognize and asked whether she could spend the night, to which they agreed. Genara hence had witnesses to back her statement that Manuel had not "enjoyed her virginity that night." Until here, then, the case ran along typical lines of deflowerment accusations that would have been familiar to nineteenth-century elite jurists.

However, subsequent statements from the young couple then complicated the picture. Manuel agreed that he had made a promise of marriage "which he would keep when the time came," and confirmed he had not "enjoyed her virginity" that night. Yet he then added that "he had in fact done so at her house, that is, Genara's house; and that he had lived there and been supported by her parents for around two months, although her parents did not know about this [their sexual relations]." Genara subsequently confirmed this, and Manuel even added later that "as Genara herself has told him, she is pregnant."

Unsurprisingly, the result of these revelations was that the judge did not accept the charge of *seducción*, since these "carnal acts" showed that Genara "was not of an honest state" in the first place. In fact, all the people in the case had apparently very different understandings of what was permissible sexual behavior for this young woman. Her mother apparently allowed Manuel to stay at her house since there had been a promise of marriage, and it was only when Genara rebelliously left home that Carlota made her accusation. She was more concerned, perhaps, to ensure control over her young daughter than to enforce strictly virginity-related notions of honor. Manuel made seemingly strategic use of elite notions of virginal honor, mentioning "carnal relations" to discredit Genara in the judge's eyes and make him drop her mother's case. Genara's attitude was different again. Spending a night together was a strategy often employed by young couples to force unwilling parents to accept a marriage or partnership, yet she denied this had been the case, attributing her night's absence purely to the "displeasure" with her mother. At the same time, she admitted "carnal acts" had occurred on many other occasions, which she apparently felt— given the marriage promise and Manuel's custom of staying at her mother's house—could be engaged in without shame. Genara thus challenged both her mother's and the judge's ability to interfere with her choice of partner or decisions about her sexuality.[64]

Sixteen-year-old recently freed *parda* Genoveva Gálvez perhaps took her cues from young free women like Genara when, a few months later in September 1884, she left her mother's house in Alquízar, a small town to the southwest of Havana, and went to the capital. It was again her mother, Josefa, who took action over her disappearance. Josefa, thirty-four, stated that "an individual who said his name was Don Enrique Marcelino de las Traviesas" had come to her house, saying he had a letter from one Don

Serafín Ramos that requested Genoveva to come to Havana. This was supposedly in order to receive the freedom document (*cédula de libre*) which Josefa herself had opened a suit for recently, on her daughter's behalf, at the provincial *junta* in Havana. Josefa let Genoveva go, accompanied by a family friend, *morena* Evarista Hava. Yet three days later, Evarista came back saying that "Genoveva had refused to return to her mother, staying with Traviesas at the inn at Cuatro Caminos." Josefa added pointedly that "her daughter Genoveva had been a virgin [*doncella*]." Not only this, but Josefa then learned that her daughter was at a *casa de citas* (brothel) on Teniente Rey Street, owned by one Doña Ramona Marty. Josefa thus resolved to go to nearby Havana herself. Perhaps using the quick train service between Alquízar and the capital city, she arrived on 25 October and went straight to Marty's house. She was accompanied by a *moreno*, Julián, possibly her partner or even Genoveva's father.

Josefa said that Ramona Marty, the brothel-owner, refused to let her see her daughter. Marty said Genoveva was "working as a prostitute" and that Josefa "had no right of any kind to take [Genoveva] away from that place: that she was now a free woman and she had obtained the necessary *cartilla de meretriz* and also she had a man who paid her a maintenance of two *pesos* per day: to which the declarant replied that she was her mother and she wanted to take her in order to keep her with her."[65] Marty told Josefa she had better go and complain to the local judicial authorities, which she promptly did; but the judge said he would do nothing, because "[Genoveva] had got herself into something that it would now be difficult to get her out of."

Genoveva's version was different, and even more complex. She said that "she did not want to be with her mother, the *morena* Josefa Gálvez, firstly because she does not attend to her needs and also because she wanted her to live in concubinage with the aforementioned Don Serafín Ramos, which she does not wish to do." She alleged it was Ramos who had taken her off to Havana, and that he had subsequently abandoned her on the street. She went to live with Evarista's sister for a few days, and meanwhile she met Don Marcelino, with whom she had had "amorous relations" for some time. She went willingly with him to the inn at Cuatro Caminos and, a few days later, to live with Ramona Marty. Marcelino explained this was because it was too expensive for them to live together, while at D. Ramona's house Genoveva could live very cheaply. Genoveva denied that she was engaged in prostitution, because of the maintenance Marcelino paid her, "so that the declarant would not need to engage in carnal acts with any man" other than him. Nonetheless, she confirmed that she had got herself a *cartilla de meretriz*. Contradicting her mother, Genoveva added that she had not, in fact, been a virgin when she came to Havana, but had been deflowered the previous year by one Don Mariano Llorente and lived in his house.

As in the case of Genara, the conclusion was simple only from the judge's perspective: the charge, this time of the corruption of a minor, had not been proven, since Genoveva "was not of an honest state" in the first place. Gazing from the heights of juridical authority, he was certainly not interested in the different perspectives on the relationship between legal freedom and sexuality of the three women involved. Having apparently played an active role in securing Genoveva's freedom, Josefa now aimed at controlling her daughter's choices of partner, perhaps seeing Ramos as a good strategic option for her daughter or for the family. To this end, she used the tools the law provided—claims related to honor and virginity—although this does not seem to have been her primary concern. Genoveva countered with an assertion of independence over her sexuality and her choice of partner, residence, and lifestyle. Being able to choose Marcelino in a brothel over "concubinage" with Serafín was more important than preserving any public image of herself as a virgin. Unproblematically accepting her close connections to the world of prostitution in Havana, she nonetheless clarified that she herself was not engaging in it. Genoveva, then, sought to make good on her newfound free status by reclaiming the enjoyment and uses of her body for herself, against not only the formal eyes of the law but also against Ramos and her mother.

Meanwhile, for Doña Ramona Marty, in whose house Genoveva was now living, the fact that "she was now a free woman" signified the right to sell her own body, earning her living through prostitution.[66] Indeed, Havana's prostitutes were used to defending their position as "public women." A daring, if short-lived, publication called *La Cebolla* (*The Onion*), produced by prostitutes, circulated in the capital during the 1880s, declaring: "The horizontals of this capital pay higher contributions to the State than those which are required to vote and to run for office. And despite this, although we contribute to the Treasury with the sweat of our brows, we are treated as if we were slaves, and as if we were outside the law."[67] The analogy with slavery, made in that institution's dying days, was significant.

The abolition process helped make enslaved and freed women's bodies in general as well as prostitution in particular a major topic of public debate in both Havana and Rio.[68] María del Carmen Barcia has noted that the numbers of Cuban women among Havana's prostitutes grew by the 1880s, thanks to dislocation and poverty caused by war and economic crisis.[69] Migration to the capital as a result of the emancipation process surely played a part. For young women like Genoveva—herself recently freed and newly arrived in the city—Marty's perspective is worth taking seriously: while prostitution might lead to newfound forms of exploitation, it might also offer a means of securing a new way of life and increased earnings.

The multiple "meanings" of slave women's bodies found expression in the drive against prostitution that occurred in Rio de Janeiro in 1871. One of the women caught up in the events was Efigênia, whose owners were the heirs of the late Eva Joaquina de Oliveira, whose story has unfolded throughout this chapter. Efigênia's *curador*, Carlos Honório de Figueiredo, said Efigênia had been bought by the late Eva at age fourteen and put, along with other women Eva owned, "to prostitution in an open house" on the notorious red-light street, the Rua da Conceição.[70] He alleged the considerable "profit from this repugnant commerce" all went to Eva and her young children, as well as to Manoel Furtado de Mendonça, with whom he noted that Eva had lived "in concubinage," attempting thus to discredit Eva morally.[71] Efigênia and the other women had been forced into prostitution by one Maria de São Pedro, herself a former slave whom Eva had bought and later freed. Although Efigênia had become infected with syphilis, her owners refused her medical care.

Naturally, Manoel and his lawyers countered that Eva had never prostituted her slaves. In his version, if Efigênia had been prostituted, it was all the fault of her *depositário*, who, in league with the *curador*, had been exploiting Efigênia's labor for over a year while the case was being heard—a loss of income which Manoel bitterly resented, as we have seen. He declared: "If she became vice-ridden and her health was ruined, it was . . . because she was walking the streets selling *quitanda*,[72] during which activity, which was for the profit of the *depositário*, she acquired venereal diseases." Eva, on the other hand, "whenever she heard about any . . . lax morals she had the delinquent taken to the Casa de Correção."[73]

Women like Efigênia were thus in an almost impossible position when it came to actually attaining freedom through the claim of prostitution.[74] Her *curador* wrote, with a zeal reminiscent of abolitionist tracts, that as this "indignant commerce" was "prohibited and repudiated by all laws— both Brazilian and those of the civilized nations—it is not permitted for *anyone* to force their slave into dishonorable acts; and only because of an abominable and monstrous abuse of the power of dominion was the Claimant obliged to destroy her body through the most wanton and scandalous prostitution."[75] Yet the preoccupation on all sides was less about the welfare of women like Efigênia than it was about "hygienic" concerns: cleansing both moral corruption and the physical threat of venereal disease from the vice-ridden streets of Rio de Janeiro.

But what really undermined Efigênia's case, like so many other suits of prostituted women, was the underlying assumption that an enslaved, black woman was likely to have engaged in prostitution *of her own volition*. Manoel did not quite accuse the *depositário* of forcing her into prostitution. Rather, he simply implied that he had been lax in controlling Efigênia, allowing her out on the street and receiving money from her in his own self-interest. The counterpoint was Eva's supposedly tight moral rein over her women slaves, sending them for physical punishment at the Casa de Correção at any sign of "loose" behavior. The implication was that the moral looseness was essentially Efigênia's. By this logic, victim became perpetrator: far from forcing her into selling her body, her owner's role was to restrain her from doing so. Pronouncing his sentence, Judge Joaquim Francisco de Faria concluded that although it had been proved that she engaged in prostitution, none of the prosecution witnesses "affirms positively that the defendants forced her into a life of prostitution." This was despite six witnesses testifying to having seen "Efigênia and others practicing prostitution with the consent of their mistress"; seeing Efigênia "many times at the window[76] with . . . Maria de São Pedro in order to attract customers for libidinous acts"; and declaring that Maria de São Pedro forced Efigênia "with blows"; another witness "knew" that Efigênia's mistress consented to her being prostituted because Maria de São Pedro had said so.[77] In the end, although proving Efigênia's "corruption" was simple, the logic that such women were *naturally* corrupt was virtually watertight. One lawyer, defending an owner against another 1872 charge of prostituting an enslaved woman, retorted: "If the claimant, . . . on her own initiative, gave herself up to prostitution, what fault can be found with the defendant for the nymphomania that the claimant suffers from? The common people generally engage in prostitution inside and outside their owners' houses; who can prevent it?"[78] In Efigênia's case, both sentences ruled for enslavement, not freedom. Twelve years later, in 1884, when fifteen of her former enslaved companions had now bought themselves and their children out or otherwise attained manumission, Efigênia remained one of the five slaves still owned by Eva's heirs.[79]

The difficulties of disentangling Efigênia's own views about the uses and abuses of her enslaved body from this web of male, literate opinion are tremendous. Efigênia "spoke" only through her *curador*, who constructed arguments in her defense using his own legal and social cosmology, a world away from Efigênia's violent life in Rio de Janeiro's red-light district. Yet the case does provide some clues about the images of freedom that Efigênia might have fashioned from such a life. The fact that several of the women allegedly prostituted by Eva and Manoel were all litigating simultaneously reminds us of the collective context of freedom claims. Although the cases were initiated by others on their behalf, these women surely shared information about the law and their expectations about the outcome of their suits.

The trajectories of the women who held power over Efigênia also provide some clues about how the experience of prostitution might have shaped her *definitions* of freedom. Former slave Eva de Oliveira had built up wealth by purchasing other women and exploiting their labor. Maria de São Pedro, by all accounts, was one of them; she may also have been prostituted by Eva, before attaining manumission and then prostituting others. In some ways, these women acted not just as brutal slaveholders, using violence to force Efigênia into sex with strange men, but also as examples of what a life in freedom might look like. Neither Eva nor Maria de São Pedro had escaped the broader economy of the selling of women's bodies for profit; rather, both had repositioned themselves within that economy, gaining more control over their own bodies along the way. Like in the Cuban case of Genoveva, these gains were more relevant than elites' concerns over prostitution, expressed in the language of honor versus lasciviousness or "hygiene" versus corruption.

Defending property, territory, and bodily integrity, freed women struggled to fashion their own meanings out of freedom. Influenced by other women around them and by their own specific experiences of enslavement, these meanings were far more complex and multifaceted than elites' limited notions about them. As the different visions met and clashed, they helped to define not just freedom but womanhood itself. Notions of womanhood were bound up, more than anything else, with motherhood. As Tomasa put it, although she was a slave, her daughter could expect something different because "she is free." The expectations of freedom that women forged for their children and for themselves as mothers are the subject of the final chapter.

CHAPTER EIGHT

My Mother Was Free-Womb, She Wasn't a Slave

Conceiving Freedom

[My children] are taught nothing more than in olden times
(if you will allow the phrase), like donkeys[,] to work to be useful to their Masters.
—*Ramona Oliva to Gobernador General, Havana, 9 August 1883*

Jeronymo José de Mello, the Rio de Janeiro artisan whom the reader met at the beginning of Chapter 7, had owned at least two other women as well as his *parda* slave Gabriella, who used her newfound freedom to resist removal from the city of Rio de Janeiro. At the same 1886 emancipation ceremony in which Gabriella was freed, he also received compensation from the municipal council in exchange for freeing another young *parda* woman, eighteen-year-old Maria.[1] Urban freedom, for Maria, surely held the kinds of significances it did for Gabriella—the ability to remain in the city; greater autonomy over her working and living conditions; enhanced chances to accumulate property; and bodily and sexual autonomy. Yet for Maria, all of these considerations had an added twist: she was the mother of an *ingênuo* child. Freedom offered her the possibility of avoiding one more of the mother-child separations that had become both an abolition-ist rallying-cry on both sides of the Atlantic and a central concern in so many women's quests for manumission. Once achieved, freedom might also allow Maria more scope to raise her child according to her own defi-nitions of mothering—shaped by African cultural inheritances as well as European ones. This chapter returns to the theme of motherhood, which, more than any other, marked out women's specific relationship with the law and with freedom. What were the links, for women like Maria, between visions of freedom and definitions of motherhood? What visions or expectations about freedom did such women hold for their children? And what would be the impact of those visions upon the changing societies in which the last generation of enslaved women lived?

"THE RIGHT TO BE A MOTHER":
MATERNITY AND THE MEANINGS OF FREEDOM

In October 1885, Rita, an enslaved *parda* woman, made an appeal via her representative, Francisco Pinto da Silva, to Rio de Janeiro's municipal council. The council was busily collecting the names of enslaved people—mainly women—to free at its next emancipation ceremony on 2 December. Rita, said her appeal, had been incarcerated by her owner at the Casa de Detenção, a prison used to punish slaves. However, she was "in an advanced state of pregnancy, that is, in the last stage." Would she be left to give birth in prison? Rita, said the letter, "begs the beneficent protection of the Illustrious Municipal Council, under whose auspicious protection she humbly places herself," and hoped for the "charitable granting" of her request.[2]

Rita's appeal might hit home with councilors who had read the *Gazeta da Tarde* newspaper's biting criticism only a month before of the continuing practice of forcibly taking enslaved mothers' newborn infants away, in order for the mothers to nurse slaveholders' children. Freeing Rita might grant her something that the article said was still being denied to enslaved women despite 1871: "the right to be a mother."[3] Even as such mother-child separations continued to occur, nonetheless the 1870s and 1880s undoubtedly saw increased legal and social currency for this idea of the "right to be a mother" for enslaved and freed women—pushed, of course, by women like Rita as much as by anyone else.

Yet the existence and quality of such a "right" was, as we have seen, deeply contested. Only a year previously, discussing the school for Rio's *ingênuas*, councilor Fernandes Couto had argued that ex-slave parents had nothing to teach their children except their own "imperfect" habits.[4] Indeed, the womb-based transition process was subjecting the very definition of motherhood for ex-slave women to considerable controversy. How did Rita envisage her relationship with her soon-to-be-born child, the "fruit" of her legally "free" womb? How might their relationship change if she gained freedom? While councilors weighing up her petition had very different understandings of mothering from her own, there was also enough overlap between the different notions for the question to be *discussable*.[5] In the syncretic spaces opened up by negotiations about legal freedom, different definitions met and vied. In the process, women sought the chance to reclaim motherhood for themselves.

Josepha Gonçalves de Moraes, whose case we have followed throughout this book, ultimately failed in her attempt to convince judge Oliveira Andrade to give her custody of her daughter Maria. Andrade reasoned she was not suitable to care for Maria because she was "recently freed" and in an unmarried relationship (*amasiada*). Central to his notions of "good" mothering, then, were intertwined notions about sexual honor and proximity to slavery. Almost by definition, it seemed, freed slaves could not be "good" mothers.

Yet while Josepha lost out on legal custody of her daughter, she did achieve a series of smaller, but important, victories. In the process of making her case, she drew upon the testimony of a network of local people—male and female, enslaved and free—who lived and worked close to the Gonçalves de Pinho household. Portuguese businessman Paulo Barboso Graça, Pará-born laborer Manoel Angelo Maria de Moraes, barber João Hespanhol, and Pernambucan freed ironess Raymunda Maria da Conceição all testified that the Gonçalves de Pinho couple had neglected Maria, while Josepha had provided her daughter with food, clothing, and care, as had they themselves. The witnesses could provide this information because they were intimately involved in the lives of mother and daughter. Manoel had, according to the Gonçalves de Pinhos's lawyer, "seduced"—literally and figuratively—several of their women slaves, including possibly Josepha herself, helping them seek freedom. Was it he who had provided Josepha with her second surname? João, meanwhile, had heard tales of the Gonçalves de Pinho couple beating the girl from "a black slave woman" who worked in their household. Raymunda, one of Josepha's former companions in slavery in the same household, had met Maria at her mother's house, and heard her complain of ill-treatment. Various witnesses had seen the ragged, hungry young girl on the streets, buying food in the local taverns.[6]

These statements helped support Josepha's legal case, which was based on the November 1872 regulations to the Rio Branco Law. The regulations stated that, while owners had the right to keep *ingênuos* and use their "services" until they were twenty-two years old, they would forfeit this right if they abused or neglected them.[7] Yet, by rallying local people to speak for her, Josepha was not only bolstering her legal claim; she was also publicly questioning whether the couple were acceptable guardians for her daughter. Many of Josepha's statements were written on her behalf by one Joaquim Monteiro dos Santos, in whose local household she had previously worked and lived while a hired slave. Santos now appeared to be acting as her patron or collaborator, perhaps with his own agenda in mind. He may even have been the lover to whom Oliveira Andrade referred in his statement, although this is not clear from Josepha's case.

Even as Josepha built allies in the neighborhood, her former owners were subjected to an assault on both their public dignity and their private household. In July 1886 they were visited by local judicial officials, who tried to take Maria away for questioning. José Gonçalves de Pinho threw them out and later vigorously protested that he had been "the victim of a violent act committed at his household, which left his whole family in a state of desolation." Although they refused to let Maria leave—and thus were surely able to influence her testimony—he and his wife did allow the officials into the house to question the girl.[8] They won the case, but the whole episode was surely highly embarrassing, significantly undermining their moral claim to a "parental" role over Maria in their neighborhood.

Although Josepha herself was a Brazilian-born *parda*, her understandings about mothering, shared by the enslaved and freed women with whom she worked and socialized, surely grew out of a cultural matrix that was African as well as European. Her argument for her right to custody was based on the claim that she fed and provided for Maria, while her owners neglected her. This would chime better with West African understandings of economic provision for families being a part of mothering than with European middle-class ideals of purely domestic motherhood.[9] At the same time, she engaged in the very Brazilian strategy of seeking the patronage—perhaps through ties of intimacy—of local men who could support her legal case. The neighbors' testimony suggests that many of them were more inclined to agree with Josepha's definitions than with those of the judge. Within the small space of a few densely populated streets of this Rio de Janeiro neighborhood, Josepha's legal struggles helped build a set of contestatory cultural understandings about what mothering, as well as freedom, meant.

The process raised not just the question of what mothering involved, but to whom the term referred. While the word "mother" was used with reference to Josepha alone, her former owners portrayed themselves as acting as "parents" in her daughter's best interests. Meanwhile, a wide set of local people were also involved to some degree in caring for Maria. The idea that caring for children is undertaken by more individuals than just the biological mother, and especially by the women of the extended family, has been noted by scholars of the African Diaspora across time and space.[10] "Family" relations in both Brazil and Cuba extended far beyond blood ties to adoptive kin networks, godparents, and associations like religious brotherhoods. How would the emancipation process affect family relationships?

In the summer of 1884, *patrono* Don Jorge Méndez of Regla, Havana, dealt with two cases involving the custody of children who were legally his *patrocinados*. As we saw earlier in this book, on 10 July, Don Jorge ceded his rights over two young brothers, Gavino and Vicente, in favor of their mother, in compensation for her "good services."[11] Compare this with Don Jorge's attitude only a month previously, when challenged to cede control of Juana, another minor in his custody. Juana's godmother, a freed laundress named Paulina Perdomo, had been born in Santiago de Cuba and officially lived in the city of Matanzas, but she was as mobile as many of the other characters who have peopled the pages of this book, appearing at Havana's Junta Local de Patronato in June 1884.[12] Perhaps encouraged by the struggles of other *patrocinados* living near Juana and Don Jorge on Calle Santuario—some of whom we met in Chapter 5—and now claiming to represent Juana, Paulina accused Don Jorge of not having given the girl the primary education, clothing, and shoes stipulated by the 1880 law.

Don Jorge dismissed Paulina's claims. He was apparently backed up by Juana, who supposedly declared that "what her godmother declares is untrue," that "the only thing her godmother has done was bring her a pair of shoes last week and a suit of clothing," and that she was "happy with her *patrono*." Paulina countered that she had made the claim at Juana's own request, "in view of the fact that [Juana] is completely separated from her mother and she has no other support than the declarant who is her godmother from baptism . . . daring to recommend that this *junta* . . . inquire whether it is true that the *patrocinada* Juana Méndez is, or is not, abandoned and separated from her mother."

Both Paulina and Don Jorge invoked the wishes of Juana's biological mother, a *patrocinada* woman working on a rural property of Don Jorge's in Matanzas, to back up their respective claims to "parenthood" of the girl. Thus, Don Jorge countered "That the mother of the *parda* Juana Méndez is to be found on the *Ingenio* 'Ojo de Agua' in the *jurisdicción* of Matanzas from where the declarant brought the *parda* Juana four or five years ago at her mother's request and in order to educate her in the family and not in order to separate them, which had never been his intention." Paulina, then, was set up as an interloper in this happy "family" arrangement. According to Méndez:

> not once since [Juana] was born had [Paulina] sought after her until about eight or ten days ago she appeared in El Cerro at the house of his daughter Doña Nieves Méndez, where he is having her educated since he does not have a family himself, bearing clothing [and] some sashes which were really inappropriate for a *patrocinada* who should dress very modestly: that in the position he has put her in, because of her mother, he has always seen her more as a daughter than as a slave because she was born into his care.

Like Josepha's former owners in Rio, Méndez painted himself as the best "parental" figure to care for Juana. By calling Paulina's gifts "immodest" he subtly discredited her morality and hence suitability as a mother figure. On both occasions—whether ceding control over Gavino and Vicente or refusing custody to Paulina—he was careful to base his arguments on the rights and wishes of the biological mothers involved.

Had Juana really asked Paulina to intercede on her behalf? Had Paulina come at the request of Juana's mother—her *comadre*, who lived, like her, in Matanzas? Don Jorge signed Juana's statement because—although he was supposedly "educating" her—she "does not know how to sign." We can only guess at the real wishes and circumstances of the absent mother and illiterate daughter. What is clear is that Don Jorge and Paulina both appealed on the grounds of the wishes of Juana's biological mother. In her absence, Don Jorge unquestionably had the upper hand in staking his claim as Juana's "parent," the local *junta* ceding to his wishes without argument. Paulina was only one of many godmothers, grandmothers, and other female relatives who made legal claims on behalf of children in this period, reflecting social understandings among the enslaved and their relatives that mothering was something performed by much wider networks of people—and especially women—than by biological mothers alone. Yet, like Paulina, they were rarely successful if their claims could be portrayed by "affectionate" owners as clashing with those of the biological mothers who were still in owners' control. To the limited degree that it was able to help wrest children away from the owners or former owners of their mothers, transition legislation's preoccupation with wombs meant that it enforced only a limited, *biological* definition of motherhood. It had little to say about the broader *social* definitions that were often a reality for families. As we have seen, this was useful for many enslaved or freed women, helping them to claim the rights of their wombs over the "parental" claims of owners. Yet it was also restrictive, closing off avenues for claims to "motherhood" from the wider circles of people often intimately involved in a child's life. Thus, Juana continued in the custody of Don Jorge, while Gavino and Vicente were handed over to their mother "for her to make the use [of them] that she wishes."[13] But what kind of "use" might she choose to make?

MOTHERS' EXPECTATIONS FOR
FREE WOMB CHILDREN

Long before transition legislation widened their grounds for appeal, enslaved mothers aimed at achieving legal freedom for their children. Freedom was a beginning, not an end: a crucial step in a much broader quest to improve children's life chances more generally. In Rio de Janeiro in 1865, an enslaved *parda* woman, Dorothea, petitioned Emperor Pedro II on behalf of her twelve-year-old *pardo* son, Eustáquio. Dorothea had followed in the footsteps of many enslaved parents by purchasing Eustáquio's freedom at the time of his birth, ensuring he was baptized "as if of a free womb."[14] Eustáquio was born in Campo Grande, a rural parish on the outskirts of the capital. Dorothea perhaps purchased his manumission with the help of one of his wealthy godparents, Albino de Oliveira Santos—owner of a *fazenda* in the neighboring parish of Irajá— and Francisca Mathilde dos Santos.[15] Freeing Eustáquio and naming well-off godparents was only the first step in Dorothea's attempts to secure a good future for her son. Her request of the emperor, in 1865, was that the twelve-year-old should be allowed to enter the Instituto de Menores Artesãos (Young Artisans' Institute) in the capital. The request was granted, allowing Eustáquio an opportunity to learn a trade at which he could then earn a living in the city. In turn, he might help free or support Dorothea in the future.[16]

Ramona Oliva, whose story we have followed throughout this book, similarly saw freedom, custody rights, and the ability to help children to a better future as part and parcel of the same struggle. Her petition accused bluntly: "one need only examine the children, and it will be clear that they are taught nothing more than in olden times (if you will allow the phrase), like donkeys[,] to work to be useful to their Masters." In part, this was simply a legal argument to support her claim to custody over the children who, born after September 1868, were entitled to "primary education" under the 1880 *patronato* law. If she could prove they were not receiving it, the *patrono* was legally obliged to relinquish his control over them. Yet at another level, her statement also suggests Ramona's expectations: that the "olden times" had ended, and that her freeborn children thus might become something more than "donkeys to work to be useful to their masters." Thus Ramona's case was not only about attaining freedom or custody, but about the expectations she held that this freedom should deliver something more for her children than had been available to her own generation.

In his classic study of Brazilian abolition, historian Robert Conrad berated the limitations of the 1871 Rio Branco Law, arguing that:

> the children whose freedom [the Rio Branco Law] guaranteed could not derive much practical benefit from their status until they reached their legal maturity. By then, . . . reared and trained in an environment of slavery, the ingenuos [*sic*] would be slaves by disposition if not by law, ill-equipped and little motivated for much more than a life of labor and servility on the plantations of their mothers' masters.[17]

Writing from a very different time and viewpoint, Cuban lawyer Francisco de Armas y Céspedes nonetheless employed a rather similar logic when he argued in 1866 against a "free womb" law as a means of ending slavery in Cuba. He said it would provoke widespread fraud, "inciting the owner to alter the record of the dates when the slave women give birth, which in many cases would be extremely easy, given the stupidity of the slaves," and that owners would fail to educate the children, so that they would be just as "stupid" as their parents.[18]

In pointing out the very real shortcomings of the law and the state's failure to take more serious measures to educate this generation of children, such statements nonetheless assume enslaved mothers were both ignorant of the law's potential and lacking in even minimal ability to help realize that potential. Ramona's story points us toward a different conclusion: aware, in her own case, of the "ignorance in which I have been raised," she nonetheless hoped freedom might promise something better for her children. Surely, she would pass on to them a consciousness that they were part of the first "free" generation, with different life chances from her own. Italian-born British journalist Antonio Gallenga, writing in 1873 about his visit to Cuba, made the following oft-quoted comment:

> The mere word "liberty," it is true, has already acted as a talisman among the blacks. I have seen the *Cria*, or negro nursery, in many of the estates, and it is touching to see with what pride the slave mother lifts

up in her arms the little naked *pickaninny* who is one day to become a free man. Only a few years ago . . . the negro woman equally shrank from the pains and from the duties of maternity. . . . But all that is changed now, and the nursery is crowded to an extent, and tended with a care never known before.[19]

Gallenga's racist views about enslaved families were shaped partly by his visits to the plantations of infamous Cuban slaveholders Julián de Zulueta and Juan Poey.[20] We do not need to accept his views—or the frequent assertion that enslaved women resisted reproduction *en masse* before the 1870s—to appreciate that mothers, conscious of the implications of legal change, worked to shape their children for a future social role as free people, just as they might in the past have tried to prevent them from future suffering by preparing them for life in slavery.[21] Interviewed in 1987 as part of a project on black family history in rural São Paulo, centenarian Maria Francisca Bueno emphasized that the only enslaved members of her family had been her grandparents, since her mother was of the "free-womb" generation: "When I came into the world, my mother was free-womb, she wasn't a slave."[22] Citing such examples, historians Ana Lugão Rios and Hebe Mattos have shown how 1871 became central to periodization for families descended from slaves, who clearly demarcated divides between "slave" and "free womb" generations.[23] Thus, the womb—simply about the transmission of property rights as far as the law and slaveholders were concerned—held a range of much richer cultural and historical significances for those who lived through the ending of slavery, shaping family histories and individual identities. Claiming the rights of "free-womb" status for their children, enslaved women—the holders of these newly "free" wombs—were at the forefront of building this consciousness of a new generation and a break from the past.

Mothers' awareness of the potential implications of legal change for their children, and their attempts to put those implications into practice, did at least challenge many elites' postemancipation assumptions that free womb children would continue to perform similar work under similar servile conditions as their parents. So argued Brazilian journalist José do Patrocinio in November 1886, responding to a slur from his arch-rival in municipal politics, Conservative councilor José Ferreira Nobre. During a bitterly contested local council election campaign, Nobre allegedly said of Patrocinio that "an individual who has left the breast of slavery will necessarily share the odious character of his progenitors, who were victims of an absolute lack of moral education." Patrocinio, the son of a slave woman, responded angrily: "This insult, which is directed towards the memory of my mother, fortunately cannot harm her. Descendants of the exploited race, she black and I mulatto, we learned through the martyrdom of our flesh, the blood of our blood, that dedication which may be ridiculed in the present, but will be respected in the future!"[24] He refuted roundly the idea that the children of the enslaved were doomed to follow their parents' fate, arguing his own excellent education would make him a faithful public servant. Rejecting the "scientific" claims of the era about slavery's defects being passed from mother to child, Patrocinio instead evoked a generational movement toward freedom and social belonging, shared between his enslaved mother and her free, successful son. Patrocinio's comments remind us, then, that this was an era in which women sought to make good on the promises of freedom by reclaiming custody and mothering rights, but also that, in so doing, they were simultaneously conceiving visions of a new society, in which their children would have a part to play.

CONCEIVING CITIZENSHIP

Mothers shaped their children's future in many senses. The place that such children could claim in the shifting societies into which they were born, and the recognition of this place by those around them, depended to a very large degree upon the circumstances of their birth.[25] For this reason, people born in mysterious circumstances provided a juicy plot for many a nineteenth-century novel. In his 1881 *Romualdo, uno de tantos*, Cuban novelist Francisco Calcagno depicted the harsh life of the book's central character, an enslaved *mulato* man, Romualdo, who labors on an isolated sugar plantation in Puerto Príncipe (present-day Camagüey). His "owner," Don Juan Castaneiro, maintains he was born on the plantation and that his mother was a slave woman, now dead, while his father was a French peddler. Yet Romualdo is assailed by dreamlike memories of his real mother and remembers snatches of songs and prayers, which he recounts to the sympathetic local priest. The novel displays the ability of Romualdo's master, and of the trader who sold him, to invent "truths" about his past through falsification of documentation, yet the old African slaves on the plantation have other stories to tell: "*Ese no son la jijo francé, ése viene langenio chiquitico*" (He is not the son of the Frenchman, he came to the plantation when he was small).[26]

The mystery is solved when the priest goes to Havana and finds Felicia, Romualdo's real mother. The counterpoint to the fraudulent written "truths" about his life is provided by the oral testimonies of the women of his family in Havana, who recite the same songs that Romualdo remembers from childhood and whose memories provide the missing pieces to the mystery. It turns out that Romualdo was born free, to a black laundress, and fathered by a rich young white man—who, through the twists of plot that underpin the novel's moral message, has unknowingly ended up enslaving and brutalizing his own son.

Like so many other nonwhite people, Romualdo's skin color made him vulnerable to illegal enslavement as long as he could be removed from the social and family context that recognized him as free and, crucially, from the mother whose womb dictated his status. Already a historical novel when it was published, the story was set in the dark days of the 1830s, when importing slaves and working them to death was cheaper than investing in reproduction.[27] Yet its themes were informed by abolitionist perspectives developed later in the century, placing the horrors of mother-child separations at the center of the novel's organization, while their moment of reunion is the key to the discovery of Romualdo's real legal status.[28]

Calcagno was a historian as well as a novelist, and *Romualdo*'s themes reflect closely the struggles of enslaved people that sometimes reached the pens of scribes and eventually Cuba's archive collections. Forced to deal with an official, written culture while overwhelmingly illiterate themselves, and often lacking basic documentation to prove their origins, people relied on living witnesses, usually their families and especially their mothers, to "prove" their status, just as they did in other parts of the diaspora.[29]

The case of free Cuban *parda* Clara Linares shows the difficulties of validating freedom for those who did not know their origins. Resident in Santiago de las Vegas (Havana province), Clara petitioned the Gobierno General in 1874. Having freed herself, she was now attempting to bring her four children into full freedom. This effort was, however, in jeopardy. Not only did she not have her baptism certificate, but she also lacked basic information about circumstances of her own birth. The husband of her deceased *señora*, Don Ramon Rojas, had been refusing to give her her baptism certificate for four years, despite her asking for it "day by day and night by night." The document was vital "in order that I may marry and learn whether I was born a slave or free"—a crucial distinction. However, when she asked Rojas, he told her dismissively that "he didn't (even) know if I was a Jew or a Christian." The ex-owner's disregard for her origins, or perhaps deliberate obfuscation of them, and the fact that she could not apparently draw on information about them from her mother or other family members, rendered Clara's "freedom" virtually meaningless: "so I find myself, Excellent Sir, . . . with the letter of freedom in my possession [but] without a document or baptism record with which I could learn my real name or who my parents are or my age."[30]

Luckier in her mother's ability to act on her behalf was the *liberta* Juana Inés Zamora, whose mother Mercedes Zamora "found herself in Madrid" in 1883, having heard that her daughter, born after September 1868, was being badly treated and beaten by her *patronos*. With the help of powerful patrons in Madrid—the foreign minister and the Count of Xiqueña—she was afforded a passage back to Havana. On finding Juana, and "convinced of the pitiable state she was in," Mercedes took her to the Junta Provincial de Patronato in Havana, which had her deposited. Meanwhile Mercedes "presented herself a few days afterwards to his Excellency the Governor General Don Luis Prendergast, with a petition." The well-connected Mercedes made use of her evident knowledge of the law on her daughter's behalf, arguing that, as well as beating her, Juana's *patronos* had not complied with the stipulations of the 1880 Patronato Law about clothing, medicine, and education.

After Mercedes spent months petitioning, the Gobierno General finally prodded the slow Havana *junta* to check whether Juana was really a *liberta* born after September 1868. In fact, the *junta* replied that "there is nothing . . . that confirms the age of the said minor and it is only from her mother's word that I know she is fourteen." Yet despite the lack of any other written evidence, "her mother's word" proved enough for the *junta* and the Gobierno. Both authorities proceeded to treat Juana as a *liberta* covered by the 1880 Patronato law, and by late December 1883, Mercedes was granted custody of her daughter. Juana was lucky to have a mother with the freedom, connections, and knowledge to plead her case convincingly with the right authorities. Despite the absence of other documentation that would prove her age, her illiterate mother's oral testimony was enough to satisfy authorities. Women like Mercedes were thus fundamental to forming both a social and a legal identity for their children, the first fully "free" generation.[31]

Indeed, women had been active in forming their children's "place" long before the 1870s and 1880s. The Brazilian case of Maria Luiza da Conceição suggests a link between individual freedom appeals and much wider questions of national belonging. The case spanned the watershed period of the final abolition of the Atlantic slave traffic. In 1847,

Margarida, who was Brazilian-born and was described at different points as a dark-skinned *parda* and as a *cabra*, appealed for the *manutenção* of her own freedom and that of her eight-year-old *parda* daughter, Safira Luiza da Conceição.[32] Margarida's former owner, Dona Custódia Maria de Jesus, had allegedly granted her conditional freedom in 1832, specifying, like many slaveholders, that she must serve her until Custódia's death. Around seven years later, in 1839, Safira was thus born of a *conditionally* free womb, making this another among the many nineteenth-century Brazilian cases of conditionally freed women giving birth to children whose status would subsequently be disputed. In March 1847, D. Custódia died, and *manutenção* of freedom was granted by a first-instance court in Rio. However, Custódia's granddaughter and her husband then attempted to overturn the ruling and reenslave mother and daughter.

Among the arguments that Margarida's *curador*, Antonio Felipe Nery Carneiro da Cunha, made throughout this long and complex case was that returning Margarida to slavery would be prejudicial to "the Nation, which desires to have more free citizens than slaves like the Supplicant, [who is] *parda*, or *cabra*, born in this Empire, and who may have children and grandchildren who are useful to the faith and to the *Pátria* [homeland], fitted for any occupation, becoming Brazilian citizens . . . when the abolition of the infamous slave traffic is being discussed, as is the emancipation of those currently enslaved."[33] The abolition of the African traffic, a defining moment in Brazil's history, occurred the same year he wrote these lines. His statement linked Margarida's specific fate to the broader destiny of the nation. If they remained free, Brazilian-born Margarida and her daughter, although not described as potential "citizens" themselves, might in future *bear* citizens.[34]

The term "citizenship" was used with great frequency in imperial Brazil, and it lay at the heart of the tension between the state's liberal foundations and its maintenance of slavery. Its changing, complex relationship with notions of race has recently been analyzed in depth. Scholars have combed the 1824 constitution—described by Eduardo Spiller Pena as "our black code written in footnotes" for its attempts to avoid overt mentions of slavery—mined juridical debates, scrutinized the daily workings of the law, and explored military recruitment practices, revealing much about the silent racism that underpinned Brazilian approaches toward citizenship but also about the quest by many men of color to carve out citizenship rights for themselves in the spaces opened by ambiguities.[35] Less attention had been paid to the potential meanings of national belonging for women, excluded from definitions of active citizenship regardless of skin color or birth.

Yet just as men who were far beyond the reach of official active citizenship still claimed inclusion in the broader political or social life of the country, so women from across the racial and status spectrum made similar attempts, despite the additional constraints they faced within a slave-based society that operated according to gender as well as race.[36] The act of formal petition, for example, was employed by women from diverse social and racial groups, often as a substitute for the many activities from which they were barred—engagement in the military, voting, full control of property, and so on. Women's arguments for broader inclusion or contributions to the "nation" were at their strongest when they spoke in the language of motherhood, presenting their claims to be heard and answered by the state as an extension of their private family roles.

While Margarida's case was being decided, for example, free Brazilian women Maria Isabel de Araújo Lírio and Maria Joaquina d'Annunciação Bastos were busy making formal petitions for their husbands' pardon or release from military service. Long before them in 1824, in newly independent Brazil, Anna Luiza de São José had petitioned the emperor for her son's pardon, pleading "the impulsive cause of Maternal love, whose voices of nature sound silently in the Heart of the Supplicant." In 1868, Hermelinda Maria de Campos pleaded with Emperor Pedro II to review her husband's murder conviction. She took care to begin her letter by recognizing that she wrote on Empress Teresa Cristina's birthday, just as freedwoman Maria Rosa would do some years later, linking her own fate with that of the women of the Imperial Family and with the significance of imperial birthdays more broadly for the nation.[37] Again, the common thread binding together petitioner and petitioned, individual and nation, was maternity. Campos was the mother of "five young children, in the greatest misery, and her husband was her only means of support."[38]

In other words, throughout the nineteenth century, free as well as enslaved Brazilian women used formal petition to make limited claims upon the broader sphere of public life. Indeed, Roderick Barman has hypothesized that, given the political importance of family connections and personal patronage, elite women perhaps played a significant role in political life "behind the scenes."[39] Motherhood was women's best defense when they extended their "private" family roles to make a claim on the public political world—indeed, it was even used by a woman who had more claim than any other Brazilian woman to a political life. After signing the "Golden Law" of 13 May 1888, Princess Isabel of Brazil justified her actions as acting head of state on the grounds of her role "as a mother":

> My children, should you later on read this paper, please realize that if your mother acted thus in the great question of abolition, it was out of a conviction that it would be best for the nation, which she had a duty to watch over, to whom she would leave her reputation as a mother and the throne free of any blemish of egotism or of weakness. God aided me, my children, in acting entirely in accord with my conscience.[40]

In colonial Cuba, too, it was not only enslaved women who made use of petition and litigation throughout the nineteenth century to express a sense of belonging to a broader public sphere. For the eighteenth century, Sherry Johnson has explored how military widows' petition campaign for the pension they were entitled to helped shape the key relationship between the military and the Spanish colonial power, while, for the nineteenth century, Sarah Franklin has considered how the "humble" language of petition could be employed by free women in divorce cases.[41] Like in Brazil, women in Cuba actively intervened in male relatives' careers by petitioning for their exemption from service.[42] Through petitioning, women of color played an important role in protesting about the persecution of their families after the 1844 Escalera Conspiracy, as well as in the widespread resistance to a Spanish army draft during the 1850s.[43] In 1862, a military widow and her daughter, from Nueva Gerona on the Isla de Pinos (now Isla de la Juventud), complained stridently about what they felt was unfair treatment by local officials, which had prevented them from purchasing a *mulata* slave girl. Writing directly to the Captain General, then Francisco Serrano, the widow's daughter protested: "the judge [either] does not know how to perform his role, or he wishes to override . . . all the laws and practices of the country," while "The Shoemaker of this town [,] who so poorly carries out the role of Síndico Procurador, has made common cause with the *comandante*[,] and the two . . . formulated the proceedings with the most damaging and culpable intentions . . ." She added witheringly: "Also, this unfortunate island urgently needs better and better-informed Governors, who understand their duties to the people."[44]

Thus, despite their exclusion from attributes of citizenship like voting or military service, the act of petition could take on highly political significance in women's hands. The claims made by the women whose stories this book has sketched had implications far beyond the attainment of a piece of paper pronouncing legal freedom. Engaging authorities at a variety of levels, these women expected to be heard and answered by the mechanisms of the state, whether national in Brazil or colonial in Cuba. Their claims also imply that their ideas about freedom for themselves or their children were far-reaching. For themselves, they wanted custody, increased autonomy in work and family life, access to property accumulation that would put social distance between themselves and slavery, and enhanced control over their own bodies. For their children, they expected something better than what they had had themselves: education, opportunity, inclusion. Surely, where they could, they instilled those expectations in the minds and hearts of their children. Thus, from these women's perspective, the politics of the womb were about much more than rights in property or elites' sterile debates over work, obedience and social control. Instead, their "free" wombs conceived not just new workers or "new citizens," but new social identities, and a new historical moment, remembered by many ex-slave families as marking a watershed from what had gone before, even if many of the hopes for what this new time would bring would soon be dashed.

Women's petitions drew on a venerable European-derived tradition of female petitioning as a means of engaging the state, employed by women of all races and statuses in both Brazil and Cuba, in the absence of other political tools. Yet they perhaps also drew on African-derived political and cultural models which did not recognize, for example, European dichotomies of mothering and nurturing on the one hand versus active engagement in the life of the polity on the other. Indeed, in many West and Central African societies it was precisely motherhood which conferred status and political power and privilege among women.[45] Their expectations were surely also shaped by their political engagement in the communities around them. Women of color played more active roles in Afro-Brazilian or Afro-Cuban associative and cultural life than did women in white society.[46] These experiences surely also influenced their expectations for their own and their children's social roles in freedom. In seeking and defining freedom, they were also helping to conceive citizenship.

Conclusion

Neither Josepha Gonçalves de Moraes nor Ramona Oliva was successful in achieving her immediate aims. In Rio de Janeiro in August 1886, the judge ruled categorically in favor of Josepha's owners. Her ten-year-old daughter, who several witnesses had said was being beaten and starved, remained in their custody. Three years earlier, in Havana, Ramona's quest for custody of her four children ended in stalemate. The petitions to the Gobierno General, which she had traveled weary miles to make, were passed back to her local *junta de patronato* in Bolondrón. The *junta* confirmed what Ramona said: that she had previously made two claims there on the basis that her former owner Manuel Oliva was not giving the children the education to which they were entitled under the 1880 *patronato* law. However, said the *junta*, on "examining" the children, it had been established that they were all receiving this "education"—although, as we have seen, exactly what this comprised was extremely ill-defined, and it is not clear how exactly the *junta* came to its conclusion. Ramona had appealed to the regional *junta* in Matanzas and received the same answer. Yet, said the Bolondrón *junta*, she had not been "expelled," as she had alleged, but had been properly heard, although her claim was refused. This statement, passed back to the regional *junta de patronato* in Matanzas and from there to Havana, was apparently accepted by the Gobierno General, which ordered in September 1883 that Ramona be notified of the outcome. Thus, coming to the law under two different legal systems—Ramona trying to make strategic use of the various channels and geographical strategies offered by the colonial administration in Cuba, and

Josepha approaching the local courts in Rio—each freedwoman nonetheless had the door to custody of her children summarily slammed in her face.

Many of those whose stories we have tried to tell in this book had more success than they did, but the outcomes of these two women's cases serve as an important reminder of the enormous challenges faced by enslaved and freed women as they sought to stamp their own meanings upon life in freedom. It would be misleading to portray them as "heroic" agents, single-handedly winning out against slavery. Nonetheless, the work of following their lives and analyzing their actions helps us map out many of the hidden contours of the gradual abolition process in the countries they inhabited. This book has explored how, in each city, enslaved and freed women were at the front line of daily battles for freedom that collectively helped speed and shape the ending of slavery. In order to explain why, we have had to rethink where their stories start and finish. Attaining legal freedom was not the end, but merely the beginning of a broader struggle to conceive what that freedom meant.

LAW

Women's struggles were bound up with a process of legal change that, beginning with the "free womb" laws of the 1870s, redrew the landscape of legal struggle for the enslaved and their relatives. Women's particular relationship to the law was not new, but very old: indeed, the *partus sequitur ventrem* rule and women's own desire to free their children meant that throughout the history of New World slavery, women had played an active part in negotiating legal freedom. The "free womb" laws—which were themselves partly a product of long-term legal struggles by the enslaved— altered the ancient relationship between women's bodies and the law. Partly for this reason, women apparently made increased numbers of legal claims during the transition period, often on different grounds from those of men. Particularly striking was the quest to apply the law's theoretical provisions to the lived experiences of their "freeborn" children. The resulting legal battles did not affect only their own lives or those of their immediate families. As we saw with Ramona's case, even when individual cases were turned down, they collectively helped shape the development of jurisprudence itself, influencing debates about how the law should be applied or modified. This in turn influenced what kinds of new legal provisions might be introduced.

Neither Josepha's nor Ramona's case was built on legal arguments alone. Instead, the rhetoric employed in many women's petitions appealed to a set of notions about the rights and responsibilities of maternity—and to whom those rights and responsibilities belonged—which were being contested and remade as part of the abolition process itself. Of course, the law was neither written nor practiced in a social vacuum. Legal struggles were only one element in a wider Atlantic discursive crucible that helped forge new gendered rhetoric and grant it social currency. The scribes, lawyers, and judges who wrote and read the claims of the enslaved drew on a gendered repertoire of ways of thinking and writing about slavery and abolition that had grown up gradually, over the nineteenth century and across the Atlantic World. Metaphors and tropes that influenced the early British abolition campaigns and, in turn, those of the United States, were recycled in new, creative ways in the contexts of late-nineteenth-century Brazil and Spanish Cuba. Along with rhetoric about "moral," "charitable," and "impulsive" womanhood, abolitionism mobilized flesh-and-blood women too, involving them in politics in unprecedented ways. Central to depictions of enslaved women's suffering, and to the notion of a shared essence of all women's femininity, was motherhood. It was this discursive framework that gave force and meaning, for example, to Ramona's appeal "as the mother that I am."

Studying the language of such petitions also suggests that these documents were a syncretic space where very different groups' understandings of motherhood, womanhood, and freedom encountered one another. By their nature, such documents resist any simple interpretations, whether as tales of unmitigated slave agency, of "heroic" elite abolitionists, or of the operation of legal change removed from the social and political actors who helped shape and implement it. Rather, they invite us to take the study of abolition in a much-needed new direction, away from increasingly stale debates about structure and agency or top-down and bottom-up. This approach would accept, and then analyze in the depth deserved, the myriad and profoundly intertwined ways in which enslaved agency, abolitionist campaigning, and legal and social shifts combined to help bring about the sea-change that was abolition.[1]

CITIES AND CONNECTIONS

While cases might be filed as individual, slaves' petitions are shot through with references to a collective urban culture of claims-making, which underpinned individuals' relationship with the law. Josepha's case, for example, was deeply influenced by a rich local nexus of connections, as accuser and defendants each mobilized the testimony of a variety of neighbors, while a lively street-by-street emancipation movement touched the lives of other women living nearby. In each city, freed women of color lived in close quarters with one another, shared cramped accommodations, looked after each other's children, and worked in similar jobs. They shared lives, goals, and struggles with their husbands and the fathers of their children, but the particular themes and strategies that emerge from women's claims-making suggest that their hopes and expectations were shaped by watching and talking to other women.

In many senses, then, the stories of Josepha and Ramona have a lot to teach us about connections. They help us identify and unravel the complex ties that bound elite and popular discourses, that connected one part of the Atlantic world with another, or that ensured that the effects of one woman's struggle rippled out to touch the lives of her neighbors. They also remind us of the links between the cities and their rural hinterlands. People's lived experiences involved constant flux and mobility, blurring the lines between "rural" and "urban" slavery. Josepha journeyed to Rio as a slave; yet once in the capital she gained her own freedom and sought custody of her daughter. Ramona traveled to Havana as a freedwoman, following in the footsteps of so many men and women who hoped to obtain justice in the capital city. Female litigants used the claims-making process to wrest control over their own geographical positioning, hoping to unite their children in cities away from plantation work. Although most enslaved people preferred to be in cities, women had particular access to both urban slavery and urban freedom.

Before and after abolition, women who arrived in the cities contributed in important ways to their demographic growth and cultural and economic life. Waves of free(d) northeastern migrants swelled Rio de Janeiro's population, reconstituting Bahian life and customs in the Cidade Nova area, hailed today as the birthplace of samba. The vitality of these communities was made possible by African-descended women like the famous Tia Ciata.[2] Their trajectories would have been familiar to one young *parda*, Emilia Córdoba, who arrived on the streets of Havana in the late 1870s after the Cienfuegos *ingenio* where she had previously lived fell prey to the ravages of the Ten Years' War. When her male companions were taken away to fight, Emilia and other enslaved women "each left for where she could best find work to support herself." In practice, this led—at least in Emilia's case—to a working life on the Calzada de Luyanó in a popular Havana neighborhood, saving money through her earnings and eventually, like several of her female neighbors, making a legal claim for formal free status.[3] Cities molded the social contexts in which women sought freedom, while their journeys profoundly altered those contexts themselves.

The broader political and social process of the gradual ending of slavery looked very different in each city. Major, popular abolition campaigns in Rio contrasted with the muffled dissent that was expressed in censored Havana. The tug-of-war between the Spanish government, laws, and institutions, and the machinations of the island's slaveholders, created a different series of legal avenues for slaves in colonial Cuba than for their counterparts in imperial Brazil. Yet in each case, women found creative ways to negotiate freedom through legal means, making connections with a variety of allies or patrons and exploiting legal avenues of petition-making. Rio de Janeiro and Havana, and their countries' particular experience of gradual emancipation, were in some ways unique. Yet the complex, three-way relationship between urban life, women of color, and access to mechanisms for legal freedom that existed in each had clearly also been shared by other cities of the slaveholding Americas. Increasingly, then, studies of urban slavery and urban freedom appear incomplete without a close analysis of both the gendering of urban slave life and women's roles in opening avenues toward urban freedom.

DEBATING WOMANHOOD, CONCEIVING FREEDOM

Gradual abolition became a space in which very different visions of freedom were debated and contested. One difference can be seen at the level of elite versus ex-slave definitions. This is in some ways a simplistic division, since each contained a broad spectrum of opinion; yet the judge's decision to deny Josepha custody of her daughter reminds us of how stark the differing visions could be and of how high the stakes were. His decision also reminds us of how, because women like Josepha represented the biological and social means through which the first fully "free" generation would be formed, defining freedom implied debating the roles and meanings of womanhood itself. By the last decades of the nineteenth century, the intellectual toolkit of an educated Atlantic World commentator could be expected to include notions of what we would today call scientific racism, often coexisting quite comfortably with the kinds of liberal abolitionist ideas examined in Chapter 4. The social upheaval threatened by abolition fanned fears about biological and moral infection, projected onto the female bodies through which emancipation would occur. Thus, the 1870s and 1880s saw a spate of debates about how to educate the children of women who worked as domestic servants, or how to prevent the transmission of moral and physical threats from wet nurses of color to the children they nursed. Like the liberal abolitionist arguments, the racialized language of moral corruption had potentially powerful results. Josepha's former owners and their lawyers marshaled it forcefully enough to convince the judge that they were better able to raise Maria than was her own mother.

Another range of understandings of freedom operated *among* enslaved and freed people. Women and men lived, suffered, and struggled in slavery together, but enslavement acted on them in often different ways. Thus, freedom also held differing significances for them. Slavery denied all enslaved people the right to choose their sexual partners; but for women this lack of bodily autonomy had specifically painful consequences, leaving them with little recourse against rape and little say in whether and under what circumstances they would bear children. All slaves were subject to separation from children and other family members, but while enslavement negated paternity for legal purposes, its perpetuation through the womb placed enslaved and freed mothers at the center of struggles to make freedom yield custody of children. Any number of their stories contained in this book could be seen as just as much struggles for custody as for freedom. Indeed, the women whose lives hung in the balance probably wasted little time on whether the two concepts were distinct at all; instead, they embraced each as a fundamental part of their broader quest to give lived meaning to their newfound legal status.

Rather than accepting their children's fate as "slaves by disposition if not by law," mothers took the "free womb" promise seriously, expecting more for their children than they had had for themselves.[4] While Josepha failed to convince the judge of her maternal right of custody, her case shows how she mobilized considerable local support for that right, stamping her own definitions of motherhood and freedom upon a neighborhood and, in the process, upon the historical record. After abolition, women's struggle to "conceive freedom" would use the same tools of formal petition and legal redress learned under slavery.[5] The habit of expecting something better, and of pursuing it through official channels, helped them stake a claim within two societies that were beginning, in different ways, to define the roles of former slave men and women within new notions of nationhood.

Epilogue
Conceiving Citizenship

*The patrono, as a master and a rich man, does as he pleases, and . . . thus violates
the articles of the law, which, like every subject resident in the place where it has been
promulgated, he is obliged to obey, or suffer the consequences of his disobedience.*
—*Ramona Oliva to Gobierno General, Havana, 9 August 1883*

With these words, Ramona Oliva's 1883 petition proclaimed a radical
vision of freedom: that the force of the law should apply equally to all,
regardless of status, wealth, sex, or skin color, and that, in the same way, its
protection might be actively sought by all who were entitled to it. Written
in the dying days of a slave regime, and a few years before a new uprising
in Cuba would transform the language of "subjecthood" to that of "citizenship," the words evoke a hope not just of combating slavery through the
law, but of staking a broader claim within national life. Despite the denial
to them of active citizenship rights, formal petition and legal redress had
long allowed women of all classes and colors to make demands of public authorities and polities beyond their own families and acquaintances.
Petitioning bridged the gulf between the public and the private that cir-
cumscribed elite women's worlds, while, for nonelites, it helped span the
yawning chasm between literate culture and the oral worlds of the illiterate majority. As we have seen, in the process claims-making also crossed
(although it could not eliminate) another divide: between the notions
about womanhood held by these different worlds.

In her study of women's antislavery campaigns in the nineteenth-
century United States, historian Susan Zaeske examines petition as a tool

for political change, out of which would emerge much broader women's rights claims.[1] While antislavery mobilization in Brazil and in the Spanish colonial world did not directly produce calls for women's suffrage, nonetheless it did constitute a new form of popular politics, bringing new groups into the public arena to influence an issue of national importance, and these groups included women from different social sectors. Linked to this process, ordinary enslaved and free(d) women's claims-making influenced not only their own destinies but those of their societies more broadly. Defending their rights, space, property, families, and bodily integrity, they sought their "rightful share" in postabolition society.[2] In this sense, they staked a claim to a citizenship that, formally, they would continue to be denied.[3]

Soon after coming across Ramona's petition in the Cuban National Archives, I made a visit to the beautiful colonial town of Trinidad. Visiting the city museum, I was drawn to the part that recounts the history of slavery and abolition. Representing the resistance of the enslaved was an artist's impression of "El Cimarrón" (the maroon), a black-and-white sketch depicting a black man with a bare, rippling torso, a broken shackle on his foot, and a machete in his hand, running through the Cuban countryside pursued by dogs and a man on horseback. Leaving the quiet cool of the museum to walk the bustling streets of the town—named, like so many streets in revolutionary Cuba, after familiar male heroes of the wars of independence like Antonio Maceo and José Martí—I began to wonder where Ramona's story fitted into these narratives about abolition and nation-building.

Not long afterwards, researching a paper on gender and marronage in the Americas, I spent time analyzing public memories of slave resistance in Brazil, most commonly represented by the figure of Zumbi dos Palmares. Zumbi, the leader of Brazil's longest-lived *quilombo*, has monuments dedicated to him in a number of Brazilian cities, while 20 November, the anniversary of Palmares's final destruction, has become a national holiday, symbolizing the achievements of the black movement in celebrating "freedoms won" rather than the "freedoms given" by Princess Isabel on 13 May 1888.[4] Although he has been chosen to represent universal black struggle in Brazil, Zumbi's masculinity is actually a central part of his image, as can be seen from a scandal whipped up by historian and gay rights activist Luis Mott in 1995, during the celebrations marking the four hundredth anniversary of the destruction of Palmares. Partly in an attempt to create awareness about gay rights, Mott published a series of articles in leading national newspapers, suggesting he had uncovered evidence that Zumbi was gay. The lessons of the incident have less to do with the rather flimsy evidence marshaled in support of his arguments than with the importance of gender to the memory of slave resistance. His perceived attack on Zumbi's masculinity was punished with attacks on his home and car and with death threats. Predictably, his attempts to point out that Zumbi's sexuality did not detract from his manliness—since "only really manly guys have the courage to love another man"—only provoked further outrage. For some, Mott's actions were an insulting publicity stunt; for others, they were a clever way of unmasking homophobia in some sectors of the Black Movement. Either way, the incident leaves us in no doubt about the importance of masculinity within narratives of resistance.[5]

How does someone like Josepha fit with the "manly" narratives immortalized by Zumbi? Zumbi wielded a weapon; other "heroic" figures in the antislavery canon in Brazil, such as mulatto *bacharéis* Luiz Gama, José do Patrocinio, or André Rebouças, wielded pens. Like the vast majority of women whose stories this book has tried to tell, Josepha in Rio—like Ramona in Havana—wielded neither, for these were generally tools reserved for men. No statues have been built to them, and they carry relatively little weight even within detailed historical accounts, let alone in the public memories of the nations they helped to construct. Yet their stories are deeply embedded in the very foundations of each of these postabolition societies. Their paths to freedom began with their own lives and those of their families, but along the way they profoundly influenced the course of emancipation, the hopes and destinies of the first fully "free" generation to whom they gave birth, and indeed the very notion of freedom itself. It is time we allow their conceptions of freedom to alter our own understandings of the past and of its lessons for our present.

Notes

ABBREVIATIONS

AGCRJ	Arquivo Geral da Cidade do Rio de Janeiro, Brazil
E:E	Coleção Escravidão: Emancipação
AHMIP	Arquivo Histórico do Museu Imperial, Petrópolis, Brazil
AGP	Arquivo Grão-Pará
CPOB	Coleção Pedro d'Orleans e Bragança
ANB	Arquivo Nacional, Rio de Janeiro, Brazil
CAE	Corte de Apelação, Escravos
ANC	Archivo Nacional de Cuba, Havana
AH	Fondo Audiencia de La Habana
CA	Fondo Consejo de Administración
CB	Fondo Casa de Beneficencia
GG	Fondo Gobierno General
GSC	Fondo Gobierno Superior Civil
ME	Fondo Miscelánea de Expedientes
ROC	Fondo Reales Órdenes y Cédulas
VI	Fondo Valle Iznaga
BNJM	Biblioteca Nacional José Martí, Havana
MMR	Archivo del Museo Municipal de Regla, Havana, Cuba
JLPR	Documentos de la Junta Local de Patronato de Regla
NAL	National Archives, London, UK
FO	Foreign Office Papers

INTRODUCTION

1. "Documentos conteniendo instancia de Ramona Oliva, sobre sus hijos María Fabiana y Agustina," ANC, ME, legajo 3724, expediente T, 1883.

2. "Josepha/José Gonçalves de Pinho," ANB, Juízo de Órphãos, ZM, número 2198, maço 2292, 1884.

3. Throughout this book, Brazil and Cuba are referred to as "countries" for convenience, although Cuba remained a Spanish colonial possession until 1898.

4. For a brief statistical overview, see Chapter 2.

5. See, especially, Chalhoub, *Visões da liberdade*; Mattos de Castro, *Das cores da liberdade*; Scott, *Slave Emancipation*; Scott, "Reclamando la mula de Gregoria Quesada."

6. The need to consider gender when thinking through the "meanings of freedom" has been pointed to by scholars; this book builds on their observations. See, for

example, Mattos de Castro and Rios, "O pós-abolição como problema histórico," 173–74; Scott, "Exploring the Meaning of Freedom," 423.

7. This may be because such activities were indeed mainly pursued by men, and/or may reflect masculinist bias in the sources or their interpretation. For a recent analysis, see Thompson, "Gender and *Marronage* in the Caribbean."

8. Landers, "Maroon Women in Colonial Spanish America," 3. Landers' own piece remains one of relatively few studies of women and marronage.

9. On the problem both of insisting on seeing only "resistance" or "accommodation," as well as the way "resistance" is defined as being only "collective," see Chalhoub, *Visões da liberdade*, 250–52; W. Johnson, "On Agency." On women and "resistance," see, for example, Bush, "Towards Emancipation."

10. Stubbs, "Social and Political Motherhood of Cuba"; Stubbs, "Race, Gender and National Identity." On women's roles in the wars and rebellions, see Prados-Torreira, *Mambisas.*

11. On Isabel's "Redeemer" image before and after her death, see Daibert, *Isabel*. For a recent gendered analysis of her life, see Barman, *Princess Isabel of Brazil*. For the new interpretations of abolition in the 1980s, see, for example, Damasceno and Giacomini, *Caminhada estudiantil pela verdadeira abolição.*

12. On women and abolitionism, see Castilho and Cowling, "Funding Freedom"; Cowling, "Debating Womanhood"; Ferreira et al., *Suaves Amazonas*; Kittleson, "Women and Notions of Womanhood"; Kittleson, "Campaign of All Peace and Charity."

13. For the term "black city" for Rio, see Chalhoub, *Visões da liberdade*, chapter 3. For Havana as an "African city," see Matt D. Childs's forthcoming research project, "An African City in the Americas: The Transatlantic Slave Trade and Havana, Cuba, 1762–1867."

14. The literature on women of color in the cities of the slaveholding Americas is very large. For two broad collections whose essays focus on urban life to a significant degree, see Gaspar and Hine, *More than Chattel* and *Beyond Bondage*. For a study whose findings on gender, geography, manumission, and urban life are often similar to those of the present study, see Hünefeldt, *Paying the Price of Freedom*, 1, 93–94, 117–28, 183, 205. On enslaved and freed women of African descent in Rio, see, for example, Faria, "Sinhás Pretas"; Farias et al., *No labirinto das nações*, ch. 5; Karasch, "Anastácia." On Havana, see Hevia Lanier, *Mujeres negras libres*; Mena, "Stretching the Limits."

15. Alencastro, *O trato dos viventes*, 345–53; see also Marquese, "The Dynamics of Slavery in Brazil."

16. For reflections on this for Brazil, see Alencastro, *O trato dos viventes*, 352–53.

17. The literature on manumission, and the tendency for women to be manumitted, is vast. On Brazil, see Karasch, *Slave Life in Rio de Janeiro*, 335–61; Libby and Graça Filho, "Notarized and Baptismal Manumissions"; Mattoso, *To Be a Slave in Brazil*, 164–68; Schwartz, "The Manumission of Slaves in Colonial Brazil"; Slenes, "The Demography and Economics of Brazilian Slavery," 521–22. For a survey of some of the recent quantitative studies of manumission in Brazil, see Klein and Luna, *Slavery in Brazil*, 250–67. For the Hispanic American context, see, for example, Lyman Johnson, "Manumission in Colonial Buenos Aires," 262; for Cuba and the comparison with other parts of the Americas, see Bergad et al., *The Cuban Slave Market*, 131–41.

18. Broadening Peter Burke's description of "notarial cultures," Sandra Lauderdale Graham describes nineteenth-century Brazil as a "juridical culture." Graham, "Writing from the Margins," 615–17. Rebecca Scott refers to a "legal culture" for nineteenth-century Cuba. Scott, *Slave Emancipation*, 280. On slaves' use of this culture in Cuba, see Barcia Zequeira, *La otra familia*, 54–57; Perera and Meriño, "Yo, el Notario."

19. Bergad et al., *The Cuban Slave Market*, 128; Castilho and Cowling, "Funding Freedom," 102–4; Karasch, *Slave Life in Rio de Janeiro*, 336, 344; Paiva, *Escravos e libertos nas Minas Gerais*, 84.

20. See, for example, de la Fuente, "Slave Law and Claims-Making in Cuba"; Grinberg, *Liberata*.

21. For example, Castañeda, "Demandas judiciales"; Chalhoub, *Visões da liberdade*; Grinberg, *Liberata*; Mendonça, *Entre a mão e os anéis*; Pena, *Pajens da Casa Imperial*; Cowling, "Negotiating Freedom"; de la Fuente, "Slaves and the Creation of Legal Rights"; Scott, *Slave Emancipation*.

22. On the interconnectedness of Brazil, Cuba, and the "second slavery," see Berbel et al., *Escravidão e política*; Marquese, *Feitores do corpo*; Rood, "Plantation Technocrats"; Schmidt-Nowara, "Empires against Emancipation"; Tomich, "The Second Slavery"; Tomich, *Through the Prism of Slavery*; Tomich and Zeuske, "The Second Slavery" (special editions of *Review: Journal of the Fernand Braudel Center*).

23. Schmidt-Nowara, *Slavery, Freedom and Abolition in Latin America*, 123.

24. See *Voyages: The Transatlantic Slave Trade Database* (http://www.slavevoyages .org/tast/assessment/estimates.faces, accessed 8 July 2012), which is constantly being updated. Note that the total number of enslaved laborers arriving in Cuba would have been higher, since this estimate does not include the significant amount of intraregional trading, representing instead voyages directly from Africa. The figure given here is for those who disembarked, out of an estimate of almost 900,000 who embarked for Cuba from African shores.

25. Scott, *Slave Emancipation*, 3.

26. Gott, *Cuba*, 46–47. This increase was mainly thanks to imports since—as in Brazil—the enslaved population did not increase naturally.

27. Ibid. Pérez, *Cuba between Reform and Revolution*, 87; González-Ripoll et al., *El rumor de Haití en Cuba*; Portuondo Zúñiga, *José Antonio Saco*, 96–100; 132–80.

28. See *Voyages: The Transatlantic Slave Trade Database* (http://www.slavevoyages .org/tast/assessment/estimates.faces, accessed 8 July 2012).

29. John V. Crawford to Earl Granville (6 September 1873), in "Correspondence respecting Slavery in Cuba and Puerto Rico, and the State of the Slave Population and Chinese Coolies in Those Islands," NAL, FO 881/2598, 1873–74, p. 11.

30. Schmidt-Nowara, *Empire and Antislavery*, 161–69.

31. On the war and Afro-Cuban participation, see Ferrer, *Insurgent Cuba*, chapters 1–3.

32. Graham, "1850–1870," 115.

33. Alencastro, *O trato dos viventes*, 9–10, 345–53.

34. See *Voyages: The Transatlantic Slave Trade Database* (http://www.slavevoyages .org/tast/assessment/estimates.faces, accessed 8 July 2012). Note that, as for the figures for Cuba, these numbers represent those who disembarked from voyages directly

from Africa, and do not include those who died in the Middle Passage or who arrived in the significant intraregional American slave trade.

35. Ibid.

36. Conrad, *World of Sorrow*, 1–3, 171.

37. On Britain and the abolition of the trade, see Bethell, *The Abolition of the Brazilian Slave Trade*. On the role of public health fears, see Chalhoub, *Cidade febril*, 68–76. For the internal trade, see Slenes, "The Demography and Economics."

38. For connections between Spanish and Brazilian laws and transition policies, see Lamounier, "Between Slavery and Free Labor," 20.

39. I use quotation marks to indicate some doubt about the expression "free womb" laws, following Sidney Chalhoub's observation that, in Brazil, the exact legal status of enslaved women's offspring was left open by lawmakers in 1871 and had to be negotiated in practice afterward. Although the debates in the Spanish case were different, negotiation about the practice and interpretation of the law played a similar role. Chalhoub, *Machado de Assis*, 171–82, 266–69.

40. "Josepha/José Gonçalves de Pinho," ANB, Juízo de Órphãos, ZM, número 2198, maço 2292, 1884, pp. 1, 2–2v, 7–12v, 15–16v, 18–18v, 21, 34, 39–39v, 42.

41. "Documentos conteniendo instancia de Ramona Oliva, sobre sus hijos María, Fabiana y Agustina," ANC, ME, legajo 3724, expediente T, 1883.

42. Bergstresser, "The Movement for the Abolition of Slavery"; Machado, *O plano e o pânico*; Silva, *As camélias do Leblon*.

43. "Discurso del Sr. Nabuco," in Sociedad Abolicionista Española, *Sesión del 23 de Enero de 1881*, 4.

44. On the differences between abolishing slavery from inside and from outside a slave society, see Azevedo, *Abolitionism in the United States and Brazil*, 14–19.

45. For a useful summary of the recent historiography on abolition, see Weinstein, "The Decline of the Progressive Planter." On the need to understand the pluralities, complexities, and contradictions of a society in transition, see Albuquerque, *O jogo da dissimulação*, 38–42.

46. Nabuco, *O abolicionismo*, 207.

47. For the comparative point, see Maia Mata, "Sentidos da liberdade." On responses to 13 May, see, for example, Albuquerque, *O jogo da dissimulação*, chapter 2; Fraga Filho, *Encruzilhadas da liberdade*, chapters 4–5.

48. Drescher, "Brazilian Abolition in Comparative Perspective," 442–51.

49. Schmidt-Nowara, *Empire and Antislavery*, 2–3, 6–7.

50. For analysis of this play of different forces in the construction of postemancipation societies, see Scott, *Slave Emancipation*, 280–82; Scott, *Degrees of Freedom*, 258–64.

51. For the developments of theories about human similarities and differences over the eighteenth and nineteenth centuries, see Schwarcz, *The Spectacle of the Races*, chapter 2. On some of the consequences of the growth of Social Darwinism in Brazil at the same time as abolitionist and antiracist struggles of a "liberal matrix," see Mattos de Castro, *Escravidão e cidadania*, 58.

52. The database "Açoes de liberdade," compiled by Keila Grinberg, is in the author's possession. Many thanks to Keila Grinberg for sharing her data with me from the

earliest stages of my work with these documents. For her own statistical analysis of these second-instance *ações de liberdade* (slave civil suits), see Grinberg, *Liberata*, 109–17.

53. Unlike some of the main government *fondos*, the Miscelánea is far too vast to count all the appeals it contains. I took a sample count from a spread of 30 *legajos*, chosen because they contained large numbers of appeals (these were *legajos* 3484; 3513–16; 3543–49; 3585–93; 3642–48; 3661; and 3724). This count yielded a total of 710 appeals made by individuals (discounting a small number made by more than one person). On the collection itself, see Giovannetti and Cowling, "Hard Work with the *Mare Magnum* of the Past."

54. In Brazil in 1872, 99.1 percent of male slaves and 99.5 percent of female slaves were recorded as illiterate. *Recenseamento da População do Municipio Neutro* (1872), 1–61. In 1861 in Havana *jurisdicción*, literate people of color as a whole—enslaved and free(d)—were recorded as representing 6 percent of the total population of color. This small number was almost certainly mainly made up of free people. Pezuela, *Diccionario geográfico*, 3:8–9. On access to literate culture even by illiterates in Cuba, see Ferrer, *Insurgent Cuba*, 116.

55. See Chalhoub, "The Precariousness of Freedom"; Varella Fernández, "Esclavos a sueldo," 416–17.

56. For the need to combine the interest in slave "agency" with closer attention to elite and slaveholding groups, see Weinstein, "The Decline of the Progressive Planter," 94–95.

57. For the notion of "Atlantic port cities," see Knight and Liss, *Atlantic Port Cities*.

58. The classic description of this function for African-descended women remains Freyre, *Casa-grande e senzala*, chapter 4. Freyre's descriptions of Brazilian families have of course been substantially revised; for overviews, see Metcalf, *Family and Frontier in Colonial Brazil*, 20–21 and chapter 6; Slenes, *Na senzala, uma flor*, chapter 1.

59. Tannenbaum, *Slave and Citizen*.

60. For a cogent summary of this very extensive historiography, see de la Fuente, "Slave Law and Claims-Making in Cuba," 342–53.

61. Ibid. For responses, see Díaz, "Beyond Tannenbaum," and Schmidt-Nowara, "Slavery and the Law: A Reply."

62. For the ongoing relevance of Tannenbaum's discussion of manumission, see de la Fuente, "Slave Law and Claims-Making in Cuba," 346–47.

63. For classic comparative studies of Cuba or Brazil with a non-Iberian "variant," see, for example, Degler, *Neither Black nor White*; Klein, *Slavery in the Americas*; Hall, *Social Control in Plantation Societies*. Studies of the United States and an Iberian country have continued to spark historians' interest more recently, albeit within new historiographical trajectories. See, for example, Azevedo, *Abolicionismo*; Grinberg, *Freedom Suits and Civil Law*. For examples of the burgeoning interest in comparing across Brazil and Cuba, see, for example, Assunção and Zeuske, "'Race,' Ethnicity and Social Structure"; Bergad, *The Comparative Histories of Slavery*; Lamounier, "Between Slavery and Free Labor"; Maia Mata, "Sentidos da liberdade."

64. Berbel et al., *Escravidão e política*, chapter 1.

65. Terborg-Penn, "Through an African Feminist Theoretical Lens," 4, 9.

66. For different suggestions about how to look across or beyond national boundaries while retaining the focus on microhistory or the agency of ordinary people, see Seigel, *Uneven Encounters*, xii–xiv; Townsend, *Tales of Two Cities*, 13–15.

67. Scott, *Degrees of Freedom*, 4–6.

68. For Brazil, see Lima, *Cores, marcas e falas*; Mattos de Castro, *Das cores da liberdade*; Mattos de Castro, *Escravidão e cidadania*. For Cuba, see de la Fuente, *A Nation for All*; Helg, "Race in Argentina and Cuba"; Helg, *Our Rightful Share*; Martínez-Alier, *Marriage, Class and Color*; Zeuske, "Hidden Markers, Open Secrets." For comparison, see Assunção and Zeuske, "'Race', Ethnicity. and Social Structure."

69. Chalhoub, "The Precariousness of Freedom."

70. For the "racialization" term, see Fields, "Ideology and Race in American History." For a recent application of the idea for Brazil, see Albuquerque, introduction to *O jogo da dissimulação*. For notions about "racialization" and its intersection with shifting notions about womanhood of color in postabolition Brazil, see Côrtes, "Coisa de pele."

CHAPTER 1

1. For example, Hazard, *Cuba with Pen and Pencil*, 89; Kidder, *Brazil and the Brazilians*, 167; Tyng, *Stranger in the Tropics*, 59.

2. For Brazil, see, for example, Agassiz, *A Journey in Brazil*, 46–51. For Cuban examples, see Martínez-Fernández, *Fighting Slavery*, 20.

3. See Tomich, *Through the Prism of Slavery*, 56–71.

4. Knight, *Slave Society*, 23; S. Johnson, *The Social Transformation of Eighteenth-Century Cuba*, 57–64; Venegas Fornias, "La Habana y su región," 333–43, 362.

5. Cuba exported 12,867,698 *arrobas* of sugar in 1841–45, and 23,139,245 by 1856–59. Guerra, *Azúcar y población*, 61. An *arroba* was the equivalent of just over twenty-five pounds. See Rood, "Plantation Technocrats," 70.

6. Martínez-Fernández, *Fighting Slavery in the Caribbean*, 19.

7. Le Riverend, *La Habana*, 151–54.

8. Scott, *Slave Emancipation*, 22.

9. Stein, *Vassouras*.

10. Viotti da Costa, "1870–1889," 165. On São Paulo, see Font, *Coffee, Contention and Change*, 15.

11. Merrick and Graham, *Population and Economic Development*, 14–15.

12. On the Brazilian food supply, see Ciro Cardoso, "The Peasant Breach in the Slave System"; Graham, "1850–1870," 120; Graham, *Feeding the City*; Linhares, *História do abastecimento*. On Cuba, see Fernández, *Cuba agrícola*, chapter 5; Le Riverend, *La Habana*, 142.

13. Childs, *The 1812 Aponte Rebellion*, 37; Cowling, "Across the Miles."

14. Gomes, "Quilombolas do Rio de Janeiro no século XIX," 270–81; Barcia Paz, *Seeds of Insurrection*, 50–51.

15. See Assunção and Zeuske, "'Race', Ethnicity and Social Structure," 406.

16. Around half the city's 112,000 population were slaves in 1821. By midcentury, slaves made up roughly the same proportion of a population that had almost doubled to 200,000. Lobo, *História do Rio de Janeiro*, 1:122–23, 135–36, 225–26.

17. There were 48,939 slaves out of a total population of 274,972 residents. *Recenseamento da População do Município Neutro* (1872), 1–61.

18. Pezuela, *Diccionario geográfico*, 3:349–50, 372.

19. Ibid. There were 21,988 slaves out of the total population of 106,968 inhabitants. Because Pezuela does not give complete breakdowns of racial and legal status for Casablanca, El Cerro, Horcón, Jesús del Monte, Luyanó, Regla, and Guanabacoa, this figure does not include these areas.

20. Pezuela, *Diccionario geográfico*, 3:349–50, 372.

21. Karasch, "Anastácia," 81–86, 100.

22. Algranti, *O feitor ausente*, 100–104; 113–14; Walker, *No More, No More*, 19–40.

23. Lauderdale Graham, *House and Street*, 73–87; Slenes, *Na senzala, uma flor*, 47, chapter 2; Walker, *No More, No More*, 25–26.

24. Algranti, *O feitor ausente*, 48–50; Deschamps, *El negro en la economía habanera*, 50–51; L. Soares, *O "Povo de Cam,"* chapter 5.

25. For comparative overviews, see Bergad et al., *The Cuban Slave Market*, 137–38; Klein and Luna, *Slavery in Brazil*, 250–72.

26. Bergad et al., *The Cuban Slave Market*, 123–24, 134.

27. Lauderdale Graham, *House and Street*, 17–18, 40–41, 53–55. *Parente*: member of blood or adoptive family, often of similar African ethnic identity.

28. Algranti, *O feitor ausente*, 20–21, 49; Reis, "De olho no canto"; Reis, *Domingos Sodré*, 196–97.

29. Santos, *Além da senzala*.

30. For population statistics, see Lobo, *História do Rio de Janeiro*, 1:122–23, 135–56, 225–26; Pezuela, *Diccionario geográfico*, 3:372.

31. See Chalhoub, *Cidade febril*; A. Azevedo, *O cortiço*.

32. For Rio, see Chalhoub, *Visões da liberdade*, 212–25, 235–39; Karasch, *Slave Life in Rio de Janeiro*, chapter 9. For Havana, see Deschamps, *Los cimarrones urbanos*, 5–14.

33. Reis, *Death Is a Festival*, 39–41; Reis, *Domingos Sodré*, 205–25.

34. On such links, see Childs, *The 1812 Aponte Rebellion in Cuba*, 115–16; Reis, *Domingos Sodré*, 21–25.

35. On brotherhoods and religious culture in Cuba, see, for example, Barcia Zequeira, *Los ilustres apellidos*, 48–57; Childs, *The 1812 Aponte Rebellion*, 95–119; Howard, *Changing History*. For Brazil, see, for example, Chalhoub, *Machado de Assis*, 240–49; Karasch, *Slave Life in Rio de Janeiro*, 265–87; Sweet, *Recreating Africa*, 144–54, chapters 9 and 10; M. Souza, *Reis negros no Brasil escravista*; Reis, *Death is a Festival*, chapter 2. For a comparative overview, see Bergad, *The Comparative Histories of Slavery*, 180–88.

36. Grinberg, "Freedom Suits," 78.

37. Needell, *A Tropical Belle Epoque*, 20.

38. Ferrer de Couto, *Los negros en sus diversos estados y condiciones*, 96. On Ferrer, see Schmidt-Nowara, "'Spanish' Cuba," 121n. 42.

39. "Expediente promovido a consecuencia del telegrama del Ministro de Ultramar, sobre libertad de la morena Felipa Galuzo," ANC, ME, legajo 3527, expediente Cc, 1872.

40. For Brazil, see Petition, Allidia Maria das Dores (Rio de Janeiro, 27 September 1883), NAL, FO, Embassy and Consular Archives: Brazil—From and To, Miscellaneous,

1882–83, 128–29. For a British consul in Havana complaining about the "trouble and expense" being caused to him by four enslaved claimants' cases, see British Consulate-General (Havana, 18 April 1881), NAL, FO, 72/1606. On British consuls in Havana in an earlier period, see also Martínez-Fernández, *Fighting Slavery*.

41. According to abolitionist municipal councilor José do Patrocinio, by 1887 there were 7,421 slaves in the Município Neutro, and a total of 3,189 owners—an average of only 2.3 slaves per owner. Speech by José do Patrocinio to Confederação Abolicionista, 1 May 1887, *Boletim* (14 May 1887): 79–80. Karasch has emphasized that it was not wealthy rural planters who were most likely to manumit their slaves, but middling urban slave owners. Karasch, *Slave Life in Rio de Janeiro*, 335–36, 344. On Rio's middling groups and their changing relationship to slaveholding, see Frank, *Dutra's World*.

42. Bergstresser, "The Movement for the Abolition of Slavery," 68–76, 189–90; Lauderdale Graham, "The Vintem Riot," 440–42.

43. Casanovas, *Bread, or Bullets!*, 3–5, 9–11, 84–86; Scott, *Slave Emancipation*, 136–38; Schmidt-Nowara, *Empire and Antislavery*, 163–65.

44. Women made up 60 percent of Havana City's enslaved population in 1791, and half the population of the *jurisdicción* of Havana by 1861. Pezuela, *Diccionario geográfico*, 3:8–9, 349. According to one 1871 survey, there were 21,782 slaves in the *jurisdicción* of Havana, among whom women made up 51 percent. Gobierno Superior Político de la Isla de Cuba, "Resumen de los esclavos comprendidos en el padrón de 1871, clasificados por edades, sexos, ocupaciones y estado," in Ministerio de Ultramar, *Cuba desde 1850 á 1873*, 154–55. Fe Iglesias's study of the most reliable version of the 1877 census puts the number of slaves in Havana *jurisdicción* at 39,014, of which around 47 percent were female. Iglesias, "El censo cubano de 1877," 214. Since the *jurisdicción* also included rural slaves, we can assume numbers of women in the urban parts of Havana were higher still.

45. Pérez, *Cuba between Reform and Revolution*, 87.

46. Ibid., 88; Pezuela, *Diccionario geográfico*, 3:8–9.

47. There were 91,625 white males and 46,820 white females in 1861. Pezuela, *Diccionario geográfico*, 3:8–9. On the seclusion of elite white women, see Martínez-Fernández, *Fighting Slavery*, 65–83. For an attempt to complicate Martínez-Fernández's vision of the divisions between public and private spaces, see McCabe, "Parameters of the Public," 53–54 and 140.

48. Gallenga, *The Pearl of the Antilles*, 36.

49. Paquette, *Sugar Is Made with Blood*; Reid, *The Year of the Lash*.

50. For these statistics, see Karasch, "Anastácia," 81.

51. *Recenseamento da População do Municipio Neutro* (1872), 1–61; Conrad, *The Destruction*, 286.

52. There were 96,255 white men in Rio in 1872, and only 55,544 white women. *Recenseamento da População do Municipio Neutro* (1872), 1–61.

53. On slaves' occupations, see *Recenseamento da População do Municipio Neutro* (1872), 1–61; Algranti, *O feitor ausente*, 47–95; Franklin, *Women and Slavery*, 130–34, 142–45; L. Soares, *O "Povo de Cam,"* chapters 4–7; Venegas Fornias, "La Habana Vieja," 35.

54. On enslaved women's occupations in Rio, see Lauderdale Graham, *House and Street*, chapter 2; Karasch, "Anastácia," 87–90. There is less specific work for Havana; for an overview, see López Valdés, *Pardos y morenos*, 57–58.

55. Fifty-nine percent of Rio's female slaves—14,184 women—were listed under this occupation in 1872, as opposed to only 35 percent—8,658—of male slaves. *Recenseamento da População do Municipio Neutro* (1872), 1–61. With abolition, domestic service would become even more female-dominated. See Hahner, "Women and Work," 103. In a survey of domestic slaves in Havana's Third District, taken in 1853–54, 63 percent of those included were women, although "domestic slaves" was a broad category that may well have included most slaves living in urban households and considered "domestic" (as opposed to field slaves) for tax purposes. "Varios padrones de esclavos de ambos sexos destinados al servicio doméstico y sujetos al pago de Capitación," ANC, GSC, legajo 48, expediente 33528, 1853–54.

56. In Rio in 1872, for example, around 13 percent of slave men—3,330 male slaves—worked in more specialized occupations such as sailors, fishermen, metalworkers, carpenters, leather workers, tailors, hatters, and shoemakers. The only skilled occupation open to women was that of seamstress. The city's 1,384 enslaved seamstresses represented 6 percent of enslaved women. Women were also less likely, at least officially, to work as *jornaleiro/as*. Only 3 percent of slave women, compared with one fifth of male slaves, were listed as *criados & jornaleiros*. *Recenseamento da População do Municipio Neutro* (1872), 1–61. These 1872 statistics on slave occupations tally closely with those discussed by Karasch for an earlier period. Karasch, *Slave Life in Rio de Janeiro*, 185–213.

57. On free women of color in Brazil, see Faria, "Sinhás pretas"; Faria, "Sinhás pretas, damas mercadoras"; Farias et al., *No labirinto das nações*, 243, 248; Paiva, *Escravos e libertos nas Minas Gerais*, 75–76; C. Soares, "Comércio, nação e gênero." On Cuba, see Mena, "Stretching the Limits," 91–93; Hevia Lanier, *Mujeres negras libres*.

58. For the ancient intersections between slavery and sex, see Lerner, "Women and Slavery."

59. See Collins, "Intimacy, Inequality, and *Democracia Racial.*"

60. See, for example, Franklin, *Women and Slavery*, 135–36; Venâncio, "Maternidade Negada."

61. On Rio, see Caulfield, "O nascimento do Mangue"; Chalhoub, *Visões da liberdade*, 152–55; Lauderdale Graham, "Slavery's Impasse," 669–94; L. Soares, "Prostitution in Nineteenth-Century Rio de Janeiro"; Vainfas, "Meretrizes e doutores." On Havana, see Barcia Zequeira, "Entre el poder y la crisis"; Díaz Martínez, *La peligrosa Habana*, 79–81; "Expediente criminal seguido de oficio por corrupción de la menor parda Genoveva Valdés" (Escribanía de Bonachea y Palmero), ANC, ME, legajo 2928, expediente Aj, 1884.

62. For this important observation, see Paiva, *Escravos e libertos nas Minas Gerais*, 116–17.

63. Karasch, *Slave Life in Rio de Janeiro*, 342–47. Following such observations, Frank "Trey" Proctor III has recently argued that, at least in the context of New Spain, women's higher rate of manumission owed more to intimate ties of domesticity and

child-rearing with women owners than to sexual relationships between enslaved women and male owners. See Proctor, "Gender and the Manumission of Slaves in New Spain."

64. For example, as Sarah Franklin has pointed out, Bergad, Barcia, and Iglesias attribute women's higher rate of manumission in Cuba to prostitution, but they are not able to provide any Cuban examples of how this worked in practice. Franklin, "Suitable to her Sex," 239; Bergad et al., *The Cuban Slave Market*, 139. Frank Proctor III provides a useful synthesis and critique of historians' tendency to assume that sexual relationships with slaveholding men necessarily explained women's higher rate of manumission in the Iberian Americas. Proctor, "Gender and the Manumission of Slaves in New Spain."

65. For example, Bergad et al., *The Cuban Slave Market*, 123, 138–39.

66. Schmidt-Nowara, *Slavery, Freedom, and Abolition*, 143.

67. See the following essays in Falola and Childs, *The Yoruba Diaspora in the Atlantic World*: Reid, "The Yoruba in Cuba"; Reis and Mamigonian, "Nagô and Mina"; M. Soares, "From Gbe to Yoruba." See also Lauderdale Graham, "Being Yoruba in Rio de Janeiro."

68. On language groups and ethnicities, see, for example, Barcia Paz, *Seeds of Insurrection*, 15–24; Farias et al., *No labirinto das nações*, chapter 1; Karasch, *Slave Life in Rio de Janeiro*, chapter 1; Ortiz, *Los negros esclavos*, 20–45; Slenes, *Na senzala, uma flor*, 142–49; M. Soares, *Devotos da Cor*; Valdés Acosta, *Los remanentes de las lenguas bantúes en Cuba*; Walker, *No More, No More*.

69. Conrad, *World of Sorrow*, 171–91; Mattos de Castro, *Das Cores do Silêncio*, 119–36.

70. Graham, "1850–1870," 125.

71. Slenes, "The Demography and Economics," 124.

72. Karasch, *Slave Life in Rio de Janeiro*, 4–8, 266.

73. Graham, "Another Middle Passage?," 315; Slenes, "The Brazilian Internal Slave Trade," 327.

74. Graham, "Another Middle Passage?," 299–300; Slenes, "The Brazilian Internal Slave Trade," 351.

75. For the links between mobility of enslaved and free colored people and the Cuban Aponte conspiracy of 1812, see Childs, *The 1812 Aponte Rebellion in Cuba*, 2–3, 48, 120, 123.

76. See Cowling, "Across the Miles"; Varella Fernández, "Esclavos a sueldo," 208–56, 375–87.

77. Slenes estimates that the city of Rio de Janeiro lost 31 percent of its slaves under 40 between 1872 and 1881, for example, mainly to the internal trade. For males these figures were even higher. Slenes, "The Brazilian Internal Slave Trade," 352–53. Manumission rates for slaves in the city of Rio during slavery's last years were also far higher than for other areas. Slenes, "The Demography and Economics," 495, 501, 504, 542. For Cuba, the percentage of slaves in Havana province fell much more than in any other western province between 1862 and 1877. By 1877, Havana province only had 43 percent of its 1862 slave population, while Matanzas had 72 percent. Domestic slaves'

numbers also fell faster than those of field slaves. Domestic slaves made up 20 percent of the Cuban slave population in 1871, but only 15 percent by 1879. Scott, *Slave Emancipation*, 86–89.

78. Drescher, "Brazilian Abolition," 437. See also Bergad et al., *The Cuban Slave Market*, 85; Graham, "Another Middle Passage?," 298–99; Varella Fernández, "Esclavos a sueldo," 375–87.

79. Scott, *Slave Emancipation*, 88–89.

80. Naranjo and García González, *Racismo e inmigración en Cuba*; Naranjo, *Cuba vista por el emigrante español*.

81. See Gladys Ribeiro, *A liberdade em construção*.

82. Lauderdale Graham, "The Vintem Riot," 433–34.

83. Scott, *Slave Emancipation*, 28–35.

84. For some edited collections, see, for example, Araujo, *Viajeras al Caribe*; Machado and Huber, *(T)races of Louiz Agassiz*; M. Leite et al., *A mulher no Rio de Janeiro no século XIX*.

85. Needell, *A Tropical Belle Epoque*, 25–26.

86. Ibid., 32.

87. "Coisas da atualidade," *Revista Illustrada*, 16 November 1885, 4–5.

88. Viotti da Costa, *The Brazilian Empire*, 199.

89. Pezuela, *Diccionario geográfico*, 3:8–9, 349–50, 372.

90. Roig de Leuchsenring, *La Habana*, 88.

91. On Jesús María, see Adrián López Denis, "El incendio de Jesús María." On El Cerro, see Martínez-Fernández, *Fighting Slavery*, 28–30. On the coexistence of urban elegance and squalor, see Díaz Martínez, *La peligrosa Habana*, 45–54.

92. Venegas Fornias, *La urbanización de las murallas*, 45; see also Marrero Cruz, *Julián de Zulueta*, 36–37.

93. Santamaría García, "Los ferrocarriles," 485–89.

94. Le Riverend, *La Habana*, 143–44.

95. Needell, *A Tropical Belle Epoque*, 25–26. On trains in Brazil, see, for example, Vasquez, *Nos trilhos do progresso*.

96. For U.S. designs on Cuba, see Pérez, *Cuba in the American Imagination*, 25–42.

97. Corwin, *Spain and the Abolition of Slavery*, 153–73; Pérez-Prendes, "La revista *El Abolicionista*," 215–40; Schmidt-Nowara, "'Spanish' Cuba," 101–22.

98. For different perspectives on the *junta*, see Cepero Bonilla, *Azúcar y abolición*, 72–73; Corwin, *Spain*, 190–213. For the *junta* debates, see España, *Información sobre reformas*.

99. Pérez, *Cuba between Reform and Revolution*, 93.

100. Corwin, *Spain*, 213.

101. Cepero Bonilla, *Azúcar y abolición*, chapters 15–18; Ferrer, *Insurgent Cuba*, chapter 1.

102. Schmidt-Nowara, *Empire and Antislavery*, 137–38; Scott, *Slave Emancipation*, 63–65.

103. For differing assessments of the sugar industry in this period, see Moreno Fraginals, *El ingenio*, 1:220–21; Scott, *Slave Emancipation*, 5, 85.

104. Barcia Zequeira, *Burguesía esclavista*, 176; Cepero Bonilla, *Azúcar y abolición*, 65–66, 112–54; Guerra, *Azúcar y población*, 171–85; Pérez, *Cuba between Empires*, 18, 131.

105. Pérez, *Cuba between Empires*, 24–29; Stubbs, *Tobacco on the Periphery*, 18–21.

106. A general amnesty at the end of the war in 1878 saw the emancipation of 16,000 slaves who had fought on both the rebel and loyalist sides. Scott, *Slave Emancipation*, 115.

107. Pérez, *Cuba between Reform and Revolution*, 89.

108. Scott, *Slave Emancipation*, 193.

109. Conrad, *The Destruction*, 74–77, 86–89. On war, recruitment, and race in Brazil, see Beattie, *The Tribute of Blood*.

110. Chalhoub, *Machado de Assis*, 137–55, 164–92; Conrad, *The Destruction*, chapter 6.

111. Sandra Lauderdale Graham long ago made this point in "Slavery's Impasse," 670–71.

112. On the passage and effects of the law, see Mendonça, *Entre a mão e os anéis*.

113. Furtado, *The Economic Growth of Brazil*, 125–26, 189.

114. See Conrad, *The Destruction*, chapters 12 and 13. For Ceará's influence on the politics of antislavery in other northeastern provinces, see Castilho, "A New Canada."

115. Dean, *Rio Claro*, 125–27; Machado, *O plano e o pânico*, 91–121.

116. Bergstresser, "The Movement for the Abolition of Slavery," 108–11.

117. On a new political style emerging in the 1880s and its connections to abolitionism, see Castilho, "Abolitionism Matters," vi–xxxi; Lauderdale Graham, "The Vintem Riot"; Kittleson, *The Practice of Politics*, chapter 4.

118. Bergstresser, "The Movement for the Abolition of Slavery," 18–19; Needell, 189–91.

119. Castilho and Cowling, "Funding Freedom"; Cowling, "Debating Womanhood."

120. On the role of the imperial family, see Daibert, *Isabel, A "Redentora" dos Escravos*, 110–34; E. Silva, *As Camélias do Leblon*, 7–18. On the friction between municipal and national government, see Castilho and Cowling, "Funding Freedom," 96–97.

121. Conrad, *The Destruction*, 234–36.

122. "Eleição municipal," *Gazeta da Tarde*, 28 June 1886, 1; "A vitória," *Gazeta da Tarde*, 2 July 1886, 1; "O regulamento negro," *Gazeta da Tarde*, 5 July 1886, 1.

123. "Ata da sessão ordinária," *Boletim*, 5 August 1886, 39–41.

124. *Quilombo:* community of fugitive slaves. On links between the actions of enslaved people and abolitionists, see Bergstresser, "The Movement for the Abolition of Slavery," 18–19, 123; Machado, *O plano e o pânico*, 15–16; E. Silva, *As camélias do Leblon*, chapter 2. For examples from the *Gazeta da Tarde* newspaper, see "Serafim, escravo," 20 October 1885, p. 1; "Juízo cível," 16 December 1885, 2; "O crime de Botafogo," 12 March 1886, 1; "História lúgubre," 19 April 1886, 2.

125. Schmidt-Nowara, *Empire and Antislavery*, 163–65; Scott, *Slave Emancipation*, 136–38.

126. Zambrana, *El negro Francisco*.

127. Schmidt-Nowara, *Empire and Antislavery*, 6–7, 101, 173–74.

128. For example, Castilho, "Brisas atlânticas"; Chalhoub, *Machado de Assis*, 142.

129. Sociedad Abolicionista Española, *Sesión del 23 de enero de 1881*, 1.

130. For an examination of how comparison between Brazil and the United States helped shape how each nation thought about slavery, race, and abolition, see C. Azevedo, *Abolitionism in the United States and Brazil*.

131. On proslavery ideas, see Berbel et al., *Escravidão e política*; Marquese, *Feitores do corpo*.

132. See Bethell and Carvalho, *Joaquim Nabuco*.

133. Duque-Estrada, *A abolição*, 105.

134. Sociedad Abolicionista Española, *Sesión del 23 de enero de 1881*, 2; Midgley, *Women against Slavery*, 37–38, 97–100.

135. For abolitionist perspectives among Cuban exiles in the United States, see, for example, Lazo, *Writing to Cuba*, chapter 4.

CHAPTER 2

1. Grinberg, *Liberata*, 21–27. See also Mattos de Castro, *Das cores do silêncio*, chapter 9.

2. See especially Chalhoub, *Visões da liberdade*, chapter 2; also Lara, *Campos da violência*, 248–68. For a historiographical overview, see Grinberg, *Liberata*, 30–35. On the law as presenting a more open field of possibilities for social struggles than had been previously recognized, see E. P. Thompson, *The Making of the English Working Class*, 19–23.

3. Chalhoub, *Visões da liberdade*, 27, 159–60, 173.

4. For example, E. Azevedo, *Orfeu de carapinha*, chapter 4; Mendonça, *Entre a mão e os anéis*; Pena, *Pajens da Casa Imperial*.

5. Scott, *Slave Emancipation*. For comparative perspectives, see Scott, "Exploring the Meaning of Freedom"; Scott, "Defining the Boundaries of Freedom"; and Scott, *Degrees of Freedom*.

6. Barcia Paz, *Seeds of Insurrection*, 90–104; Barcia Zequeira, *La otra familia*; Castañeda, "The Woman Slave in Cuba"; Castañeda, "Demandas judiciales"; de la Fuente, "Slave Law and Claims-making in Cuba"; García, *La esclavitud desde la esclavitud*, 3–5, 42–44.

7. Until 1874 appeals courts were located only in Bahia, Rio de Janeiro, Maranhão, and Pernambuco. After this date, others were founded in Ouro Preto, Goiás, Mato Grosso, Belém, and Fortaleza. Occasionally, cases also reached the Supreme Court. Grinberg, *Liberata*, 23–24.

8. Varella Fernández, "Esclavos a sueldo," 133.

9. Keeping a close eye on Spain's Moret Law, the Brazilians discussed the idea of adopting similar *juntas* to oversee the transition process. However, the idea was not taken up, because of the fear that it would undermine owners' private authority over slaves. Chalhoub, *Machado de Assis*, 142–43.

10. For a recognition of this problem and an attempt to prevent it, see "Decreto del Gobierno Superior Civil mandando que los Gobernadores y Tenientes gobernadores entiendan en primer término de las quejas de los esclavos contra sus dueños y las de éstos contra las resoluciones de los Síndicos," Joaquín Vigil de Quiñones, Director de

Administración Local, Havana, 8 June 1868, in Cano and Zalba, *El libro de los síndicos*, 50–51.

11. Varella Fernández, "Esclavos a sueldo," 126–29.

12. "Expediente promovido por el Síndico de Bejucal sobre el negro Domingo, esclavo de Dn. Antonio Almora, vecino de Güines," ANC, GSC, legajo 955, expediente 33856, 1863.

13. The Gobierno Superior Civil collection contains appeals made by claimants both in Havana and on other parts of the island, made from 1800 to 1866 (after which date the institution was replaced by other government bodies).

14. These figures are taken from a count of all the claims involving slaves in the collection's card index. Claims were made from people living across the island. By contrast, across Cuba as a whole, women made up only 38 percent of the slave population at midcentury, so while their presence as claims-makers grew, they still appear underrepresented in claims-making at this point. See Pérez, *Cuba between Reform and Revolution*, 87.

15. Among Rio-based appellants identifiable by sex (individuals or same-sex groups), 16 were women (47 percent) and 18 were men (53 percent). Keila Grinberg, database "Ações de liberdade." . This does not include the multiple claims that reached only first-instance courts. These have now been merged, along with the appeals court cases, criminal court cases, and miscellaneous other judicial documents involving slaves, into an electronic database available at the ANB.

16. Women comprised 40 percent of Rio's slaves in both 1838 and 1849. Plantations' enslaved populations, on the other hand, were often 70–80 percent male. See Karasch, "Anastácia," 81.

17. At the time I undertook this survey (2004), these appeals had been collated in a printed catalogue at the Brazilian National Archive, called: Corte de Apelação (Escravos): 1785–1951 (código do fundo: 20; SDJ 033). Among these, women defendants made up just 2 of 24 appeals cases sent by first-instance courts within the city of Rio (8 percent) where the defendant was identifiable by sex. For appeals sent by courts elsewhere in the country, female defendants made up 21 of 249 cases (also 8 percent). Although these printed catalogues still exist, the criminal and civil appeals, along with first-instance appeals and a variety of other documentation involving slaves have been merged into a general database, also available at the ANB. Thus, broader surveys of this kind will be possible in the future.

18. For example: Algranti, *O Feitor Ausente*, 173; Algranti, "Slave Crimes"; Chalhoub, *Visões da liberdade*, 29–174; Amantino, "O perfil demográfico do escravo fugitivo"; Gómez Véliz et al., "Algunas reflexiones sobre el cimarronaje femenino." Alvin Thompson suggests there may have been more women in maroon communities than is often acknowledged: see A. Thompson, "Gender and *Marronage* in the Caribbean." Broadly, though, fewer women appear in crime and marronage statistics across space and time. For nineteenth-century Jamaica, for example, Diana Paton found women numbered between 13 percent and 30 percent of advertized slave fugitives, while convicts were between 17 percent and 26 percent female. Paton notes that this phenomenon was not unique to slave societies: late-nineteenth-century British prisons, for example, contained roughly similar percentages of women. Paton, *No Bond but the*

Law, 38. Malcolm Feeley and Deborah Little have noted women's presence in British and US crime statistics was once higher, but declined rapidly from about the 1830s. Nonetheless, for Geltner, crime and imprisonment have been conceived as a largely male preserve since medieval times. See Feeley and Little, "The Vanishing Female"; Geltner, "No-Woman's Land?"

19. Karasch, *Slave Life in Rio de Janeiro*, 347.

20. This is a very broad summary of a complex set of legal and customary practices that evolved significantly over the nineteenth century. For differing perspectives on *coartación*, see Aimes, "*Coartación*"; de la Fuente, "Slaves and the Creation of Legal Rights"; García, *La esclavitud desde la esclavitud*, 43–44, 143–51; Ortiz, *Los negros esclavos*, 191–96, 391–92; and Varella Fernández, "Esclavos a sueldo."

21. Paiva, *Escravos e libertos nas Minas Gerais*, 77–85.

22. For Cuba, see Reglamento de Esclavos, 14 November 1842, Articles 34 and 37, reproduced in Cano and Zalba, *El libro de los síndicos*, 28.

23. For estimates, see Bergad et al., *The Cuban Slave Market*, 123; Scott, *Slave Emancipation*, 13–14.

24. De la Fuente, "Slaves and the Creation of Legal Rights," 675, 692.

25. Bergad et al., *The Cuban Slave Market*, 123.

26. Scott, *Slave Emancipation*, 13–14. There were 1,247 female *coartadas* and 890 males—particularly significant in a slave population still dominated by males. Scott's findings in terms of urban slavery and women in *coartación* are confirmed by Bergad et al., *The Cuban Slave Market*, 122–31. In a survey of newspaper advertisements of slaves for sale or rent in Havana and Matanzas in the 1830s and 1840s, Sarah Franklin found that among the *coartados* advertised, women made up 78.6 percent. Observing the high number of *coartada* wet nurses who appeared in the ads, Franklin hypothesizes that wet-nursing proved a route toward savings and eventual self-purchase for women. Franklin,141–46.

27. Scott, *Slave Emancipation*, 13–14.

28. On the ancient connections between the development of the institutions of slavery and concubinage, and the way in which these institutions also helped define the meaning of "woman," see Lerner, "Women and Slavery."

29. In the Spanish context this can be traced back as far as the thirteenth-century Siete Partidas legal code. See "Ley I, Tít. XXII, Part. IV. Sobre la potestad de dar el señor la libertad á [*sic*] sus esclavos," reproduced in Cano and Zalba, *El libro de los síndicos*, 151.

30. The Castilian Siete Partidas forbade prostitution of enslaved women. See "Ley IV, Tít. XXII, Part. IV, que declara libre la esclava prostituida públicamente por su dueño," reproduced in Cano and Zalba, *El libro de los síndicos*, 152.

31. Lauderdale Graham, "Slavery's Impasse," 679.

32. The Spanish *Real Cédula* of 1789, which codified slave law for the Indies, prohibited owners from putting women slaves to work at "labors unsuitable to their sex," including work that brought them into contact with men. *Real Cédula de su Majestad*, chapter 3, p. 5. The stipulation was carried over into the 1842 slave code: see "Reglamento de esclavos," November 1842, article 14, in Cano and Zalba, *El libro de los síndicos*, 23. For a comparative example, for Jamaica, see Paton, *No Bond but the Law*, 6–7.

33. For example, the 1789 *Real Cédula* stipulated that where slaves of different owners married, in order for them to stay together, the husband's owner should buy the wife in the first instance. Thus the woman followed her husband. This was carried over into the 1842 slave code. *Real Cédula de su Majestad*, chapter 7, p. 7; "Reglamento de esclavos," November 1842, article 30, in Cano and Zalba, *El libro de los síndicos*, 7.

34. See Pena, *Pajens da casa imperial*, 179–85.

35. On connections between slavery and gendered systems of power, see, for example, Beckles, *Natural Rebels*; Beckles, *Centering Woman*; Fox-Genovese, *Within the Plantation Household*; Gautier, *Les Soeurs de Solitude*; White, *Ar'n't I a Woman*; Jones, *Labor of Love, Labor of Sorrow*; Lerner, "Women and Slavery"; Mathurin, *The Rebel Woman in the British West Indies*; Moitt, *Women and Slavery in the French Antilles*; Morgan, *Laboring Women*; Morrissey, *Slave Women in the New World*.

36. Given its centrality to the formation of the slave societies and economies of the Americas, it is surprising how little specific attention *partus sequitur ventrem* has received from historians. For an important exception, see especially Dorsey, "Women without History." See also Beckles, *Natural Rebels*, 115–35; Millward, "'That All Her Increase May Be Free.'"

37. "Ley II, tít. XXI, part. II. Que dispone que es esclavo el nacido de madre esclava, aunque el padre sea libre," reproduced in Cano and Zalba, *El libro de los síndicos*, 149.

38. This term, in nineteenth-century Brazil, became *pai de família*, denoting patriarchal authority as well as paternal affection. Graham, *Patronage and Politics*, 18. The notion is present in the Spanish 1789 *Real Cédula*, which stipulated that slaves must venerate their masters as family fathers (*padres de familia*). *Real Cédula de su Majestad*, chapter 8, p. 8. The same stipulation appears in the 1842 slave code, as well as in the 1872 *Reglamento* for the 1870 Moret Law. "Reglamento de esclavos," November 1842, article 41, in Cano and Zalba, *El libro de los síndicos*, 29–30; "Real Decreto aprobando el Reglamento para la ejecución de la ley de 4 de julio sobre abolición gradual de la esclavitud," article 39, in Cano and Zalba, *El libro de los síndicos*, 118.

39. "Illegitimacy" and the absence of nonelite men in the records did not necessarily equate to matrifocality in practice; see Perera and Meriño, *Esclavitud, familia y parroquia en Cuba*, 157–88.

40. Dorsey, "Women without History," 173.

41. For parliamentary and juridical debates about *partus sequitur ventrem* and "free womb" laws in Brazil, see Abreu, "Slave Mothers"; Chalhoub, *Machado de Assis*, 137–38, 168–82; Pena, *Pajens da Casa Imperial*, 80–116.

42. On "free womb logic," a term coined by Hebe Mattos in discussing my work in 2004, see Cowling, "Debating Womanhood," 287–88.

43. Conrad, *The Destruction*, 90.

44. Padre Felix Varela, "Proyecto de decreto sobre la abolición de la esclavitud en la Isla de Cuba y sobre los medios de evitar los daños que puedan ocasionarse a la población blanca y a la agricultura," 1822, reproduced by Ortiz, *Los negros esclavos*, 298–307.

45. On Perdigão Malheiro's proposal, see Pena, *Pajens da Casa Imperial*, 286. On Pimenta Bueno's project and the Council of State's discussions of it, see Chalhoub, *Machado de Assis*, 139–55.

46. For Cuba, see, for example, Armas y Céspedes, *La esclavitud en Cuba*, 376–77. For Brazil, see Abreu, "Slave Mothers and Freed Children," 577.

47. Chalhoub, *Visões da liberdade*, 159.

48. For copies of the respective laws, see Ortiz, *Los negros esclavos*, 317–20, and Conrad, *The Destruction*, 305–9.

49. Chalhoub, *Machado de Assis*, 274.

50. The Rio Branco law followed an earlier precedent from 1869, which banned the separate sale of children under 15 from parents. "Decreto no. 1695, de 15 de setembro de 1869," cited by Chalhoub, *Machado de Assis*, 163.

51. The ability to work to earn money, however, still depended on the owner's consent. On the effects of the self-purchase provisions of 1871 see Mendonça, *Entre a mão e os anéis*, 221–56.

52. For the fund's gendered priorities, see Dauwe, "A libertação gradual," 72–77, 82, 100–101, 108.

53. Conrad, *The Destruction*, 104–5, 110–16; Lamounier, "Between Slavery and Free Labor," 100–106; Viotti da Costa, *The Brazilian Empire*, 165. For a reappraisal of the fund, see Dauwe, "A libertação gradual," 9–33.

54. Castilho and Cowling, "Funding Freedom."

55. Sociedad Abolicionista Española, *La abolición de la esclavitud en el Brasil y en España*, 6–8, 10–13.

56. Sociedad Abolicionista Española, *Sesión del 23 de Enero de 1881*, 4–6, 11–18.

57. There were various precedents for this in Cuba, where the Spanish colonial state was keen on taking counts and censuses of slaves as well as other sectors of the population. See "Real decreto aprobando el reglamento para la formación de padrones y de un registro civil de los esclavos," 22 March 1854, in Cano and Zalba, *El libro de los síndicos*, 186–87. A similar unsuccessful attempt to register slaves followed the 1866 law that finally ended the transatlantic slave trade. See Kiple, *Blacks in Colonial Cuba*, 65–66.

58. Chalhoub, *Machado de Assis*, 203–27; Scott, *Slave Emancipation*, 81–82.

59. Scott, *Slave Emancipation*, 172–76.

60. See Conrad, *The Destruction*, 237–38.

61. For the text of the law, see Ortiz, *Los negros esclavos*, 331–34.

62. Chalhoub, *Machado de Assis*, 142–43.

63. Lamounier, "Between Slavery and Free Labor," 21.

64. "Reglamento del patronato de esclavos," in Ortiz, *Los negros esclavos*, 320–29.

65. Barcia Zequeira, "Táctica y estrategia de la burguesía esclavista," 125; Scott, *Slave Emancipation*, 133.

66. Women had played an important role in this tradition since at least the eighteenth century. See Russell-Wood, "'Acts of Grace'"; Karasch, *Slave Life in Rio de Janeiro*, 339–41; Schultz, *Tropical Versailles*, 165–76.

67. Chalhoub, *Machado de Assis*, 138, 203–4.

68. Ibid., 137, 183, 226–27; Scott, *Slave Emancipation*, 73–74.

69. Such a notion bears a striking resemblance to today's fetal rights discourse, in which, as Katherine de Gama has argued, "the status of the pregnant woman is reduced to . . . reproductive object while the foetus is presented as the personification of abstract

individualism." Thus, "the framing of the abortion issue in terms of [fetal] rights has robbed women of the potential to develop any notion of property in their bodies." De Gama, "A Brave New World?," 116, 128. Thanks to Diana Paton for inspiring me to think about some of these contemporary connections.

70. Grinberg also notes that more cases were resolved by the appeals court *against* freedom after 1871, and speculates that the effect of the Rio Branco Law was actually to tighten up the law regarding the grounds on which slaves could appeal. Grinberg, *Liberata*, 95–100. This would suggest that the legislators anticipated precisely what happened: that more people would seek to make claims for freedom following the passage of the law. See also Grinberg, *O fiador*, 255.

71. Forty-two individual appeals initiating in Rio reached the appeals court from 1850 to 1870 and 35 from 1871 to 1888; the rest were other or had no date. Database "Ações de liberdade," compiled by Keila Grinberg.

72. Samples from the main *fondos* at the ANC suggest increased slave petitioning over time. The Gobierno Superior Civil collection, which spans the nineteenth century, contains 70 slave claims from 1800 to 1849 but 278 from 1850 to 1866. The Consejo de Administración collection contains 147 appeals by individuals identifiable by sex from after 1880, and only a handful from before 1880. The biggest single repository for slave claims at the ANC is the Miscelánea de Expedientes collection, wherein slave appeals come overwhelmingly from the 1870s and 1880s. While appeals in the Gobierno Superior Civil and Gobierno General and Consejo de Administración *fondos* might come from anywhere across the island, the Miscelánea cases—which form the majority of the cases of this kind I identified at the archive—come overwhelmingly from the city of Havana or nearby areas.

73. Nor can this be explained by the presence of women among the general enslaved population: by 1871, the city's male and female slave populations remained roughly level. Women represented 49.1 percent of city's total slave population in 1872. *Recenseamento da população do Município Neutro* (1872), 1–61.

74. This sample count taken from the vast Miscelánea de Expedientes *fondo* at the ANC was taken from a spread of 30 *legajos*, chosen because they contained large numbers of appeals. These were *legajos* 3484, 3513–3516, 3543–3549, 3585–3593, 3642–3648, 3661, and 3724. This count yielded a total of 710 appeals made by individuals (discounting a small number made by more than one person).

75. Note that these samples represent only the appeals' titles as they appear in the catalogues, not a reading of all the appeals themselves. In fact, in opening one of these documents, an appeal whose title suggests it was made by a male slave often turns out to be on behalf of a child, and being made by his mother. This may mean that these figures significantly under-represent women's role in claims-making.

76. This argument is advanced for Cuba by Castañeda, "Demandas judiciales," 230, and for the Hispanic Caribbean more broadly by Dorsey, "Women without History," 173.

77. Iglesias, "El censo cubano de 1877," 194. There were 1,568 female *coartadas* and 1,134 male *coartados*.

78. For the link between mothers and *coartação*, see Paiva, *Escravos e libertos nas Minas Gerais*, 121–23.

79. For a detailed discussion of the role and origins of *síndicos* in Cuba, see Varella Fernández, "Esclavos a sueldo," 124–81, 472–74. Varella Fernández emphasizes that while the *síndicos* had their origin in the tradition of legal representation for all legal minors, the *síndico* in Cuba came to exercise separate functions from *procuradores*, who acted on behalf of women and children. See also Barcia Zequeira, *La otra familia*, 47–54, and de la Fuente, "Slaves and the Creation of Legal Rights," 665. On *síndicos'* defense of *asiáticos*, see, for example, "Los síndicos del Ayuntamiento de esta Capital piden se les exima de defender los esclavos y colonos en todos los casos en que no exista oposición entre sus derechos y los de sus dueños y patronos," ANC, AH, legajo 233, expediente 18, 1868. On *curadores* in Brazil, see Grinberg, *Liberata*, 63–70.

80. The quotation is from "Expediente promovido por el moreno Lucas Xiqués por libertad de su suegra Julia Ginés," ANC, ME, legajo 3537, expediente W, 1868.

81. Varella, "El canal administrativo de los conflictos entre esclavos y amos," 116.

82. "Los síndicos del Ayuntamiento de esta Capital piden se les exima de defender los esclavos y colonos todos los casos en que no exista oposición entre sus derechos y los de sus dueños y patronos," ANC, AH, legajo 233, expediente 18, 1868.

83. "Efigênia, preta, por seu curador," ANB, CAE, caixa 3687, ap. 14298, 1872, 13–14.

84. The *depósito* process was an important source of income for these charitable public institutions, as well as a lucrative earner for some private individuals. Varella, "Esclavos a sueldo," 257–318.

85. "Expediente promovido por Tomasa esclava de D. Luis Salgado en solicitud de libertad por haber sido prostituida por su amo," ANC, ME, legajo 3516, expediente Ae, 1880.

86. Mendonça, *Entre a mão e os anéis*, 230–32.

87. "Contra los asiáticos Estanislao y José, por heridas al negro esclavo Ciriaco Sánchez," ANC, ME, legajo 2805, expediente J, 1863. Thanks to Benjamin Narváez for passing me this document.

88. Grinberg, *O fiador*, 271–72.

89. The level of training varied. Many first-instance lawyers who represented slaves in Brazil had less formal training than those who took on slave cases at the appeals court level, who were a small, highly trained group. See Grinberg, *O fiador*, 256–60. For Cuba, many of the key provisions about how *síndicos* should proceed and the latest legislation and ordinances on slave law were compiled in 1875 in Cano and Zalba, *El libro de los síndicos*.

90. Differences have emerged between Brazilian historians over the degree to which both *curadores* and judges were influenced by their own personal or political views. Grinberg's meticulous study of the workings of Brazilian slave law finds an increasingly limited scope for personal interpretation as the previous welter of legislation (from which judges were relatively free to pick and choose) gave way to a much more restrictive set of possibilities ushered in by the Portuguese Lei de Boa Razão in 1789. Meanwhile, others have shown how judges and lawyers acted from their own personal and political convictions to a significant degree. The difference may be partly due to the fact that these scholars have often focused on the abolition period, when—as Grinberg discusses—political positions on the slavery question hardened in Brazilian society and took on a newfound intensity. The different emphases are each useful: appreciating the

limits imposed by the law and jurisprudence is vital for interpreting these documents, yet clearly the political and social context also influenced the law's implementation and significance. See: E. Azevedo, *Orfeu de carapinha*, 233–34; Chalhoub, *Visões da liberdade*, 106–7; Grinberg, *O fiador*, 233–53, 274–77; Mendonça, *Entre a mão e os anéis*, 246, 260; Pena, *Pajens da casa imperial*, 364.

91. For Azcárate's and Morales Lemus's actions as *síndicos*, see, for example, Nicolás Azcárate to Gobierno Superior Civil, Guanabacoa, 23 September 1862, ANC, GSC, legajo 954, expediente 33713, 1862; "Expediente promovido por el Lic. Dn. José Morales Lemus, Síndico Segundo en el bienio de 60 y 61, acompañando un estado de las quejas y reclamaciones en que ha intervenido y cuya mayor parte ha terminado por acuerdo," ANC, GSC, legajo 954, expediente 33747, 1862.

92. Schmidt-Nowara, *Empire and Antislavery*, 163–65.

93. Sociedad Abolicionista Española, *Sesión del 23 de Enero de 1881*, 2.

94. Perera and Meriño, *El cabildo carabalí viví de Santiago de Cuba: Familia, cultura y sociedad (1797–1909)*, 108n. 284.

95. Calcagno, *Diccionario biográfico*, 2:435–36; Cepero Bonilla, *Azúcar y abolición*, 144–53, 155–59, 169–74, 181.

96. E. Azevedo, *Orfeu de carapinha*, 193, 199, 262–64.

97. Clóvis Moura, *Dicionário da escravidão negra no Brasil*, 373.

98. "O bacharel Ferreira Nobre: V," *Gazeta da Tarde*, 12 November 1886, 3; see also *Gazeta da Tarde*, 8 November 1886, 3. The *Livro de Ouro* fund was originally conceived as a conservative emancipationist gesture, but later took on a more stridently abolitionist significance, thanks to a proslavery conservative turn by the national government by late 1885. See Castilho and Cowling, "Funding Freedom," 95–97.

99. "Josepha liberta, justificante/José Gonçalves de Pinho, justificado," ANB, juízo de órfãos da 2ª vara, ZM, maço 2292, número 2198, 1884, 2–2v, 31–31v, 34, 39–39v, 42, 49v.

100. This book is mainly concerned with the process by which claims were made, as part of an increased push by the enslaved to take freedom into their own hands. It does not make quantitative claims about whether they were more likely to be resolved in favor of the enslaved person from the 1870s. Even if this could be done in the Brazilian case, many of the Cuban cases do not contain a final verdict, making comparison impossible.

101. Claudia Varella Fernández hypothesizes that the minimum time given to petitioners by *síndicos* was fifteen minutes, following a statement made by a *síndico* in the case of an enslaved woman, Estefanía, in 1866. Varella Fernández, "Esclavos a sueldo," 144, n. 69.

CHAPTER 3

1. For one legal debate on this question, conclusively resolved in favor of owners' right to refuse manumission even if slaves could pay their freedom price, see Conrad, *Children of God's Fire*, 267–73.

2. On socially constructed notions of "good slavery," see Mattos de Castro, *Das cores do Silêncio*, 119–36.

3. Grinberg, *O fiador*, 221, 253–77.

4. Moraes, *A campanha abolicionista*, 282.

5. Graham, *Patronage and Politics*, 6, 65–69, 84, 232; Grinberg, *O fiador*, 198; Pena, *Pajens*, 35–44.

6. "O visitador apostólico da Ordem Carmelita/Laudelina, por seu curador," ANB, CAE, caixa 3684, numero 12189, 1868, microfilm: AN 083–2006, pp. 5–30, 82–83, 91–96, 103–28.

7. José Alamo was Havana's first *síndico* around this time (there were now four *sindicaturas*); the first *sindicatura* was based at Galiano, number 90. See Varella Fernández, "Esclavos a sueldo," 472–74. Around this time, Alamo also represented many other enslaved people living close by, including the *morena* Felipa Galuzo, whose legal claim is mentioned in Chapter 1 of this book.

8. Secretaría del Gobierno Superior Civil, "Reglamento para las Sindicaturas á la presentación de esclavos en queja de sus amos," Havana, January 1863, Article 7, reproduced in Cano and Zalba, *El libro de los síndicos*, 42–43.

9. We can assume that if Santiago was old enough to be earning *jornales*, then he was not a post-1870-born free womb child. Even if he had been, there was no specific legal stipulation about rights of mothers to *coartar* such children.

10. "Expediente promovido por Luisa Criolla (sobre su libertad) (esclava de Doña Cándida Vidal) en queja de no haber efectuado su coartación a pesar de haber puesto una cantidad en depósito," ANC, ME, legajo 3527, expediente Bñ, 1873.

11. "Expediente promovido por la morena Juana Romero para que se le permita coartar a su madre Lucía, esclava de José Antonio Ibarra," ANC, ME, legajo 3586, expediente T, 1874. The appeal's title suggests that Juana wished to *coartar* Lucía; during the case, she also mentions purchasing her outright, as well as Lucía's right to be freed as a *sexagenaria*. In this sense, the case is similar to many freedom claims, in which the aim of those appealing (freedom, or as close to freedom as possible) is more important than the various attempted means of attaining it.

12. *Sindicatura*: *síndico*'s office. *Finca*: Plantation; estate; farm. As the petition still calls María a slave rather than a *patrocinada*, so the *patrono* is referred to as the owner ("dueño").

13. For the "humble" rhetoric, see Varella Fernández, "Esclavos a sueldo," 189–90. For the particular use women made of it, see Russell-Wood, "Acts of Grace."

14. Corwin, *Spain and the Abolition of Slavery*, 307.

15. "Instancia de María Forbes, sobre su hijo José," ANC, ME, legajo 3589, expediente Y, 1882.

16. Maria Rosa to Empress Teresa Cristina, 6 March 1886, AGCRJ, E:E, Book 6.1.41, p. 35.

17. For Teresa as "mother of the Brazilians" see Schwarcz, *As barbas do imperador*, 94. On the children's births and deaths, see, for example, Calmon, *A Princesa Isabel*, 9–18.

18. Pereira Peixoto to Municipal Council, 13 March 1886, AGCRJ, E:E, Book 6.1.41, p. 34.

19. See AGCRJ, E:E, Book 6.1.41, 14 March 1886, 41–43; Castilho and Cowling, "Funding Freedom"; Cowling, "Debating Womanhood."

20. "Expediente promovido por Juana Sánchez y Sánchez esclava de de D. Gregorio Masá pidiendo su libertad por haber tenido una hija con su amo," ANC, GSC, legajo 954, expediente 33696, 1862. The phrase "leaving one's blood in slavery" was the frequent subject of debate in 1860s Brazil. See Pena, *Pajens da casa imperial*, 145–252.

21. "Expediente promovido por la mulata Paula esclava de D. Vicente Martínez pidiendo su libertad por haberla disfrutado su dueño y tener un hijo con él," ANC, GSC, legajo. 954, expediente 33705, 1862.

22. "Expediente promovido por la morena Dolores Chacón, esclava de D Joaquín Chacón en queja contra su amo," ANC, ME, legajo 3514, expediente N, 1870; Cowling, "Negotiating Freedom," 382.

23. Barcia Zequeira, *La otra familia*, 45, 51.

24. For a copy of this rule (Siete Partidas, Ley I, Tit. XXII, Partida IV), see Cano and Zalba, *El libro de los síndicos*, 151.

25. Ibid., 27.

26. On the Moret Law as a continuation of this longer process, see Perera and Meriño, *La cesión de patronato*.

27. On Busch e Varella's career, see Grinberg, *O fiador*, 266, 273.

28. "Apelantes Benta e outras; apelado Antonio José da Silva Ribeiro," ANB, CAE, caixa 3689, número 2623, 1879, microfilm AN 094–2006, pp. 5–11, 71, 102–6, 119, 135, 144, 176, 210.

29. "Carta de liberación, Catalina González," MMR, Expedientes del Ayuntamiento, legajo 21, expediente 7, 21 August 1878.

30. "Crônica do Bem," *Gazeta da Tarde*, 29 July 1884, 1. The abolitionist paper described the woman as being "restored" to freedom in a pointed attempt to argue that freedom rightfully belonged to enslaved people, from whom it had been taken.

31. "Expediente promovido por la morena Isabel Casas, esclava de D José López y Robert, pidiendo la libertad que le había ofrecido por criarle un hijo," ANC, ME, legajo 3600, expediente Bh, 1872.

32. Scott, *Slave Emancipation*, 167.

33. Faustino would have been born in 1864—he was thus a slave, not a *liberto*.

34. Due to massive fluctuation in the value of *billetes* in this period, there were endless disputes between owners and slaves about how amounts should be paid. In 1874, it was resolved that slaves should pay their *jornales* in *billetes*, not gold. "Expediente promovido por el Síndico Segundo consultando si los esclavos coartados deben pagar sus jornales en oro," ANC, ME, legajo 3586, expediente Bc, 1874. The value of payments in notes was roughly half that of gold. Scott, *Slave Emancipation*, 153.

35. If Inés was over 60, she would seem rather old to have a son aged 12. Possibly her age had been exaggerated, or Faustino's underestimated, for the purposes of making the appeal.

36. Scott, *Slave Emancipation*, 133–38, 147.

37. Marrero Cruz, *Julián de Zulueta*, 83–84; Pérez, *Cuba between Reform and Revolution*, 131.

38. See Barcia Zequeira, *La otra familia*, 93; Barcia Zequeira, *Los ilustres apellidos*, 126–31; Basso Ortiz, *Los gangá en Cuba*, 52–54.

39. "Expediente y cuaderno de notas promovido en la sindicatura 3a con motivo de la coartación del moreno Faustino hijo de Inés morena libre," ANC, GG, legajo 356, expediente 17063, 1876.

40. Italics mine.

41. "Informe del expediente instruido a consulta del Caballero Síndico 3° de esta Capital relativa a que si los esclavos menores de 14 años hijos de madres libres pueden venderse separados de estas," ANC, CA, legajo 44, expediente 4927, 1876.

42. See, for example, "Comunicaciones de los tres colectores de la provincia (Habana) sobre Patrocinados," ANC, GG, legajo 271, expediente 13574, 1877; "Oficio dirigido al señor capitán pedáneo del partido de Banao por D. Rafael Pereira apoderado de Don Roque de Lara, manifestándole el traslado de los esclavos Tranquilino y Tomás, que pertenecían a la dotación del potrero 'Vallejos,'" ANC, VI, caja V-B, legajo 2, expediente 23, 1872.

43. "Consulta sobre lo promovido por el Excmo Sr Gobernador Civil de Santiago de Cuba en solicitud de que se declare que las antiguas esclavas que por cualquier causa queden exentas de patronato pueden llevarse a sus hijos libertos," ANC, CA, legajo 69, expediente 6970, 1881–82. A similar consultation in the same year was resolved in the same way: see "Consulta sobre si los nacidos desde el 17 de Setiembre de 1868 de antiguas esclavas declaradas libres con arreglo al artículo 19 de la ley de 4 de julio de 1870 deben ser entregados a sus padres sin exigirles la indemnización prevista por el art. 11 segundo párrafo de la propia Ley," ANC, CA, legajo 76, expediente 7374, 1882.

44. "Consulta sobre la R.O. de 10 de Octubre de 1883 disponiendo que los padres libertos pueden revindicar el patronato de sus hijos menores nacidos desde 17 de Septiembre de 1868 sin indemnización," ANC, CA, legajo 80, expediente 7513, 1883.

45. "Documento conteniendo instancia de Ramona Oliva, sobre sus hijos María Fabiana y Agustina," ANC, ME, legajo 3724, expediente T, 1883.

46. "Expediente relativo a la renuncia graciosa que de los derechos de patronato hace Dn Jorge Mendez a favor de la madre de sus patrocinados Gavino y Vicente criollos," MMR, JLPR, legajo 16, expediente 002965, 1884.

47. On this question as debated by the Instituto de Advogados Brasileiros in the 1850s, see Pena, *Pajens da casa imperial*, 32–33, 80–116. By contrast, for Cuba, the question of whether *coartación* of mothers altered the status of their children in any way had long since been resolved. It was decided that *coartación* was personal only and had no effect on children born to *coartadas*. Aimes, "Coartación," 418–20. Nonetheless, Cuba deputies to the Madrid Junta de Información in the 1860s did state their belief that if a mother was *coartada*, this ought to grant her an advantage in the process of seeking *coartación* for her child. España, *Información sobre reformas*, 1:68.

48. See Chalhoub, *Visões da liberdade*, 114–17.

49. "Henrique preto menor por seu curador Joaquim Pereira Bastos," ANB, CAE, caixa 3682, número 13335, 1870, microfilm AN 087–2006.

50. Abreu, "Slave Mothers," 576; see also Chalhoub, *Machado de Assis*, chapter 4.

51. Some lawyers were even more explicit about the political implications of courts' decisions. The *curador* of the slave Isaac, whose case reached the Supreme Court in September 1871, mentioned that the case was being judged at a "solemn moment:

Brazilian society repudiates the shameful and infamous canker of slavery." "Isaac, por seu curador," ANB, CAE, caixa 3687, apelação 13433, 1871, microfilm AN 029–2006.

52. "Ismael (escravo), Domiciano, Laurelio, Basília," ANB, CAE, caixa 3687, número 8140, 1872, microfilm AN 029–2006.

CHAPTER 4

1. Drescher, "Brazilian Abolition," 450.

2. Alonso, *Idéias em movimento*, 284; C. Azevedo, *Abolitionism in the United States and Brazil*, x, 3–7; Bethell and Carvalho, *Joaquim Nabuco*. For a Spanish pamphlet on the history of Atlantic abolitions, which discussed the British and American cases in detail as well as France, Sweden, Holland, and Russia, see Barón Fortacín, *Cuestión de Cuba*. Spanish-born Barón Fortacín, a Spanish Abolitionist Society member, became a deputy for Puerto Rico, whose 1873 abolition law he drafted.

3. For example: Alonso, "The Cosmopolitan Abolitionist"; Castilho, "Brisas atlânticas"; Chalhoub, *Machado de Assis*, 141, 148.

4. Castelar, *Discurso pronunciado por el ciudadano Emilio Castelar*, 4, 21.

5. Franklin, *Women and Slavery*, 135.

6. "El Proyecto del Señor Moret," *La Revolución* (June 1870), 481–82 in Unos abolicionistas, *La abolición de la esclavitud*, 83.

7. *La Igualdad*, 415 (June 1870), reproduced in Unos abolicionistas, *La abolición de la esclavitud*, 88.

8. Aguilera, *Notes about Cuba*, 12.

9. Abreu, "Slave Mothers."

10. "A Nossa Missão," *O Abolicionista: Orgão da Sociedade Brasileira contra a Escravidão* 1 (1 November 1880): 1.

11. Célia Maria Azevedo has argued that Brazilian antislavery arguments focused much more on slavery as an impediment to progress than on moralistic rhetoric about slaves as "brothers" or fellow human beings. By comparison with the United States, and for most of the nineteenth century, she is undoubtedly right. However, as this chapter shows, the use of sentimental, impassioned, and moralizing rhetoric did become an important way of mobilizing popular support for abolitionism during the 1880s in particular. The example also demonstrates that, in any case, there was not necessarily a contradiction between modernizing versus moralizing arguments—here, *O Abolicionista* combines both. C. Azevedo, *Abolitionism in the United States and Brazil*, 8–14.

12. For the notion of charity and humanity as "modern" feminine sentiments, contrasting with foreign travelers' observations earlier in the century about Brazilian women's inhumane treatment of their slaves, see Gomes Costa, "Entre práticas escravistas e caritativas."

13. "Mãe, filho e senhor," *Gazeta da Tarde*, 7 January 1884, 1. The *roda dos expostos* was a reference to the practice employed by charitable institutions that took in abandoned children, where mothers unable to care for children placed them on a revolving wheel that took them inside the institution, preserving the anonymity of the person who left them.

14. Pareceres: Sr Dr Rodrigues dos Santos," *Boletim* (26 February 1877): 18; "Portarias," *Boletim* (10 April 1880): 3; "Resumo do mapa demonstrativo do movimento dos partos da Maternidade Municipal, de abril a dezembro de 1881," *Boletim* (26 January 1882): 21–23.

15. "Abolición de la esclavitud en Cuba," España, *Información sobre reformas*, 2:259–60.

16. "The model Plantation of Paraizo," *Anglo-Brazilian Times* (7 October 1874): 2.

17. Gallenga, *The Pearl of the Antilles*, 123.

18. Castelar, *Abolición de la esclavitud*, 28. Note that Castelar, like Nabuco in the 1880 *O Abolicionista* example cited above, conflated "the sentiment of humanity" with the "modernity" sought by Spanish and Brazilian abolitionists alike. Again, there was not necessarily any opposition between the two ideas.

19. Ibid., 9–10.

20. See Grinberg, *Liberata*, 75–77; Pena, *Pajens da casa imperial*, 87.

21. Christopher Schmidt-Nowara convincingly analyzes distinctions in emphasis and portrayals of enslaved people between metropolitan and colonial writers. The former were more likely to envision idealized harmonious (although certainly not equal) labor relations between former masters and former slaves along the lines of their hopes for reforming class relations in Spanish society; the latter were more likely to view ex-slaves as violent and threatening. Ultimately, neither group genuinely envisioned racial equality in postemancipation societies. Schmidt-Nowara, *Empire and Antislavery*, 119–22; 174–76.

22. See Bronfman, *Measures of Equality*; Helg, "Race in Argentina and Cuba"; Schwarcz, *The Spectacle of the Races*, 44–70; Stepan, *"The Hour of Eugenics,"* 21–62.

23. Hoganson, "Garrisonian Abolitionists," 569–75; Midgley, *Women against Slavery*, 95–99, 102; Zaeske, *Signatures of Citizenship*, 62–65. On how this imagery stamped itself upon Atlantic imaginings of emancipation, see Wood, *The Horrible Gift of Freedom*, 58–89.

24. Suárez y Romero, *Francisco*; Tanco y Bosmoniel, *Petrona y Rosalía*; Villaverde, *Cecilia Valdés*. For analysis, see Fivel-Démoret, "The Production and Consumption of Propaganda Literature"; Acosta and Montoto, *Historia de la literatura cubana*, 1:115–24, 141–50, 203–10.

25. Gómez de Avellaneda, *Sab*; Fivel-Démoret, "The Production and Consumption of Propaganda Literature," 8–10.

26. Casasnovas, *Bread, or Bullets!*, 86.

27. Ibid.

28. Guimarães, *A escrava Isaura*. Of course, Isaura was white-skinned, making the quest for sympathy from white, elite readers much easier to achieve.

29. Castilho, "Performing Abolitionism"; Midgley, *Women against Slavery*, 145–49.

30. Chalhoub, *Machado de Assis*, 192–97.

31. On Romantic rhetoric and its appearance in political oratory as well as literary texts, see A. Souza, *Formação da literatura brasileira*, 2:23–44; Kirkendall, *Class Mates*, chapter 2; Needell, *Party of Order*, chapter 1, n. 87. Thanks to Jeffrey Needell for these references and for his helpful insights about nineteenth-century rhetoric.

32. Alencar, *Mãe*. In his prologue to the collection, R. Magalhães Jr. argues that although the play was not intended as such, "there is no doubt that *Mãe* became, *malagré lui*, an abolitionist drama." Magalhães, "Sucessos e insucessos de Alencar no teatro," in *José de Alencar: Teatro completo*, 1:18. For the significance the drama took on during the debates of the Instituto de Advogados Brasilieiros in the 1840s and 1850s about the status of children sired by slaveholders, see Pena, *Pajens da casa imperial*, 175–76.

33. On abolitionism and theatre, see Castilho, "Performing Abolitionism"; and Marzano, *Cidade em cena*, 72–80.

34. "Pelos teatros," *Revista Illustrada* (21 November 1886), 6. For *Uncle Tom's Cabin*'s translation into Spanish, and on the popularity of theatre representations in favor of abolition, see Labra y Ladrana, *La abolición y la Sociedad Abolicionista Española*, 9, 53.

35. "Ingênuo espancado," *Gazeta da Tarde*, 28 January 1884, 2.

36. As Sharon Block insightfully analyzes for early America, the very definition of whether a sexual encounter could be conceived of as "rape" was a function of the relative power (gender, race, economic independence or lack of it) of the individuals involved. Block, *Rape in Early America*, 4, 239.

37. See Midgley, *Women against Slavery*, 97, 102, 200. On historical portrayals of women of color, see Bush, *Slave Women in Caribbean Society*, 11–22; Côrtes, "Coisa de pele," 75–76, 92, 104–15; Morgan, *Laboring Women*, 26–30; Nagel, *Race, Ethnicity, and Sexuality*, 91–97; Simms, "Controlling Images."

38. Sociedad Abolicionista Española, *La abolición de la esclavitud en el Brasil y en España*, 9–10, 14–15.

39. "A Emancipação na Tribuna Sagrada," *O Abolicionista* (1 January 1881): 7–8. Dots in original text. On abolitionism in Rio Grande do Sul, see Kittleson, *The Practice of Politics*, 118–48; Kittleson, "Women and Notions of Womanhood," 99–120.

40. For the history of the festival and brotherhood, see M. Souza, *Reis negros no Brasil escravista*.

41. Here I build on Roger Kittleson's point about Porto Alegre that "the traditional sphere of women's activities provided abolitionists with an extra-political space in which to defuse the explosive effects of antislavery measures." Kittleson, "Campaign of All Peace and Charity," 84.

42. I am indebted for this realization to Kristin Hoganson's insightful analysis of Garrisonian abolitionists in the United States. Hoganson, "Garrisonian Abolitionists," 559–63.

43. Kirkendall, *Class Mates*, chapter 2.

44. On the *pai de família* term, see Graham, *Patronage and Politics*, 19. For "manly" rhetoric directed to Emperor Pedro II, see João Pereira Lopes, speech on 7 September 1886, *Boletim* (16 September 1886): 89–93. On the different gendered praise given to women and men who supported the Paraguay War effort, see Ipsen, "Delicate Citizenship," 161.

45. "A mulher brazileira é escravocrata?," *Gazeta da Tarde*, 14 January 1884, 2. On Reis, see Moraes, *A campanha abolicionista*, 59, n.56.

46. A similar point is made by Hoganson on United States abolitionism. Male abolitionists, seeking political credibility "as men," praised each other for their "Christian

manliness" and "manly hostility" toward slavery. Hoganson, "Garrisonian Abolitionists," 586.

47. Moraes, *A campanha abolicionista*, 100.

48. "Antônio Francisco de Couto (Autor) / Francelina, por seu Curador (Ré): Libelo Civel de Escravidão," ANB, CAE, caixa 3679, número 7633, 1870, microfilm: AN 25–2006, pp. 2–7, 13, 28–30, 36–38,55–56, 82–83.

49. Castilho, "With Grace and Delicacy"; Hahner, *A mulher brasileira*, 44–50; Midgley, *Women against Slavery*; Schmidt-Nowara, *Empire and Antislavery*, 117–18; Zaeske, *Signatures of Citizenship*.

50. Conrad, *The Destruction*, 141–43; Drescher, *Abolition*, 338.

51. Kittleson notes the similarity in mobilizing women and notions of femininity between Britain, the United States, and Brazil, though he does not mention any actual links between the movements. Kittleson, "Women and Notions of Womanhood," 99–101.

52. Schmidt-Nowara, *Empire and Antislavery*, 118; *Birmingham Daily Post*, 6 May 1871; "Às senhoras brasileiras," *O Abolicionista*, 1 December 1880, 3–4. Interestingly, *O Abolicionista* translated the name of the Birmingham society as the "Sociedade amiga das mulheres negras" (society of the friends of black women). On the Birmingham societies, see Hall, *Civilizing Subjects*, 290–379, and Midgley, *Women against Slavery*, 45–47, 189.

53. Franklin, *Women and Slavery*, 21.

54. Schmidt-Nowara, *Empire and Antislavery*, 92.

55. Joaquín Sanromá, *Educación social de la mujer* (Madrid: Rivadeneyra, 1869), 20–21, quoted and translated into English by Schmidt-Nowara, *Empire and Antislavery*, 94.

56. Concepción Arenal, "La esclavitud de los negros," in Sociedad Abolicionista Española, *El cancionero del esclavo*, 17–36. On Arenal, see Schmidt-Nowara, *Empire and Antislavery*, 97.

57. Joaquina García Balmaseda, "¡Caridad en favor del esclavo! A las Madres de Familia," in Sociedad Abolicionista Española, *El cancionero del esclavo*, 80. Among her other works, García Balmaseda's *La madre de familia* stands out: it ran into at least twelve editions and was re-published up until 1920.

58. García Balmaseda, "Caridad a favor del esclavo," 85. On the separate spheres notion, see Schmidt-Nowara, 117–18.

59. García Balmaseda, *La mujer sensata*, 66.

60. Ipsen, "Delicate Citizenship," Chapter 2.

61. Kittleson, "Campaign of All Peace and Charity," 92–93.

62. *Gazeta da Tarde*, 11 August 1886, 1. On Bulicioff's visit, see also "Crônica do bem," *Gazeta da Tarde*, 12 August 1886, 2.

63. "Uma bela festa," *Revista Illustrada*, 20 August 1886, 6–7. The empress may have had particular reasons for crying, other than her emotion over the emancipations, since Pedro II and Nadina had reportedly become lovers. See Marzano, *Cidade em cena*, 76. Thanks to Celso Castilho for alerting me to this reference.

64. Castilho, "Performing Abolitionism."

65. See Alonso, *Idéias em movimento*, 263–313; Castilho, "Abolition Matters," viii–x; Kittleson, "Campaign of All Peace and Charity," 98.

66. "Confederação Abolicionista: Reunião de senhoras no edifício da Municipalidade," AGCRJ, E:E, Book 6.2.42, 22 June 1883.

67. "Festa de 25 de março," *Gazeta da Tarde*, 23 February 1884, 3. On the repercussions and celebrations of abolition in Ceará in Rio, see França Ferreira, "Nas asas da imprensa."

68. *Gazeta da Tarde*, 28 February 1884, 1; *Gazeta da Tarde*, 20 March 1884, 2. The female relatives of prominent male abolitionists often appeared in the abolitionist press, such as D. Maria Cândida Jardim, wife of the Portuguese ambassador and mother-in-law of João Clapp, who got a special mention on her death. "D. Maria Cândida Jardim," *Gazeta da Tarde*, 14 December 1885, 1.

69. On this phenomenon elsewhere in Brazil, see Kittleson, "Campaign of All Peace and Charity." Religious language and sentiment as expressed in Brazilian abolitionism was certainly much more muted than in the United States, as Célia Maria Azevedo has argued. Many Brazilian abolitionists were also anticlerical and Republican. However, arguments based on Christian principles still appeared quite frequently in Brazilian abolitionist language. Elite feminine identities were also bound up with religiosity, so when women were mobilized into abolitionist campaigning, they frequently expressed religious sentiments. See C. Azevedo, *Abolitionism in the United States and Brazil*, 11–12. For the role of religious and humanitarian rhetoric in the debates prior to the 1871 law, see Chalhoub, *Machado de Assis*, 140–41, 166.

70. "Festival abolicionista," *Gazeta da Tarde*, 14 January 1884, 1; "Matinée abolicionista," *Gazeta da Tarde*, 19 January 1884, 1'; "Grande matinee," *Gazeta da Tarde*, 28 January 1884, 2; *Gazeta da Tarde*, 1 February 1884, 1. Also involved were the Abolitionist Confederation's Júlio Lemos, and the *mestiço* actor and abolitionist Francisco Correa Vasques.

71. "Grande matinee," *Gazeta da Tarde*, 28 January 1884, 2. On Josefa Águeda Felisbela Mercedes de Oliveira's career, see Castilho, "With Grace and Delicacy"; Hahner, *Emancipating the Female Sex*, 56–60.

72. Oliveira's speech appears in "A mulher brasileira é esclavocrata?," *Gazeta da Tarde*, 30 January 1884, 2.

73. "Colaboração: Às senhoras brasileiras," *Gazeta da Tarde*, 13 September 1884, 3; *Gazeta da Tarde*, 16 September 1884, 2. The piece was signed simply "O menor dos brasileiros" (the humblest of the Brazilians). The emperor sometimes signed in this way, but it is unlikely that this radical abolitionist piece was his doing.

74. Hahner, *A mulher brasileira*, 44; Kittleson, "Women and Notions of Womanhood," 100, 113; Viotti da Costa, *The Brazilian Empire*, 247–65. Drescher adds that Brazilian abolitionism more generally "lacked the means of political reproduction," failing to translate into other social and political reform movements of any kind. Drescher, "Brazilian Abolition in Comparative Perspective," 460. On the other hand, Clare Midgley notes that in any case, there was no straightforward passage from abolitionism to suffragism in Britain; rather, there was a tension within abolitionism between upholding socially conservative views about women's sphere, and the undermining of

such views that women's mobilization could imply. Midgley, *Women against Slavery*, 200–203.

75. On women's education in Brazil, see Ipsen, "Delicate Citizenship," 221–23; Hahner, *Emancipating the Female Sex*, chapter 2; Schueler, "Culturas escolares," 64, 116–19, 139, 144. For the argument that women's mobilization, both during the Paraguayan War and then in the cause of abolitionism, created an opening in which elite women began to claim a greater inclusion in the nation's political life, see Ipsen, "Delicate Citizenship," 312. For the nineteenth-century reevaluation of girls' education in Cuba, and a survey of works about similar processes in several European countries, see Franklin, *Women and Slavery*, 71–72. Matt Childs points out that the interest in women's education in Cuba was also specifically linked to the desire to preserve "civilization" in the face of huge African imports: see Childs, "'Sewing' Civilization."

76. "O eterno feminino," *Revista Illustrada*, 16 January 1886, 6. On "O eterno feminino" and its treatment of some women's claims for suffrage rights in the 1880s and early 1890s, see Ipsen, "Delicate Citizenship," 298.

77. "O eterno feminino," *Revista Illustrada*, 12 December 1885, 6.

78. Nagel, *Race, Ethnicity and Sexuality*, 14–18.

79. For elite fears or controls of "ethnosexual" crossings, see Martínez-Alier, *Marriage, Class and Color*; Mena, "Stretching the Limits," 95–97, 100–102.

80. See Kittleson, *The Practice of Politics in Postcolonial Brazil*, 133–34.

81. Vera y González, *La esclavitud*, 278.

82. Quoted in Spanish by Vera y González, *La esclavitud*, 286. The original English version, used here, is from O'Kelly, *The Mambi-Land*, 65.

83. Several Cuban and Puerto Rican Abolitionists, *The Abolition of Slavery*, 15.

84. C. Vianna, "O lote!," *Gazeta da Tarde*, 17 January 1884, 2.

85. Anselmo Suárez y Romero, "Después de seis años," BNJM, Manuscritos, CM Suárez R, vol. 6, no. 30, 1877, 506–7.

86. Ibid., 512–15.

87. On the difficulty of conceiving of a nongendered humanity, see Hoganson, "Garrisonian Abolitionists," 562.

88. Segismundo Moret y Prendergast, "Del porvenir de las clases obreras de mujeres," *Gaceta Economista* (Madrid) 1, no. 3(July 1861): 184–88. Quoted in Schmidt-Nowara, *Empire and Antislavery*, 90.

89. España, *Información sobre reformas*, 2:258.

90. Gomes Costa, "Entre práticas escravistas e caritativas."

91. "O crime de Botafogo," *Gazeta da Tarde*, 12 March 1886, 1.

92. For example: "Notas e impressões," *Revista Illustrada*, 16 January 1886, 3, 8; "Notas e impressões," *Revista Illustrada*, 18 February 1886, 3; "Francisca de Castro," *Gazeta da Tarde*, 15 April 1886, 1; "O julgamento de ontem," *Gazeta da Tarde*, 25 October 1886, 1.

93. Moraes, *A campanha abolicionista*, 157–58. On depictions of slaveholding women's cruelty, including one piece in a Porto Alegre newspaper entitled, as in Rio's *Gazeta da Tarde*, "A mulher brasileira é escravocrata?," see Kittleson, "Campaign of All Peace and Charity," 96.

94. "A mulher brasileira é escravocrata?," *Gazeta da Tarde*, 14 January 1884, 2.

95. "A mulher brasileira é escravocrata?," *Gazeta da Tarde*, 22 January 1884, 1. Italics in original.

96. Aluízio Azevedo, "A mulher brasileira é escravocrata?," *Gazeta da Tarde*, 29 January 1884, 2. Aluízio Azevedo, *O Mulato*, 16–17, 39–41, 56.

97. João Clapp, "A mulher brasileira é escravocrata?," *Gazeta da Tarde*, 19 January 1884, 1.

98. Luiz Gonzaga Duque Estrada, "A mulher brasileira é escravocrata?," *Gazeta da Tarde*, 22 January 1884, 2.

99. "A mulher brasileira," *Gazeta da Tarde*, 25 January 1884, 1.

100. Speech by Sr. Dr. Adolpho Bezerra de Menezes, *Boletim*, 14 March 1876, 31. Italics in original.

101. Speech by João Pereira Lopes, 14 March 1886, *Boletim* (18 March 1886): 122.

102. Castelar, *Los crímenes de la esclavitud*, 3.

103. Several Cuban and Puerto Rican Abolitionists, *The Abolition of Slavery*, 30n. 10.

104. Mena, "Stretching the Limits," 96, 100.

105. Castillo de González, "La mujer cubana," 2–4.

106. Liddell, "Nature, Nurture and Nation."

107. Speech by unnamed member of the Confederação Abolicionista, Rio de Janeiro, 1 May 1887, to Câmara Municipal, *Boletim*, 14 May 1887, 79. Flávia Fernandes de Souza found no fewer than nineteen projects presented to the Municipal Council in the 1880s and 1890s for the regulation of domestic servants. See F. Souza, "Para casa de família e mais serviços," 170. On wet-nursing, domestic service, and "hygiene," see also the following articles in *Boletim*: "Projeto de posturas sobre amas de leite," 16 April 1884, 22–23; "Projetos de posturas: Sobre a locação de serviços domésticos no Município Neutro," 29 August 1885, 90–93; "Projeto de postura sobre locação de serviços," 24 March 1887, 93–95; "Regulamento do Serviço Domestico," 4 October 1888, 3–4. For analysis, see Chalhoub, *Cidade febril*; Lauderdale Graham, *House and Street*, 108–32; Lauderdale Graham, "A abolição na cidade"; Meade, *"Civilizing" Rio*.

108. On attempts to control prostitution in Rio, see Caulfield, "O nascimento do Mangue"; Lauderdale Graham, "Slavery's impasse"; L. Soares, *O "Povo de Cam,"* 176–85; Engel Vainfas, "Meretrizes e doutores." For Havana, see Barcia Zequeira, "Entre el poder y la crisis"; Guy, "Medical Imperialism Gone Awry," 77.

109. "Proposta, vereador Candido Alves Pereira de Carvalho," *Boletim*, 22 November 1888, 55–56.

110. Macedo, *As vítimas-algozes*, 7. On Macedo's novel and the political context that produced it, see Chalhoub, *Machado de Assis*, 157–63.

111. On how metaphors shape how we think, see Pérez, *Cuba in the American Imagination*.

CHAPTER 5

1. "Apelantes Benta e outras; apelado Antonio José da Silva Ribeiro," ANB, CAE, caixa 3689, núm 2623, 1879, microfilm AN 094–2006, 71.

2. "A lei negra," *Gazeta da Tarde*, 19 November 1885, 1. Robert Conrad also discusses part of this quotation; I have followed his translation into English. Conrad, *The Destruction*, 233.

3. Zambrana, *El negro Francisco*, 117.

4. For the perceptive argument that internal trades shaped the life of *all* slaves, see W. Johnson, *Soul by Soul*, 19.

5. For example, Childs, *The 1812 Aponte Rebellion*, 76, 115–16, 130–31, 138–39, 149; García, *La esclavitud desde la esclavitud*, 36–41; Machado, *O plano e o pânico*, 15–16, 104–6, 143–65.

6. For the mobility of "slave-insurgents" see Ferrer, *Insurgent Cuba*, 32–37. For the impact of war on central Cuba, see Scott, *Degrees of Freedom*, 94–104, 113–14, 129–53. On migration strategies—although often temporary and involving different members of a family at different points, rather than the mass exodus that planters feared—see Scott, *Slave Emancipation*, 242–44, 247–54. For recruitment during the Paraguay War in Brazil, see Beattie, "The House, the Street and the Barracks," 444–51. On slave mobility and trains, see Machado, *O plano e o pânico*, 91–92.

7. On the southeast, see Machado, *O plano e o pânico*, 15–16, 104–6, 143–65; Machado, "From Slave Rebels to Strikebreakers"; Moraes, *A campanha abolicionista*, 36–39, 163–64, 235–50; E. Silva, *As camélias do Leblon*. On the underground railroad in the northern provinces, see Castilho, "A New Canada."

8. "Expediente promovido por el negro Paulino Criollo esclavo de Dn José Francisco de la Vega que reside en su ingenio 'Ecuador' situado en la jurisdicción de Colón o Cárdenas; y coartado en 250 p. pide papel porque se le tiene en los trabajos de la finca como los demás," ANC, GSC, legajo 954, expediente 33742, 1862.

9. *Potrero*: cattle-raising ranch or farm, often with sugar plantation attached.

10. "Expediente promovido por la morena Severina Hernández de D. Bernardo Lastra que solicita variar de dueño," ANC, ME, legajo 3540, expediente Aj, 1878.

11. For the various bodies to which Cuban slaves might appeal in the nineteenth century, see Varella Fernández, "Esclavos a sueldo," 124–81.

12. *Dotaciones*: the slaves belonging to a particular plantation; slave gangs. Conde de Cañongo, President of Junta Protectora de Libertos, to Gobernador Superior Político, Havana, 3 October 1873, in "Junta Protectora de Libertos de la Habana," ANC, ME, legajo 3576, expediente K, 1873.

13. On the "rival geography" created by enslaved people in the U.S. South, see Camp, *Closer to Freedom*, 7, 47–51.

14. "Orden del Gobierno Superior Político disponiendo que, cuando el dueño de un esclavo, presentado en jurisdicción extraña, reclame el fuero de domicilio, al contestar al Síndico le provea de lo necesario para el viaje del siervo y del alguacil que ha de conducirlo," 26 May 1871, reproduced in Cano and Zalba, *El libro de los síndicos*, 60.

15. For example, "Expediente promovido por la morena Juliana esclava de D. Vicente Bocalandro, en queja de que su amo le ha cobrado tres onzas y media por la libertad de una hija suya nacida después del 18 de Septiembre de 1868," ANC, ME, legajo 3518, expediente A1, 1871.

16. Cano and Zalba, *El libro de los síndicos*, 50.

17. Scott, *Slave Emancipation*, 88–89, 137, 168, 191.

18. Watson, *Slave Law in the Americas*, 51.

19. Scott, *Slave Emancipation*, 76.

20. Like the system established in Brazil in 1885, this meant that prices were not dictated by the market, but in a uniform manner. The introduction of the scale in Cuba seems to have marked the end of a period of conflict over the rights of *coartado* slaves. On the 1880 provision, see Scott, *Slave Emancipation*, 129–30.

21. García, *La esclavitud desde la esclavitud*, 43.

22. For example: "Sobre el cobro de la capitación del segundo semestre de 1845 sobre los esclavos al servicio doméstico que establece la Real Orden de 29 de Julio de 1844," ANC, GSC, legajo 33295, expediente 944, 1845; "Varios padrones de los esclavos de ambos sexos destinados al servicio doméstico y sujetos al pago de Capitación," ANC, GSC, legajo 948, expediente 33528, 1853–54; "Real Orden relativa a derechos de capitación de esclavos residentes en la isla de Cuba," ANC, ROC, legajo 180, expediente 17, 1854. For the 1872 tax, see "Resolución de la Intendencia General de Hacienda para el establecimiento y cobranza del impuesto extraordinario de guerra sobre los esclavos alquilados y los destinados al servicio doméstico en poblados acordado por el Excmo. Sr. Gobernador Superior Político en 11 de octubre último y aprobado por Real Orden de 7 de Noviembre siguiente," (1872), in Cano and Zalba, *El libro de los síndicos*, 341–46.

23. "Circular de Gobierno Superior Político declarando que los esclavos de campo no adquieren por la coartación el derecho de cambiar de dueño," 1 May 1871, in Cano and Zalba, *El libro de los síndicos*, 59.

24. "Expediente promovido por la negra Justa Morales esclava de D. Cayetano Rosich en solicitud de no ser vendida para el campo," ANC, ME, legajo 3527, expediente Dd, 1873.

25. "Expediente promovido a consecuencia de consultar el Síndico de Regla sobre la esclava Juana de D Francisco Muro deba considerarse como de campo o del servicio doméstico," ANC, ME, legajo 3546, expediente S, 1875; "Decreto del Gobierno General disponiendo que los esclavos de campo que permanezcan cuatro meses en las poblaciones sean considerados como del servicio doméstico," 1 April 1876, in Cano and Zalba, *El libro de los síndicos*, 7.

26. For this estimate, see the report of Consejo de Administración official Federico Zalla in "Expediente promovido a consecuencia de consultar el Síndico de Regla sobre la esclava Juana de D Francisco Muro deba considerarse como de campo o del servicio doméstico," ANC, ME, legajo 3546, expediente S, 1875.

27. "Expediente promovido por la morena María de Regla esclava de D. Lorenzo Toro pidiendo sea tazada en la Sindicatura Segunda de esta Capital," ANC, ME, legajo 3594, expediente Ah, 1875.

28. "João Cândido da Teixeira Chaves, morador em Magé, pedindo a entrega do menor Aleixo filho de Anna parda liberta," ANB, juízo de órfãos da 2ª vara (ZM), maço 324, núm. 6057, 1888.

29. On the Peñalver family, see Martínez-Fernández, *Fighting Slavery*, 80; Moreno Fraginals, *El ingenio*, 1:112, 137.

30. "Instancia de Pedro Peñalver a nombre de Margarita de D. Ignacio Peñalver sobre faltar a la Ley su patrono," ANC, ME, legajo 3527, expediente A11, 1884.

31. See, for example, Camp, *Closer to Freedom*, 28–59; Landers, "Maroon Women in Colonial Spanish America."

32. Women were seen as less threatening, perhaps allowing women runaways to blend in better. Observing that for Rio between 1808 and 1850, 85 percent of enslaved fugitives were males, historian Mary Karasch also noted that more women were advertized as runaways than feature among lists of those captured, and suggests that it may have been easier for women fugitives to pass unobserved among the general population of color. Women based in the city of Rio traded with runaway groups established around its fringes, exchanging goods and money but also news and information. Karasch, *Slave Life in Rio de Janeiro*, 305–7.

33. Italics in the original.

34. España, *Información sobre reformas*, 1:42, 68.

35. Bergad et al., *The Cuban Slave Market*, 85, 92; Drescher, "Brazilian Abolition in Comparative Perspective," 437.

36. See Cowling, "Across the Miles"; Sartorius, "Uncommon Winds"; Varella, "Esclavos a sueldo," 182–256.

37. On the gendered distinctions in Cuba between urban and rural slavery, see Franklin, "Suitable to Her Sex," 128–30.

38. "Expediente promovido por la mulata Dorotea Criolla, esclava de Dn José Mariano Herrera, pidiendo variar de amo," ANC, ME, legajo 3724, expediente H, 1877.

39. Suárez y Romero, "Después de seis años," BNJM, Manuscritos, CM Suárez R, vol. 6, no. 30, 1877, 512–15.

40. For example, "O estado da pátria," *Gazeta da Tarde*, 16 Jan 1884, 1; *Gazeta da Tarde*, 7 February 1884, 1–2; "Jurisprudência idiota," *Gazeta da Tarde*, 11 February 1884, 1; "Notas e impressões," *Revista Illustrada*, 9 April 1886, 7; "Os mercados de gente," *Gazeta da Tarde*, 9 June 1886, 1.

41. "Novos aspectos," *Revista Illustrada*, 30 April 1886, 3. The paper alternates the term "slaves" with "enslaved people" (*escravizados*), a common linguistic strategy adopted by abolitionists.

42. For a recent discussion, see Paton, "The Flight from the Fields."

43. Childs, *The 1812 Aponte Rebellion*, 116.

44. This figure is given by Conrad, *World of Sorrow*, 175.

45. Graham, "Another Middle Passage?," 300.

46. "Classificação dos escravos residentes no Município da Corte para se libertarem aqueles, cujo valor poder ser indenizado pela quota de 71:391$319 distribuída do fundo de emancipação," AGCRJ, E:E, Book 6.2.2, 27–33.

47. "Josepha liberta, justificante/ José Gonçalves de Pinho, justificado," ANB, juízo de órfãos da 2ª vara, ZM, maço 2292, número 2198, 1884, 15.

48. For a recent summary of the broad consensus on these two points in the Brazilian literature, see Libby and Graça Filho, "Notarized and Baptismal Manumissions," 220–23. Libby and Graça Filho point out that urban-rural distinctions among the manumission statistics need to be more clearly established. This important point has also been developed recently in a different context by Rosa Bezerra, *As chaves da liberdade*, 20–21. Nonetheless, proximity to cities and urban lifestyles did seem to play a significant role in the possibility of attaining manumission.

49. Firmina preta to Juízo de Órfãos da 2ª Vara, Rio de Janeiro, 21 August 1883, ANB, Juízo de Órfãos da 2ª Vara, ZM, maço 107, número 2073, 1883.

50. Emília crioula to Juízo de Órfãos da 2ª Vara, ANB, Juízo de Órfãos da 2ª Vara, ZM, maço 162, número 3248, 1882.

51. On this practice, see Mendonça, *Entre a mão e os anéis*, 343–45.

52. Inventário, Carolina Umbelina de Sá, ANB, 1ª Vara Cível do RJ, 3J, SDJ, notação 9681, maço 0493, Gal B, 1884.

53. Castilho and Cowling, *Funding Freedom*, 103, 108.

54. "Relação dos escravos, que neste Juízo de Órfãos da Segunda Vara apresentaram e têm quantia para pecúlio, as quais se acham por empréstimo no Tesouro Nacional," AGCRJ, E:E, Book 6.2.1, 21 August 1880, 9.

55. Conrad calculates this was 575 *mil-réis*. Conrad, *The Destruction of Brazilian Slavery*, 302.

56. *Boletim*, 2 June 1885, 102–3.

57. Josepha to Municipal Council, n.d. [approx. November 1887], AGCRJ, E:E, Book 6.2.9, 161–62; *Boletim*, 2 December 1887.

58. For the term "city hideout," see Chalhoub, *Visões da liberdade*, 219.

59. "Monica Maria da Conceição, por seu curador o solicitador Domingos Gomes dos Santos, justificação para manutenção," ANB, CAE, maço 1745, núm. 4212, 1886, 2, 5, 9v, 14, 46–49v, 61–63, 67–85.

60. Trouillot, *Silencing the Past*, 27, 54–55. For the idea that authorities deliberately avoided any collective negotiation over freedom, preferring to deal with claimants on an individual basis only, see Chalhoub, *Machado de Assis*, 254.

61. Works on Brazilian slaves' family manumission strategies are numerous; for a recent overview, see Klein and Luna, *Slavery in Brazil*, 178–88, 212–49. On manumission and slave families in Cuba, see Perera and Meriño, *Para librarse de lazos*.

62. On fathers, see Walker, *No More No More*, 88–90.

63. Joaquim Pereira de Souza on behalf of Manuel Vicente, to Presidente e Vereadores da Illma Câmara Municipal, 29 July 1885, AGCRJ, E: E, Book 6.2.6, 24; João Francisco Diogo to Presidente e Vereadores da Illma Câmara Municipal, 29 June 1885, AGCRJ, E:E, Book 6.2.6, 25.

64. "Expediente promovido por Juan Vázquez padre de la párvula Blanca Andrea esclava de Doña Concepción Vázquez sobre excesivo precio de su coartación," ANC, ME, legajo 3527, expediente Db, 1873.

65. Manoel Caetano Alves d'Oliveira and Benedicta Caetana to Câmara Municipal, AGCRJ, E:E, Book 6.2.6, 20 June 1885, 28.

66. It is not clear whether Cecilio was the father of some or all of the children. Antonia and two of the children were described as *morenos*, while the other was described as *pardo*. He may have had a white father.

67. Standard proceedings in the evaluation of slaves' prices were for the *síndico* and owner to each name one assessor. If the assessments were different, a third assessor would be called in to choose one of the prices.

68. "Expediente promovido por los morenos José Ernesto, José Casimiro y Manuela Fernández, esclavos de Luisa Fernández en queja contra el Síndico de Guanabacoa," ANC, ME, legajo 3585, expediente Ay, 1878.

69. Relations of *compadrio* were important at all levels of Iberian societies. For their significance among people of color, see Barcia Zequeira, *La otra familia*, 113–36; Barcia Zequeira, *Los ilustres apellidos*; Childs, *The 1812 Aponte Rebellion*, 95–119; Reis, *Death is a Festival*, 39–65; M. Soares, "From Gbe to Yoruba," 239–42.

70. For example, "Expediente promovido por la morena libre Josefa Achondo para que se le expida carta de libertad a su ahijada la párvula Francisca hija de la parda Genoveva esclava de Doña Rosario Aguirre de Ecay," ANC, ME, legajo 3597, expediente J, 1869.

71. "Congo" in nineteenth-century Cuba referred broadly to Africans who had embarked at one of the ports of West Central Africa, between the ports of Luanda and Benguela. See Barcia Paz, *Seeds of Insurrection*, 22–23.

72. "Expediente en que el negro Pedro Real se queja del mal trato que le da Don Angel Arechavaleta a su esclava María Luisa," ANC, GSC, legajo 948, expediente 33540, 1854.

73. "Varios padrones de los esclavos de ambos sexos destinados al servicio doméstico y sujetos al pago de Capitación," ANC, GSC, legajo 948, expediente 33528, 1853–54. In 1853–54 the Third District comprised the following neighborhoods: San Leopoldo, Monserrate, San Lázaro, Tacón, Guadalupe, Colón, Dragones, and La Punta. This covered what would now be parts of Centro Habana, along the Malecón up as far as Animas, into today's Barrio Chino and the streets which now cluster behind the Capitolio. Domestic slaves were defined for this *padrón* simply as those registered as living and working in Havana. They included washerwomen, seamstresses, and *jornaleras*, as well as those actually working as domestic servants. The *padrón* for the Third District listed 1,839 slaves in total. The Spanish government took many of these counts or *padrones* throughout the nineteenth century. Kenneth Kiple rightly argued that they are too partial and unreliable to be used to provide a broader picture of the island's population. However, they can certainly help us build up a picture of a particular neighborhood at a given point in time. Kiple, *Blacks in Colonial Cuba*, 9–20.

74. "Planilla correspondiente al Padrón de Patrocinados de La Habana, año económico de 1881–2," ANC, ME, legajo 3539, expediente B, 1882. This *padrón* is roughly, not exactly, comparable to the 1853–54 *padrón*. The 1881–2 *padrón* contained fewer *patrocinados* (220) than the slaves of the earlier *padrón* (reflecting the decline of slavery by this point) and was taken from a wider range of *barrios*. It included most of those mentioned for the 1853–54 *padrón* but also San Juan de Dios, San Nicolás, la Ceiba, San Isidro, Santa Clara, San Francisco, del Angel, Jesús del Monte, Peñalver, and Atarés.

75. *Recenseamento da população do Município Neutro* (1872), 58–59.

76. "Varios padrones de los esclavos de ambos sexos destinados al servicio doméstico y sujetos al pago de Capitación," ANC, GSC, legajo 948, expediente 33528, 1853–54.

77. "Planilla correspondiente al Padrón de Patrocinados de La Habana, año económico de 1881–2," ANC, ME, legajo 3539, expediente B, 1882.

78. The relationship between slaves classified for freedom and slaves actually freed through the Emancipation Fund is not completely clear. Fabiano Dauwe has shown that from 1876, it was stipulated that only those slaves who could realistically be freed with the resources available should be classified. If this is the case, then the classification

tables of 1876, 1880, 1882, and 1883 found for the Corte show that a total of 1001 slaves were freed in these years. However, this is significantly different from Robert Slenes' estimate that the Fund freed a total of 656 slaves in the Corte between 1871 and early 1885. It is also much higher than Dauwe's own estimate, using Ministry of Agriculture reports, that by 1883 the Fund had freed 627 slaves in the Corte. Dauwe, "A Libertação Gradual," 30, 81; Slenes, "The Demography and Economics," 644.

79. *Gazeta da Tarde*, 15 April 1884, 1.

80. "Brazilia (escrava) por seu curador," ANB, CAE, caixa 9688, ap. 14318, 1872. On female-headed households among poor women in Brazil, see Barickman and Few, "Ana Paulina de Queirós"; Dias, *Power and Everyday Life*, 15–20. For slaves' independent living strategies in Rio, see Santos, *Além da senzala*.

81. On Rio, see Chalhoub, *Cidade febril*; on Havana, see Arriaga and Delgado, "Contribución al estudio de la vivienda pobre en La Habana"; González-Quiñones et. al., "Hogares y familias en los barrios populares de La Habana."

82. For this analysis of the 1861 *padrones* for Alambique Street, which would make up part of the 1861 island-wide census, see McCabe, "Parameters of the Public," 138–41.

83. "Padrón de morenos y pardos libres de la jurisdicción de La Habana," ANC, ME, legajo 3413, expediente S, 1870.

84. Racial definitions as recorded on the *padrón* forms presumably reflected the racial gaze of the census-taker rather than any self-description by the inhabitants, but in some cases additional scribbles imply an intervention or disagreement by residents about the way they had been listed. Census-takers, probably under time constraints, also tended to list the characteristics of the household head and then fill in "ditto" marks for all other members. Thus they may have ignored racial distinctions within household groupings—*mulato* children of *morena* mothers, and so on. On the mutability and negotiability of racial terms of individuals and families' racial "strategies," see Perera and Meriño, *Familias, agregados y esclavos*, Chapter 4.

85. "Juicio de falta contra la morena Alejandra Calisto por insultos al pardo José de la Paz Balsa," ANC, ME, legajo 3092, expediente Bs, 1884.

86. See Varella, "Esclavos a sueldo," 145–46.

87. "Documento con instancia de Lucía Collazo en queja de la Junta de Patronato de la Habana, sobre demora de un expediente," ANC, ME, legajo 3724, expediente Aa, 1883.

88. "Mapa dos libertandos e libertandas que receberão carta de liberdade no faustoso aniversario de S.M. a Imperatriz e que deverão comparecer ao Paço Municipal às 9 horas da manhã," AGCRJ, E:E, Book 6.1.41, p. 41.

89. For the table in which Sebastiana appears, see AGCRJ, E:E, Book 6.1.61, p. 74.

90. "Classificação dos escravos residentes no Município da Corte . . . ," AGCRJ, E:E, Book 6.2.1, anexo, 1880.

91. "Expediente promovido por la morena Teresa Baez patrocinada a cargo de los Herederos de Dn. Benito Mateos y Mendo," MMR, JLPR, legajo 16, expediente 002984, 1882.

92. "Expediente promovido por el moreno Anselmo patrocinado que dice ser de los Herederos de D. Juan Pedro Torres," MMR, JLPR, legajo 16, expediente 002990, 1884.

93. In Brazil, an owner's death during these final years of slavery often led enslaved people to conclude their time as "reasonably" enslaved was over. Chalhoub, *Visões da liberdade*, 110–12.

94. Francisca and Guadalupe Criollas to Junta Local de Patronato de Regla, MMR, JLPR, legajo 16, expediente 002994, 1883; "Documento conteniendo instancia de Ursula Canton sobre sus hijas Francisca y Guadalupe," ANC, ME, legajo 3724, expediente Q, 1883.

95. "Cuaderno de audiencia de los autos seguidos por D Antonio Beltrán de Gazurieta contra D Bernardo Lastra para que le entregue la cédula y certificado de empadronamiento de la esclava Micaela que le vendió, o la recisión del contrato y entrega del precio," ANC, AH, legajo 56, expediente 11, 1874; "Expediente promovido por la morena Severina Hernández de D. Bernardo Lastra que solicita variar de dueño," ANC, ME, legajo 3540, expediente Aj, 1878; "Demanda de la parda Seferina Perez [subsequently spelled Ceferina] contra un acuerdo de la Junta de Patronato de la Habana que la declaró sujeta al patronato de Dn Bernardo Lastra," ANC, CA, legajo 65, expediente 6577, 1881; "Expediente formado por instancia de Ceferina Perez en queja contra su dueño," ANC, ME, legajo 3589, expediente Z, 1882.

96. Antonio Beltrán de Gazurieta, against whom Lastra was involved in litigation over Micaela in 1874, had had a suit for freedom brought against him by his slave Petrona, on behalf of herself and her two children, in 1868. See "Decreto del Gobierno Superior Civil fijando jurisprudencia acerca de las reclamaciones que se produzcan contra los Síndicos de Ayuntamiento por autos de Sindicatura," in Cano and Zalba, *El libro de los síndicos*, 53.

97. Mendonça, *Entre a mão e os anéis*, 263–64.

98. "Monica Maria da Conceição, por seu Curador o Solicitador Domingos Gomes dos Santos, justificação para manutenção," ANB, CAE, maço 1745, núm. 4212, 1886, 79–79v.

CHAPTER 6

1. The phrase is taken from Chalhoub, *Visões da liberdade*.

2. Chalhoub, *Machado de Assis*, 161–62.

3. See, for example, Moore and Johnson, *Neither Led nor Driven*, 96–136, 151.

4. On Allo, the Cuban exiles, and *El Mulato*, see Lazo, *Writing to Cuba*, 127–28, chapter 4, and 215 (n. 61).

5. Allo, *Domestic Slavery*, 8.

6. Ibid., 14.

7. Armas y Céspedes, *La esclavitud en Cuba*, 334.

8. Ibid., 350–51.

9. For notions about African women and their "fecundity" see Morgan, *Labouring Women*, Chapter 1.

10. Armas y Céspedes, *La esclavitud en Cuba*, 376–77. For the effects of such views in the United States, see Roberts, *Killing the Black Body*, 8–21.

11. Armas y Céspedes, *La esclavitud en Cuba*, 408.

12. España, *Información sobre reformas*, vol. 1, 73–76.

13. Gutiérrez y Salazar, *Reformas de Cuba*, 9–10, 12. Similar arguments were made in Brazil by, for example, Romantic writer and Conservative party member José de Alencar. See Chalhoub, *Machado de Assis*, 196–97.

14. *Conuco*: slave provision grounds. Gutiérrez y Salazar, *Reformas de Cuba*, 13.

15. For a copy of the original statutes of the Sociedad, see http://www.economic amatritense.com/ (accessed 27/2/2011).

16. Schmidt-Nowara, *Empire and Antislavery*, 73–74.

17. Ibid., 89–90.

18. Quoted and translated by Schmidt-Nowara, "'Spanish' Cuba," 114.

19. See Abreu, "Slave Mothers."

20. Ibid., 579.

21. Ibid., 577.

22. Quoted in translation in Ipsen, "Delicate Citizenship," 215–16.

23. Ipsen, "Delicate Citizenship," 215–17.

24. For a national overview, see Dauwe, "A libertação gradual," 76–77, 100–101. For classifications of slaves to be freed by the Fund in Rio, see "Classificação dos escravos residentes no Município da Corte, para que se libertarem aqueles, cujo valor puder ser indenizado pela quota de 115:361$660 do fundo de emancipação," 17 October 1876, AGCRJ, E:E, Book 6.1.40, pp. 1–3; "Classificação dos escravos residentes no Município da Corte . . . ," 13 December 1880, AGCRJ, E:E, Book 6.2.1, p. 36; "Classificação dos escravos residentes no Município da Corte . . . ," 17 July 1882, AGCRJ, E:E, Book 6.2.2, pp. 27–33; "4a classificação dos escravos residentes no Município da Corte . . . ," 11 December 1883, AGCRJ, E:E, Book 6.2.2, pp. 25–32 (page numbers repeat).

25. Dauwe, "A libertação gradual," 100–101.

26. *A Republica* (12 November 1871): 2.

27. For these visual representations, see Castilho and Cowling, "Funding Freedom."

28. Moraes, *A Campanha Abolicionista*, 401. Scott, *Slave Emancipation*, 272–75.

29. Article 7, "Ley de vientres libres," 4 June 1870, in Ortiz, *Los negros esclavos*, 318, and "Ley de abolición de la esclavitud," 13 February 1880, in Ortiz, *Los negros esclavos*, 331.

30. For such initiatives by slaves, *libertos* and *patrocinados*, see Scott, *Slave Emancipation*, 157–71.

31. See Chalhoub, *Machado de Assis*, 279–80.

32. Schueler, "Culturas escolares," 205.

33. Ibid., 205–14.

34. For example: Albuquerque, *O jogo da dissimulação*; Cunha and Gomes, *Quase-Cidadão*; Carvalho, *Cidadania no Brasil*; Grinberg, *O fiador dos brasileiros*; Lima, *Cores, marcas e falas*; Mattos de Castro, *Escravidão e cidadania*.

35. Schueler, "Culturas escolares," 212–26.

36. On notions of citizenship in the nineteenth-century Spanish Empire, see Sartorius, "Limits of Loyalty."

37. Vera y González, *La esclavitud*, 312. Italics in original.

38. Ibid., 312.

39. Gutiérrez y Salazar, *Reformas de Cuba*, 47.

40. Articles 41–42, "Reglamento del patronato de esclavos," 5 August 1872, in Ortiz, *Los negros esclavos*, 328–29.

41. The regulations appeared some five years after the 1872 Reglamento of the 1870 Moret Law stipulated that they be drafted. "Reglamento para el régimen de las Juntas Protectoras de Libertos," 5 June 1877, art. 12, reproduced in Cano and Zalba, *El libro de los síndicos*, 27.

42. Scott, *Slave Emancipation*, 68.

43. Calcagno, *Romuldo, uno de tantos*, 298.

44. "Consulta sobre si los patronos que infrinjan las leyes de abolición de 4 de Julio de 1870 y 13 de Febrero de 1880 en cuanto concierne a la enseñanza primaria que debe darse a los menores libertos," ANC, CA, legajo 86, expediente 7940, 1884.

45. Gallenga, *The Pearl of the Antilles*, 123.

46. "Colégio Felipe Nery," *Gazeta da Tarde*, 14 December 1885, 2.

47. The 1880 electoral reform stipulated that only literates could vote, with devastating consequences for the suffrage. See Chalhoub, *Machado de Assis*, 279–86; Graham, *Patronage and Politics*, Chapter 7.

48. "Asilo de meninos desvalidos," *Gazeta da Tarde*, 4 December 1885, 1–2.

49. For such imagery, see Wood, *The Horrible Gift of Freedom*, 123–25.

50. Speech, Oliveira Rosário, "Ata da sessão solene extraordinária," *Boletim*, 14 May 1888, 63.

51. Cottrol, "The Long Lingering Shadow," 58.

52. Speech, Cláudio da Silva, 2 December 1885, *Boletim*, 5 December 1885, 17–132 (page numbers out of sequence in original document).

53. "Dr Rabello, Relatório da Fundação da Escola de Santa Isabel," *Boletim*, 5 August 1886, 44.

54. On the slaughterhouse and municipal corruption, see *Revista Illustrada*, 17 October 1885, 1. On the politics of the meat supply in Rio, see also Juliana Teixeira Souza, "A Autoridade Municipal na Corte Imperial," 50–53. References to the slaughterhouse appear constantly in the Municipal Council's *Boletim* in the 1880s.

55. Speech, Luiz de Moura, *Boletim*, 5 August 1886, 43. For the insidious uses of metaphors of childhood in a different context but with similar implications, see Pérez, *Cuba in the American Imagination*, 95–174.

56. For example, "Crônica do Bem," *Gazeta da Tarde*, 18 December 1885, 2; "Festa municipal," *Gazeta da Tarde*, 2 December 1887, 2; *Gazeta da Tarde*, 3 December 1887, 2.

57. *The Rio News*, 15 March 1875, 5.

58. "Os educandos do Pão de Açúcar," *A Republica*, 209, 14 December 1871, 2.

59. On girls and domestic service, see Olívia Maria Gomes da Cunha, "Criadas para servir: domesticidade, intimidade e retribuição," in *Quase-cidadão*, ed. Cunha and Gomes, 377–417.

60. Dr. Ennes de Souza, "A educação republicana," *Gazeta da Tarde*, 18 December 1885, 2. The Republicans had a particular desire to improve popular education. See, for example, "Instrução Pública," *A República*, 223, 30 December 1871, 2. Here the newspaper reproduced an article from the Washington paper *Daily National Republican* (6 November 1871) concerning education in Brazil following the Rio Branco law.

61. For Brazil, see Schueler, "Culturas escolares," 115–59; for Spain, see Schmidt-Nowara, *Empire and Antislavery*, 92–93, 96–97; for Cuba, and for links to broader nineteenth-century ideas about girls' education in Europe, see Franklin, *Women and Slavery*, 71–73.

62. In 1872, women made up 44 percent of teachers in Rio's public primary schools; by 1884, they outstripped men's numbers in this capacity. Associated with poorer women and poorly-paid, the profession potentially included many women of color; as Jerry Dávila shows, the numbers of teachers of color would decrease over the first half of the twentieth century. Dávila, *Diploma of Whiteness*, chapter 3; Schueler, "Culturas escolares," 127, 154–59. Havana had a long tradition of women of color working as popular teachers (*maestras amigas*), although the repression following the 1844 Escalera conspiracy had an important detrimental impact on their numbers. Deschamps, *El negro en la economía habanera*, 119–32; Mena, "Stretching the Limits," 98–99.

63. On the maternity hospital, see Chapter Four; on the school, see *Gazeta da Tarde*, 3 December 1886, 2; on the asylum, see "Ordem do dia," *Boletim*, 10 January 1887, 7; "Ordem do dia," *Boletim*, 12 December 1887, 73, 80.

64. Gutiérrez y Salazar, *Reformas de Cuba*, 63–64.

65. Cowling, "Negotiating Freedom," 379.

66. "Portarias: da professora D. Theresa Pizarro Filha, apresentando um projeto de fundação de internato para educação de ingênuas," *Boletim*, 7 February 1884, 69.

67. Although Couto discussed "ingênuos" generally, the subjects of his speech were girls only, as the pupils of the planned school. Speech, Torquato J. Fernandes Couto, *Boletim*, 13 March 1884, 123–24.

68. Speech, Torquato J. Fernandes Couto, *Boletim*, 13 March 1884, 124; see also *Boletim*, 19 March 1884, 130.

69. "Regulamento para o Externato de ingênuas, mantido pela Illma Câmara Municipal," *Boletim*, 26 June 1884, 119–20.

70. Castillo de González, "Una raza que se levanta," 1882, BNJM, Manuscritos, CM Casti, no. 35, pp. 2–4.

71. Castillo y González, "Reflexiones sobre la conciencia," 21 August 1878, BNJM, Manuscritos, CM Casti, no. 30, pp. 14–16.

72. Antonio Bachiller y Morales to Gobierno Superior Civil, 1863, quoted in Fe Iglesias, "El censo cubano de 1877," 193.

73. Ipsen, "Delicate Citizenship," chapter 5.

74. "Autos de requerimento para renúncia," Bernardo José de Oliveira Bastos / a parda Leonor, ANB, juízo de órfãos da 2ª vara (ZM) maço 2287, núm. 298, gal. A, 1875.

75. "Expediente promovido por Da Elvira Perovany pidiendo tener a su cuidado un hijo menor, libre, de su esclava Matilde Criolla," ANC, ME, legajo 3724, expediente AK, 1873.

76. For nonelite social actors' use of patronage, see Castilho and Cowling, "Funding Freedom," 100–101.

77. Dr. Luiz de Moura, H.A. de Carvalho, and Dr Pinto Guedes, "Relatório da comissão de instrução sobre as escolas municipais," *Boletim*, 18 December 1884, 153–54.

78. Schueler, "Culturas escolares," 212.

79. Otovo, "From *Mãe Preta* to *Mãe Desamparada*," 166.

80. Moura, Carvalho and Guedes, "Relatório da comissão de instrução sobre as escolas municipais," *Boletim*, 18 December 1884, 153–54. The use of the "enslavement" metaphor when discussing domestic service, and the tensions about whether "hygienic" motherhood could be practiced by all women or was racially exclusive, remained prominent themes in the press of early-twentieth-century Rio. See Garzoni, "Arena de combate," chapter 2.

81. As inculcators of moral values, teachers were increasingly required to be "moral" themselves. New regulations began to be set out the Corte in 1882 which obliged women teachers (not their male counterparts) to produce a marriage, divorce, or widowhood certificate, or for unmarried women, proof that they lived with their parents and of parental consent. *Boletim*, September–December 1882.

82. Farias, "Greve nas Marinhas."

83. Otovo, "From *Mãe Preta* to *Mãe Desamparada*," 184.

84. Franklin, *Women and Slavery*, 138.

85. On the relationship between the Ministry and the Municipal Council, see Schueler, "Culturas escolares," 207.

86. "Ata da 3ª sessão ordinária em 3 de fevereiro de 1887," *Boletim*, 3 February 1887, 37–38.

87. Chalhoub, "The Politics of Silence," 73–76. For broader reflections on the "silencing" of color in Brazilian historical records, see Mattos de Castro, *Das cores do silêncio*.

88. Proposta, Torquato Couto, *Boletim*, 5 April 1888, 9–10.

89. Ipsen, "Delicate Citizenship," 225.

90. On women and discourses of womanhood in associations for people of color, see Barcia Zequeira, "Mujeres en torno a Minerva"; Hevia Lanier, "Otra contribución a la historia de los negros sin historia," 81–82.

CHAPTER 7

1. "Inventário, Eva Joaquina de Oliveira," ANB, Juízo de Órfãos da 1ª Vara, Caixa 972, núm. 4084, 1868, 2.

2. For example, "Serafim, escravo," *Gazeta da Tarde*, 20 October 1885, 1.

3. On Mello, see Frank, "Layers, Flows and Intersections."

4. *Boletim*, 18 March 1886, 122.

5. João Coelho Bastos, Secretaria de Polícia da Corte, to Secretário da Câmara Municipal, AGCRJ, E:E, Book 6.1.61, 17 March 1886, 59.

6. Frank, "Layers, Flows, and Intersections," 317.

7. See Chalhoub, "Solidariedade e liberdade," 219–20.

8. Socolow, *The Women of Colonial Latin America*, 112–29.

9. On the *mina* women of Rio de Janeiro, see Faria, "Sinhás pretas"; C. Soares, "Comércio, nação e gênero." For women's commercial strategies in Minas Gerais, see Paiva, *Escravos e libertos*, chapter 3. For a rural Cuban counterpoint, showing rural women's tendency to accumulate property, see Zeuske, "Two Stories of Gender and Slave Emancipation."

10. Lauderdale Graham, "Being Yoruba in Rio de Janeiro," 18–19.

11. On these roles, see Kevin Roberts, "Yoruba Family, Gender, and Kinship Roles," 251.

12. Rosa's case was reported by the *Gazeta da Tarde*, 24 May 1886, p 2. For the ceremony at which Rosa was freed, see *Boletim*, 18 March 1886, 122.

13. Mena, "Stretching the Limits," 91.

14. See Mendonça, *Entre a mão e os anéis*; Scott, *Slave Emancipation*, 149–57. For Cuba and Puerto Rico, the *juntas de libertos* were specifically charged with helping administer slaves' savings: see Reglamento del Patronato de Esclavos, 5 August 1872, art. 6, part 9, reproduced in Ortiz, *Los negros esclavos*, 322.

15. All the documents describe them both as *lucumí* except for one of the baptism documents, which describes Águeda as *arará*. One of the children had a *lucumí* godfather, implying the family's connections to *lucumí* networks.

16. This theory would fit with Michael Zeuske's claim, for central Cuba, that the emancipation period saw many ex-slaves seek to escape the shadow of slavery represented by their owners' former surnames. This suggestion is disputed in a more detailed and longue-durée study of naming practices for enslaved families in Cuba by Aisnara Perera and María de los Ángeles Meriño, who argue that rather than seeking to cast off former owners' surnames, ex-slaves sought during the emancipation period to acquire two surnames (often those of two former owners) rather than one. While the issue has not been definitively resolved, clearly the complex negotiations over freedom's meanings were reflected in naming practices. See Perera and Meriño, *Esclavitud, familia y parroquia*, 87–109; Zeuske, "Ciudadanos 'sin otro apellido': nombres esclavos, marcadores raciales e identidades en la colonia y en la República, Cuba 1879–1940," in *Ciudadanos en la nación*, vol. 1, eds. Portuondo and Zeuske, 102. The surname Del Rey for Cuban slaves had its origins in the slaves "of the king," the best example being those of El Cobre in Santiago de Cuba (see Díaz, *The Virgin, the King, and the Royal Slaves of El Cobre*, and Perera and Meriño, *Esclavitud, familia y parroquia*, 100). All slaves who belonged to the state were declared free in 1870 (see Ortiz, *Los negros esclavos*, 318). It is not clear how this particular family acquired this surname.

17. Varela, "Esclavos a sueldo," 59–60.

18. Lauderdale Graham, "Being Yoruba in Rio de Janeiro," 18.

19. "La morena Águeda del Rey contra el moreno Florindo del Rey sobre alimento," ANC, Escribanía de Brezmes, legajo 106, expediente 9, 1878.

20. For the most famous Brazilian example—of many—see Furtado, *Chica da Silva*, 128–156.

21. Mena, "Stretching the Limits," 91.

22. On property ownership by women of color in nineteenth-century Cuba, see Hevia Lanier, *Mujeres negras libres y propietarias*. For indications of the extent of women's acquisition of property, see, for example: "Beatriz Camberana morena vecina de la calle San Cipriano no 36. Solicitud de reedificar su casa y sus planos," MMR, Expedientes del Ayuntamiento, legajo 15, expediente 002953, 1874; "Expediente seguido por la morena Brígida Pedroso en cobro de pesos por su casa del Águila 189 (Habana)," ANC, ME, legajo 121, expediente K, 1882; "Expediente de apremio contra la morena Ana Sotalongo," ANC, ME, legajo 278, expediente M, 1881; "Expediente promovido por

la morena libre Antonia Cadaval, solicitando exención" ANC, ME, legajo 295, expediente J, 1878.

23. "Expediente promovido por la morena libre Mercedes Estévez, para que se le exima de pagar contribuciones por una casa en Sitios 60, en La Habana," ANC, ME, legajo 4360, expediente Az, 1879. *Carabalí* was a term used in Cuba to refer to the many different African ethnic groups who had embarked from the Bight of Biafra, in present-day southeastern Nigeria. Barcia Paz, *Seeds of Insurrection*, 18–19.

24. "Expediente formado por incendio en la casa de la negra Teresa Maleón," ANC, ME, legajo 2892, expediente An, 1854; "Actuación de audiencia formado por incendio en la casa de la morena," ANC, ME (Escribanía de del Río), legajo 2548, expediente Ll, 1859; "Causa criminal por incendio de una casa de la morena Martirio Campa," ANC, ME (Escribanía de Salinas), legajo 2620, expediente X, 1862.

25. On rising real estate prices in Rio from midcentury, see Frank, *Dutra's World*, 167.

26. Because of the "non-existence of color"—as Hebe Mattos has described the practice of "silencing" the issue of race in Brazilian nineteenth-century records—nowhere in Eva's inventory is the color of her skin or her legal origin noted. However, in a subsequent freedom suit by Efigênia, one of her slaves (discussed further below), Eva is described as a *preta forra*. "Efigênia, preta, por seu curador," ANB, CAE, caixa 3687, apelação 14298, 1859, 79; Mattos de Castro, *Das cores do silêncio*, 106–14.

27. Zephyr Frank shows this for Rio up to midcentury. Although slaves became more expensive after the end of the Atlantic trade in 1850, slaveholding and to a lesser degree property were still more accessible routes to wealth in the city than, say, investment in stocks and shares, as Manoel himself would explain. Frank, *Dutra's World*, 39–45.

28. "Inventário, Eva Joaquina de Oliveira," ANB, Juízo de Órfãos da 1ª Vara, Caixa 972, núm. 4084, 1868, especially pp. 2, 17–19, 27–33v, 34–34v, 44, 52, 55–55v, 59, 61–62, 68–69v, 83–84v, 113–14, 124–33, 148–49, 151, 199, and loose pages at the back of the file, s/n. On death, see Reis, *Death Is a Festival*, 13, 66–90.

29. Expediente criminal por robo de varias prendas a las morenas Rosario Martínez y Asención [*sic*] Herrera (Escribanía de Soroa), ANC, ME, legajo 2453, expediente Ad, 1864.

30. The role of gossip in resolving disputes, and the profoundly social nature of most aspects of life in Rio de Janeiro's *casas de cômodos*, is discussed in Abreu, *Meninas perdidas*, 198–201, and throughout Chalhoub, *Trabalho, lar e botequim*.

31. "Expediente criminal formado por hurto de aves a la morena Rita Foles" (Escribanía de Ozeguera), ANC, ME, legajo 2547, expediente Ao, 1881.

32. "Galeria Policial," *Gazeta da Tarde*, 18 August 1886, 2.

33. For Rio, Sidney Chalhoub has noted the depth and importance of relationships of reciprocity and mutual aid between relatives and friends in the intimacy of shared housing arrangements. Chalhoub, *Trabalho, lar e botequim*, 184–202.

34. "Expediente criminal contra Belén Carvallo por estafa a la parda Rosenda Valera," (Escribanía de Galletti), ANC, ME, legajo 2868, expediente D, 1878.

35. Díaz Martínez, *La peligrosa Habana*, 25–26.

36. "A população pobre," *Gazeta da Tarde*, 14 February 1884, 1.

37. Díaz Martínez, *La peligrosa Habana*, 21–27, 49; Holloway, *Policing Rio de Janeiro*.

38. "Expediente criminal contra María Mercedes Romana por hurto a la morena Asunción Castañeda," ANC, ME (Escribanía de D. Arturo Galletti), legajo 2870, expediente G, 1887.

39. "Galeria policial," *Gazeta da Tarde*, 7 September 1886, 2; "Galeria policial," *Gazeta da Tarde*, 16 September, 1886, 2.

40. See Cruz, "Suburbanização e racismo no Rio de Janeiro," 16.

41. "Galeria policial," *Gazeta da Tarde*, 14 September 1886, 2.

42. "Galeria policial," *Gazeta da Tarde*, 5 October 1886, 2.

43. As Iacy Maia Mata reminds us, in 1879 the Spanish Penal Code of 1870 was applied to Cuba. It contained various modifications regarding race and slavery like this one. Mata, "Sentidos da liberdade."

44. "Causa criminal contra la morena Agustina Briones por contusión a Doña María de los Ángeles Pino Santana," ANC, ME, legajo 2483, expediente Ap, 1884. The title "Doña"/ "Don" was normally applied only to whites in Cuba. This book follows the convention of the time, in the hope that they will remind us of the relations of power between one group and another.

45. "Diligencias sumarias instruidas a consecuencia de la reyerta habida entre Felicia González y Dolores Pérez, de las cuales ha salido golpeada la primera," ANC, ME, legajo 2669, expediente A1, 1876.

46. Frank, *Dutra's World*, 2–3, 8–9, 167–68.

47. Dias, *Power and Everyday Life*, 9–19, 28–32, 74–93; Hahner, "Women and Work in Brazil," 93–94; Samara, *As mulheres, o poder e a família*, 7–14.

48. Frank, *Dutra's World*, 160.

49. For a Havana example of a *lucumí* woman who purchased two female slaves listed as being from different African nations from her own (Gangá and Congo), see: "Expediente promovido por la morena libre Rita Moinelo pidiendo el empadronamiento de dos esclavas Rosario y Lutgarda," ANC, ME, legajo 3514, expediente Ai, 1872.

50. "Acta da sessão de 17 de setembro," *Boletim*, 13 October 1887, 3; "Mapa dos libertandos e libertandas que têm de receber carta de liberdade pelo Livro de Ouro no 65 aniversário da Independência do Império," AGCRJ, E:E, Book 6.1.41, 7 September 1887, 44.

51. The other suspicion one might have on seeing this purchase of large numbers of very young women is that the supposed laundry business was actually a cover for prostitution. "Expediente promovido por D. Santiago Chenevar solicitando certificado de exención por las esclavas de su propiedad dedicadas a los trabajos de un tren de lavado de su pertenencia," ANC, ME, legajo 241, expediente F, 1876. Thanks to Jorge Giovannetti for passing me this reference.

52. "Expediente promovido por D. Pedro Sar solicitando exención del impuesto por su esclava Enriqueta, en razón de tenerla ocupada en la industria de modista que ejerce su esposa," ANC, ME, legajo 3124, expediente Bñ, 1878.

53. These included *mina*, *congo*, and the broadly Bantu/Angola "nations," *monjolo*, *cassange*, and *cabinda*.

54. For Manoel's petitions about Theodora, see Manoel Furtado de Mendonça to President & Councilors of Municipal Council, 19 June 1885, AGCRJ, E:E, Book 6.2.6, 22–23, 29–31; for the table of freed slaves in which she appears, see *Boletim*, 29 July 1885, 29.

55. "Inventário, Eva Joaquina de Oliveira," ANB, Juízo de Órfãos da 1ª Vara, caixa 972, núm. 4084, 1868, 2, 17–19, 27–33v, 34–34v, 44, 52, 55–55v, 59, 61–62, 68–69v, 83–84v, 113–14, 124–33, 148–49, 151, 199, and loose pages at back of file, s/n; "Efigênia, preta, por seu curador," ANB, CAE, caixa 3687, apelação 14298, 1872, 1–3, 5–6, 7, 23–24, 79, 111–15, 135, 150.

56. Tomasa subsequently declared that she was the slave of Don Leonardo Fernández, although she and Candelaria shared the Oñas' surname. The relationship between the two families, and the fixed residence of mother and daughter, is not clear from the statements. Nor is it clear where Tomasa was at the time Candelaria was raped.

57. "Tuvo que ver con."

58. On rape of slave women in the Hispanic Caribbean, see Dorsey, "It Hurt Very Much at the Time"; for Brazil, see Caulfield, *In Defense of Honor*, 25; "A Master Abuses His Adolescent Slave Girl: A Court Case, 1882–1884," in Conrad, *Children of God's Fire*, 73–81; Machado, "Corpo, gênero e identidade." On rape of enslaved women of in a different context, see Block, *Rape and Sexual Power in Early America*, 239–41.

59. "Expediente criminal formado por violación de la negrita libre Canderlaria Oña" (Escribanía de del Río), ANC, ME, legajo 2889, expediente Am, 1871 [case commenced 1868].

60. Brown, "'What Has Happened Here,'" 304.

61. *Forçada*. The paper distinguished between the use of physical force and *enganada* (deceived), applied to women "seduced" into sex with promises of marriage.

62. *Gazeta da Tarde*, 28 September 1885, 2.

63. Abreu, *Meninas perdidas*, 160–63; Caulfield, *In Defense of Honor*, 130–33; Martínez-Alier, *Marriage, Class and Color*, 112–19.

64. "Expediente criminal contra Manuel Hernández y Herrera por rapto de la morena Genara Carricarte" (Escribanía de Mazón), ANC, ME, legajo 2284, expediente J, 1884.

65. *Cartilla de meretriz:* a registration card for prostitutes, as part of contemporary attempts to enforce control over prostitution in the city. On these attempts from 1873 in Havana, see Guy, "Medical Imperialism Gone Awry," 77.

66. "Expediente criminal seguido de oficio por corrupción de la menor parda Genoveva Valdés" (Escribanía de Bonachea y Palmero), ANC, ME, legajo 2928, expediente Aj, 1884. Genoveva's surname is mainly registered as Gálvez throughout the case, like that of her mother, but the judge referred to her as Valdés in an apparent error.

67. Barcia Zequeira, "Entre el poder y la crisis," 272.

68. On the links between the abolition of slavery and discussions about prostitution in early-twentieth-century Rio de Janeiro, see Schettini, *Que tenhas teu corpo*, 131–40.

69. Barcia Zequeira, "Entre el poder y la crisis," 267–68.

70. On the Rua da Conceição, see Lauderdale Graham, "Slavery's Impasse," 671.

71. Most of the slaveholders targeted were poor—and often immigrant—women, who were more vulnerable to defamation of their reputations than wealthier, male slaveholders. Lauderdale Graham, "Slavery's Impasse," 681.

72. The phrase used in Portuguese was "por andar quitandando," which was often used as a euphemism for prostitution.

73. "Efigênia, preta, por seu curador," ANB, CAE, caixa 3687, apelação 14298, 1872, 24.

74. Theoretically, in both Cuba and Brazil, it was possible to make a legal argument that the prostitution of a slave by the owner led to freedom. Lawyers prosecuting owners for prostitution of slaves in 1870s Rio invoked Roman law principles to this effect. The Spanish Siete Partidas contained a similar provision. The Spanish 1870 Moret Law stipulated that *libertos* would be freed if prostituted. In practice, however, in both contexts the claim was extremely difficult to prove. See Lauderdale Graham, "Slavery's Impasse," 688, n.55; "Ley IV, Título XXII, Partida IV," reproduced in Cano & Zalba, *El libro de los síndicos*, 152; Ortiz, *Los negros esclavos*, 318.

75. Italics in original.

76. Prostitutes commonly displayed their "wares" by standing at windows to attract clients. Being "at the window" thus became a euphemism for engaging in prostitution.

77. "Efigênia, preta, por seu curador," ANB, CAE, caixa 3687, apelação 14298, 1872, 79–110.

78. "Eva, escrava, por seu curador," ANB, CAE, caixa 3686, apelação 14133, 1872, 47–49.

79. Nine others had died since 1868. "Inventário, Eva Joaquina de Oliveira," ANB, Juízo de Órfãos da 1ª Vara, caixa 972, núm. 4084, 1868, 68–69v.

CHAPTER 8

1. *Boletim*, 18 March 1886, 122.

2. Francisco Pinto da Silva on behalf of Rita, parda, to President of Municipal Council, 12 October 1885, AGCRJ, E:E, Book 6.1.61, 45. The ceremony would free 133 adults, of whom 88 were childless women, 25 were women with children, and 20 were men; it is not clear whether Rita was among them. "Dois de Dezembro," *Gazeta de Notícias*, 2 December 1885, 1.

3. "Casas de maternidade," *Gazeta da Tarde*, 4 September 1885, 1.

4. Report, Councilor Fernandes Couto, AGCRJ, *Boletim*, 13 March 1884, 123–24.

5. My understanding of this was clarified by Paton, "The Flight from the Fields Reconsidered." See also Priore, *Ao sul do corpo*, 18–20.

6. "Josepha / José Gonçalves de Pinho," ANB, Juízo de Órphãos, ZM, número 2198, maço 2292, 1884, pp. 7–12v, 25v–32.

7. See articles 18 and 19, Decree 5135, 13 November 1872, in *Elemento servil: Lei no. 2,040 de 28 de Setembro de 1871*, 64.

8. "Josepha / José Gonçalves de Pinho," ANB, Juízo de Órphãos, ZM, número 2198, maço 2292, 1884, pp. 39–39v, 45–50.

9. For African and diaspora perspectives on mothers and economic provision, see, for example, Hill Collins, "Shifting the Center: Race, Class, and Feminist Theorizing

about Motherhood," 50–51; Lauderdale Graham, "Being Yoruba in Rio de Janeiro," 18; Niara Sudarkasa, "The 'Status of Women' in Indigenous African Societies," in *Women in Africa and the African Diaspora*, ed. Terborg-Penn et al., 34; Sutton, Foreword, xi. On the struggles of African mothers for custody of children and the ability to bring them up according to their own cultural norms, in a context of official repression of African culture in 1850s Salvador, see Collins, "Domestic Servitude and the Difference a Race Makes."

10. For example, Hill Collins, "Shifting the Center," 55–56; Paton, "The Flight from the Fields," 185; K. Roberts, "Yoruba Family, Gender, and Kinship Roles."

11. "Expediente relativo a la renuncia graciosa que de los derechos de patronato hace Dn Jorge Mendez a favor de la madre de sus patrocinados Gavino y Vicente criollos," MMR, JLPR, legajo 16, expediente 002965, 1884.

12. Nor was this the first time she had come to the capital: four years previously, she had had a fight in Regla with one Doña Filomena Hernández, who sustained injuries. Eduardo Gómez Luaces, "Efemérides Reglanas, 1796–1881," unpublished ms., p. 533; consulted at MMR, Colección Manuscritos Eduardo Gómez Luaces.

13. "Expediente promovido por la parda libre Paulina Perdomo en reclamación de su ahijada la menor parda Juana Méndez a cargo de Dn Jorge Méndez," MMR, JLPR, legajo 16, expediente 002996, 1884.

14. The difference between someone born free and someone *subsequently* freed was important: freedmen could vote only in primary elections, while those born free potentially had access to full voting rights. See Chalhoub, "The Politics of Silence," 76–78.

15. Albino de Oliveira Santos' property was worth 19 *contos* and 460 *mil-réis* at the time of his death in 1896. "Inventário, Albino de Oliveira Santos: 2ª vara de órfãos. Inventariante: Jacintha de Barros Oliveira dos Santos," ANB, Inventários, caixa 4202, número 609, 1896, 20–21.

16. Dorothea, through Pedro Augusto Varella, ANB, Série Justiça: Chancelaria, Comutação de Penas e Graças, Ofícios com Anexos de Petições ao Imperador, 1834–1878, IJ3/ 25, document 1, 17 January 1865.

17. Conrad, *The Destruction*, 104.

18. Armas y Céspedes, *La esclavitud en Cuba*, 375.

19. Gallenga, *The Pearl of the Antilles*, 123. Italics in original.

20. For the argument that Gallenga was "bought" by Zulueta, see Marrero Cruz, *Juliían de Zulueta*, 77–78.

21. For an argument against notions that enslaved women engaged in higher levels of abortion or infanticide than other groups of women, see Perera and Meriño, *Esclavitud, familia y parroquia*, 133–34. Sara Ruddick's thoroughly critiqued yet still valuable exploration of the "discipline" of mothering discusses the aim of mothers to prepare children to fit their future social roles. Applying Ruddick's definitions of mothering's "interests" to enslaved mothers in the antebellum American South, Stephanie J. Shaw has suggested that enslaved mothers would prepare their children for the harsh discipline of life under slavery in order to preserve them. It stands to reason that the preparation would change as the new status of these children became apparent. See

Ruddick, "Maternal Thinking"; Shaw, "Mothering under Slavery in the Antebellum South," 250–53.

22. Rios and Mattos de Castro, *Memórias do cativeiro*, 164.

23. Ibid., 46, 178.

24. José do Patrocinio, "O bacharel Ferreira Nobre," *Gazeta da Tarde*, 11 November 1886, 3.

25. On the importance of social recognition of one's status in legal cases for freedom, see Mattos de Castro, *Das cores do silêncio*, 195–96. On the invention of genealogy as part of constructing a social identity for oneself as master of dependents, see Chalhoub, *Machado de Assis*, 70.

26. Calcagno, *Romualdo*, 294.

27. Moreno Fraginals, *El ingenio*, 1:272–73.

28. Calcagno, *Romualdo*, 273–380.

29. Loren Schweninger has noted enslaved mothers' concern with preserving family genealogy in the United States. Rosalyn Terborg-Penn discusses African Diaspora women's role, in migrant families in the twentieth century, in recording and recounting family genealogies. Schweninger, "Slave Women Petitioners"; Terborg-Penn, "Migration and Trans-Racial/National Identity Re-Formation."

30. "Expediente promovido por la parda libre Clara Linares pidiendo la libertad de sus cuatro hijos esclavos de D Juan Fernández Salgas," ANC, GG, legajo 566, expediente 28174, 1874.

31. "Documento conteniendo instancia de Mercedes Zamora sobre su hija Juana Inés a cargo de D. Manuel de S. Suárez por no cumplir el mismo con la ley," ANC, ME, legajo 3724, expediente Ad, 1883.

32. *Cabra* had a wide array of uses, varying according to region and time, in nineteenth-century Brazil. Mary Karasch defines it as "a person of indeterminate racial mixture but at least of some African ancestry." For João José Reis, for Bahia earlier in the century, it meant the "offspring of a mulatto and a black parent" or more broadly "persons who skin color was somewhere between black and brown." Ivana Stolze Lima reminds us that "citizens' colors should not be understood as simply a physical attribute" but as imbued with much more complex, and shifting, political meanings. Karasch, "Free Women of Color in Central Brazil"; Lima, *Cores, marcas e falas*, 20; Reis, *Death Is a Festival*, 19, 30.

33. "Apelante: Maria Luiza da Conceição; apelado José Rodrigues de Oliveira Vereza," ANB, CAE, caixa 4466, número 3682, 1855, 61–63.

34. Had Margarida been a man, there would have been nothing to stop her gaining a vote if she acquired minimum property rights because she was Brazilian-born (African-born freedpeople were denied voting rights). Access to voting was relatively wide in Brazil in this period, although it would be drastically curtailed by stringent literacy qualifications imposed by the 1881 electoral reform act.

35. For example: Albuquerque, *O jogo da dissimulação*; Beattie, *The Tribute of Blood*; Cunha and Gomes, *Quase-Cidadão*; Carvalho, *Cidadania no Brasil*; Grinberg, *O fiador*; Mattos de Castro, *Escravidão e cidadania*. For the quotation, see Pena, *Pajens da casa imperial*, 75.

36. On the "practice of politics" by nonelites, see Kittleson, *The Practice of Politics*, 9.

37. On days of national festivity, including imperial family birthdays, see Kraay, "Definindo nação e estado."

38. For the respective appeals to the emperor described in this paragraph, see ANB, série Justiça, AG, CODES, IJ3 26, documents 15, 11, s/n, 14, respectively.

39. Barman, "Gender and the Public Sphere in Brazil."

40. Untitled narrative by Princess Isabel, dated by her as December 1888, AHMIP, CPOB, Cat. A, maço 199, doc. 9030, 8. For this reference and the translation into English, see Barman, *Princess Isabel of Brazil*, 183–84.

41. Franklin, *Women and Slavery*, 63; S. Johnson, *The Social Transformation*, 116–18.

42. For example, "Expediente promovido por D. Elvira Rivero solicitando la exención de servicios de milicia a favor de su hermano D. Secundino," ANC, ME, legajo 3441, expediente Q, 1876.

43. Reid, *The Year of the Lash*, chapter 5. On the loyalty shown Spain by people of color, see Sartorius, "Limits of Loyalty."

44. "Expediente promovido por Doña Ana María Fernández y Bellido vecina de Nueva Gerona (Isla de Pinos) sobre coartación de la parda Encarnación, esclava del Párroco de la población," ANC, GSC, legajo 954, expediente 33736, 1862.

45. Lauderdale Graham, "Being Yoruba in Rio de Janeiro," 18; Sutton, "Motherhood Is Powerful"; Walker, "No More, No More," 97–98, 103.

46. Barcia Zequeira, *Los ilustres apellidos*, 86–88, 92–102, 220–24; Chalhoub, "Solidariedade e liberdade," 234–35; Reis, *Death Is a Festival*, 48–50.

CONCLUSION

1. For a recent study that takes such an approach with fascinating results, see Albuquerque, *O jogo da dissimulação*.

2. Moura, *Tia Ciata e a Pequena África no Rio de Janeiro*, 96–107.

3. Emilia's case is described in an extract from the *Boletín Oficial de la Provincia de la Habana*, Friday, 18 July 1884, contained in "Expediente relativo a la renuncia graciosa que de los derechos de patronato hace Dn Jorge Mendez a favor de la madre de sus patrocinados Gavino y Vicente criollos," MMR, JLPR, legajo 16, expediente 002965, 1884.

4. For the quotation, see Conrad, *The Destruction*, 104.

5. Rebecca Scott observed that the very process of gradual emancipation helped provide ex-slaves with juridical tools and habits which they would also use after emancipation. Scott, *Slave Emancipation*, 280–82.

EPILOGUE

1. Zaeske, *Signatures of Citizenship*.

2. The term is borrowed from Helg, *Our Rightful Share*.

3. Women gained the vote in Brazil in 1932 and in Cuba in 1934, although arguably voting rights made little difference to the lives of poor women. See Hahner, *Emancipating the Female Sex*, and Stoner, *From the House to the Streets*.

4. For these phrases, see Butler, *Freedoms Given, Freedoms Won*.

5. For a summary of Mott's argument and his account of the controversy, see Mott, *Crônicas de um gay assumido*, 155–60. For a fairly balanced account of the episode, see Maestri, "Palmares: una comuna negra."

Bibliography

PRIMARY SOURCES: ARCHIVES AND LIBRARIES

Brazil

Arquivo Geral da Cidade do Rio de Janeiro (AGCRJ)
    Coleção Escravidão: Emancipação (E:E)
Arquivo Histórico do Museu Imperial, Petrópolis (AHMIP)
    Arquivo Grão-Pará (AGP)
    Coleção Pedro d'Orleans e Bragança (CPOB)
Arquivo Nacional, Rio de Janeiro (ANB)
    Slave civil and criminal court cases compiled within ANB database which includes
        material from: the appeals formerly catalogued as "Corte de Apelação:
        Escravos;" 1ª Vara Cível; 2ª Vara Cível; Tribunal de Relação do Rio de
        Janeiro; Supremo Tribunal de Justiça (CAE)
    Inventários
    Série Justiça e Polícia
Biblioteca Nacional, Rio de Janeiro
    Newspaper collections
Casa Rui Barbosa, Rio de Janeiro
    Newspaper collections
Database, "Ações de liberdade," compiled by Keila Grinberg, copy in author's
    possession
Instituto Histórico e Geográfico Brasileiro, Rio de Janeiro

Cuba

Archivo del Museo Municipal de Regla, Havana (MMR)
    Colección Manuscritos Eduardo Gómez Luaces
    Expedientes del Ayuntamiento
    Documentos de la Junta Local de Patronato de Regla (JLPR)
Archivo Nacional de Cuba, Havana (ANC)
    Audiencia de La Habana (AH)
    Casa de Beneficencia
    Consejo de Administración (CA)
    Escribanías (Barreto, Salinas)
    Fondo Valle Iznaga (VI)
    Gobierno General (GG)
    Gobierno Superior Civil (GSC)

Miscelánea de Expedientes (ME)
Reales Órdenes y Cédulas (ROC)
Biblioteca Nacional José Martí, Havana (BNJM)
Printed Nineteenth-Century Materials Collection
Manuscript collections:
Abreu
Alfonso
Bachiller
Castillo
Echeverría
Escoto
Franco
Lobo
Morales
Pérez
Ponce
Sociedad
Suárez
Oficina del Historiador de La Habana
Untitled assorted manuscript collections

Puerto Rico

Centro de Investigaciones Históricas (Universidad de Puerto Rico, Recinto Río
Piedras)
Published/printed sources

Spain

Biblioteca Nacional, Madrid
Published/printed sources

United Kingdom

British Library
British & Overseas Nineteenth-Century Newspaper Collections
National Archives, London (NAL)
Foreign Office Papers (FO)

PUBLISHED AND PRINTED NINETEENTH-CENTURY MATERIALS

Agassiz, Louis, and Mrs. Agassiz. *A Journey in Brazil*. Boston: Ticknor & Fields, 1868.
Aguilera, Francisco Vicente. *Notes about Cuba*. New York: N.p., 1872.
Alencar, José de. *Mãe: Drama em quatro atos*. In *José de Alencar, teatro completo*, Rio
de Janeiro: Serviço Nacional de Teatro, 1977, vol. 2, pp. 253–310.

Allo, Lorenzo. *Domestic Slavery in Its Relations with Wealth: An Oration Pronounced in the Cuban Democratic Athenaeum of New York on the Evening of the 1st of January, 1854*. Translated by Goicuria. New York: W. H. Tinson, 1855.

Armas y Céspedes, Francisco de. *La esclavitud en Cuba*. Madrid: Establecimiento Tipográfico de T. Fortanet, 1866.

Arrieta, J. J. *Cuestión de Cuba*. Madrid: Imprenta F. Nozal, 1879.

Azevedo, Aluísio. *O cortiço*. 1890. Reprint, Porto Alegre: L & PM Editores, 2007.

———. *O mulato*. 1881. Reprint, Belo Horizonte: Crisálida, 2005.

Bachiller y Morales, Antonio. *Los negros*. Barcelona: Gorgas, 1887.

Baron Fortacín, M. *Cuestión de Cuba: La abolición de la esclavitud*. Madrid: Imprenta de J.M. Pérez, 1879.

Calcagno, Francisco. *Romualdo, uno de tantos*. 1881. In *Noveletas cubanas*, vol. 1, edited by Imeldo Álvarez García. Havana: Editorial de Arte y Literatura, 1974.

Câmara Municipal da Capital. *Relatório, Assembléa Legislativa Provincial da Parahyba do Norte* (30 July 1887), 34. ANB, IJJ9 571.

Câmara Municipal do Rio de Janeiro. *Boletim da Câmara Municipal* (1876–88). AGCRJ.

Cano, Bienvenido, and Federico de Zalba, eds. *El libro de los Síndicos de Ayuntamiento y de las Juntas Protectoras de Libertos: Recopilación cronológica de las disposiciones legales a que deben sujetarse los actos de unos y otras*. Havana: Imprenta del Gobierno y Capitanía General, 1875.

Castelar, Emilio. *Abolición de la esclavitud: Discurso pronunciado por Don Emilio Castelar en la sesión de las Cortes Constituyentes celebrada el día 20 de junio de 1870*. Madrid: Imprenta de J.A. García, 1870.

———. *Los crímenes de la esclavitud*. Madrid: Publicaciones Populares de la Sociedad Abolicionista Española, 1866.

Cuba. *Juntas Protectoras de Libertos. Reglamento para el regimen y procedimientos de las Juntas Protectoras de Libertos establecidas en las jurisdicciones de la Isla de Cuba. Formado en virtud y con arreglo al artículo 18 del de 5 de Agosto de 1872, para la ejecucion de la Ley de 4 de Julio de 1870, sobre abolicion de la esclavitud*. Havana: Imprenta del Gobierno y Capitanía General por S.M., 1877.

Cuban Anti-Slavery Committee. *Slavery in Cuba. A Report of the Proceedings of the Meeting, Held at Cooper Institute, New York City, December 13, 1872, by the Cuban Anti-Slavery Committee. Newspaper Extracts, Official Correspondence, Etc. Etc.* New York: n.p., 1872.

Del Valle Hernández, Antoine. *Recueil de diverses pieces et des discussions qui eurent lieu aux Cortes Générales et extraordinaires d'Espagne, en l'annee 1811, sur la traite et l'esclavage des negres. Traduit de l'espagnol*. Paris: n.p., 1814.

Dupierris, Marcial. *Cuba y Puerto Rico. Medios de conservar estas dos Antillas en su estado de esplendor, por un negrófilo concienzudo*. Madrid: Imprenta de José Cruzado, 1866.

Elemento servil: Lei no. 2,040 de 28 de Setembro de 1871, com os decretos no. 4835 de 1 de Dezembro de 1871 e no. 5135 de 13 de Novembro de 1872, edited and with annotations by V. A. de P. P. Rio de Janeiro: Instituto Typographico do Direito, 1875.

España. *Información sobre reformas en Cuba y Puerto-Rico celebrada en Madrid en 1866 y 67, por los representantes de ambas islas. Con un prólogo por un emigrado cubano*, 2 vols. New York: Imprenta de Hallet y Breen, 1877.

Ferrer de Couto, José. *Los Negros en sus diversos estados y condiciones; Tales como son, como se supone que son, y como deben ser*. New York: Imprenta de Hallet, 1864.

Gallenga, Antonio Carlo Napoleone. *The Pearl of the Antilles*. London: Chapman and Hall, 1873.

García Balmaseda, Joaquina. *La madre de familia: Diálogos instructivos sobre la religión, la moral y las maravillas de la naturaleza*. Madrid: Imprenta Santa Coloma, 1860.

———. *La mujer sensata (educación de sí misma). Consejos útiles para la mujer y leyendas morales*. Madrid: Imprenta de la Correspondencia, 1882.

Gómez de Avellaneda, Gertrudis. *Sab*. 1841. Edited and with an introduction, critical analysis, notes, and vocabulary by Catherine Davies. Manchester: Manchester University Press, 2001.

Guimarães, Bernardo. *A escrava Isaura*. 1875. Reprint, Santa Catarina: Avenida Gráfica e Editora, 2005.

Gutiérrez y Salazar, Pedro. *Reformas de Cuba. Cuestión social*. Madrid: Imprenta de Manuel G. Hernández, 1879.

Hazard, Samuel. *Cuba with Pen and Pencil*. Hartford, Conn.: n.p., 1871.

Intendencia General de Hacienda. *Instrucción para el establecimiento y cobranza del impuesto sobre los esclavos alquilados y destinados al servicio doméstico en poblado*. Havana: Imprenta del Gobierno y Capitanía General, 1872.

Kidder, Daniel P. *Brazil and the Brazilians, Portrayed in Historical and Descriptive Sketches*. Philadelphia: Childs & Peterson, 1857.

Labra y Ladrana, Rafael María de. *La abolición y la Sociedad Abolicionista Española en 1874*. Madrid: Sociedad Abolicionista Española, 1874.

———. *Un reto del esclavismo. El reglamento esclavista de 8 de mayo de 1880*. Madrid: A. J. Alaria, 1881.

Macedo, Joaquim Manoel de. *As vítimas-algozes: Quadros da escravidão*. 1869. Reprint, Porto Alegre: Editora Zouk, 2005.

Madden, R. R., ed. *Poems by a Slave in the Island of Cuba, Recently Liberated; translated from the Spanish by R. R. Madden, with the history of the early life of the negro poet, written by himself; to which are prefixed two pieces descriptive of Cuban slavery and the slave-traffic, by R. R. M.* London: Thomas Ward, 1840.

Márquez Sterling, Adolfo, and Francisco Giralt. *En nombre del honor y de Dios: Folleto*. Havana: Librería e Imprenta La Publicidad, 1882.

Martí, José. *Obras completas*, vol. 3. Havana: Editorial de Ciencias Sociales, 1975.

Ministerio de Ultramar. *Cuba desde 1850 á 1873: Colección de Informes, Memorias, Proyectos y Antecedentes sobre el gobierno de la isla de Cuba, relativos al citado período, que ha reunido por comisión del gobierno D. Carlos de Sedano y Cruzat, ex-diputado á Córtes*. Madrid: Imprenta Nacional, 1873.

Nabuco, Joaquim. *O abolicionismo*. 1883. Reprint, Recife: Editora Massangana, 1988.

Nobre, José Ferreira, Bernadino José Borges, and Julio Benedicto Ottoni. *Classificação dos escravos residentes no Municipio da Côrte para se libertarem aquelles, cujo valor puder ser indemnizado pela quota de 71:391$319 distribuida do fundo de emancipação*. Rio de Janeiro: n.p., 17 July 1882. Consulted at AGCRJ, E:E, Book 6.2.2, Anexo.

———. *4a classificação dos escravos residentes no Municipio da Côrte para se libertarem aquelles, cujo valor puder ser indemnizado pela quota de 94:000$000 distribuida do fundo de emancipação*. Rio de Janeiro: n.p., 11 December 1883. Consulted at AGCRJ, E:E, Book 6.2.2, pp. 25–32.

O'Kelly, James. *The Mambi-Land, or, Adventures of a Herald Correspondent in Cuba*. Philadelphia: J. B. Lippincott & Co., 1874.

Pereira, Antônio Barroso, Manoel Paulo Vieira Pinto, and J. E. Sayão de Bulhões Carvalho. *Classificação dos escravos residentes no Municipio da Côrte para se libertarem aquelles, cujo valor puder ser indemnizado pela quota de 115:351$660 do fundo de emancipação*. Rio de Janeiro: n.p., 17 October 1876. Consulted at AGCRJ, E:E, Book 6.1.40, pp. 1–13.

Pezuela, Jacobo de la. *Diccionario geográfico, estadístico, histórico de la Isla de Cuba*, vol. 3. Madrid: Imprenta de Mellado, 1863.

Recenseamento da População do Municipio Neutro e Provincia de Parana a Que se Procedeu em 1o de Agosto de 1872, n.a. Rio de Janeiro: n.p., 1872.

Several Cuban and Puerto Rican Abolitionists. *The Abolition of Slavery in Cuba and Porto Rico*. New York: William C. Bryant & Co., 1865.

Several Planters of Cuba. *Project for the Extinction of Slavery in Cuba and Porto Rico*. New York: S. Hallet, 1865.

Silió y Gutiérrez, Evaristo. *El esclavo, leyenda en verso*. Madrid: Imprenta de Tomás Fortanet, 1868.

Sociedad Abolicionista Española. *Conferencias Anti-Esclavistas*, vol. 3. Madrid: Secretaria de la Sociedad Abolicionista Española, 1872.

———. *El cancionero del esclavo: colección de poesías leídas en el certamen de 1866*. Madrid: Fortanet, 1866.

———. *La abolición de la esclavitud en el Brasil y en España. Discurso pronunciado por D. Salvador Torres Aguilar, catedrático de la Universidad de Madrid*. Madrid: Secretaria de la Sociedad Abolicionista Española, 1872.

———. *La experiencia abolicionista de Puerto Rico: Exposiciones de la Sociedad Abolicionista Española al Excmo Sr Ministro de Ultramar*. Madrid: n.p., July 1874.

———. *Sesión del 23 de enero de 1881*. Madrid: Imprenta de A. J. Alaria, 1881.

Spain, *Real Cedula de su Majestad sobre la educación, trato y ocupaciones de los esclavos en todos sus dominios de Indias, e Islas Filipinas, bajo las reglas que se expresan*. Madrid: Imprenta de la Viuda de Ibarra, 1789.

Suárez y Romero, Anselmo. *Francisco, el ingenio o las delicias del campo*. 1839. Reprint, Havana: Ministerio de Educación, 1947.

Tanco y Bosmoniel, Félix. *Petrona y Rosalía*. 1925. Reprint, Havana: Editorial Letras Cubanas, 1980.

Tyng, C.D. *Stranger in the Tropics: Being a Hand-book for Havana*. New York: American News Co., 1868.

Unos abolicionistas. *La abolición de la esclavitud y el proyecto del señor Moret*. Madrid: Tipología de Fortanet, 1870.

Vera y González, Enrique. *La esclavitud en sus relaciones con el estado social de los pueblos*. Toledo: Imprenta de Fando e hijo, 1881.

Villanova, Manuel. *Estadísica de la abolición de la esclavitud en la Isla de Cuba*. Havana: n.p., 1885.

Villaverde, Cirilo. *Cecilia Valdés, o la Loma del Ángel*. 1839. Reprint, Havana: Editorial Letras Cubanas, 1996.

Ward Howe, Julia. *A Trip to Cuba*. Boston: Ticknor and Fields, 1860.

Zambrana, Antonio. *El negro Francisco: Novela de costumbres cubanas*. 1873. Reprint, Havana: Imprenta P. Fernández y Cia, 1951.

REFERENCE WORKS

Calcagno, Francisco. *Diccionario biográfico cubano*. 2 vols. New York: Imprenta y Librería de N. Ponce de León, 1878.

Moura, Clóvis. *Dicionário da escravidão negra no Brasil*. São Paulo: Editora da Universidade de São Paulo, 2004.

Serrano, Nicolás María. *Diccionario universal de la lengua castellana, ciencias y artes*. 16 vols. Madrid: Biblioteca Universal Ilustrada, 1878.

Verdecia Hernández, Miriam, Esther Calderín Friol, Marta Casals Reyes, and Reyna Guevara Rodríguez. *Guía breve de los fondos procesados del Archivo Nacional*. Havana: Editorial Academia, 1990.

NEWSPAPERS

Anglo-Brazilian Times (Rio de Janeiro)
Anti-Slavery Reporter (London)
A Republica (Rio de Janeiro)
Birmingham Daily Post (Birmingham, UK)
Boletín Oficial de la Provinicia de La Habana (Havana)
Diário de Notícias (Rio de Janeiro)
Gazeta da Tarde (Rio de Janeiro)
New York Sun
O Abolicionista (Rio de Janeiro)
O País (Rio de Janeiro)
Revista Illustrada (Rio de Janeiro)
Rio News (Rio de Janeiro)

PUBLISHED SECONDARY SOURCES

Abreu, Martha. *Meninas perdidas: Os populares e o cotidiano do amor no Rio de Janeiro da Belle Epoque*. Rio de Janeiro: Paz e Terra, 1989.

———. "Slave Mothers and Freed Children: Emancipation and Female Space in Debates on the 'Free Womb' Law, Rio de Janeiro, 1871." *Journal of Latin American Studies* 28, no. 3 (1996): 567–80.

Acosta Cubierta, Rinaldo, and Alfredo Montoto, eds. *Historia de la literatura cubana*, vol. 1. Havana: Instituto de Literatura y Lingüística, 2005.

Aguirre, Carlos. *Agentes de su propia libertad: Los esclavos de Lima y la desintegración de la esclavitud 1821–1854*. Lima: Universidad Católica, 1993.

Aimes, Hubert. "Coartación: A Spanish Institution for the Advancement of Slaves into Freedmen." *Yale Review* 17 (February 1909): 412–31.

Albuquerque, Wlamyra R. *O jogo da dissimulação. Abolição e cidadania negra no Brasil*. São Paulo: Companhia das Letras, 2009.

Alencastro, Luiz Felipe de. *O trato dos viventes: Formação do Brasil no Atlântico Sul*. 2000. Reprint, São Paulo: Companhia das Letras, 2006.

Algranti, Leila Mezan. *O feitor ausente: Estudo sobre a escravidão urbana no Rio de Janeiro, 1808–1822*. Petrópolis: Vozes, 1988.

———. "Slave Crimes: Use of Police Power to Control the Slave Population of Rio de Janeiro." *Luso-Brazilian Review* 25, no. 1 (Summer 1988): 27–48.

Alonso, Angela. *Idéias em movimento. A geração 1870 na crise do Brasil-Império*. São Paulo: Paz e Terra, 2002.

Amantino, Marcia Sueli. "O perfil demográfico do escravo fugitivo." *Estudos Afro-Asiáticos* 31 (1997): 169–88.

Andrade, Manuel Correia de, and Eliane Moury Fernandes. *Atualidade e Abolição*. Recife: Editora Massangana, 1991.

Andrews, George Reid, Hebe Maria Mattos de Castro, Seymour Drescher, Robert M. Levine, and Rebecca J. Scott. *The Abolition of Slavery and the Aftermath of Emancipation in Brazil*. Durham: Duke University Press, 1988.

Aptheker, Herbert. "Resistance and Afro-American History: Some Notes on Contemporary Historiography and Suggestions for Further Research." In *In Resistance: Studies in African, Caribbean and Afro-American History*, edited by Gary Y. Okihiro, 10–20. Amherst: University of Massachusetts Press, 1986.

Araujo, Nara, ed. *Viajeras al Caribe*. Havana: Casa de las Américas, 1983.

Argüelles Espinosa, Luis Ángel. "La abolición de la esclavitud a través de algunos diarios habaneros de la epoca (1880–1886)." *Anuario de Estudios Americanos* 43 (1986): 241–57.

Arriaga Mesa, Marcos, and Andrés Delgado Valdés. "Contribución al estudio de la vivienda pobre en La Habana del siglo XIX: Ciudadelas y accesorias." *Revista de Indias* 204 (1995): 453–83.

Assunção, Matthias Röhrig, and Michael Zeuske. "'Race,' Ethnicity and Social Structure in Nineteenth Century Brazil and Cuba." *Ibero-Amerikanisches Archiv* 24: 3–4 (1998): 375–444.

Awe, Bolande. "Writing Women into History: The Nigerian Experience." In *Writing Women's History: International Perspectives*, edited by Karen Offen, Ruth Roach Pierson, and Jane Rendall, 211–20. Bloomington: Indiana University Press, 1991.

Azevedo, Célia Maria Marinho de. *Abolitionism in the United States and Brazil: A Comparative Perspective*. New York: Garland, 1995.

———. *Onda Negra, Medo Branco: O negro no imaginário das elites—século XIX*. Rio de Janeiro: Paz e Terra, 1987.

Azevedo, Elciene. *Orfeu de Carapinha: A trajetória de Luiz Gama na imperial cidade de São Paulo*. Campinas: Editora Unicamp, 1999.

Baer, Werner. *The Brazilian Economy: Growth and Development*. Westport, Conn.: Praeger, 2001.

Baptist, Edward E. "'Cuffy,' 'Fancy Maids' and 'One-Eyed Men': Rape, Commodification and the Domestic Slave Trade in the United States." In *The Chattel Principle: Internal Slave Trades in the Americas*, edited by Walter Johnson, 165–202. New Haven: Yale University Press, 2005.

Barcia Paz, Manuel. "A Black Bahamian Family's Odyssey in Turbulent 1840s Cuba." In *The Chattel Principle: Internal Slave Trades in the Americas*, ed. Walter Johnson, 275–90. New Haven: Yale University Press, 2005.

———. *Seeds of Insurrection: Domination and Resistance on Western Cuban Plantations, 1808–1848*. Baton Rouge: Louisiana State University Press, 2008.

Barcia Zequeira, María del Carmen. *Burguesía esclavista y abolición*. Havana: Editorial de Ciencias Sociales, 1987.

———. "Entre el poder y la crisis, las prostitutas se defienden." In *Mujeres latinoamericanas: Historia y cultura, siglos XVI al XIX*, edited by Luisa Campuzano, 1:263–74. Havana: Editorial Casa de las Américas, 1997.

———. *La otra familia: Parientes, redes y descendencia de los esclavos en Cuba*. Havana: Editorial Casa de las Américas, 2003.

———. *Los ilustres apellidos: Negros en La Habana colonial*. Havana: Ediciones Boloña, 2008.

———. "Mujeres en torno a *Minerva*." *La Rábida* 17 (1998): 113–21.

———. "Táctica y estrategia de la burguesía esclavista de Cuba ante la abolición de la esclavitud." *Anuario de Estudios Americanos* 43 (1986): 111–26.

Barickman, B. J. *A Bahian Counterpoint: Sugar, Tobacco, Cassava, and Slavery in the Recôncavo, 1780–1860*. Stanford: Stanford University Press, 1998.

Barickman, B. J., and Martha Few. "Ana Paulinha de Queirós, Joaquina da Costa, and Their Neighbors: Free Women of Color as Household Heads in Rural Bahia (Brazil)." In Gaspar and Hine, *Beyond Bondage*, 169–201.

Barman, Roderick J. *Princess Isabel of Brazil: Gender and Power in the Nineteenth Century*. Wilmington: Scholarly Resources, 2002.

Barnet, Miguel. *Biografía de un cimarrón*. 1964. Reprint, Havana: Editorial Letras Cubanas, 2001.

Basso Ortiz, Alessandra. *Los gangá en Cuba*. Havana: Fundación Fernando Ortiz, 2005.

Beattie, Peter. *The Tribute of Blood: Army, Honor, Race, and Nation in Brazil, 1864–1945*. Durham: Duke University Press, 2001.

Beckles, Hilary McD. "Black Female Slaves and White Households in Barbados." In Gaspar and Hine, *More than Chattel*, 111–25.

———. *Centering Woman: Gender Relations in Caribbean Slave Society*. Kingston: Ian Randle, 1999.

———. "Emancipation by War or Law? Wilberforce and the 1816 Barbados Slave Rebellion." In *Abolition and Its Aftermath: The Historical Context, 1790–1916*, edited by David Richardson, 80–104. London: Frank Cass, 1985.

———. "Freeing Slavery: Gender Paradigms in the Social History of Caribbean Slavery." In Moore, Higman, Campbell, and Bryan, *Slavery, Freedom, and Gender*, 197–231.

———. "Historicising Slavery in West Indian Feminisms." *Feminist Review* 59 (Summer 1998): 34–56.

———. *Natural Rebels: A Social History of Enslaved Women in Barbados*. New Brunswick: Rutgers University Press, 1989.

———. "Sex and Gender in the Historiography of the Caribbean." In Shepherd, Brereton, and Bailey, *Engendering History*, 125–40.

Bellini, Ligia. "Por amor e por interesse: A relação senhor-escravo em cartas de alforria." In *Escravidão e invenção da liberdade: estudos sobre o negro no Brasil*, edited by João José Reis, 73–86. São Paulo: Editora Brasiliense, 1988.

Berbel, Márcia Regina, and Rafael Bivar Marquese. "The Absence of Race: Slavery, Citizenship and Pro-Slavery Ideology in the Cortes of Lisbon and the Rio de Janeiro Constituent Assembly (1821–4)." *Social History*, 32:4 (November 2007): 415–33.

Berbel, Márcia Regina, Rafael Marquese and Tâmis Parron. *Escravidão e política entre impérios e nações: Brasil e Cuba, c. 1790–1850*. São Paulo: Hucitec/Centro Universitário Mariantonia, 2010.

Bergad, Laird W. *The Comparative Histories of Slavery in Brazil, Cuba, and the United States*. New York: Cambridge University Press, 2007.

———. *Slavery and the Demographic and Economic History of Minas Gerais, Brazil, 1720–1888*. Cambridge: Cambridge University Press, 1999.

Bergad, Laird W., Fe Iglesias, and María del Carmen Barcia. *The Cuban Slave Market, 1790–1880*. Cambridge: Cambridge University Press, 1990.

Berger, Iris. "Rebels or Status-Seekers? Women as Spirit-Mediums in East Africa." In *Women in Africa*, edited by Nancy J. Hafkin and Edna G. Bay, 157–82. Stanford: Stanford University Press, 1976.

Besse, Susan. *Restructuring Patriarchy: The Modernization of Gender Inequality in Brazil, 1914–1940*. Chapel Hill: University of North Carolina Press, 1996.

Bethell, Leslie. *The Abolition of the Brazilian Slave Trade: Britain, Brazil and the Slave Trade Question, 1807–1869*. Cambridge: Cambridge University Press, 1970.

Bethell, Leslie, and José Murilo de Carvalho, eds. *Joaquim Nabuco, British Abolitionists and the End of Slavery in Brazil: Correspondence, 1880–1905*. London: Institute for the Study of the Americas, 2009.

Bezerra, Nielson Rosa. *As Chaves da Liberdade: Confluências da escravidão no Recôncavo do Rio de Janeiro (1833–1888)*. Niterói: Editora da Universidade Federal Fluminense, 2008.

Bhana, Hershini. "La mujer conjuro, el obeah y la quema de la casa del amo." *Del Caribe* 34 (2001): 57–60.

Blackburn, Robin. *The Overthrow of Colonial Slavery, 1776–1848*. London: Verso, 1988.

Blassingame, John W. "Bibliographical Essay: Foreign Writers View Cuban Slavery." *Journal of Negro History* 57, no. 4 (October 1972): 415–24.

Block, Sharon. *Rape and Sexual Power in Early America*. Chapel Hill: University of North Carolina Press, 2006.

Brana-Shute, Rosemary. "Approaching Freedom: The Manumission of Slaves in Suriname, 1760–1808." *Slavery and Abolition* 10, no. 3 (December 1989): 40–63.

Brereton, Bridget. "Gendered Testimonies: Autobiographies, Diaries and Letters by Women as Sources for Caribbean History." In Moore, Higman, Campbell, and Bryan, *Slavery, Freedom, and Gender*, 232–53.

Bronfman, Alejandra. *Measures of Equality: Social Science, Citizenship, and Race in Cuba, 1902–1940*. Chapel Hill: University of North Carolina Press, 2004.

Brooks, George E., 1983. "A Nhara of the Guinea-Bissau Region: Mãe Aurelia Corneia." In *Women and Slavery in Africa*, edited by Claire Robertson and Martin A. Klein, 295–319. Madison: University of Wisconsin Press, 1983.

———. "The *Signares* of Saint-Louis and Gorée: Women Entrepreneurs in Eighteenth Century Senegal." In *Women in Africa*, edited by Nancy J. Hafkin and Edna G. Bay, 19–44. Stanford: Stanford University Press, 1976.

Brown, Elsa Barkley. "'What Has Happened Here': The Politics of Difference in Women's History and Feminist Politics." *Feminist Studies* 18, no. 2 (1992): 295–312.

Bulcão, Ana Lucia, and Luiz Sérgio Dias. *Escravidão urbana*. Rio de Janeiro: Arquivo Geral da Cidade do Rio de Janeiro, 1992.

Burnard, Trevor. "'Do Thou in Gentle Phibia Smile': Scenes from an Interracial Marriage, Jamaica, 1754–86." In Gaspar and Hine, *Beyond Bondage*, 82–105.

Bush, Barbara. "'The Family Tree Is Not Cut': Women and Cultural Resistance in Slave Family Life in the British Caribbean." In *In Resistance: Studies in African, Caribbean and Afro-American History*, edited by Gary Y. Okihiro, 117–32. Amherst: University of Massachusetts Press, 1986.

———. "Hard Labor: Women, Childbirth and Resistance in British Caribbean Slave Societies." In Gaspar and Hine, *More than Chattel*, 193–217.

———. *Slave Women in Caribbean Society, 1650–1838*. London: James Currey, 1990.

———. "Towards Emancipation: Slave Women and Resistance to Coercive Labour Regimes in the British West Indian Colonies, 1790–1838." In *Abolition and Its Aftermath: The Historical Context, 1790–1916*, edited by David Richardson, 27–54. London: Frank Cass, 1985.

Butler, Kim. *Freedoms Given, Freedoms Won: Afro-Brazilians in Post-Abolition São Paulo and Salvador*. New Brunswick: Rutgers University Press, 1998.

Callou, Hélvia. *Abolição sem libertação*. Campina Grande, Paraíba: FUNCESP, 2002.

Calmon, Pedro. *A Princesa Isabel: A "Redentora."* São Paulo: Companhia Editorial Nacional, 1941.

Calwell, Kia Lily. *Negras in Brazil: Re-Envisioning Black Women, Citizenship, and the Politics of Identity*. New Brunswick: Rutgers University Press, 2007.

Camp, Stephanie. *Closer to Freedom: Enslaved Women and Everyday Resistance in the Plantation South*. Chapel Hill: University of North Carolina Press, 2004.

Campuzano, Luisa. "Blancas y 'blancos' en la conquista de Cuba." In *Mujeres latinoamericanas: historia y cultura, siglos XVI al XIX*, edited by Luisa Campuzano, 1:35–52. Havana: Editorial Casa de las Américas, 1997.

Cardoso, Ciro Flamarion. "The Peasant Breach in the Slave System: New Developments in Brazil." *Luso-Brazilian Review* 25:1 (1988): 49–57.

Carrera Damas, Germán. "Flight and Confrontation." In *Africa in Latin America: Essays on History, Culture, and Socialization*, translated by Leonor Blum and edited by Manuel Moreno Fraginals, 23–37. New York: Holmes and Meier, 1984.

Carvalho, José Murilo de. *Cidadania no Brasil: O longo caminho*. 2001. Reprint, Rio de Janeiro: Civilização Brasileira, 2008.

———. "Political Elites and State-Building: The Case of Nineteenth-Century Brazil." In *Constructing Culture and Power in Latin America*, edited by Daniel H. Levine, 403–28. Ann Arbor: University of Michigan Press, 1993.

Casanova-Marengo, Ilia. *El intersticio de la colonia: Ruptura y mediación en la narrativa antiesclavista cubana*. Madrid: Vervuert Iberoamericana, 2002.

Casanovas, Joan. *Bread, or Bullets! Urban Labor and Spanish Colonialism in Cuba, 1850–1898*. Pittsburgh: Pittsburgh University Press, 1990.

Castañeda, Digna. "Demandas judiciales de las esclavas en el siglo XIX cubano." *Temas* 5 (January–March 1996): 60–65.

———. "The Woman Slave in Cuba during the First Half of the Nineteenth Century." In Shepherd, Brereton, and Bailey, *Engendering History*, 141–54.

Castilho, Celso. ""Brisas atlánticas: La abolición gradual y la conexión brasileña-cubana." In *Haití: Revolución y emancipación*, edited by Rina Cáceres Gómez and Paul E. Lovejoy, 128–39. San José: Editorial Universidad de Costa Rica, 2008.

———. "Performing Abolitionism, Enacting Citizenship: The Social Construction of Political Rights in 1880s Recife, Brazil." *Hispanic American Historical Review* 93 (2013), forthcoming.

Castilho, Celso, and Camillia Cowling. "Funding Freedom, Popularizing Politics: Abolitionism and Local Emancipation Funds in 1880s Brazil." *Luso-Brazilian Review* 47, no. 1 (Spring 2010): 89–120.

Castro, Hebe Maria Mattos de. "Beyond Masters and Slaves: Subsistence Agriculture as a Survival Strategy in Brazil during the Second Half of the Nineteenth Century." In *The Abolition of Slavery and the Aftermath of Emancipation in Brazil*, edited by George Reid Andrews, Hebe Maria Mattos de Castro, Seymour Drescher, and Robert M. Levine, 55–83. Durham: Duke University Press, 1988.

———. *Das cores do silêncio. Os significados da liberdade no sudeste escravista—Brasil século XIX*. Rio de Janeiro: Arquivo Nacional, 1995.

———. *Escravidão e cidadania no Brasil monárquico*. Rio de Janeiro: Jorge Zahar Editora, 2000.

———. Introduction to Livro de Ouro collection, n.d. Arquivo Geral da Cidade do Rio de Janeiro.

———. "Os Combates da Memória: Escravidão e liberdade nos arquivos orais de descendentes de escravos brasileiros." *Tempo* (History Department, Universidade Federal Fluminense) 3, no. 6 (December 1998): 119–38.

Castro, Hebe Maria Mattos de, and Ana Lugão Rios, "O pós-abolição como problema histórico: balanços e perspectivas." *Topói* (UFRJ) 8, no. 5 (2004): 170–98.

Caulfield, Sueann. "The History of Gender in the Historiography of Latin America." *Hispanic American Historical Review*, 82:3–4 (August–November 2001): 421–90.

———. *In Defence of Honor: Sexual Morality, Modernity and Nation in Early Twentieth-Century Brazil*. Durham: Duke University Press, 2000.

———. "O nascimento do Mangue: Raça, nação e controle da prostituição no Rio de Janeiro, 1850–1942." *Tempo* 9 (2000): 43–63. Publication of the History Department, Universidade Federal Fluminense.

Cavalcanti, Nireu Oliveira. *Rio de Janeiro: Centro histórico 1808–1998*. São Paulo: Hamburg Gráfica Editora, 1998.

Centro Juan Marinello. *Historia y memoria: Sociedad, cultura y vida cotidiana en Cuba, 1878–1917*. Havana: Centro Juan Marinello, 2003.

Cepero Bonilla, Raúl. *Azúcar y abolición*. 1948. Reprint, Barcelona: Editorial Crítica, 1976.

Chalhoub, Sidney. *Cidade febril: Cortiços e epidemias na corte imperial*. São Paulo: Companhia das Letras, 1996.

———. *Machado de Assis, historiador*. São Paulo: Companhia das Letras, 2003.

———. "The Politics of Silence: Race and Citizenship in Nineteenth-Century Brazil." *Slavery and Abolition* 27, no.1 (April 2006): 73–87.

———. "The Precariousness of Freedom in a Slave Society: Brazil in the Nineteenth Century." *International Review of Social History* 56 (2011): 405–39.

———. "Solidariedade e liberdade: Sociedades beneficentes de negros e negras no Rio de Janeiro na segunda metade do século XIX." In *Quase-Cidadão: Histórias e antropologias da pós-emancipação no Brasil*, edited by Olívia Maria Gomes da Cunha and Flávio dos Santos Gomes, 219–39. Rio de Janeiro: Editora Fundação Getúlio Vargas, 2007.

———. *Trabalho, lar e botequim: O cotidiano dos trabalhadores no Rio de Janeiro da "belle époque."* 1986. Reprint, Campinas: Editora Unicamp, 2001.

———. *Visões da liberdade: Uma história das últimas décadas da escravidão na Corte*. São Paulo: Companhia das Letras, 1990.

Childs, Matt D. *The 1812 Aponte Rebellion in Cuba and the Struggle against Atlantic Slavery*. Chapel Hill: University of North Carolina Press, 2006.

———. "'Sewing' Civilization: Cuban Female Education in the Context of Africanization." *Americas* 54, no. 1 (July 1997): 83–107.

Coatsworth, John H. "La independencia de Cuba en la historia de América Latina." In *Espacios, silencios y los sentidos de la libertad: Cuba entre 1878 y 1912*, edited by Fernando Martínez Heredia, Rebecca J. Scott, and Orlando García Martínez, 346–55. Havana: Ediciones UNIÓN, 2001.

Cohen, Deborah, and Maura O'Connor, eds. *Comparison and History: Europe in Cross-National Perspective*. New York: Routledge, 2004.

Collins, Jane-Marie. "Bearing the Burden of Bastardy: Infanticide, Child Murder, Race, and Motherhood in Brazilian Slave Society, Nineteenth-Century Bahia." In *Killing Infants: Studies in the Worldwide Practice of Infanticide*, edited by Brigitte Bechtold and Donna Cooper Graves, 199–229. Lampeter: Edwin Mellen, 2006.

―――. "Intimacy, Inequality and *Democracia Racial*: Theorizing Race, Gender and Sex in the History of Brazilian Race Relations." *Journal of Romance Studies* 7, no. 2 (2007): 19–34.

―――. "Slavery, Subversion and Subalternity: Gender and Violent Resistance in Nineteenth Century Bahia." In *Brazilian Feminisms*, edited by Solange Ribeiro de Oliveira and Judith Still, 34–56. Nottingham: University of Nottingham, 1999.

Conrad, Robert Edgar. *The Destruction of Brazilian Slavery, 1850–1888*. Berkeley: University of California Press, 1972.

―――. *World of Sorrow: The African Slave Trade to Brazil*. Baton Rouge: Louisiana State University Press, 1986.

―――, ed. *Children of God's Fire: A Documentary History of Black Slavery in Brazil*. Princeton: Princeton University Press, 1983.

Cooper, Frederick, Thomas C. Holt, and Rebecca J. Scott. *Beyond Slavery: Explorations of Race, Labor and Citizenship in Postemancipation Societies*. Chapel Hill: University of North Carolina Press, 2000.

Corwin, Arthur. *Spain and the Abolition of Slavery in Cuba, 1817–1886*. Austin: University of Texas Press, 1967.

Costa, Suely Gomes. "Entre práticas escravistas e caritativas, transformações da gestualidade feminina. (Rio de Janeiro, primeira metade do século XIX.)" *Gênero* 1, no. 1 (2000): 57–63.

Cottrol, Robert J. "The Long Lingering Shadow: Law, Liberalism, and Cultures of Racial Hierarchy and Identity in the Americas." *Tulane Law Review* 76, no. 11 (2001): 11–79.

Cowling, Camillia. "Debating Womanhood, Defining Freedom: The Abolition of Slavery in 1880s Rio de Janeiro." *Gender and History* 22, no. 2 (August 2010): 284–301.

―――. "Negotiating Freedom: Women of Color and the Transition to Free Labor in Cuba, 1870–1886." *Slavery and Abolition* 26, no. 3 (December 2005): 373–87.

Cuales, Sonia Magdalena. "In Search of Our Memory: Gender in the Netherlands Antilles." *Feminist Review* 59 (Summer 1998): 86–100.

Cubano-Iguina, Astrid. "Legal Constructions of Gender and Violence against Women in Puerto Rico under Spanish Rule, 1860–1895." *Law and History Review* 22, no. 3 (Fall 2004): 531–64.

Cunha, Olívia Maria Gomes da, and Flávio dos Santos Gomes, eds. *Quase-Cidadão: Histórias e antropologias da pós-emancipação no Brasil*. Rio de Janeiro: Editora Fundação Getúlio Vargas, 2007.

Curtin, Philip. *The African Slave Trade: A Census*. Madison: University of Wisconsin Press, 1969.

Daibert, Robert, Jr. *Isabel, a "Redentora" dos Escravos: Uma história da Princesa entre olhares negros e brancos (1846–1988)*. Bauru, São Paulo: Editora da Universidade do Sagrado Coração, 2004.

Damasceno, Caetana M., and Sônia Giacomini. *Caminhada estudiantil pela verdadeira abolição: O que Zumbi diria à Princesa Isabel*. Rio de Janeiro: Universidade Federal do Rio de Janeiro, 1988.

Dauphin, Cécile, Arlette Fage, Genevieve Fraisse, Christiane Klapisch-Zuber, Rose-Marie Lagrave, Michelle Perrot, Pierette Pfzerat, Yannick Ripa, Pauline Schmitt-Pantel, and Daniele Voldman. "Women's Culture and Women's Power: Issues in French Women's History." In *Writing Women's History: International Perspectives*, edited by Karen Offen, Ruth Roach Pierson, and Jane Rendall, 107–34. Bloomington: Indiana University Press, 1991.

Davies, Catherine, ed. Introduction to *Sab* (1841) by Gertrudis Gómez de Avellaneda. 1–28. Manchester: Manchester University Press, 2001.

Dávila, Jerry. *Diploma of Whiteness: Race and Social Policy in Brazil, 1917–1945*. Durham: Duke University Press, 2003.

Davis, David Brion. *The Problem of Slavery in the Age of Emancipation*. Ithaca: Cornell University Press, 1975.

———. *The Problem of Slavery in Western Culture*. New York: Oxford University Press, 1966.

Dean, Warren. *Rio Claro: A Brazilian Plantation System, 1820–1920*. Stanford: Stanford University Press, 1976.

De Armas, Ramón. "José Martí: La verdadera y única abolición de la esclavitud." *Anuario de Estudios Americanos* 43 (1986): 333–51.

Degler, Carl N. *Neither White nor Black: Slavery and Race Relations in Brazil and the United States*. Madison: University of Wisconsin, 1971.

De Groot, Silvia W. "The Maroons of Surinam: Agents of Their Own Emancipation." In *Abolition and Its Aftermath: The Historical Context, 1790–1916*, edited by David Richardson, 55–79. London: Frank Cass, 1985.

de la Fuente, Alejandro. *A Nation for All: Race, Inequality, and Politics in Twentieth-Century Cuba*. Chapel Hill: University of North Carolina Press, 2001.

———. "Slave Law and Claims-making in Cuba: The Tannenbaum Debate Revisited." *Law and History Review* 22, no. 2 (Summer 2004): 339–67.

———. "Slavery and the Law: A Reply." *Law and History Review* 22, no. 2 (Summer 2004): 383–87.

———. "Slaves and the Creation of Legal Rights: *Coartación* and *Papel*." *Hispanic American Historical Review* 87, no. 4 (November 2007): 659–92.

Del Priore, Mary. 1993. *Ao sul do corpo: Condição feminina, maternidades e mentalidades no Brasil colônia*. Rio de Janeiro: José Olympio, 1993.

Del Vas Mingo, Milagros. "El derecho de patronato en los proyectos abolicionistas cubanos." *Anuario de Estudios Americanos* 43 (1986): 171–84.

Deschamps Chapeaux, Pedro. *El negro en la economía habanera del siglo XIX*. Havana: UNEAC, 1971.

———. *Los cimarrones urbanos*. Havana: Editorial de Ciencias Sociales, 1983.

Dias, Maria Odila Leite da Silva. *Power and Everyday Life: The Lives of Working Women in Nineteenth-Century Brazil*. Translated by Ann Frost. Cambridge: Polity Press, 1995.

Díaz, María Elena. "Beyond Tannenbaum." *Law and History Review* 22, no. 2 (Summer 2004): 371–76.

———. "Of Life and Freedom at the (Tropical) Hearth: El Cobre, Cuba, 1709–73." In Gaspar and Hine, *Beyond Bondage*, 19–36.

————. *The Virgin, the King, and the Royal Slaves of El Cobre. Negotiating Freedom in Colonial Cuba, 1670–1780*. Stanford: Stanford University Press, 2000.

Díaz Martínez, Yolanda. *La peligrosa Habana: Violencia y criminalidad a finales del siglo XIX*. Havana: Editorial Ciencias Sociales, 2005.

Dorsey, Joseph C. "It Hurt Very Much at the Time: Rape Culture, Patriarchy, and the Slave Body-Semiotic." In *The Culture of Gender and Sexuality in the Caribbean*, edited by Linden Lewis, 294–322. Gainesville: University Press of Florida, 2003.

————. "Women without History: Slavery and the International Politics of *Partus Sequitur Ventrem* in the Spanish Caribbean." *Journal of Caribbean History* 28, no. 2 (1994): 165–207.

Drescher, Seymour. *Abolition: A History of Slavery and Antislavery*. Cambridge: Cambridge University Press, 2009.

————. "Brazilian Abolition in Comparative Perspective." *Hispanic American Historical Review* 68, no. 3 (August 1988): 429–60.

————. *From Slavery to Freedom: Comparative Studies in the Rise and Fall of Atlantic Slavery*. Houndmills: Macmillan, 1999.

Duharte Jiménez, Rafael. *Nacionalidad e Historia*. Santiago de Cuba: Editorial Oriente, 1991.

Dunernin, James. "La abolición del patronato en 1886: Los debates en Madrid." *Anuario de Estudios Americanos* 43 (1986): 185–99.

Duque, Francisco M. *La historia de Regla. Descripción política, económica y social, desde su fundación hasta el día*. Havana: Imprenta de Rambla, Bouza y Ca., 1925.

Duque-Estrada, Osório. *A abolição: Esboço histórico, 1831–1888*. With an introduction by Rui Barbosa. Rio de Janeiro: Leite Ribeiro & Maurillo, 1918.

Eltis, David. *Economic Growth and the Ending of the Transatlantic Slave Trade*. Oxford: Oxford University Press, 1987.

Falola, Toyin, and Matt D. Childs, eds. *The Yoruba Diaspora in the Atlantic World*. Bloomington: Indiana University Press, 2004.

Faria, Sheila Siqueira de Castro. *A colônia em movimento: Fortuna e família no cotidiano colonial*. Rio de Janeiro: Nova Fronteira, 1998.

————. "Sinhás Pretas: Acumulação de pecúlio e transmissão de bens de mulheres forras no sudeste escravista (sécs. XVIII–XIX)." In *Escritos sobre História e Educação. Homenagem á Maria Yedda Leite Linhares*, edited by Francisco Carlos Teixeira da Silva, Hebe Maria Mattos, and Ciro Flamirion Cardoso, 289–329. Rio de Janeiro: FAPERJ/Mauad, 2001.

Farias, Juliana Barreto. "Mercado em greve: Protestos e organização dos trabalhadores na Praça das Marinhas, Rio de Janeiro/ século XIX." *Revista ArtCultura* 11, no. 19 (2009): 35–55.

Farias, Juliana Barreto, Carlos Eugênio Líbano Soares, and Flávio dos Santos Gomes. *No labirinto das nações: Africanos e identidades no Rio de Janeiro, século XIX*. Rio de Janeiro: Arquivo Nacional, 2005.

Feeley, Malcom M., and Deborah L. Little. "The Vanishing Female: The Decline of Women in the Criminal Process, 1687–1912." *Law and Society Review* 24 (1991): 719–57.

Fernández Prieto, Leida. *Cuba agrícola: Mito y tradición, 1878-1920*. Madrid: Consejo Superior de Investigaciones Científicas, 2005.

Ferreira, Luzilá Gonçalves, et al. *Suaves amazonas: Mulheres e abolição da escravatura no nordeste*. Recife: Editora Universidade Federal de Pernambuco, 1999.

Ferrer, Ada. *Insurgent Cuba: Race, Nation and Revolution, 1868-1898*. Chapel Hill: University of North Carolina Press, 1999.

Fields, Barbara. "Ideology and Race in American History." In *Nation, Race, and Reconstruction: Essays in Honor of C. Van Woodward*, edited by J. Morgan Kousser and James M. McPherson, 143-77. New York: Oxford University Press, 1982.

Finch, Aisha. "Scandalous Scarcities: Black Slave Women, Plantation Domesticity, and Travel Writing in Nineteenth-Century Cuba." *Journal of Historical Sociology* 23, no. 1 (March 2010): 101-43.

Fivel-Démoret, Sharon Romeo. "The Production and Consumption of Propaganda Literature: The Cuban Antislavery Novel." *Bulletin of Hispanic Studies* 66 (1989): 1-12.

Florentino, Manolo, and José Roberto Góes. *A paz das senzalas: Famílas escravas e tráfico atlântico, Rio de Janeiro, c.1790-c.1850*. Rio de Janeiro: Civilização Brasileira, 1997.

Foote, Nicola. "Rethinking Race, Gender and Citizenship: Black West Indian Women in Costa Rica, 1920-1940." *Bulletin of Latin American Research* 23, no. 2 (April 2004): 198-212.

Font, Maurício A. *Coffee, Contention and Change in the Making of Modern Brazil*. Cambridge: Blackwell, 1990.

Fox-Genovese, Elizabeth. "Strategies and Forms of Resistance: Focus on Slave Women in the United States." In *In Resistance: Studies in African, Caribbean and Afro-American History*, edited by Gary Y. Okihiro, 143-87. Amherst: University of Massachusetts Press, 1986.

———. "Unspeakable Things Unspoken: Ghosts and Memories in the Narratives of African American Women." In Moore, Higman, Campbell, and Bryan, *Slavery, Freedom, and Gender*, 254-75.

———. *Within the Plantation Household: Black and White Women of the Old South*. Chapel Hill: University of North Carolina Press, 1988.

Fraga Filho, Walter. *Encruzilhadas da liberdade: Histórias de escravos e libertos na Bahia (1870-1910)*. Campinas: Editora Unicamp, 2006.

Franco Ferrán, José Luciano. *Comercio clandestino de esclavos*. 1980. Reprint, Havana: Editorial de Ciencias Sociales, 1996.

Frank, Zephyr. *Dutra's World: Wealth and Family in Nineteenth-Century Rio de Janeiro*. Albuquerque: University of New Mexico Press, 2004.

———. "Layers, Flows, and Intersections: Jeronymo José de Mello and Artisan Life in Rio de Janeiro, 1840s-1880s." *Journal of Social History* 41, no. 2 (Winter 2007): 307-28.

Franklin, Sarah L. *Women and Slavery in Nineteenth-Century Colonial Cuba*. Rochester: University of Rochester Press, 2012.

Frederickson, George. *The Comparative Imagination: On the History of Racism, Nationalism, and Social Movements*. Berkeley: University of California Press, 2000.

Freyre, Gilberto. *Casa-grande e senzala. Formação da família brasileira sob o regime da economia patriarcal*. 1933. Reprint, São Paulo: Editora Global, 2003.

Furtado, Celso. *The Economic Growth of Brazil: A Survey from Colonial to Modern Times*. Berkeley: University of California Press, 1971.

Furtado, Júnia Ferreira. *Chica da Silva e o Contrator dos Diamantes: O outro lado do mito*. São Paulo: Companhia das Letras, 2003.

Gama, Katherine de. "A Brave New World? Rights Discourse and the Politics of Reproductive Autonomy." *Journal of Law and Society* 20, no. 1 (1993): 114–30.

García, Gloria. *La esclavitud desde la esclavitud*. Havana: Editorial de Ciencias Sociales, 2003.

Gaspar, David Barry. "'To Be Free Is Very Sweet': The Manumission of Female Slaves in Antigua, 1817–26." In Gaspar and Hine, *Beyond Bondage*, 60–81.

Gaspar, David Barry, and Darlene Clark Hine, eds. *Beyond Bondage: Free Women of Color in the Americas*. Urbana: University of Illinois Press, 2004.

———. *More than Chattel: Black Women and Slavery in the Americas*. Bloomington: Indiana University Press, 1996.

Gautier, Arlette. *Les Soeurs de Solitude: La condition feminine dans l'esclavage aux Antilles du XVIIe au XIX siècle*. Paris: Editions Caribéenes, 1985.

Geggus, David P. "Slave and Free Colored Women in St. Domingue." In Gaspar and Hine, *More than Chattel*, 259–78.

Geltner, G. "No-Woman's-Land? On Female Crime and Incarceration, Past, Present, and Future." *Justice Policy Journal* 7, no. 2 (Fall 2010), http://www.cjcj.org/files/No_Woman.pdf

Giovannetti, Jorge L., and Camillia Cowling. "Hard Work with the *Mare Magnum* of the Past: Cuban Nineteenth-Century History and the *Miscelánea de Expedientes* Collection." *Cuban Studies/Estudios Cubanos* 39 (2008): 60–84.

Gomes, Flávio dos Santos. "Quilombos do Rio de Janeiro no século XIX." In *Liberdade por um fio: Histórias dos quilombos no Brasil*, edited by João José Reis and Flávio dos Santos Gomes, 263–90. São Paulo: Companhia das Letras, 1996.

Gómez Luaces, Eduardo. *Un Siglo de Periodismo en Regla, 1852–1949*. Regla: Oficina del Historiador, 1948.

Gómez Véliz, Doreya, Marta Ferriol Marchena, Bárbara Danzie León, and Hilda Otero Abreu. "Alunas reflexiones sobre el cimarronaje femenino en Cuba." In *Conferencia Internacional Presencia de Africa en América*, edited by Antonio Núñez Jiménez, 64–75. Havana: UNESCO, 1985.

González Quiñones, Fernando, Pilar Pérez-Fuentes Hernández, and Lola Valverde Lamsfús. "Hogares y familias en los barrios populares de La Habana en el siglo XIX. Una aproximación a través del censo de 1861." *Boletín de la Asociación de Demografía Histórica* 16, no. 2 (1998): 87–133.

González-Ripoll, María de los Dolores, Consuelo Naranjo Orovio, Ada Ferrer, Gloria García Rodríguez, and Josef Opatrny. *El Rumor de Haití en Cuba: Temor, Raza y Rebeldía, 1789–1844*. Madrid: Consejo Superior de Investigación Científica, 2004.

González Ruíz, Julio. "El tema de la esclavitud en la literatura femenina del S. XIX." In *IX Encuentro de la Ilustración al Romanticismo (1750-1850): Historia, memoria y ficción*, edited by A. González Troyano, 137–48. Cádiz: Universidad de Cádiz, 1999.

Gott, Richard. *Cuba: A New History*. New Haven: Yale University Press, 2004.

Gould, Virginia Meacham. "Henriette Delille, Free Women of Color and Catholicism in Antebellum New Orleans." In Gaspar and Hine, *Beyond Bondage*, 271–85.

———. "Urban Slavery—Urban Freedom: The Manumission of Jacqueline Lemelle." In Gaspar and Hine, *More than Chattel*, 298–314.

Graden, Dale T. "'So Much Superstition amongst These People!' Candomblé and the Dilemmas of Afro-Bahian Intellectuals, 1864–1871." In *Afro-Brazilian Culture and Politics: Bahia, 1790s-1990s*, edited by Henrik Kraay, 57–73. London: M. E. Sharpe, 1998.

Graham, Richard. "Another Middle Passage? The Internal Slave Trade in Brazil." In *The Chattel Principle: Internal Slave Trades in the Americas*, edited by Walter Johnson, 291–324. New Haven: Yale University Press, 2005.

———. *Britain and the Onset of Modernization in Brazil, 1850-1914*. Cambridge: Cambridge University Press, 1968.

———. *Feeding the City: From Street Market to Liberal Reform in Salvador, Brazil, 1780-1860*. Austin: University of Texas Press, 2010.

———. *Patronage and Politics in Nineteenth-Century Brazil*. Stanford: Stanford University Press, 1990.

———. "1850-1870." In *Brazil: Empire and Republic, 1822-1930*, edited by Leslie Bethell, 104–30. Cambridge: Cambridge University Press, 1989.

Greenfield, Gerald Michael. "Lighting the City: A Case Study of Public Service Problems in São Paulo, 1885–1913." In *Essays concerning the Socioeconomic History of Brazil and Portuguese India*, edited by Dauril Alden and Warren Dean, 118–49. Gainesville: University Press of Florida, 1977.

Grinberg, Keila. "Freedom Suits and Civil Law in Brazil and the United States." *Slavery and Abolition* 22, no. 3 (December 2001): 66–82.

———. *Liberata: A lei da ambigüidade: As ações de liberdade da Corte de Apelação do Rio de Janeiro no século XIX*. Rio de Janeiro: Relume Dumará, 1994.

———. *O fiador dos brasileiros: Cidadania, escravidão e e direito civil no tempo de Antônio Pereira Rebouças*. Rio de Janeiro: Civilização Brasileira, 2002.

Guerra y Sánchez, Ramiro. *Azúcar y población en las Antillas*. 1927. Reprint, Havana: Editorial de Ciencias Sociales, 1970.

Guy, Donna. "Medical Imperialism Gone Awry: The Campaign against Legalized Prostitution in Latin America." In *Science, Medicine and Cultural Imperialism*, edited by Teresa Meade and Mark Walker, 75–94. London: Macmillan, 1991.

Hahner, June E. *Emancipating the Female Sex: The Struggle for Women's Rights in Brazil, 1850-1940*. Durham: Duke University Press, 1990.

———. "Women and Work in Brazil, 1850-1920." In *Essays concerning the Socioeconomic History of Brazil and Portuguese India*, edited by Dauril Alden and Warren Dean, 87–117. Gainesville: University Press of Florida, 1977.

Hall, Catherine. *Civilizing Subjects: Metropole and Colony in the English Imagination, 1830–1867*. Cambridge: Polity Press, 2002.

Hall, Gwendolyn Midlo. *Social Control in Slave Plantation Societies: A Comparison of St. Domingue and Cuba*. Baltimore: Johns Hopkins University Press, 1971.

Hanger, Kimberley S. "Landlords, Shopkeepers, Farmers and Slave-Owners: Free Black Female Property-Holders in Colonial New Orleans." In Gaspar and Hine, *Beyond Bondage*, 219–36.

Helg, Aline. *Our Rightful Share: The Afro-Cuban Struggle for Equality, 1886–1912*. Chapel Hill: University of North Carolina Press, 1995.

———. "Race in Argentina and Cuba, 1880–1930: Theories, Policy and Popular Reaction." In *The Idea of Race in Latin America, 1870–1940*, edited by Richard Graham, 37–70. Austin: University of Texas Press, 1990.

Heuman, Gad, ed. *Out of the House of Bondage: Runaways, Resistance and Marronage in Africa and the New World*. London: Frank Cass, 1986.

Hevia Lanier, Oílda. *Mujeres negras libres y propietarias en la Habana colonial del siglo XIX*, forthcoming.

———. "Otra contribución a la historia de los negros sin historia." *Debates americanos* 4 (July–December 1997): 77–89.

———. "1880–1900. Los cabildos de nación en la provincia de Matanzas." *Debates americanos* 12 (January–December 2002): 91–98.

Higgins, Kathleen J. *"Licentious Liberty" in a Brazilian Gold-Mining Region: Slavery, Gender and Social Control in Eighteenth-Century Sabará, Minas Gerais*. University Park: Pennsylvania State University Press, 1999.

Higman, Barry W. "The Invention of Slave Society." In Moore, Higman, Campbell, and Bryan, *Slavery, Freedom, and Gender*, 57–75.

Hill Collins, Patricia. "Shifting the Center: Race, Class, and Feminist Theorizing about Motherhood." In *Mothering: Ideology, Experience, and Agency*, edited by Evelyn Nakano Glenn, Grace Chang, and Linda Rennie Forcey, 45–65. New York: Routledge, 1994.

Hoefte, Rosemarijn, and Jean Jacques Vrij. "Free Black and Colored Women in Early-Nineteenth-Century Paramaribo, Suriname." In Gaspar and Hine, *Beyond Bondage*, 145–68.

Hoganson, Kristin. "Garrisonian Abolitionists and the Rhetoric of Gender, 1850–1860." *American Quarterly* 45, no. 4 (December 1993): 558–95.

Holloway, Thomas. "Immigration and Abolition: The Transition from Slave to Free Labor in the São Paulo Coffee Zone." In *Essays concerning the Socioeconomic History of Brazil and Portuguese India*, edited by Dauril Alden and Warren Dean, 150–77. Gainesville: University Press of Florida, 1977.

———. *Policing Rio de Janeiro: Repression and Resistance in a Nineteenth Century City*. Stanford: Stanford University Press, 1993.

hooks, bell. *Ain't I a Woman? Black Women and Feminism*. London: Pluto Press, 1980.

———. *Feminist Theory: From Margin to Centre*. Boston: South End Press, 1984.

Howard, Philip A. *Changing History: Afro-Cuban Cabildos and Societies of Color in the Nineteenth Century*. Baton Rouge: Louisiana State University Press, 1998.

Hünefeldt, Christine. *Paying the Price of Freedom: Family and Labor among Lima's Slaves, 1800–1854*. Berkeley: University of California Press, 1994.

Ibarra, Jorge. "Crisis de la esclavitud patriarcal cubana." *Anuario de Estudios Americanos* 43 (1986): 391–417.

Iglesias, Fe. "El censo cubano de 1877 en sus diferentes versiones." *Santiago* 34 (June 1979): 167–214.

Instituto de Literatura y Lingüística. *Historia de la literatura cubana*, vol. 1: *La Colonia: Desde los orígenes hasta 1898*. Havana: Instituto de Literatura y Lingüística, 2005. First printed in 2002.

Johnson, Lyman L. "Manumission in Colonial Buenos Aires, 1776–1810." *Hispanic American Historical Review* 59, no. 2 (May 1979): 258–79.

Johnson, Sherry. *The Social Transformation of Eighteenth-Century Cuba*. Gainesville: University Press of Florida, 2001.

Johnson, Walter. "On Agency." *Journal of Social History* 37, no. 1 (Fall 2003): 113–24.

———. *Soul by Soul: Life inside the Antebellum Slave Market*. Cambridge: Harvard University Press, 1999.

———, ed. *The Chattel Principle: Internal Slave Trades in the Americas*. New Haven: Yale University Press, 2005.

Johnson-Odin, Cheryl, and Margaret Strobel. "Conceptualizing the History of Women in Africa, Asia, Latin America and the Caribbean, and the Middle East." *Journal of Women's History* 1, no. 1 (Spring 1989): 31–62.

Jones, Jacqueline. *Labor of Love, Labor of Sorrow: Black Women, Work, and the Family from Slavery to the Present*. New York: Vintage Books, 1995.

Kapcia, Antoni. *Cuba: Island of Dreams*. Oxford: Berg, 2000.

———. *Havana: The Making of Cuban Culture*. Oxford: Berg, 2005.

Karasch, Mary. "Anastácia and the Slave Women of Rio de Janeiro." In *Africans in Bondage: Studies in Slavery and the Slave Trade*, edited by Paul E. Lovejoy, 79–105. Madison: University of Wisconsin Press, 1986.

———. "Free Women of Color in Central Brazil." In Gaspar and Hine, *Beyond Bondage*, 237–70.

———. *Slave Life in Rio de Janeiro*. Princeton: Princeton University Press, 1987.

———. "Slave Women on the Brazilian Frontier in the Nineteenth Century." In Gaspar and Hine, *More than Chattel*, 79–96.

Karst, Kenneth, and Keith Rosen. *Law and Development in Latin America: A Case Book*. Berkeley: University of California Press, 1975.

Kiddy, Elizabeth. *Blacks of the Rosary: Memory and History in Minas Gerais, Brazil*. University Park: University of Pennsylvania Press, 2005.

King, Wilma. "Out of Bounds: Emancipated and Enslaved Women in Antebellum America." In Gaspar and Hine, *Beyond Bondage*, 127–44.

———. "'Suffer with Them until Death': Slave Women and Their Children in Nineteenth-Century America." In Gaspar and Hine, *More than Chattel*, 147–68.

Kiple, Kenneth F. *The Cuban Slave Trade, 1820–1862*. Gainesville: University Press of Florida, 1976.

Kirkendall, Andrew J. *Class Mates: Male Student Culture and the Making of a Political Class in Nineteenth-Century Brazil*. Lincoln: University of Nebraska Press, 2002.

Kittleson, Roger A. "Campaign of All Peace and Charity: Gender and the Politics of Abolitionism in Porto Alegre, Brazil, 1846–1888." *Slavery and Abolition* 22 (2001): 83–108.

———. *The Practice of Politics in Postcolonial Brazil: Porto Alegre, 1845–1895*. Pittsburgh: University of Pittsburgh Press, 2005.

———. "Women and Notions of Womanhood in Brazilian Abolitionism." In *Gender and Slave Emancipation in the Atlantic World*, edited by Pamela Scully and Diana Paton, 99–140. Durham: Duke University Press, 2005.

Klein, Herbert S. "African Women in the Atlantic Slave Trade." In *Women and Slavery in Africa*, edited by Claire Robertson and Martin A. Klein, 29–38. Madison: University of Wisconsin Press, 1983.

———. "Nineteenth-Century Brazil." In *Neither Slave nor Free: The Freedmen of African Descent in the Slave Societies of the New World*, edited by David W. Cohen and Jack P. Greene, 309–34. Baltimore: Johns Hopkins University Press, 1972.

———. *Slavery in the Americas: A Comparative Study of Cuba and Virginia*. Chicago: University of Chicago Press, 1967.

Kline, Herbert S., and Francisco Vidal Luna. *Slavery in Brazil*. New York: Cambridge University Press, 2010.

Knight, Franklin. "Cuba." In *Neither Slave nor Free: The Freedmen of African Descent in the Slave Societies of the New World*, edited by David W. Cohen and Jack P. Greene, 278–308. Baltimore: Johns Hopkins University Press, 1972.

———. "Slavery and the Transformation of Society in Cuba, 1511–1760." In Moore, Higman, Campbell, and Bryan, *Slavery, Freedom, and Gender*, 76–96.

———. *Slave Society in Cuba during the Nineteenth Century*. Madison: University of Wisconsin Press, 1970.

Knight, Franklin, and Peggy K. Liss, eds. *Atlantic Port Cities: Economy, Culture, and Society in the Atlantic World, 1650–1850*. Knoxville: University of Tennessee Press, 1991.

Kraay, Hendrik. "Definindo nação e estado: Rituais cívicos na Bahia pós-Independência." *Topoi* (Rio de Janeiro) 3 (2001): 64–90.

Kutzinsky, Vera M. *Sugar's Secrets: Race and the Erotics of Cuban Nationalism*. Charlottesville: University Press of Virginia, 1994.

Landers, Jane G. *Atlantic Creoles in the Age of Revolutions*. Cambridge: Harvard University Press, 2010.

———. "Maroon Women in Colonial Spanish America: Case Studies in the Circum-Caribbean from the Sixteenth through the Eighteenth Centuries." In Gaspar and Hine, *Beyond Bondage*, 3–18.

Landes, Ruth. *The City of Women*. 1947. Reprint, with an introduction by Sally Cole. Albuquerque: University of New Mexico Press, 1994.

Lara, Silvia Hunold. *Campos da violência: Escravos e senhores na Capitania do Rio de Janeiro, 1750–1808*. Rio de Janeiro: Paz e Terra, 1988.

Lauderdale Graham, Sandra. "A Abolição na cidade: Amas-secas, contaminação e controle." In *Atualidade e Abolição*, edited by Manuel Correia de Andrade and Eliane Moury Fernandes, 75–90. Recife: Editora Massangana, 1991.

———. "Being Yoruba in Rio de Janeiro." *Slavery and Abolition* 32, no. 1 (March 2011): 1–26.

———. *Caetana Says No: Women's Stories from a Brazilian Slave Society*. Cambridge: Cambridge University Press, 2002.

———. *House and Street: The Domestic World of Servants and Masters in Nineteenth-Century Rio de Janeiro*. Cambridge: Cambridge University Press, 1988.

———. "Slavery's Impasse: Slave Prostitutes, Small-time Mistresses, and the Brazilian Law of 1871." *Comparative Studies in Society and History* 33 (1991): 669–94.

———. "The Vintem Riot and Political Culture, Rio de Janeiro, 1880." *Hispanic American Historical Review* 60, no. 3 (August 1980): 431–49.

———. "Writing from the Margins: Brazilian Slaves and Written Culture." *Comparative Studies in Society and History* 49, no. 3 (2007): 611–36.

Lavrin, Asunción. "Women in Latin America: Current Research Trends." In *Researching Women in Latin America and the Caribbean*, edited by Edna Acosta-Belén and Christine E. Bose, 7–36. Boulder: Westview, 1993.

Law, Robin. *Ouidah: The Social History of a West African Slaving "Port," 1727–1892*. Athens: Ohio University Press / Oxford: James Currey, 2004.

Lazo, Rodrigo. *Writing to Cuba: Filibustering and Cuban Exiles in the United States*. Chapel Hill: University of North Carolina Press, 2005.

Leite, Miriam Lifchiz Moreira, Maria Lucia de Barros Mott, and Bertha Kauffman Appelenzer. *A mulher no Rio de Janeiro no Século XIX: Um índice de referências em livros de viajantes estrangeiros*. São Paulo: Fundação Carlos Chagas, 1982.

Le Riverend Brusone, Julio. *La Habana, espacio y vida*. Madrid: MAPFRE, 1992.

Lerner, Gerda. "Women and Slavery." *Slavery and Abolition* 4, no. 3 (1983): 173–98.

Libby, Douglas Cole, and Afonso de Alencastro Graça Filho. "Notarized and Baptismal Manumissions in the Parish of São José do Rio das Mortes, Minas Gerais (c.1750–1850)." *Americas* 66, no. 2 (October 2009): 211–40.

Liddell, Charlotte. "Nature, Nurture and Nation: Nísia Floresta's Engagement in the Breast-Feeding Debate in Brazil and France." *Feminist Review* 79 (2005): 69–82.

Lima, Ivana Stolze. *Cores, marcas e falas: Sentidos da mestiçagem no Império do Brasil*. Rio de Janeiro: Arquivo Nacional, 2003.

Linhares, Maria Yedda Leite. *História do abastecimento: Uma problemática em questão (1530–1918)*. Brasília: Binagri, 1979.

Lobo, Maria Lahmeyer. *História do Rio de Janeiro: Do capital comercial ao capital industrial e financeiro*, vol. 1. Rio de Janeiro: IBEMEC, 1978.

López Denis, Adrián. "El incendio de Jesús María: Situaciones de emergencia, solidaridad y sociedad civil en La Habana (1828)." *La Rábida* 20 (2001): 3–10.

López Valdés, Rafael L. *Pardos y morenos esclavos y libres en Cuba y sus instituciones en el Caribe Hispano*. San Juan: Centro de Estudios Avanzados de Puerto Rico y el Caribe, 2007.

Lovejoy, Paul E. "Fugitive Slaves: Resistance to Slavery in the Sokoto Caliphate." In *In Resistance: Studies in African, Caribbean, and Afro-American History*, ed. Gary Y. Okihiro, 71–95. Amherst: University of Massachusetts Press, 1986.

———. "The Volume of the Atlantic Slave Trade: A Synthesis." *Journal of African History* 23 (1982): 473–501.

Machado, Maria Helena Pereira Toledo. "Corpo, gênero e identidade no limiar da Abolição: A história de Benedicta Maria Albina da Ilha ou Ovídia, escrava (sudeste, 1880)." *Afro-Ásia* 42 (2010): 157–93.

———. "From Slave Rebels to Strikebreakers: The Quilombo of Jabaquara and the Problem of Citizenship in Late-Nineteenth-Century Brazil." *Hispanic American Historical Review* 86, no. 2 (2006): 247–74.

———. *O plano e o pânico: Os movimentos sociais na década da abolição.* Rio de Janeiro: UFRJ/EDUSP, 1994.

Machado, Maria Helena Pereira Toledo, and Sasha Huber, eds. *(T)races of Louiz Agassiz: Photography, Body and Science Yesterday and Today [Rastros e raças de Louis Agassiz: fotografia, corpo e ciência, ontem e hoje].* São Paulo: Capacete Entretimentos, 2010.

Maestri, Mario. "Palmares: Una comuna negra del Brasil esclavista." *Razón y Revolución* 2 (Spring 1996): 1–9.

Magalhães, R., Jr. "Sucessos e insucessos de Alencar no teatro." In *José de Alencar: Teatro completo.* Rio de Janeiro: Serviço Nacional de Teatro, 1977, 1:9–24.

Marquese, Rafael de Bivar. "The Dynamics of Slavery in Brazil: Resistance, the Slave Trade, and Manumission in the Seventeenth to Nineteenth Centuries." Translated by Anthony Doyle. *Revista Novos Estudos—CEBRAP* (Centro Brasileiro de Análise e Pesquisa, São Paulo) 74, no. 2 (March 2006): 107–23.

———. *Feitores do corpo, missionários da mente: Senhores, letrados e o controle dos escravos nas Américas, 1660–1860.* São Paulo: Companhia das Letras, 2004.

Marrero Cruz, Eduardo. *Julián de Zulueta y Amondo: Promotor del capitalismo en Cuba.* Havana: Ediciones Unión, 2006.

Martínez-Alier, Verena [later Stolke]. *Marriage, Class and Color in Nineteenth-Century Cuba: A Study of Racial Attitudes and Sexual Values in a Slave Society.* 1974. Reprint, Ann Arbor: University of Michigan Press, 1989.

Martínez-Fernández, Luis. *Fighting Slavery in the Caribbean: The Life and Times of a British Family in Nineteenth-Century Havana.* Armonk: M. E. Sharpe, 1998.

Marzano, Andrea. *Cidade em cena: O ator Vasques, o teatro e o Rio de Janeiro, 1839–1892.* Rio de Janeiro: Editora Folha Seca, 2008.

Mata, Iacy Maia. "Sentidos da liberdade e encaminhamento legal da abolição: Bahia e Cuba—notas iniciais." *Revista de História Comparada* (UFRJ) 5, no. 1 (2011): 66–90.

Mathurin, Lucille. *The Rebel Woman in the British West Indies during Slavery.* Kingston: Institute of Jamaica, 1975.

Matos-Rodríguez, Felix. *"Libertas Citadinas:* Free Women of Color in San Juan, Puerto Rico." In Gaspar and Hine, *Beyond Bondage,* 202–18.

———. *Women in San Juan, 1820–1868.* Princeton: M. Wiener, 2001.

Mattoso, Katia M. de Queiroz. *To Be a Slave in Brazil, 1550–1888*. Translated by Arthur Goldhammer. New Brunswick: Rutgers University Press, 1991.

McFarlane, Anthony. "*Cimarrones* and *Palenques*: Runaways and Resistance in Colonial Colombia." In *Out of the House of Bondage: Runaways, Resistance and Marronage in Africa and the New World*, edited by Gad Heuman, 131–51. London: Frank Cass, 1986.

Meade, Teresa. *"Civilizing" Rio: Reform and Resistance in the Brazilian City, 1889–1930*. University Park: Pennsylvania State University Press, 1997.

Meillasoux, Claude. "Female Slavery." In *Women and Slavery in Africa*, edited by Claire Robertson and Martin A. Klein, 49–66. Madison: University of Wisconsin Press, 1983.

Mena, Luz. "Stretching the Limits of Gendered Spaces: Black and Mulatto Women in 1830s Havana." *Cuban Studies/Estudios Cubanos* 36, no. 1 (2005): 87–104.

Mendonça, Joseli Maria Nunes. *Entre a mão e os anéis. A lei dos sexagenários e os caminhos da abolição no Brasil*. Campinas: Unicamp, 1999.

Méndez Rodenas, Adriana. *Gender and Nationalism in Colonial Cuba: The Condesa de Santa Cruz y Merlín*. Nashville: Vanderbilt University Press, 1998.

Meriño Fuentes, María de los Ángeles, and Aisnara Perera Díaz. *Un café para la microhistoria: Estructura de posesión de esclavos y ciclo de vida en la llanura habanera (1800–1886)*. Havana: Editorial Ciencias Sociales, 2008.

Merrick, Thomas, and Douglas H. Graham. *Population and Economic Development in Brazil, 1800 to the Present*. Baltimore: Johns Hopkins University Press, 1979.

Merryman, John Henry. *The Civil Law Tradition: An Introduction to the Legal Systems of Western Europe and Latin America*. 1969. Reprint, Stanford: Stanford University Press, 1985.

Metcalf, Alida C. *Family and Frontier in Colonial Brazil: Santana de Parnaíba, 1580–1822*. Berkeley: University of California Press, 1992.

Michel, Sonya. "The Comparative Turn: Is Women's History Ready?" *Journal of Women's History* 10, no. 2 (Summer 1998): 188–97.

Midgley, Clare. *Women against Slavery: The British Campaigns, 1780–1870*. London: Routledge, 1992.

Millward, Jessica. "'That All Her Increase May Be Free': Enslaved Women's Bodies and the Maryland Manumission Law of 1809." *Women's History Review* 21, no. 3 (2012): 363–78.

Mohammed, Patricia. "Towards Indigenist Feminist Theorizing in the Caribbean." *Feminist Review* 59 (Summer 1998): 6–33.

———. "Writing Gender into History: The Negotiation of Gender Relations among Men and Women in Post-Indenture Trinidad Society, 1917–1947." In Shepherd, Brereton, and Bailey, *Engendering History*, 20–47.

Mohanty, Chandra Talpade. "Introduction: Cartographies of Struggle." In *Third World Women and the Politics of Feminism*, edited by C. T. Mohanty, Ann Russo, and Lourdes Torres, 1–47. Bloomington: Indiana University Press, 1991.

Moitt, Bernard. "In the Shadow of the Plantation: Women of Color and the *Libres de fait* of Martinique and Guadeloupe, 1685–1848." In Gaspar and Hine, *Beyond Bondage*, 37–59.

———. "Slave Women and Resistance in the French Caribbean." In Gaspar and Hine, *More than Chattel*, 239–58.

———. *Women and Slavery in the French Antilles, 1645–1838*. Bloomington: Indiana University Press, 2001.

———. "Women, Work, and Resistance in the French Caribbean during Slavery, 1700–1848." In Shepherd, Brereton, and Bailey, *Engendering History*, 155–75.

Montaldo, Graciela. "Invisibilidad y exclusión: El sujeto femenino visto por los viajeros europeos en el siglo XIX." In *Mujeres latinoamericanas: Historia y cultura, siglos XVI al XIX*, edited by Luisa Campuzano, 2:105–9. Havana: Editorial Casa de las Américas, 1997.

Monteiro, Beatriz Moreira. "Da prisão cor-de-rosa aos arquivos: Fontes documentais sobre a mulher no Arquivo Nacional." *Revista do Arquivo Nacional* 9, nos. 1–2 (1996).

Monteiro, Marília Pessoa. "Ser mulher no Brasil: Um patriarcalismo renitente (ser mulher, negra e escrava: Triple discriminação)." In *Atualidade e Abolição*, edited by Manuel Correia de Andrade and Eliane Moury Fernandes, 67–74. Recife: Editora Massangana, 1991.

Moore, Brian W., B. W. Higman, Carl Campbell, and Patrick Bryan, eds. *Slavery, Freedom and Gender: The Dynamics of Caribbean Society*. Kingston: University of the West Indies Press, 2003.

Moore, Brian L., and Michele A. Johnson. *Neither Led nor Driven: Contesting British Cultural Imperialism in Jamaica, 1865–1920*. Mona: University of the West Indies Press, 2004.

Moraes, Evaristo de. *A campanha abolicionista, 1879–1888*. Rio de Janeiro: Leite Ribeiro, 1924.

Moreno Fraginals, Manuel. *El ingenio: Complejo económico social cubano del azúcar*, Vols. 1–3. Havana: Editorial de Ciencias Sociales, 1978.

Morgan, Jennifer L. *Laboring Women: Reproduction and Gender in New World Slavery*. Philadelphia: University of Pennsylvania Press, 2004.

Morrissey, Marietta. *Slave Women in the New World: Gender Stratification in the Caribbean*. Lawrence: University Press of Kansas, 1989.

Mott, Luíz. *Crônicas de um gay assumido*. Rio de Janeiro: Editora Record, 2003.

Mott, Maria Luiza de Barros. *Submissão e resistência: A mulher na luta contra a escravidão*. São Paulo: Contexto, 1988.

Moura, Roberto. *Tia Ciata e a Pequena África no Rio de Janeiro*. 2nd ed. Rio de Janeiro: Prefeitura da Cidade do Rio de Janeiro, 1995.

Murray, David R. "Statistics of the Slave Trade to Cuba, 1790–1867." *Journal of Latin American Studies* 3, no. 2 (November 1971): 131–49.

Nagel, Joanne. *Race, Ethnicity, and Sexuality: Intimate Intersections, Forbidden Frontiers*. New York: Oxford University Press, 2003.

Nakano Glenn, Evelyn, Grace Chang, and Linda Rennie Forcey, eds. *Mothering: Ideology, Experience, and Agency*. New York: Routledge, 1994.

Naranjo, Consuelo. *Cuba vista por el emigrante español a la isla (1900–1959)*. Madrid: Consejo Superior de Investigaciones Científicas, 1987.

Naranjo, Consuelo, and Armando García González. *Racismo e inmigración en Cuba en el siglo XIX*. Madrid: Doce Calles, 1996.

Naro, Nancy Priscilla. "Revision and Persistence: Recent Historiography on the Transition from Slave to Free Labor in Rural Brazil." *Slavery and Abolition* 13, no. 2 (1992): 67–85.

———. *A Slave's Place, a Master's World: Fashioning Dependency in Rural Brazil*. London: Continuum, 2000.

———, ed. *Blacks and Coloreds in the Formation of National Identity in Nineteenth-Century Latin America*. London: Institute of Latin American Studies, 2003.

Needell, Jeffrey D. *The Party of Order: The Conservatives, the State, and Slavery in the Brazilian Monarchy, 1831–1871*. Stanford: Stanford University Press, 2006.

———. *A Tropical Belle Epoque: Elite Culture and Society in Turn-of-the-Century Rio de Janeiro*. Cambridge: Cambridge University Press, 1987.

Nishida, Mieko. "Manumission and Ethnicity in Urban Slavery: Salvador, Brazil, 1808–1888." *Hispanic American Historical Review* 73, no. 3 (August 1993): 361–91.

———. *Slavery and Identity: Ethnicity, Gender and Race in Salvador, Brazil, 1808–1888*. Bloomington: Indiana University Press, 2003.

Núñez Jiménez, Antonio. "San Cristobal de La Habana: Fundación y mudanzas." In *La Habana*, by Manuel Méndez Guerrero, Antonio Núñez Jiménez, and Carlos Venegas Fornias, 1–30. Vitoria: Ediciones Cultura Hispánica, 1989.

N'Zengou-Tayo, Marie-Jose. "'F'am se Poto Mitan': Haitian Woman, the Pillar of Society." *Feminist Review* 59 (Summer 1998): 118–42.

Offen, Karen, Ruth Roach Pierson, and Jane Rendall, eds. *Writing Women's History: International Perspectives*. Bloomington: Indiana University Press, 1991.

Okonjo, Kamene. "The Dual-Sex Political System in Operation: Igbo Women and Community Politics in Midwestern Nigeria." In *Women in Africa*, edited by Nancy J. Hafkin and Edna G. Bay, 45–58. Stanford: Stanford University Press, 1976.

Olwell, Robert. "Loose, Idle, and Disorderly: Slave Women in the Eighteenth-Century Charleston Marketplace." In Gaspar and Hine, *More than Chattel*, 97–110.

Ortiz, Fernando. *Los negros esclavos*. 1916. Reprint, Havana: Editorial de Ciencias Sociales, 1996.

Otovo, Okezi T. "From *Mãe Preta* to *Mãe Desamparada*: Maternity and Public Health in Post-Abolition Bahia." *Luso-Brazilian Review* 48, no. 2 (2011): 164–91.

Owensby, Brian. "How Juan and Leonor Won Their Freedom: Litigation and Liberty in Seventeenth-Century Mexico." *Hispanic American Historical Review* 85, no. 1 (February 2005): 39–79.

Paiva, Eduardo. *Escravos e libertos nas Minas Gerais do século XVIII: Estratégias de resistência através dos testamentos*. São Paulo: Annablume, 2000. First printed in 1995.

Palmer, Colin A. "Africa in the Making of the Caribbean: The Formative Years." In Moore, Higman, Campbell, and Bryan, *Slavery, Freedom, and Gender*, 40–56.

Paquette, Robert. *Sugar Is Made with Blood: The Conspiracy of La Escalera and the Conflict between Empires over Slavery in Cuba*. Middletown: Wesleyan University Press, 1988.

Paton, Diana. "The Flight from the Fields Reconsidered: Gender Ideologies and Women's Labor after Slavery in Jamaica." In *Reclaiming the Political in Latin America: Essays from the North*, edited by Gilbert M. Joseph, 175–204. Durham: Duke University Press, 2001.

————. *No Bond but the Law: Punishment, Race and Gender in Jamaican State Formation, 1780–1870*. Durham: Duke University Press, 2004.

Paton, Diana, and Pamela Scully. Introduction to *Gender and Slave Emancipation in the Atlantic World*, edited by P. Scully and D. Paton, 1–33. Durham: Duke University Press, 2005.

Pena, Eduardo Spiller. *Pajens da casa imperial: Juriconsultos, escravidão e a lei de 1871*. Campinas: Unicamp, 2001.

Perera Díaz, Aisnara, and María de los Ángeles Meriño Fuentes. *El cabildo carabalí vivi de Santiago de Cuba: Familia, cultura y sociedad (1797–1909)*. Forthcoming.

————. *Esclavitud, familia y parroquia en Cuba: Otra mirada desde la microhistoria*. Santiago de Cuba: Editorial Oriente, 2006.

————. *Familias, agregados y esclavos: Los padrones de vecinos de Santiago de Cuba (1778–1861)*. Santiago de Cuba: Editorial Oriente, 2011.

————. "La cesión de patronato: Una estrategia familiar en la emancipación de los esclavos en Cuba, 1870–1880." *Revista de História* (Universidade de São Paulo) 152 (2005): 29–55.

————. *La cesión de patronato: Una estrategia familiar en la emancipación de los esclavos en Cuba, 1870–1880*. San Antonio de los Baños: Editorial Unicornio, 2009.

————. *Para librarse de lazos, antes buena familia que buenos brazos: Apuntes sobre la manumisión en Cuba*. Santiago de Cuba: Editorial Oriente, 2010.

————. "Yo, el Notario: Breve reflexión micro-histórica sobre el poder de la escritura." *Boletim de História Demográfica* (São Paulo) 33, no. 11 (September 2004), http://www.brnuede.com/boletinsenha.htm.

Pérez, Louis A., Jr. *Cuba between Empires, 1878–1902*. Pittsburgh: Pittsburgh University Press, 1982.

————. *Cuba between Reform and Revolution*. 1988. Reprint, New York: Oxford University Press, 1995.

————. *Cuba in the American Imagination: Metaphor and the Imperial Ethos*. Chapel Hill: University of North Carolina Press, 2008.

————. "In the Service of the Revolution: Two Decades of Cuban Historiography, 1959–1979." *Hispanic American Historical Review* 60, no. 1 (February 1980): 79–89.

Pérez-Prendes, J. M. "La revista *El Abolicionista* (1865–1876) en la génesis de la abolición de la esclavitud en las Antillas Españolas." *Anuario de Estudios Americanos* 43 (1986): 215–40.

Portuondo Zúñiga, Olga. *José Antonio Saco: Eternamente polémico*. Santiago de Cuba: Editorial Oriente, 2005.

Portuondo Zúñiga, Olga, and Michael Zeuske. *Ciudadanos en la nación*, vol. 1. Santiago de Cuba: Fritz Thyssen Stiftung/Oficina del Conservador de la Ciudad, 2002.

————. *Ciudadanos en la nación*, vol. 2. Bogotá: Editorial Nomos S.A., 2003.

Prados-Torreira, Teresa. *Mambisas: Rebel Women in Nineteenth-Century Cuba.* Gainesville: University Press of Florida, 2005.

Proctor, Frank "Trey," III. "Gender and the Manumission of Slaves in New Spain." *Hispanic American Historical Review* 86, no. 2 (2006): 309–36.

Ranger, Terence. "Resistance in Africa: From Nationalist Protest to Agrarian Protest." In *In Resistance: Studies in African, Caribbean, and Afro-American History,* edited by Gary Y. Okihiro, 32–52. Amherst: University of Massachusetts Press, 1986.

Rathbone, Richard. "Some Thoughts on Resistance to Enslavement in West Africa." In *Out of the House of Bondage: Runaways, Resistance and Marronage in Africa and the New World,* edited by Gad Heuman, 11–22. London: Frank Cass, 1986.

Reid-Vázquez, Michele Bernita. *The Year of the Lash: Free People of Color in Cuba and the Nineteenth-Century Atlantic World.* Athens: University of Georgia Press, 2011.

————. "The Yoruba in Cuba: Origins, Identities, and Transformations." In *The Yoruba Diaspora in the Atlantic World,* edited by Toyin Falola and Matt D. Childs, 111–29. Bloomington: Indiana University Press, 2004.

Reis, João José. *Death Is a Festival: Funeral Rites and Rebellion in Nineteenth-Century Brazil.* Translated by H. Sabrina Gledhill. Chapel Hill: University of North Carolina Press, 2003.

————. "De olho no canto: Trabalho de rua na Bahia na véspera da Abolição." *Afro-Ásia,* 24 (2000): 199–242.

————. *Domingos Sodré, um sacerdote africano. Escravidão, liberdade e candomblé na Bahia do século XIX.* São Paulo: Companhia das Letras, 2008.

————. *Slave Rebellion in Brazil: The Muslim Uprising of 1835 in Bahia.* Translated by Arthur Brakel. Baltimore: Johns Hopkins University Press, 1993.

Reis, João José, and Beatriz Mamigonian. "Nagô and Mina: The Yoruba Diaspora in Brazil." In *The Yoruba Diaspora in the Atlantic World,* edited by Toyin Falola and Matt D. Childs, 77–110. Bloomington: Indiana University Press, 2004.

Reis, João José, and Flávio dos Santos Gomes, eds. *Liberdade por um fio: Histórias dos quilombos no Brasil.* São Paulo: Companhia das Letras, 1996.

Ribeiro, Gladys Sabina. *A liberdade em construção. Identidade nacional e conflitos antilusitanos no Primeiro Reinado.* Rio de Janeiro: Relume Dumará/FAPERJ, 2002.

Rios, Ana Lugão, and Hebe Maria Mattos de Castro. *Memórias do cativeiro: Família, trabalho e cidadania no pós-abolição.* Rio de Janeiro: Civilização Brasileira, 2005.

Roberts, Dorothy. *Killing the Black Body: Race, Reproduction, and the Meaning of Liberty.* New York: Pantheon, 1997.

Roberts, Kevin. "Yoruba Family, Gender, and Kinship Roles in New World Slavery." In *The Yoruba Diaspora in the Altantic World,* edited by Toyin Falola and Matt D. Childs, 177–82. Bloomington: Indiana University Press, 2004.

Robertson, Claire. "Africa into the Americas: Slavery and Women, the Family, and the Gender Division of Labor." In Gaspar and Hine, *More than Chattel,* 3–40.

————. "Post-Proclamation Slavery in Accra: A Female Affair?" In *Women and Slavery in Africa*, edited by Claire Robertson and Martin A. Klein, 220–30. Madison: University of Wisconsin Press, 1983.

Roig de Leuchsenring, Emilio. *La Habana: Apuntes históricos*. Havana: Municipio de la Habana, 1939.

Rubiera Castillo, Daisy. *Reyita: The Life of a Black Cuban Woman in the Twentieth Century: María de los Reyes Castillo Bueno*. Introduction by Elizabeth Dore, translated by Anne McLean. London: Latin American Bureau, 2001.

Ruddick, Sara. "Maternal Thinking." In *Mothering: Essays in Feminist Theory*, edited by Joyce Treblicot, 213–30. Totowa: Rowman and Allenheld, 1983.

Russell-Wood, A. J. R. "'Acts of Grace': Portuguese Monarchs and Their Subjects of African Descent in Eighteenth-Century Brazil." *Journal of Latin American Studies* 32, no. 2 (May 2000): 307–32.

Samara, Eni de Mesquita. *As mulheres, o poder e a família: São Paulo, século XIX*. São Paulo: Marco Zero, 1989.

Santamaría García, Antonio. "Los ferrocarriles de servicio público cubanos (1837–1959)." *Revista de Indias* 204 (1995): 485–513.

Santos, Ynaê Lopes dos. *Além da senzala: Arranjos escravos de moradia no Rio de Janeiro (1808–1850)*. São Paulo: Editora Hucitec/FAPESP, 2010.

Satchell, Veront M. "Women, Land Transactions and Peasant Development in Jamaica, 1866–1906." In Shepherd, Brereton, and Bailey, *Engendering History*, 213–32.

Scheper-Hughes, Nancy. *Death without Weeping: The Violence of Everyday Life in Brazil*. Berkeley: University of California Press, 1992.

Schettini, Christiana. *"Que tenhas teu corpo": Uma história social da prostituição no Rio de Janeiro das primeiras décadas republicanas*. Rio de Janeiro: Arquivo Nacional, 2006.

Schmidt-Nowara, Christopher. *Empire and Antislavery: Spain, Cuba, and Puerto Rico, 1833–1874*. Pittsburgh: University of Pittsburgh Press, 1999.

————. *Slavery, Freedom, and Abolition in Latin America and the Atlantic World*. Albuquerque: University of New Mexico Press, 2011.

————. "'Spanish' Cuba: Race and Class in Spanish and Cuban Antislavery Ideology, 1861–1868." *Cuban Studies/Estudios Cubanos* 25 (1995): 101–22.

————. "Still Continents (and an Island) with Two Histories?" *Law and History Review* 22, no. 2 (Summer 2004): 377–82.

Schuler, Monica. "Liberated Africans in Nineteenth-Century Guyana." In Moore, Higman, Campbell, and Bryan, *Slavery, Freedom, and Gender*, 133–60.

Schultz, Kirsten. *Tropical Versailles: Empire, Monarchy, and the Portuguese Royal Court in Rio de Janeiro, 1808–1821*. New York: Routledge, 2001.

Schwarcz, Lilia Moritz. *As Barbas do Imperador: D. Pedro II, um monarca nos trópicos*. São Paulo: Companhia das Letras, 1998.

————. *The Spectacle of the Races: Scientists, Institutions, and the Race Question in Brazil, 1870–1930*. 1993. Translated by Leland Guyer. Reprint, New York: Hill and Wang, 1999.

Schwartz, Stuart. "Recent Trends in the Study of Slavery in Brazil." *Luso-Brazilian Review* 25, no. 1 (Summer 1988): 1–25.

———. *Slaves, Peasants and Rebels: Reconsidering Brazilian Slavery*. Urbana: University of Illinois Press, 1992.

———. *Sugar Plantations in the Formation of Brazilian Society*. Cambridge: Cambridge University Press, 1985.

Schweninger, Loren. "The Fragile Nature of Freedom: Free Women of Color in the U.S. South." In Gaspar and Hine, *Beyond Bondage*, 106–26.

Scott, Joan Wallach. "Deconstructing Equality-versus-Difference; or, The Uses of Poststructuralist Theory for Feminism." *Feminist Studies* 1 (Spring 1988): 33–50.

———. *Gender and the Politics of History*. New York: Columbia University Press, 1988.

———. "The Problem of Invisibility." In *Retrieving Women's History*, edited by S. Jay Kleinberg, 5–29. London: Berg, 1988.

———, ed. *Feminism and History*. Oxford: Oxford University Press, 1996.

Scott, Rebecca J. "Defining the Boundaries of Freedom in the World of Cane: Cuba, Brazil, and Louisiana after Emancipation." *American Historical Review* 99, no.1 (February 1994): 70–102.

———. *Degrees of Freedom: Cuba and Louisiana after Slavery*. Cambridge: Harvard University Press, 2005.

———. "Exploring the Meaning of Freedom: Postemancipation Societies in Comparative Perspective." *Hispanic American Historical Review* 68, no. 3 (1988): 407–28.

———. "Reclamando la mula de Gregoria Quesada: El significado de la libertad en los valles del Arimao y del Caunao, Cienfuegos, Cuba (1880–1899)." In *Espacios, silencios y los sentidos de la libertad. Cuba entre 1878 y 1912*, edited by Fernando Martínez Heredia, Rebecca J. Scott, and Orlando F. García Martínez, 23–72. Havana: Ediciones UNIÓN, 2001.

———. *Slave Emancipation in Cuba: The Transition to Free Labor, 1860–1899*. Princeton: Princeton University Press, 1985.

———. "Tres vidas, una guerra: Rafael Iznaga, Bárbara Pérez y Gregoria Quesada entre la emancipación y la ciudadanía." In *Historia y memoria: Sociedad, cultura y vida cotidiana en Cuba, 1878–1917*, Centro Juan Marinello, 83–99. Havana: Centro Juan Marinello, 2003.

Segre, R., M. Coyula, and J. L. Scarpaci. *Havana: Two Faces of the Antillean Metropolis*. Chichester: John Wiley & Sons, 1997.

Seigel, Micol. *Uneven Encounters: Making Race in Brazil and the United States*. Durham: Duke University Press, 2009.

Shapiro, Herbert. "Historiography and Slave Revolt and Rebelliousness in the United States: A Class Approach." In *In Resistance: Studies in African, Caribbean, Latin American and Afro American History*, edted by Gary Y. Okihiro, 133–42. Amherst: University of Massachusetts Press, 1986.

Shaw, Stephanie J. "Mothering under Slavery in the Antebellum South." In *Mothering: Ideology, Experience, and Agency*, edited by Evelyn Nakano Glenn, Grace Chang, and Linda Rennie Forcey, 237–58. New York: Routledge, 1994.

Shepherd, Verene, Bridget Brereton, and Barbara Bailey, eds. *Engendering History: Caribbean Women in Historical Perspective*. London: James Currey, 1995.

Silva, Eduardo. *As camélias do Leblon e a abolição da escravatura: Uma investigação de história cultural*. São Paulo: Companhia das Letras, 2003.

———. *Prince of the People: The Life and Times of a Brazilian Free Man of Color*. Translated by Moyra Ashford. London: Verso, 1993.

Silva, Maria Beatriz Nizza da. "Women's History in Brazil: Production and Perspectives." In *Writing Women's History: International Perspectives*, edited by Karen Offen, Ruth Roach Pierson, and Jane Rendall, 369–80. Bloomington: Indiana University Press, 1991.

Silvestrini, Blanca G. "Women and Resistance: 'Herstory' in Contemporary Caribbean History." In Moore, Higman, Campbell, and Bryan, *Slavery, Freedom, and Gender*, 161–82.

Simms, Rupe. "Controlling Images and the Gender Construction of Enslaved African Women." *Gender and Society* 15:6 (December 2001): 879–97.

Skidmore, Thomas E. "Racial Ideas and Social Policy in Brazil, 1870–1940." In *The Idea of Race in Latin America, 1870–1940*, edited by Richard Graham, 7–36. Austin: University of Texas Press, 1990.

Slenes, Robert W. "Black Homes, White Homilies: Perceptions of the Slave Family and of Slave Women in Nineteenth-Century Brazil." In Gaspar and Hine, *More than Chattel*, 126–46.

———. "The Brazilian Internal Slave Trade, 1850–1888: Regional Economies, Slave Experience, and the Politics of a Peculiar Market." In *The Chattel Principle: Internal Slave Trades in the Americas*, edited by Walter Johnson, 325–70. New Haven: Yale University Press, 2005.

———. "Escravidão e família: Padrões de casamento e estabilidade familiar numa comunidade escrava. Campinas, sec. XIX." *Estudos Econômicos* (São Paulo) 17, no. 2 (1987): 217–27.

———. *Na senzala, uma flor: Esperanças e recordações na formação da família escrava—Brasil, sudeste, século XIX*. Rio de Janeiro: Editora Nova Fronteira, 1999.

———. "Senhores e subalternos no Oeste Paulista." In *História da vida privada no Brasil*, vol. 2: *Império: a corte e a modernidade nacional*, edited by Fernando Novais and Luiz Felipe Alencastro, 234–90. São Paulo: Companhia das Letras, 1997.

Smith, Hilda. "Are We Ready for a Comparative History of Women?" *Journal of Women's History* 1, no. 1 (Spring 1989): 92–95.

Smith, E. Valerie. "The Sisterhood of Nossa Senhora da Boa Morte and the Brotherhood of Nossa Senhora do Rosário: African-Brazilian Cultural Adaptations to Antebellum Restrictions." *Afro-Hispanic Review* 11:1–3 (1992): 121–33.

Soares, Carlos Eugênio Líbano. "Comércio, nação e gênero: As negras minas quitandeiras no Rio de Janeiro, 1835–1900." In *Escritos sobre História e Educação. Homenagem á Maria Yedda Leite Linhares*, edited by Francisco Carlos Teixeira da Silva, Hebe Maria Mattos, and Ciro Flamirion Cardoso, 402–13. Rio de Janeiro: FAPERJ/Mauad, 2001.

Soares, Luiz Carlos. *O "Povo de Cam" na capital do Brasil: A escravidão urbana no Rio de Janeiro do século XIX*. Rio de Janeiro: FAPERJ/7 Letras, 2007.

Soares, Mariza de Carvalho. *Devotos da cor: Identidade étnica, religiosidade e escravidão no Rio de Janeiro, século XVIII*. Rio de Janeiro: Civilização Brasileira, 2000.

———. "From Gbe to Yoruba: Ethnic Change and the Mina Nation in Rio de Janeiro." In *The Yoruba Diaspora in the Atlantic World*, edited by Toyin Falola and Matt D. Childs, 231–47. Bloomington: Indiana University Press, 2004.

Socolow, Susan Migden. "Economic Roles of Free Women of Color in Cap Français." In Gaspar and Hine, *More than Chattel*, 279–97.

———. *The Women of Colonial Latin America*. Cambridge: Cambridge University Press, 2000.

Soihet, Rachel. "Mulheres em busca de novos espaços e relações de gênero." *Revista do Arquivo Nacional* 9:1–2 (1996).

Souza, Antonio Cândido Mello e. *Formação da literatura brasileira*. Vol. 2: 1836–80. 2nd ed. São Paulo: Livraria Martins Editora, 1964. First published in 1959.

Souza, Marina de Mello. *Reis negros no Brasil escravista: História da festa de coração de rei Congo*. Belo Horizonte: Editora UFMG, 2002.

Stein, Stanley J. *Vassouras: A Brazilian Coffee County, 1850–1900*. Cambridge: Harvard University Press, 1957.

Stepan, Nancy Leys. *The Hour of Eugenics: Race, Gender, and Nation in Latin America*. Ithaca: Cornell University Press, 1991.

Stolke, Verena [Martínez-Alier]. "La influencia de la esclavitud en la estructura doméstica y la familia en Jamaica, Cuba y Brasil." *Desacatos* 13 (Winter 2003): 134–51. Publication of Centro de Investigaciones y Estudios Superiores en Antropología Social, Mexico City.

Stoner, Lynn. *From the House to the Streets: The Cuban Women's Movement for Legal Reform, 1898–1940*. Durham: Duke University Press, 1991.

Stubbs, Jean. "Gender in Caribbean History." In *General History of the Caribbean*, vol. 6: *Methodology and Historiography of the Caribbean*, edited by B. W. Higman, 95–135. London: UNESCO Publishing, 1999.

———. "Race, Gender and National Identity in Nineteenth-Century Cuba: Mariana Grajales and the Revolutionary Free Browns of Cuba." In *Blacks, Coloreds and National Identity*, edited by Nancy Priscilla Naro, 95–122. London: Institute of Latin American Studies, University of London, 2003.

———. "Social and Political Motherhood of Cuba: Mariana Grajales Cuello." In Shepherd, Brereton, and Bailey, *Engendering History*, 296–317.

———. *Tobacco on the Periphery: A Case Study in Cuban Labor History*. Cambridge: Cambridge University Press, 1985.

Sutton, Constance. Foreword to *Women and the Ancestors: Black Carib Kinship and Ritual*, by Virginia Kerns, ix–xii. 1983. Reprint, Urbana: University of Illinois Press, 1997.

———. "Motherhood Is Powerful: Embodied Knowledge from Evolving Field-Based Experiences." *Anthropology and Humanism* 23, no. 2 (1998): 139–45.

Sweet, James H. *Recreating Africa: Culture, Kinship, and Religion in the African-Portuguese World, 1441–1770.* Chapel Hill: University of North Carolina Press, 2003.

Tannenbaum, Frank. *Slave and Citizen: The Negro in the Americas.* New York: Knopf, 1947.

Terborg-Penn, Rosalyn. "Black Women in Resistance: A Cross-Cultural Perspective." In *In Resistance: Studies in African, Caribbean, and Afro American History,* edited by Gary Y. Okihiro, 188–209. Amherst: Massachusetts University Press, 1986.

————. "Migration and Trans-Racial/National Identity Re-Formation: Becoming African Diaspora Women." *Black Women, Gender and Families* 5, no. 2 (Fall 2011): 4–24.

————. "Through an African Feminist Theoretical Lens: Viewing Caribbean Women's History Cross-Culturally." In Shepherd, Brereton, and Bailey, *Engendering History,* 3–19.

Terborg-Penn, Rosalyn, Sharon Harley, and Andrea Benton Rushing, eds. *Women in Africa and the African Diaspora.* Washington, D.C.: Howard University Press, 1987.

Thompson, Alvin O. "Gender and *Marronage* in the Caribbean." *Journal of Caribbean History* 39, no. 2 (2005): 262–89.

Thompson, E. P. *The Making of the English Working Class.* 1963. Reprint, Harmondsworth: Penguin, 1991.

Thornton, John. *Africa and Africans in the Making of the Atlantic World, 1400–1680.* Cambridge: Cambridge University Press, 1992.

————. "Sexual Demography: The Impact of the Slave Trade in the Family Structure." In *Women and Slavery in Africa,* edited by Claire Robertson and Martin A. Klein, 39–48. Madison: University of Wisconsin Press, 1983.

Tomich, Dale W. "The Second Slavery: Bonded Labor and the Transformation of the Nineteenth-Century Economy." In *Rethinking the Nineteenth Century,* edited by Francisco Ramírez, 103–17. Stanford: Stanford University Press, 1988.

————. *Through the Prism of Slavery: Labor, Capital and World Economy.* Lanham: Rowman and Littlefield, 2004.

Tomich, Dale W., and Michael Zeuske, eds. "The Second Slavery: Mass Slavery, World Economy, and Comparative Microhistories," parts 1 and 2, special editions of *Review: Journal of the Fernand Braudel Center* 31, nos. 2 and 3 (2008).

Townsend, Camilla. *Tales of Two Cities: Race and Economic Culture in Early Republican North and South America: Guayaquil, Ecuador, and Baltimore, Maryland.* Austin: University of Texas Press, 2000.

Trouillot, Michel-Rolph. *Silencing the Past: Power and the Production of History.* Boston: Beacon Press, 1995.

Valdés Acosta, Gema. *Los remanentes de las lenguas bantúes en Cuba.* Havana: Fundación Fernando Ortiz, 2002.

Varella Fernández, Claudia. "El canal administrativo de los conflictos entre esclavos y amos: Causas de manumisión decididas ante síndicos en Cuba." *Revista de Indias* 71, no. 251 (2011): 109–36.

Vasconcelos, Sandra Guardini Teixeira. "Mulher por mulher: Notícias do Brasil colonial." In *Mujeres latinoamericanas: Historia y cultura, siglos XVI al XIX*, edited by Luisa Campuzano, 2:129–35. Havana: Editorial Casa de las Américas, 1997.

Vasquez, Pedro Karp. *Nos trilhos do progresso: A ferrovia no Brasil Imperial vista pela fotografia*. São Paulo: Metalivros, 2007.

Venâncio, Renato Pinto. "Maternidade Negada." In *História das Mulheres no Brasil*, edited by Mary Del Priore, 189–222. São Paulo: Contexto, 2004.

Venegas Fornias, Carlos. "La Habana Vieja: Patrimonio de la Humanidad." In *La Habana*, edited by Manuel Méndez Guerrero, Antonio Núñez Jimenez, and Carlos Venegas Fornias, 31–49. Vitoria: Ediciones Cultura Hispánica, 1986.

———. "La Habana y su región: Un proyecto de organización espacial de la plantación esclavista." *Revista de Indias* 56 (1996): 333–66.

———. *La urbanización de las murallas: Dependencia y modernidad*. Havana: Editorial Letras Cubanas, 1990.

Viotti da Costa, Emilia. *The Brazilian Empire: Myths and Histories*. Chapel Hill: University of North Carolina Press, 2000. Originally published in 1985.

———. "1870–1889." In *Brazil: Empire and Republic, 1822–1930*, edited by Leslie Bethell, 131–69. Cambridge: Cambridge University Press, 1989.

Walker, Daniel. *No More, No More: Slavery and Cultural Resistance in Havana and New Orleans*. Minneapolis: University of Minnesota Press, 2004.

Watson, Alan. *Slave Law in the Americas*. Athens: University of Georgia Press, 1989.

Weinstein, Barbara. "The Decline of the Progressive Planter and the Rise of Subaltern Agency: Shifting Narratives of Slave Emancipation in Brazil." In *Reclaiming the Political in Latin American History: Essays from the North*, edited by Gilbert M. Joseph, 81–101. Durham: Duke University Press, 2001.

Williams, Eric. *Capitalism and Slavery*. 1944. Reprint, Chapel Hill: University of North Carolina Press, 1994.

Wilmot, Swithin. "'Females of Abandoned Character?': Women and Protest in Jamaica, 1838–1865." In Shepherd, Brereton, and Bailey, *Engendering History*, 279–95.

Wimberley, Fayette. "The Expansion of Afro-Bahian Religious Practices in Nineteenth-Century Cachoeira." In *Afro-Brazilian Culture and Politics: Bahia, 1790s-1990s*, edited by Hendrik Kraay, 74–89. London: M. E. Sharpe, 1998.

White, Deborah Gray. *Ar'n't I a Woman: Female Slaves in the Plantation South*. New York: Norton, 1985.

Wood, Alice L. "Religious Women of Color in Seventeenth-Century Lima: Estefania de San Ioseph and Ursula de Jesu Christo." In Gaspar and Hine, *Beyond Bondage*, 286–316.

Wood, Marcus. *The Horrible Gift of Freedom: Atlantic Slavery and the Representation of Emancipation*. Athens: University of Georgia Press, 2010.

Yuval-Davis, Nira. *Gender and Nation*. London: Sage, 1997.

Zaeske, Susan. *Signatures of Citizenship: Petitioning, Antislavery, and Women's Political Identity*. Chapel Hill: University of North Carolina Press, 2003.

Zeuske, Michael. "Ciudadanos 'sin otro apellido': Nombres esclavos, marcadores raciales e identidades en la colonia y en la República, Cuba 1879–1940." In *Ciudadanos en la nación*, vol. 1, edited by Olga Portuondo Zúñiga and Michael Zeuske, 58–108. Santiago de Cuba: Fritz Thyssen Stiftung/ Oficina del Conservador de la Ciudad, 2002.

———. "Hidden Markers, Open Secrets: On Naming, Race-Marking and Race-Making in Cuba." *New West Indian Guide* 76, nos. 3–4 (2002): 211–42.

———. "Lux veritatis, vita memoriae, magistra vitae: 116 vidas y la historia de Cuba." In *Historia y memoria: Sociedad, cultura y vida cotidiana en Cuba, 1878–1917*, 55–81. Havana: Centro Juan Marinello, 2003.

———. "Two Stories of Gender and Slave Emancipation in Cienfuegos and Santa Clara, Central Cuba: A Microhistorical Approach to the Atlantic World." In *Gender and Slave Emancipation in the Atlantic World*, edited by Pamela Scully and Diana Paton, 181–98. Durham: Duke University Press, 2005.

UNPUBLISHED SECONDARY SOURCES

Almeida, Fernanda Moutinho de. "E depois do 13 de maio? Conflitos e expectativas dos últimos libertos de Juiz de Fora (1888–1900)." M.A. thesis, Universidade Federal Fluminense, 2003.

Alonso, Angela. "The Cosmopolitan Abolitionist: Joaquim Nabuco and the Transtlantic Abolitionist Network." Paper presented to Institute for the Study of the Americas (University of London) conference on Joaquim Nabuco (1849–1910): Intellectual, Abolitionist, Statesman, 3 November 2010.

Barman, Roderick. "Gender and the Public Sphere in Brazil: The Role and Influence of Women in High Politics." Paper presented to Brazilian Studies Association, Brasília, July 2010.

Bergstresser, Rebecca Baird. "The Movement for the Abolition of Slavery in Rio de Janeiro, Brazil, 1880–1889." Ph.D. diss., Stanford University, 1973.

Brana-Shute, Rosemary. "Liberating Women: Female Manumitters in Late-Eighteenth- and Early-Nineteenth-Century Suriname." Paper presented to Association of Caribbean Historians, Havana, April 1999.

Castilho, Celso. "Abolitionism Matters: The Politics of Antislavery in Pernambuco, Brazil, 1869–1888." Ph.D. diss., University of California, 2008.

———. "A New Canada: A Maritime Route to Freedom in Northeastern Brazil." Paper presented to American Historical Association, Boston, 6–9 January 2011.

———. "With Grace and Delicacy: The *Ave Libertas* and Women's Involvement with Abolitionism." Unpublished essay. Author's collection.

Chaves, María Eugenia. "Honor y Libertad: Recursos y discursos en la estrategia de libertad de una mujer esclava." Ph.D. diss., University of Gothenburg, 2001.

Collins, Jane-Marie. "Domestic Servitude and the Difference a Race Makes: Negotiating the Politics of African Motherhood in Salvador da Bahia (1853)." Paper presented to the Institute for the Study of Slavery, University of Nottingham, 8 September 2010.

Côrtes, Giovana Xavier da Conceição. "Coisa de pele: Relações de gênero, literatura e mestiçagem feminina (Rio de Janeiro, 1880–1910)." M.A. thesis, Universidade Federal Fluminense, 2005.

Cosme Baños, Pedro, Teresa de Jesús Díaz Pena, Raisa Fornaguera de la Peña, Luís Alberto Pedroso Hernández, and Concepción Morales de la O. "Apuntes de Regla: Síntesis Histórica del Municipio." Unpublished paper, Archivo del Museo Municipal de Regla, Havana, n.d.

Cowling, Camillia. "Across the Miles: Slavery, Mobility and the Law in Nineteenth-Century Cuba." Paper presented to the American Historical Association, Boston, 6–9 January 2011.

Cruz, Alline Torres Dias da. "Suburbanização e racismo no Rio de Janeiro: Uma leitura de Madureira e Dona Clara no contexto pós-emancipação." M.A. thesis, Instituto de Pesquisa e Planejamento Urbano e Regional, Universidade Federal Rio de Janeiro, 2007.

Dauwe, Fabiano. "A Libertação Gradual e a Saída Viável: Os múltiplos sentidos da liberdade pelo Fundo de Emancipação de Escravos." M.A. thesis, Universidade Federal Fluminense, 2004.

Du Moulin, John. "Changing Conjugal Forms in 19th-Century Cuba: Gender, Race, Class, and the Colonial State." Paper presented to the Latin American Studies Association, Las Vegas, 2004.

Faria, Sheila Siqueira de Castro. "Sinhás pretas, damas mercadoras: As minas pretas nas cidades do Rio de Janeiro e de São João del Rey, 1700–1850." Thesis presented to the History Department, Universidade Federal Fluminense, for title of Professor Titular em História do Brasil, 2004.

Ferreira, Lusirene Celestino França. "Nas asas da imprensa: A repercussão da abolição da escravatura na província do Ceará nos periódicos do Rio de Janeiro, 1884–5." M.A. thesis, Universidade Federal de São João del Rei, 2010.

Franklin, Sarah L. "Suitable to Her Sex: Race, Slavery, and Patriarchy in Nineteenth-Century Colonial Cuba." Ph.D. diss., Florida State University, 2006.

Garzoni, Lerice de Castro. "Arena de combate: gênero e direitos na imprensa diária (Rio de Janeiro, início do século XX)." Ph.D. diss, UNICAMP, 2012.

Gómez Luaces, Eduardo. "Efemérides Reglanas, 1796–1881." Unpublished history of Regla events, Colección Manuscritos Eduardo Gómez Luaces, Archivo del Museo Municipal de Regla, Havana.

Ipsen, Wiebke. "Delicate Citizenship: Gender and Nation Building in Brazil, 1865–1891." Ph.D. diss., University of California, Irvine, 2005.

Lamounier, Maria Lúcia. "Between Slavery and Free Labor: Experiments with Free Labor and Patterns of Slave Emancipation in Brazil and Cuba, c. 1830–1888." Ph.D. diss., London School of Economics, 1993.

McCabe, Marikay. "Parameters of the Public: Commercial and Legal Topographies of Nineteenth-Century Havana." Ph.D. diss., Columbia University, 2003.

Rood, Daniel Brett. "Plantation Technocrats: A Social History of Knowledge in the Slaveholding Atlantic World, 1830–1865." Ph.D. diss., University of California, 2010.

Sartorius, David A. "Limits of Loyalty: Race and the Public Sphere in Cienfuegos, Cuba, 1845–1898." Ph.D. diss., University of North Carolina, 2003.

————. "Uncommon Winds: Race, Passports and the Legal Culture of Travel in Cuba." Paper presented to the Annual Meeting of the American Historical Association, Boston, 9 January 2011.

Schueler, Alessandra Frota Martínez de. "Culturas escolares e experiências docentes na cidade do Rio de Janeiro (1854–1889)." Ph.D. diss., Universidade Federal Fluminense, 2007.

Schweninger, Loren. "Slave Women Petitioners in the Chancery Courts of the United States South." Paper presented to Institute for the Study of Slavery, University of Nottingham, September 2006.

Slenes, Robert W. "The Demography and Economics of Brazilian Slavery: 1850–1888." Ph.D. diss., Stanford University, 1976.

Soares, Luiz Carlos. "Prostitution in Nineteenth Century Rio de Janeiro." Occasional Papers, Institute of Latin American Studies, University of London, 1988.

Souza, Flávia Fernandes de. "Para casa de família e mais serviços: o trabalho doméstico na cidade do Rio de Janeiro no final do século XIX." M.A. thesis, UERJ, 2010.

Souza, Juliana Teixeira. "A autoridade municipal na corte imperial: Enfrentamentos e negociações na regulação do comércio de gêneros (1840–1889)." PhD diss., UNICAMP, 2007.

Vainfas, Magali Engel. "Meretrizes e doutores: O saber médico e prostituição no Rio de Janeiro, 1845–1890." M.A. thesis, Universidade Federal Fluminense, 1985.

Varella Fernández, Claudia. "Esclavos a sueldo: La coartación cubana en el siglo XIX." Ph.D. diss., Departamento de Historia, Geografía y Arte, Universitat Jaume I, 2010.

Index

Abolitionism: and elite women, 4,
109–15, 167, 249 (n. 51), 250 (n. 69),
251 (n. 75); Atlantic world, 6–7, 17, 45,
98, 110; in Brazil, 10–11, 13, 41–42,
45, 64, 77, 98, 100–101, 104, 111–20,
125, 221, 246 (n. 11), 250 (nn. 69, 74);
and Spain, 11, 39–40, 45, 57, 77, 98,
104, 122; in Puerto Rico, 11, 45, 46,
98, 102, 116, 120, 122; discourse of,
11–12, 15, 19, 74, 77, 216; and gender,
15, 19, 108, 115–20, 122; in Havana,
29–30, 44–45, 98, 99–100, 116, 120,
122, 218; and United States, 45, 110,
114, 220–21, 248–49 (n. 46); and language of equality, 98, 104, 247 (n. 21);
and Britain, 98, 110, 114, 250–51
(n. 74); and separation of mothers
and children, 99–103, 104, 107, 122,
208; and emotional appeals, 100,
101, 106, 108, 109, 110, 246 (n. 11);
and sentiment and modernity, 103–4,
246 (n. 11), 247 (n. 18); and sympathy for slaves, 103–9, 110, 216; and
motherhood, 106–7; and masculinity,
108, 109, 117, 122, 248–49 (n. 46);
and femininity, 108–9, 118, 122, 248
(n. 41), 249 (n. 51); and corruption of
families, 115–20; and social sickness,
120–21
Abolitionist Confederation (Brazil), 43,
45, 111, 112–13
Abreu, Martha, 94
Achondo, Josefa, 142
African-derived religious and cultural
life, 28, 35, 107–8
African diaspora, 35, 46, 202, 208, 270
(n. 29)

Aguilera, Francisco Vicente, 100
Alamo, José, 75, 76, 243 (n. 7)
Aleixo (enslaved boy), 132
Alencar, José, 105–6, 248 (n. 32), 260
(n. 13)
Alencastro, Luiz Felipe, 5
Alexandrina (free child), 187
Allo Bermúdez, Lorenzo, 153, 155
Almeida, Daniel de, 161
Almeida, João Mendes de, 157
Amalia (patrocinada), 143
Andrada, Felipe Pereira de, 161
Andrade, Joaquim José de Oliveira, 151,
156, 168, 172–73, 200, 201
Ángela (enslaved daughter of Juana
Sánchez y Sánchez), 83
Anglo-Brazilian Times, 103
Angola, 8
Anna (parda freedwoman), 132
Anselmo (freedman), 146
Anselmo (enslaved man), 135
Appeals court of Rio de Janeiro: and
slave claims-making, 12, 48, 49, 50,
60, 240 (n. 70); decisions affecting
national legislation, 28, 240 (n. 70);
and enslaved women's claims-mak-
ing, 50, 60–61, 240 (n. 73); enslaved
women as criminal defendants, 51,
236 (n. 17)
Araújo, Maria Silva, 177
Araújo Lírio, Maria Isabel de, 211
A Republica, 157
Argentina, 41
Armas y Céspedes, Francisco de, 154–55,
156, 205
Atlantic World: growth of slave-produced plantation crops in, 6; and

abolitionism, 6–7, 17, 45, 98, 110; port cities of, 15, 19, 23, 25, 34–38, 45–46, 142

Azcárate, Nicolás, 44, 63–64, 83, 127

Azevedo, Aluízio, 119, 120

Azevedo, Célia Maria, 246 (n. 11), 250 (n. 69)

Bachiller y Morales, Antonio, 167

Baez, Teresa, 146, 177

Balsa, Valentina de los Dolores, 143

Barcia, María del Carmen, 52, 194, 232 (n. 64)

Barman, Roderick, 211

Basília (black freedwoman), 94–95

Basília (child), 94–95

Bastos, Bernadino José de Oliveira, 168, 169

Bastos, João Coelho, 174–75

Bastos, Maria Joaquina d'Annunciação, 211

Bastos, Miguel José Tavares, 53, 144, 187

Beltrán de Gazurieta, Antonio, 259 (n. 96)

Berbel, Márcia, 16

Bergad, Laird, 52, 232 (n. 64), 237 (n. 26)

Bezerra, Nielson Rosa, 255 (n. 48)

Block, Sharon, 248 (n. 36)

Bolívar, José, 92

Brazil: gradual emancipation in, 2, 6–10, 18, 38–39, 41–42, 56–57, 71, 125, 158, 215, 218, 235 (n. 9); law of final abolition in, 3–4; manumission levels in, 5, 16, 26, 51, 67; second slavery in, 6, 8, 25, 35, 125; slave imports in, 8, 34, 35, 134, 225 (n. 26), 225–26 (n. 34); abolitionist movements in, 10–11, 13, 41–42, 45, 64, 77, 98, 100–101, 104, 111–20, 125, 221, 246 (n. 11), 250 (nn. 69, 74); self-purchase requirements in, 32; free African-descended population in, 34; enslaved population distributed in, 35; politics in, 41, 43; location of appeals courts in, 49, 235 (n. 7); and "free womb" laws,

55, 226 (n. 39); and sexagenarian slaves, 57; and slave registers, 85–86, 124; education in, 158–59, 162; and juridical culture, 225 (n. 18); and patriarchal authority, 238 (n. 38); and voting access, 270 (n. 34), 272 (n. 3). See also Imperial family of Brazil; Rio de Janeiro, Brazil

Brazilia (parda woman), 144

Brazilian Anti-Slavery Society, 101

Briones, Agustina, 184

Britain: slave trade banned by, 7, 59; slaves seeking leverage with British consuls, 29; and abolitionist movements, 98, 110, 114, 250–51 (n. 74)

Brown, Elsa Barkley, 190

Bueno, Maria Francisca, 206

Bulicioff, Nadina, 111–13, 249 (n. 63)

Burke, Peter, 225 (n. 18)

Caetana, Benedicta, 140

Caetana, Paulina, 140

Calcagno, Francisco, 160, 207–8

Calero Lorenzo, Victoriano, 88–89, 91

Calundú ceremonies, 28

Campos, Hermelinda Maria de, 211

Canabarro, Augusto Joaquim de Siqueira, 107–8

Cañongo, Conde de, 126–27

Carmelite Order, 72–74

Carolina, Maria, 190

Carricarte, Carlota, 191–92

Carricarte, Genara, 191–92, 194

Carricarte, Marcelino, 191

Carvallo, Belén, 182

Casas, Isabel, 86–87, 142

Castelar, Emilio, 99–100, 103–4, 120, 154, 247 (n. 18)

Casteñeda, Asunción, 183

Castillo de González, Aurelia, 120, 167

Castro, Francisca da Silva, 118

Catta Pretta, Olympia Guimarães, 112

Ceferina (patrocinada), 147

Céspedes, Carlos Manuel de, 39

Céspedes, Ramón, 100

Chacón, Dolores, 84
Chacón, Joaquín, 84
Chalhoub, Sidney, 28, 152, 226 (n. 39),
  265 (n. 33)
Chaves, João Cândido Teixeira, 132
Chenevar, Paula, 186
Chenevar, Santiago, 186
Childs, Matt, 251 (n. 75)
Chile, 55
Chinese indentured laborers, 36, 62, 63,
  144
Citizenship: national belonging, 3, 12,
  210–11; and gendered norms, 3, 164,
  220; conception of, 3, 213; and edu-
  cation, 159, 160, 162, 164, 170, 172,
  173; and race, 210–11
Clapp, João, 119, 250 (n. 68)
Coartación: enslaved women's use of,
  51–52, 61, 75, 76, 88, 237 (n. 26), 243
  (n. 11), 245 (n. 47); as legal right, 52,
  56; and control over geographical
  location, 52, 75, 128–32; and Moret
  Law, 61; and enslaved children, 75,
  88–91, 244 (n. 34)
Código Negro Carolino, 84
Coffee cultivation, 6, 8, 25–26, 28, 35, 44
Collazo, Lucía, 145, 146
Comparative history, 16–17
Conceição, Camila Maria da, 184
Conceição, Isabel Maria da, 181
Conceição, Maria da, 181
Conceição, Maria Emília da, 184
Conceição, Maria Luiza da, 183, 209–10
Conceição, Maria Umbelina da, 184
Conceição, Mônica Maria da, 138, 148
Conceição, Raymunda Maria da, 200
Conceição, Safira Luiza da, 210
Congo, Agustín, 189
Conrad, Robert, 205
Consejo de Administración: and slave
  claims-making, 61, 240 (nn. 72, 75);
  and Azcárate, 64; and Moret Law,
  89–90, 91, 92–93; and tax evasion,
  130; and education, 160
Córdoba, Emilia, 217–18

Cottroll, Robert, 162
Couto, Torquato Fernandes, 166–67,
  171–72, 199
Crime: and gender, 2, 51, 224 (n. 7),
  236–37 (n. 18); and urban space, 183
Criolla, Matilde, 168
Criollo, Paulino, 126–27
Crowe (English Consul General), 79
Cuba: gradual emancipation in, 1, 2,
  6–11, 13, 18, 38–41, 42, 48, 58, 71,
  102, 125, 158, 215, 218; manumission
  levels in, 5, 16, 51, 67; second slavery
  in, 6, 25, 35, 125; slave imports in, 7,
  34, 134, 225 (nn. 24, 26); enslaved
  population of, 7, 36, 225 (n. 26);
  rebellion in, 7, 39–40, 44, 46, 100,
  158; independence of, 8, 39, 46, 173;
  colonial government institutions of,
  12–13, 49, 155, 214; sugar exports, 25,
  228 (n. 5); enslaved women of, 30,
  50, 236 (n. 14); self-purchase requirements in, 32; enslaved population
  distributed in, 36; transportation
  infrastructure of, 37–38; and United
  States, 39, 40, 45, 116; colonial status
  of, 39, 46, 58–59; and slave registers,
  57, 239 (n. 57); literary portrayals of
  slavery's excesses, 105, 117; and elite
  women's education, 114, 251 (n. 75);
  jurisprudence of geography in,
  128–32; as legal culture, 225 (n. 18);
  and voting access, 272 (n. 3). *See also*
  Havana, Cuba
Cunha, Antonio Felipe Nery Carneiro
  da, 210
Cunha, Fernandes da, 156
Curadores: as legal representatives for
  slaves, 14, 48, 62, 63, 73–74, 216; and
  depósito process, 62–63; political
  views of, 63, 64–65, 241–42 (n. 90);
  as translators, 66, 67; and sympathy
  for slaves, 104; training of, 241 (n. 89)

Dantas, Manoel Pinto de Souza, 42, 114
Dauwe, Fabiano, 157, 257–58 (n. 78)

Dávila, Jerry, 262 (n. 62)
De la Fuente, Alejandro, 16
Del Monte, Domingo, 105, 117
Depósito process, 62–63, 241 (n. 84)
Diario de la Marina, 100
Domiciano (Basília's son), 94–95
Domingo (enslaved man), 49–50
Dorothea (enslaved *parda* woman), 204
Dorsey, Joseph, 54
Douglass, Frederick, 45
Drescher, Seymour, 98, 250 (n. 74)

Eduarda (enslaved girl), 118
Education: of elite women, 114, 165,
167, 251 (n. 75); of ex-slaves, 152,
158–64, 165, 170, 199, 206–7; and Rio
Branco Law, 158, 163, 261 (n. 60);
and *patronato* law, 158, 204–5, 209,
214; and citizenship, 159, 160, 162,
164, 170, 172, 173; and teachers, 165,
262 (n. 62), 263 (n. 81); of ex-slave
women, 165–72
Eduwiges (enslaved *parda*), 168
Efigênia (prostituted slave), 195–97, 265
(n. 26)
El Abolicionista Español, 110
Elites: and abolitionism, 11–12, 99; social
and educational projects of, 19, 20;
political influence of, 29; on morality of enslaved families, 152–58; on
education of ex-slaves, 158–64; and
bodily freedom of enslaved women,
190
Elite women: and abolitionism, 4, 109–
15, 167, 249 (n. 51), 250 (n. 69), 251
(n. 75); and universal mother-love,
12; modesty of, 106; and motherhood,
106, 171, 211–12; and femininity,
108–9; moral authority of, 110–11,
155, 165, 167, 169; education of, 114,
165, 167, 251 (n. 75); and religiosity,
250 (n. 69)
El Mulato, 153
Emancipation: and Ten Years' War,
40, 234 (n. 106); emancipation

ceremonies, 43, 44, 80, 163–64, 186,
188, 221; emancipation funds, 43,
56–57, 65, 80, 135, 137, 143–44, 146,
157, 188, 242 (n. 98), 257–58 (n. 78);
political and legal context of, 50; and
debates on future of ex-slaves, 152–
58. *See also* Gradual emancipation
Emília (enslaved *crioula*), 137
Enriqueta (enslaved woman), 186
Enslaved children: and enslaved women's
claims-making, 3, 77, 88–94, 138, 189,
198–99; and "free womb" principle,
55, 60, 153, 158, 160, 205, 206; and
slave claims-making, 61; and *coartación*, 75, 88–91, 244 (n. 34); and
slave owners, 84; and enslaved men's
claims-making, 139–40; education of,
158, 160
Enslaved men: defining terms of freedom, 12; and routes toward freedom,
19, 51, 61; urban occupations of, 31,
32, 231 (n. 56); literacy of, 44, 227
(n. 54); and patriarchal authority of
slave owners, 54; and slave law, 54;
masculinity of, 117; and enforced sale,
134; as fathers, 138–40, 178
Enslaved women: routes toward freedom, 3, 6, 8–9, 10, 13, 18–19, 20, 34,
51, 55, 61, 67, 185; and "free womb"
principle, 8–9, 11, 12, 18, 40, 42, 48,
50, 55, 60, 61, 72, 199–200; and universal mother-love, 12; slave owners'
sexual relations with, 15, 32, 34, 53,
54, 83–86, 104, 106, 116, 118–19, 122,
231–32 (n. 63), 232 (n. 64); social
context of, 19; as domestic servants,
27, 31, 32–33, 34, 121, 127, 133–34,
142, 231 (n. 55), 231–32 (n. 63), 232–
33 (n. 77), 252 (n. 107), 257 (n. 73);
and urban slavery, 30–32, 34, 50–51,
142–45, 217; urban occupations of,
31–32, 231 (n. 56); and prostitution,
32, 36, 121, 144, 156, 167, 187, 190,
195–97, 266 (n. 51), 268 (nn. 72, 76);
as wet nurses, 32, 53, 84, 86–87, 99,

101, 115, 120–21, 122, 134, 138, 142, 153, 190, 199, 237 (n. 26); literacy of, 44, 227 (n. 54); and slave law, 48, 53–55, 61–62, 237 (n. 32); abolition-ist sympathy for suffering of, 104–6, 115, 116, 122, 152, 216

—claims-making: and separation of mothers from children, 1–2, 84–85, 88–95, 98, 99, 101, 134, 138–39, 141, 165, 199, 244 (n. 33); and children's manumission, 3, 77, 88–94, 138, 189, 198–99; and second-instance courts of Rio de Janeiro, 13, 50, 236 (n. 15); motivations of, 13–14, 17, 46, 52–53, 122; and maternity, 19, 71, 72–81, 87, 97, 98, 141, 187, 216; and motherhood, 19, 71–72, 74–81, 87, 95, 99, 169, 198–99, 201, 203–7, 213, 219; and appeals court of Rio de Janeiro, 50, 60–61, 240 (n. 73); and manumission, 51, 52; and "free womb" principle, 67, 74–75, 87–88, 94–95, 204–7, 213, 215, 219; and slave owners' sexual relations, 83–86; and wet nurse role, 84, 86–87; and femininity, 98, 216; and geo-graphical location, 130–31, 217; and gossip, 145–48; influence of, 221
Escalera Conspiracy, 31, 212, 262 (n. 62)
Estévez, Mercedes, 179
Estrada, Luis Gonzaga Duque, 119–20
Eu, Conde d', 41
Eusébio de Queiroz Law (1850), 8
Eustáquio (*pardo* boy), 204
Ewe-Fon language, 35
Ex-slaves: and "scientific" racial theories, 15; slave owners' rights over, 27, 58, 174–75; gendered debates on future of, 152, 155; education of, 152, 158–64, 165, 170, 199, 206–7; moralizing families of, 152–58, 163, 172; and child metaphors, 160, 164; surnames of, 181, 264 (n. 16)
Ex-slave women: morality of, 152–54, 156–57; domestic labor of, 164, 165, 166, 170, 172–73, 176, 263 (n. 80);

education of, 165–72; and freedom, 176

Fabré, Joaquín, 88, 90
Faria, Joaquim Francisco de, 196
Faustino (enslaved son of Inés Gangá), 88–91, 92, 93, 244 (nn. 33, 35)
Feeley, Malcolm, 237 (n. 18)
Felicia (*patrocinada*), 147
Femininity: and legal freedom, 3; and enslaved women's claims-making, 98, 216; and abolitionism, 108–9, 118, 122, 248 (n. 41), 249 (n. 51); and freedwomen, 184, 185
Fernández, Antonia, 140–41
Fernández, Isabel, 143
Fernández, José Casimiro, 140
Fernández, José Ernesto, 140
Fernández, Leonardo, 267 (n. 56)
Fernández, Luisa, 140, 141
Fernández, Manuela, 140
Fernández, Rosa, 189
Ferrer de Couto, José, 28–29
Fetal rights discourse, 239–40 (n. 69)
Figueiredo, Carlos Honório, 195
Firmina (enslaved woman), 137
First-instance courts, and slave claims-making, 9, 12, 48, 49, 60
Flores, José María de, 169
Floresta, Nísia, 121
Folles, Rita, 180–81
Fonseca, Tenente, 72
Fontes, Alexandre Cardoso, 65
Forbes, José, 77–80
Forbes, María, 77–80, 81
Former slaves. *See* Ex-slaves; Ex-slave women
Francelina (freed girl), 109
Francisca (Genoveva's daughter), 142
Francisca (*parda patrocinada*), 146–47
Frank, Zephyr, 265 (n. 27)
Franklin, Sarah, 99, 171, 212, 232 (n. 64), 237 (n. 26)
Freedmen: elites' molding destinies of, 20; in Cuba, 30; urban occupations

of, 31, 32; and property ownership, 176; and fatherhood, 178–79; voting rights of, 269 (n. 14)

Freedom: defining of, 2, 3, 11, 12, 20, 66–67, 99, 122, 148, 151–52, 167, 172, 175, 177, 183, 197, 201, 213, 215, 218, 219, 222, 269 (n. 14); gendered notions of, 2, 3, 12, 19–20, 176, 223 (n. 6); enslaved women's routes toward, 3, 6, 8–9, 10, 13, 18–19, 20, 34, 51, 55, 61, 67, 185; enslaved men's routes toward, 19, 51, 61; legal routes to, 40, 41, 45, 46, 50, 51, 52, 55, 59, 60, 67, 132, 200, 204–7, 215, 218; restoration of, 86, 244 (n. 30); legal and philosophical arguments on, 104, 154; and family strategies, 132–33, 152–58; bodily meanings of, 188–97, 198, 219; validation of, 208–9

Freedwomen: claims for custody of children, 1–2, 4–5, 30, 71, 77, 92, 215, 217; struggles for freedom, 12, 20, 180, 219; elites' molding destinies of, 20; in Havana, 30; in Rio de Janeiro, 31; and separation from children, 91–92; poverty of, 144, 179; and property ownership, 176–82, 186, 198; and motherhood, 179, 197, 199, 201, 203–4; and womanhood, 182, 185, 197; and urban space, 182–85; and bodily meanings of freedom, 188–97, 198, 219; and prostitution, 193–95, 267 (n. 65). *See also* Ex-slave women

Freemason movement, 65

Free people of color, 5, 14, 27. *See also* Women of color

"Free womb" principle: and enslaved women, 8–9, 11, 12, 18, 40, 42, 48, 50, 55, 60, 61, 72, 199–200; effect on enslaved population, 26, 41; and enslaved children, 55, 60, 153, 158, 160, 205, 206; and slave law, 55–59; and enslaved women's claims-making, 67, 74–75, 87–88, 94–95, 204–7, 213,

215, 219; debates on, 99, 100, 153–55, 156, 158

Fugitive slaves: communities of, 26; and urban slavery, 28, 44; and rural slavery, 42; and gender, 51; enslaved women as, 236 (n. 18), 255 (n. 32)

Funeral rites, 28, 180

Gabriella (enslaved *parda* woman), 174–75, 176, 198

Galdina (free child), 187

Gallenga, Antonio Carlo Napoleone, 30, 103, 161, 205–6

Galuzo, Felipa, 29

Gálvez, Genoveva, 192–95

Gálvez, Josefa, 192–94

Gama, Katherine de, 239–40 (n. 69)

Gama, Luiz, 64–65, 222

Gangá, Inés, 88–91, 92, 93, 244 (n. 35)

García, Francisca, 165

García, Leocadia, 86–87

García, Magdalena, 63

García Balmaseda, Joaquina, 110–11, 249 (n. 57)

Gassie, Don Antonio, 86

Gavino (*patrocinado*), 93, 147, 202, 203, 204

Gazeta da Tarde, 65, 101, 106, 108, 111, 113, 114, 118, 161, 181, 183–84, 190, 199

Geltner, G., 237 (n. 18)

Gender: and defining freedom, 2, 3, 12, 19–20, 176, 223 (n. 6); and marronage, 2, 51, 224 (nn. 7, 8), 236 (n. 18); and crime, 2, 51, 224 (n. 7), 236–37 (n. 18); and armed conflict, 2, 224 (n. 7); slavery as gendered concept, 3; and citizenship, 3, 164, 220; and manumission, 5, 12, 32, 34, 51, 52, 53, 67, 143, 231–32 (n. 63), 232 (n. 64); and "scientific" racial theories, 12; and abolitionism, 15, 19, 108, 115–20, 122; and legal routes to freedom, 46; and slave law, 47, 53–55, 59; and slave claims-making, 50–53, 67; and slave mobility, 133–36; and debates on future of ex-slaves, 152. *See also* Enslaved men; Enslaved women; White men; White women

Genoveva (Francisca's mother), 142

Gertrudes (enslaved *preta*), 135

Girand, Enrique, 140–41

Glória, Maria da, 86

Gobierno General, Havana: and slave claims-making, 49, 65, 79–80, 127, 146, 209, 214, 240 (n. 72); and Moret Law, 90, 91

Gobierno Superior Civil, Havana: and slave claims-making, 49, 50, 236 (n. 13), 240 (n. 72); and enslaved women's claims-making, 76; and geographical movement, 129

Gomes, Carlos, 161

Gomes Costa, Suely, 118

Gómez de Avellaneda, Gertrudis, 105, 153

Gonçalves de Moraes, Josepha: claim for custody of daughter, 1–2, 4–5, 6, 9, 10, 12, 15, 43, 97, 136, 146, 151–52, 156, 168, 169–70, 173, 200–201, 203, 214–15, 216, 217, 218, 219, 222; claim for freedom, 9, 99, 151–52; illiteracy of, 14; Ramona Oliva compared to, 16–17; as *parda*, 18; in Rio de Janeiro, 23, 26, 35–36, 42, 44, 135–36; as domestic servant, 36; lawyer representing, 65

Gonçalves de Pinho, José, 1, 9, 200, 201

González, Catalina, 86

González, Felicia, 184–85

González de Valés, Vicente, 76

Graça, Paulo Barboso, 200

Graça Filho, Afonso de Alencastro, 255 (n. 48)

Gradual emancipation: in Cuba, 1, 2, 6–11, 13, 18, 38–41, 42, 48, 58, 71, 102, 125, 158, 215, 218; and women claimants, 1–2, 3; and laws and legislation, 2, 3, 8–11, 16, 18; in Brazil, 2, 6–10, 18, 38–39, 41–42, 56–57, 71, 125, 158,

215, 218, 235 (n. 9); and sexagenarian slaves, 9, 11, 42, 114; debates on, 19; and "free womb" principle, 48, 60, 156; and motherhood, 72

Grajales, Mariana, 3, 173

Gran Colombia, 55

Grinberg, Keila, 13, 28, 48, 50, 60, 240 (n. 70), 241 (n. 90)

Guadalupe (*parda patrocinada*), 146–47

Guanajay, Cuba, 25

Guerra Chiquita (Little War), 40

Guillermí, Cecilio, 140–41, 256 (n. 66)

Guimarães, Bernardo, 105

Guimarães, Francisco Gomes da Rocha, 94

Guimarães, José da Costa, 94, 95

Güines, Cuba, 25

Gutiérrez y Salazar, Pedro, 155, 159, 165

Haiti, 7, 55

Hava, Evarista, 193

Havana, Cuba: freedwomen's claims for custody of children, 1–2, 4–5; slaves' court cases in, 3; tradition of freedom in, 5; and plantation-based economy, 5, 25–26, 28, 125; and enslaved women as claimants, 13; labor regime of, 18, 23; docks of, 25; population of, 26; enslaved population of, 26, 127, 229 (n. 19), 232–33 (n. 77); urban slavery in, 26–30, 185; politics in, 28–29, 44–45, 46; abolitionist movements in, 29–30, 44–45, 98, 99–100, 116, 120, 122, 218; enslaved women's population in, 30, 143, 230 (n. 44), 257 (n. 73); freedwomen in, 30, 176, 183, 184; markets of, 31; enslaved women as prostitutes in, 32; peninsular Spaniard population of, 36; European visitors to, 36–37; North American visitors to, 36–37; growth of, 37, 182–83; transportation infrastructure of, 37–38, 125; *coartación* in, 52; women of color in, 144–45; literacy of people of color, 227 (n. 54);

Index / 317

enslaved women as domestic servants in, 231 (n. 55), 232–33 (n. 77)

Henrique (*preto* son of *preta* Marianna), 94, 95

Hernández, Filomena, 269 (n. 12)

Hernández, Severina, 126, 128–29, 147

Hernández y Herrera, Manuel, 191–92

Herrera, Ana, 191

Herrera, Asunción, 180

Herrera, Dorotea, 134

Hespanhol, João, 200

Higinio (alleged rapist), 189

Hoganson, Kristin, 248 (n. 42), 248–49 (n. 46)

Humility, gendered language of, 81

Igbo language, 35

Iglesias, Fe, 52, 230 (n. 44), 232 (n. 64)

Imperial family of Brazil: and abolitionism, 3–4, 13, 44; and slave claims-making, 28, 59, 80, 95, 211, 239 (n. 66); and emancipation ceremonies, 43, 44, 80. *See also* Isabel, Princess Imperial of Brazil; Pedro II; Teresa Cristina

Infant mortality, 26

Instituto de Advogados Brasileiros, 74

Instituto de Menores Artesãos, 204

Ipsen, Wiebke, 157, 167

Isaac (enslaved man), 245–46 (n. 51)

Isabel, Princess Imperial of Brazil: image as "Redeemer," 3–4; and abolitionist movement, 10, 41; legal representatives addressing, 15; and emancipation ceremonies, 43, 163–64, 186, 188, 221; and education of ex-slaves, 162; and education of ex-slave women, 166; and motherhood, 212

Isabel II (queen of Spain), 110

Ismael (Basília's son), 94–95

Jamaica, 236 (n. 18)

Jardim, Antônio Pedro, 132, 250 (n. 68)

Jardim, Maria Cândida, 250 (n. 68)

Jaruco, Cuba, 25

Jesus, Custódia Maria de, 210

Joana (enslaved girl), 118

Johnson, Sherry, 212

Jornal por su cuenta, 27, 75

José (aka Lechuza; Chinese worker), 63

Josepha (enslaved woman), 137

Josepha (enslaved *parda* girl, daughter of Rachel), 146

Julián (*moreno*), 193

Juliana (enslaved *moreno*), 127

Junta de Información, 39, 64, 101–2, 117–18, 133–34, 154, 155, 245 (n. 47)

Juntas de libertos in Cuba, 13, 49, 59, 126, 160

Juntas de patronato in Cuba, 13, 49, 59, 93, 214

Jurisprudence, and motherhood, 87–96

Karasch, Mary, 32–33, 34, 51, 230 (n. 41), 231 (n. 56), 255 (n. 32), 270 (n. 32)

Kimbundu language, 35

Kiple, Kenneth, 257 (n. 73)

Kittleson, Roger, 248 (n. 41), 249 (n. 51)

Labra y Ladrana, Rafael María de, 57

La Cebolla (The Onion), 194

Ladies' Negro's Friend Society, 110, 249 (n. 52)

Lahmeyer, Henrique Gaspar de, 138

La Igualdad, 100

Lamounier, Maria Lúcia, 58

Landers, Jane, 2, 224 (n. 8)

La Revolución, 100

Lastra, Bernardo, 126, 129, 147, 259 (n. 96)

Latin America, 2, 12

Laudelina (daughter of Quitéria Maria da Piedade), 72, 73, 74, 77

Lauderdale Graham, Sandra, 225 (n. 18)

Laurentino (son of enslaved woman), 180

Lauriano (Basília's son), 94–95

Laws and legislation: and gradual emancipation, 2, 3, 8–11, 16, 18; and legal recourse, 6; and legal change, 11, 41–42; influence of courts on, 28; and elites' political influence, 29; political contexts of, 46; influence of slave claims-making on, 48; and "free womb" principle, 72, 215; influence of enslaved women's claims-making on, 85, 93, 215. *See also* Moret Law; *Patronato* law; Rio Branco Law; Saraiva-Cotegipe Law; Slave law

Lawyers, as legal representatives for slave claims-making, 65, 216. See also *Curadores*; *Síndicos*

Legitimacy/illegitimacy, 54, 238 (n. 39)

Leocádia (enslaved woman), 101

Leonor (freed girl), 168

Lerma, Delfino, 177

Libby, Douglas Cole, 255 (n. 48)

Lima, Ivana Stolze, 270 (n. 32)

Linares, Clara, 208–9

Lincoln, Abraham, 55

Literacy: slaves' lack of, 14, 44, 77; of enslaved men and women, 44, 227 (n. 54); of ex-slaves, 47, 158, 208; and scribes, 65–66; and voting rights, 161, 261 (n. 47)

Little, Deborah, 237 (n. 18)

Livro de Ouro slave emancipation fund, 43, 65, 80, 137, 144, 146, 188, 242 (n. 98)

Llorente, Mariano, 194

Lopes, João Pereira, 120

Lopes Robert, José, 86–87

Lucía (enslaved woman), 243 (n. 11)

Ludovina (enslaved woman), 85

Ludovina (enslaved woman, daughter of Maria Rosa), 80, 81, 174

Luisa (enslaved woman), 75–77

Macedo, Joaquim Manoel de, 121, 152

Maceo, Antonio, 3, 45, 221

Madden, Richard, 105

Magalhães, R., Jr., 248 (n. 32)

Malheiro, Perdigão, 55

Mande language, 35

Manhood: renegotiation of, 18; and citizenship, 19; gendered imaginaries of, 98

Manumission: children's manumission, 3, 77, 88–94, 138, 189, 198–99; and gender, 5, 12, 32, 34, 51, 52, 53, 67, 143, 231–32 (n. 63), 232 (n. 64); in Brazil, 5, 16, 26, 51, 67; in Cuba, 5, 16, 51, 67; and religious brotherhoods, 28, 142; and urban slavery, 34, 51, 136–37, 255 (n. 48); and emancipation funds, 43, 56–57, 65, 135, 137, 143–44, 146, 157, 188, 257–58 (n. 78); and middling urban slave owners, 230 (n. 41); and rural slavery, 255 (n. 48)

Marcelina (enslaved woman), 144

Margarida (enslaved woman), 210–11, 270 (n. 34)

Margarita (enslaved woman), 143

Maria (daughter of Josepha Gonçalves de Moraes): mother's claim for custody of, 1, 43, 97, 146, 151, 168, 200–201, 214, 219; as "free womb" daughter, 9; birth of, 35; in Rio de Janeiro, 135–36

Maria (enslaved *parda* woman), 198, 199

María Luisa (enslaved *congo* woman), 142

Marianna (conditionally freed *preta* woman), 94

Maria Rosa (black freedwoman), 80–81, 144, 174, 211

Marquese, Rafael, 16

Marronage, and gender, 2, 51, 224 (nn. 7, 8), 236 (n. 18)

Martí, José, 221

Martínez, Rosario, 180

Martinha (enslaved woman), 175

Marty, Ramona, 193–95

Masá, Gregorio, 83

Masculinity: and legal freedom, 3; and abolitionism, 108, 109, 117, 122, 248–49 (n. 46)

Mata, Iacy Maia, 266 (n. 43)

Mateos y Mendo, Benito, 146

Maternity: and enslaved women's claims-making, 19, 71, 72–81, 87, 97, 98, 141, 187, 216; and leveling rhetoric, 77–81; and ex-slave women, 167, 171, 176; and modernity, 170

Mathilde (enslaved *fazenda* woman), 85, 124, 139

Mattos, Hebe, 206, 238 (n. 42), 265 (n. 26)

Mello, Jeronymo José de, 174–75, 198

Men. *See* Enslaved men; Freedmen

Méndez, Jorge, 93, 147, 202–3, 204

Méndez, Juana, 202–3, 204

Méndez, Nieves, 203

Mendonça, Joseli, 147–48

Mendonça, Manoel Furtado de, 179–80, 186–88, 195–97

Menezes, Adolpho Bezerra de, 120, 195

Merced (*patrocinada*), 143

Meriño, María de los Ángeles, 264 (n. 16)

Micaela (enslaved woman), 259 (n. 96)

Middle Passage, 35

Midgley, Clare, 250–51 (n. 74)

Miscegenation, 5

Miscelánea de Expedientes collection, Havana National Archive, 13, 60, 61, 227 (n. 53), 240 (nn. 72, 74)

Mónica (enslaved woman), 143, 148

Monte Carmello, Francisco Fausto do, 73

Monteiro, João Pereira, 157

Monteiro, João Pereira, Jr., 157

Moraes, Evaristo de, 118, 158

Moraes, Manoel Angelo Maria de, 200

Morales, Justa, 129–30

Morales Lemus, José, 63–64

Moret Law: as "free womb" law, 8–9, 10, 40, 41, 56, 117; whipping banned by, 11, 57; and slave owners, 40, 57, 58, 59; reaction to, 44, 57, 58, 235 (n. 9); and sexagenarian slaves, 57; and mothers separated from children, 84, 88–94, 100, 103, 129; and geographical movement, 129; and enslaved families, 155; and education, 158;

Regulation of, 160, 261 (n. 41); and prostitution, 268 (n. 74)

Moret y Prendergast, Segismundo, 40, 99–100, 117, 156

Motherhood: political context of, 12, 19, 211; and enslaved women's claims-making, 19, 71–72, 74–81, 87, 95, 99, 169, 198–99, 201, 203–7, 213, 219; meanings of, 20, 71–72, 201–4, 213, 219; rhetoric on, 72, 74, 76–81; and family connections between owners and slaves, 83–87; and jurisprudence, 87–96; and elite women, 106, 171, 211–12; and abolitionism, 106–7; and ex-slave women, 168, 173, 176; and freedwomen, 179, 197, 199, 201, 203–4

Mott, Luis, 221–22

Moura, Luiz de, 164

Muro, Juan, 130

Nabuco, Joaquim, 10, 45, 57, 247 (n. 18)

Nagel, Joanne, 115

National belonging, 3, 12, 210–11

Needell, Jeffrey, 28

Nobre, José Ferreira, 65, 206

O Abolicionista, 101, 107, 110, 249 (n. 52)

O'Kelly, James, 115–16

Olazabal, Caridad, 84

Oliva, Agustina, 1, 47, 71, 123

Oliva, Luis, 1, 10, 47, 71, 123

Oliva, Manuel, 1, 10, 47, 214

Oliva, María de las Nieves, 1, 10, 47, 71, 123

Oliva, María Fabiana, 1, 47, 71, 123

Oliva, María Josefa, 143

Oliva, Ramona: freedom purchased by, 1, 9–10; claim for custody of children, 1–2, 4–5, 6, 7, 9, 10, 12, 15, 28, 30, 45, 47, 71, 93, 123–24, 173, 204–5, 214–15, 216, 217, 220, 221, 222; illiteracy of, 14, 47; Josepha Gonçalves de Moraes compared to, 16–17; as *morena*, 18; in Havana, 23, 28, 30, 35,

42, 44, 77, 123, 125–27; scribe writing petitions of, 65

Oliveira, Balbino, 188
Oliveira, Elvira, 187
Oliveira, Eva Joaquina de, 179–80, 186–88, 195–97, 265 (n. 26)
Oliveira, Manoel Caetano Alves d', 140
Oliveira, Josefa Águeda Felisbela Mercedes de, 113
Oña, Candelaria, 188–90, 197, 267 (n. 56)
Oña, Tomasa, 188–90, 197, 267 (n. 56)
Orixá (orisha) worship, 28
Ortiz, Dolores, 143
Otovo, Okezi, 170
Oviedo, Adelaida, 181
Oyo Empire, 35

Pact of Zanjón, 40
Palmares, Zumbi dos, 221–22
Paraguay, 8, 41, 120
Paraguay War, 64, 111, 251 (n. 75)
Para inglês ver, 59
Paraíso Plantation, 103
Parron, Tâmis, 16
Partus sequitur ventrem, 53–56, 75, 139, 157, 158, 215, 238 (n. 36)
Paternalism, 175
Paton, Diana, 236 (n. 18)
Patriarchal authority, 54, 155, 156, 157, 158, 168, 238 (n. 38)
Patrocinados (apprentices): slaves renamed as, 9, 40, 77; stipend for, 58; and enslaved women's claims-making, 78–79, 143, 145; population of, 127, 143, 145, 257 (n. 74), 258 (n. 84)
Patrocinio, José do: and abolitionist movement, 44, 65, 111, 124–25; as radical journalist, 138, 222; and education of ex-slaves, 161, 162, 206–7; and education of ex-slave women, 165; on enslaved population, 230 (n. 41)
Patronato (apprenticeship) law (1880): passage of, 9; and self-purchase, 10, 128; and apprenticeship period, 40–41, 57–58; debates on, 64; and freedwomen's claims for custody of children, 71, 77, 92; and education, 158, 204–5, 209, 214
Paula (enslaved mulata), 83, 84
Pedro II (emperor of Brazil), 10, 114, 163, 204, 211, 249 (n. 63), 250 (n. 73)
Pedroso, Margarita, 132–33
Peixoto, José Pereira, 81
Pena, Eduardo Spiller, 210
Peñalver, Ignacio, 132, 133
Peñalver, Pedro, 133
Perdomo, Paulina, 202–3, 269 (n. 12)
Pereira, Luiz de Santa Bárbara, 72, 73
Perera, Aisnara, 264 (n. 16)
Pérez, Dolores, 184–85
Pérez, Juana, 130, 132, 134
Pérez, Salvador Miguel, 168–69
Perovany, Elvira, 168–69
Petrona (enslaved woman), 259 (n. 96)
Pezuela, Jacobo de la, 229 (n. 19)
Philippines, 155, 165
Phoenix Dramática theatre, 106
Piedade, Quitéria Maria da, 72–74, 76–77
Pimenta Bueno, José Antônio, 55
Pineapples, export of, 26
Pinho, Maria Amélia da Silva, 1, 9, 200
Pizarro Filha, Teresa, 165, 166, 170
Plácida (enslaved girl), 91
Poey, Juan, 206
Portillo, Manuel, 188
Portocarrero y Gassie y Valdés, Margarita de la Soledad, 86
Portugal, 55
Power relations: and slave claims-making, 14, 47, 50; and gender, 53; and geography, 124–25; and enslaved women's claims-making, 151–52, 169
Prado, Antônio, 109, 124
Prendergast, Luis, 79, 209
Proctor, Frank "Trey", III, 231–32 (n. 63), 232 (n. 64)
Prostitution: and enslaved women, 32, 36, 121, 144, 156, 167, 187, 190,

195–97, 266 (n. 51), 268 (nn. 72, 76); and slave law, 53; and freedwomen, 193–95, 267 (n. 65); and manumission, 232 (n. 64); and Moret Law, 268 (n. 74)

Puerto Rico: politics in, 7; abolitionist movements in, 11, 45, 46, 98, 102, 116, 120, 122; slavery issue in, 38, 39, 40, 64; and Junta de Información, 154

Punishment: whipping banned as, 11, 57; and urban slavery, 27; and abolitionism, 118–19

Rabello, Thomas, 163

Race: and gendered norms, 3; "scientific" racial theories, 12, 15, 98, 103, 104, 115, 190, 218; and citizenship, 210–11; silencing of, 265 (n. 26)

Rachel (enslaved woman classified for freedom), 146

Railroads, development of, 37–38

Ramos, Serafín, 192–94

Real, Pedro, 142

Rebouças, André, 222

Regadas, Luiza, 112–13

Regla, María de, 130–32, 134

Reis, João José, 270 (n. 32)

Reis, José Agostinho dos, 108–9

Religious brotherhoods, 28, 107–8, 142, 202

Resistance, characterization of, 2–3

Revista Illustrada, 37, 106, 111–12, 114, 135, 168

Rey (O'Reilly), Águeda del, 177–79, 264 (n. 15)

Rey (O'Reilly), Florindo, 177–79

Rey (O'Reilly), Simona del, 177–78

Rhetoric: and abolitionist discourse, 11–12, 100, 108, 216; of slave claims-making, 14, 216; on womanhood, 19, 121, 216; on motherhood, 72, 74, 76–81; leveling rhetoric, 77–81

Ribeiro, Antonio José da Silva, 85

Rio Branco, José Paranhos, Viscount, 161

Rio Branco Law (1871): passage of, 9; and abolitionism, 10–11, 58; and "free womb" principle, 41, 56, 107, 156, 168–69; and emancipation fund, 56–57; and appeals courts, 60, 240 (n. 70); and slave registers, 85; debates on, 94–95, 187; and separation of mothers and children, 100–101, 239 (n. 50); opposition to, 106; and self-purchase, 136; and enslaved families, 157; and education, 158, 163, 261 (n. 60); regulations to, 200; limitations of, 205

Rio de Janeiro, Brazil: freedwomen's claims for custody of children, 1–2, 4–5; slaves' court cases in, 3, 12; tradition of freedom in, 5; and plantation-based economy, 5, 25–26, 28, 125; abolitionist movements in, 10, 13, 29, 43–44, 45, 65, 105–6, 122, 124–25, 134–35, 143, 161, 218; appeals court of, 12, 28, 48, 49, 50, 51, 60–61, 236 (n. 17), 240 (nn. 70, 73); second-instance courts of, 13, 50, 236 (n. 15); labor regime of, 18, 23; docks of, 25; population of, 26; enslaved population of, 26, 36, 60, 228 (n. 16), 229 (n. 17), 230 (n. 41), 232 (n. 77); urban slavery in, 26–30, 185; politics in, 28–29, 43–44, 46; and urban riots, 29; social inequality in, 29, 37; free population of color in, 31; enslaved women's population in, 31, 143, 144, 236 (n. 16), 240 (n. 73); markets of, 31, 176; freedwomen in, 31, 176, 183–84, 217; and prostitution, 32, 53, 135, 195–97; Portugese population of, 36; European visitors to, 36–37; North American visitors to, 36–37; growth of, 37, 182–83; transportation infrastructure of, 38, 125; "Black Regulation," 43–44, 134–35; and enslaved women's self-purchase, 136–38; and education of ex-slaves, 161, 165, 170, 199; enslaved women as domestic servants in, 231 (n. 55); manumission rates in, 232 (n. 77)

Rio Preto, Baron of, 103

Rios, Ana Lugão, 206

Rita (freedwoman), 146

Rita (enslaved *parda* woman), 199, 268 (n. 2)

Roda dos expostos, 101, 113–14, 246 (n. 13)

Rodrigues, José Braga, 97

Rodrigues, Manoel Jorge, 73

Rojas, Ramon, 208

Romana, Mercedes, 183

Roman law, 53, 268 (n. 74)

Romanticism, 105, 106, 108, 260 (n. 13)

Romero, Juana, 76, 88, 243 (n. 11)

Rosa (*parda* freedwoman), 176–77

Rosário, Oliveira, 162

Roselló, Eufemio, 183

Rosich, Cayetano, 129

Ruddick, Sara, 269 (n. 21)

Rural areas, 26, 29, 37

Rural slavery: and sale of urban slaves to plantations, 26, 27, 36, 44, 52, 123, 125, 126, 128, 130, 133–34, 138; legal arguments based on status of, 36, 124–25, 128–29, 148; and fugitive slaves, 42; and gender, 50–51; and manumission rates, 255 (n. 48)

Sá, Carolina Umbelina de, 137

Sabina (freedwoman), 185–86

Saint Domingue, 55

Salvador da Bahia, Brazil, 28

San Antonio de los Baños, Cuba, 25

Sánchez, Ciriaco, 63

Sánchez, Luisa, 145

Sánchez y Sánchez, Juana, 83, 84

Sanromá, Joaquín María, 110

Santana, María de los Ángeles Pinto, 184

Santiago (*pardo* boy), 75, 243 (n. 9)

Santiago de Cuba, Cuba, 28

Santos, Albino de Oliveira, 204, 269 (n. 15)

Santos, Domingos Gomes dos, 65, 138

Santos, Francisca Mathilde dos, 204

Santos, Joaquim Monteiro dos, 9, 65, 201

Santos, Maria Meirelles dos, 183–84

São José, Anna Luiza de, 211

São Paulo, Brazil, 25, 36, 64

São Pedro, Maria, 195, 196, 197

Sar, Carmen Bujia de, 186

Saraiva, José Antônio, 42

Saraiva-Cotegipe Law (1885), 9, 42, 43, 57, 58, 124

Schmidt-Nowara, Christopher, 7, 34–35, 64, 110, 247 (n. 21)

Schoelcher, Victor, 45

Schweninger, Loren, 270 (n. 29)

"Scientific" racial theories, 12, 15, 98, 103, 104, 115, 190, 218

Scott, Rebecca, 17, 36, 48, 52, 127, 225 (n. 18), 237 (n. 26), 271 (n. 5)

Scribes, 65–66, 67, 76, 140, 216

Sebastiana (freedwoman), 146

Second-instance courts of Rio de Janeiro, 13, 50, 236 (n. 15)

Self-purchase: and manumission, 6; and gradual emancipation, 9; and urban slavery, 27; and owner's consent, 32; savings for, 32, 56, 136, 137–38, 177, 188; and slave claims-making, 49–50; and *partus sequitur ventrem*, 55–56; as legal right, 56, 187; price scales for, 58, 128, 254 (n. 20); in Rio de Janeiro, 136–38; and lottery, 178. See also *Coartación*

Senespleda Battaglia, Giuseppina de, 112

Serrano, Francisco, 212

Sexagenarian slaves, 9, 11, 42, 57, 114, 243 (n. 11)

Shaw, Stephanie J., 269 (n. 21)

Siete Partidas legal code, 54, 84, 268 (n. 74)

Silva, Cláudio da, 162

Silva, Francisco Pinto da, 199, 268 (n. 2)

Síndicos: as legal representatives for slaves, 14, 48, 62, 63, 75–76, 126, 130, 141, 216; and municipal councils, 49; bribery of, 62; and *depósito* process,

62–63; political views of, 63–64;
as translators, 66, 67; and enslaved
women's claims-making, 101; and
evaluation of slaves' prices, 141, 256
(n. 67); as legal representatives for
legal minors, 241 (n. 79); training of,
241 (n. 89); time given to petitioners,
242 (n. 101)

Skin color, 18, 208, 210, 211, 220, 270
(n. 32). *See also* Race

Slave agency, 3, 14, 15, 16, 47–48

Slave families: and slave law, 53, 238
(n. 33); and *partus sequitur ventrem*,
55–56; and "free womb" principle,
56, 153; and abolitionism, 102–3,
115; and urban slavery, 138–42; and
godparents, 142, 257 (n. 69)

Slave law: and enslaved agency, 16,
47–48; and gender, 47, 53–55, 59; and
enslaved women, 48, 53–55, 61–62,
237 (n. 32); and *coartación* as right,
52, 56; and patriarchal authority, 54,
238 (n. 38); and "free womb" principle, 55–59

Slave owners: role in manumission,
5–6; and abolitionist movements,
10, 115–20; enslaved women's sexual
relations with, 15, 32, 34, 53, 54,
83–86, 104, 106, 116, 118–19, 122,
231–32 (n. 63), 232 (n. 64); rights
over ex-slaves, 27, 58, 169, 174–75;
role in self-purchase, 32, 56; women
as, 34, 116, 118–20, 185–88, 231–32
(n. 63), 268 (n. 71); geographic
transfer of slaves, 36, 92; and Moret
Law, 40, 57, 58, 59; and Rio Branco
Law, 41; and slave claims-making,
50, 78, 127; and *coartación*, 52;
males as *paterfamilias*, 54; and "free
womb" principle, 56, 60, 88; and
depósito process, 62–63; and leaving
one's blood in slavery, 83, 244 (n. 20);
and education of enslaved children,
158, 160; and slaves' ability to earn

money, 239 (n. 51); death of, 259
(n. 93)

Slavery: legal routes out of, 2–3, 5–6, 11,
18–19; as gendered concept, 3; negotiating conditions of, 14; harsh conditions of, 14–15, 154; racist defenders
of, 29; genealogical inheritance of,
53–54; injustice of, 87; meanings
of, 176. *See also* Enslaved children;
Enslaved men; Enslaved women;
Rural slavery; Urban slavery

Slave trade: and slave imports, 7, 8, 225
(nn. 24, 26); abolition of, from Africa,
7, 26, 59, 125, 134, 209, 210; intraregional, 8, 35, 42, 43, 125, 134, 135,
225 (n. 24), 226 (n. 34), 232 (n. 77);
gendered geographies of, 133–36;
deaths resulting from, 226 (n. 34)

Slenes, Robert, 258 (n. 78)

Social inequality, and urban slavery, 29

Sociedad Matritense de Amigos del País,
155

Solano López, Francisco, 41

Sota, João Antônio Mendes, 137

Souza, Ennes de, 164

Souza, Flávia Fernandes de, 252 (n. 107)

Souza, José da Costa e, 72, 73, 74

Spain: gradual abolition laws enacted
by, 1, 8–9, 11, 44, 55, 58, 226 (n. 39);
slave trade banned by, 7; rebellion
in Cuba, 7, 39–40, 44; abolitionist
movements in, 11, 39–40, 45, 57, 77,
98, 104, 122

Spanish Abolitionist Society, 10, 39, 45,
57, 64, 105, 107, 110–11

Spanish Anti-Slavery Society, 45

Stowe, Harriet Beecher, 15, 105, 106

Suárez y Romero, Anselmo, 105, 116–17,
134

Sugar cultivation, 6, 7, 8, 25–26, 28, 36,
40, 127, 129, 228 (n. 5)

Tanco y Bosmoniel, Félix, 105

Tannenbaum, Frank, 16

Tello, Francisco d'Albuquerque Muniz, 85–86

Ten Years' War (1868–78), 39–40, 41, 217, 234 (n. 106)

Terborg-Penn, Rosalyn, 17, 270 (n. 29)

Teresa Cristina (empress of Brazil), 80–81, 112, 144, 211, 249 (n. 63)

Theodora (enslaved woman), 188

Theresa (enslaved *preta*), 135

Thompson, Alvin, 236 (n. 18)

Tia Ciata, 217

Tobacco cultivation, 19, 25, 45, 105

Toro, Lorenzo del, 130–31

Torres, Manoel Martins, 94

Torres Aguilar, Salvador, 107

Trabalhar ao ganho, 27

Traviesas, Enrique Marcelino de las, 192–94

Trouillot, Michel-Rolph, 139

Uncle Tom's Cabin (Stowe), 15, 105, 106

United States: second slavery in South, 6; abolition following Civil War, 7, 55; slave imports of, 8; and Cuba, 39, 40, 45, 116; abolitionist movements in, 45, 110, 114, 220–21, 248–49 (n. 46); education of ex-slaves in, 159

Urban slavery: and plantation-based economy, 5, 26; legal recourse to, 6; and sale to plantation labor, 26, 27, 36, 44, 52, 123, 125, 126, 128, 130, 133–34, 138; living conditions of slaves, 26–27; plantation labor compared to, 26–27, 217; and domestic slaves, 27, 31, 129, 231 (n. 55), 232–33 (n. 77); and daily wages, 27, 131, 187; and fugitive slaves, 28, 44; and social inequality, 29; and abolitionist movements, 29–30; and enslaved women, 30–32, 34, 50–51, 142–45, 217; and manumission rates, 34, 51, 136–37, 255 (n. 48); legal arguments based on status of, 36, 124–25, 128–29, 148; and Saraiva-Cotegipe Law, 42;

coartación associated with, 52, 128, 129; and taxation, 130; and enslaved families, 138–42; women as slave owners, 185–88, 268 (n. 71)

Urban space, 182–85

Urrutia, Gregoria, 181

Uruguay, 41

Valdés, José Celestino, 169

Valera, Rosenda, 181–82

Valés, Vicente González de, 169

Varela, Felix, 55

Varella, Carlos Busch e, 85, 124

Varella Fernández, Claudia, 49, 241 (n. 79), 242 (n. 101)

Vassouras, Brazil, 25

Vázquez, Juan, 139–40

Vera y González, Enrique, 115–16, 159–60, 162

Vianna, Ferreira, 86

Vicente (*patrocinado*), 93, 147, 202, 203, 204

Vicente, Manoel, 139

Victorina (enslaved woman), 187

Vidal, Cándida, 75, 76

Villa da Barra, Baron, 156–57

Villaverde, Cirilo, 105

Virginia (freed girl), 157

Vivano, Bráulio de, 140–41

Voduns, 28

Wanderley, João Maurício, Baron of Cotegipe, 42, 43

Wedgewood, Josiah, 45, 105

White men, 18, 31, 66

White women, 18, 30, 31, 168. *See also* Elite women

Womanhood: political context of, 12; renegotiation of, 18, 114–15, 173; rhetoric on, 19, 121, 216; gendered imaginaries of, 98; conceptions of, 151–52, 218–19, 220; and ex-slave women, 167, 168, 172; and freedwomen, 182, 185, 197

"Womanliness," definitions of, 12
Women. *See* Elite women; Enslaved women; Ex-slave women; Freedwomen; Women of color
Women of color: and miscegenation, 5; diversity of, 17–18; in Atlantic port cities, 23; role of, 121, 173; in Havana, 144–45; and property ownership, 179, 180–81; petitions of, 212, 213. *See also* Enslaved women; Freedwomen

Xiqueña, Count of, 209

Zaeske, Susan, 220–21
Zalazar, Timotea, 191
Zambrana, Antonio, 44, 125
Zamora, Juana Inés, 209
Zamora, Mercedes, 209
Zeferina (enslaved woman), 187
Zeuske, Michael, 264 (n. 16)
Zulueta y Amondo, Julián de, 206